BUILDING
MODERN TURKEY

CULTURE, POLITICS,
AND THE BUILT ENVIRONMENT

Dianne Harris, Editor

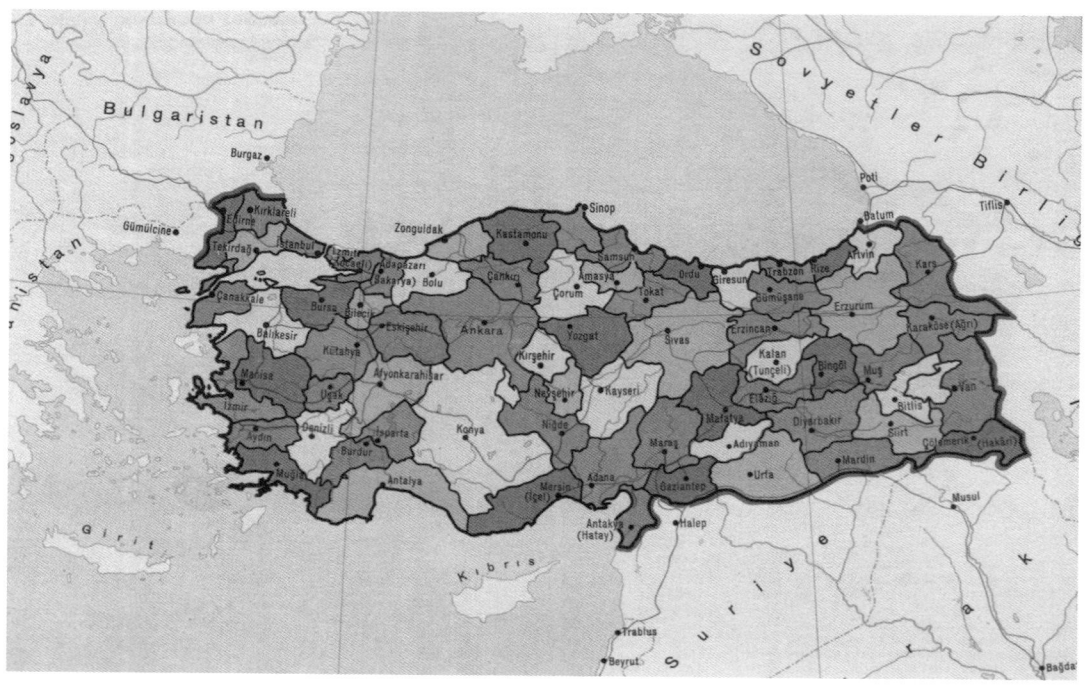

BUILDING MODERN TURKEY

STATE, SPACE,
AND IDEOLOGY IN
THE EARLY REPUBLIC

Zeynep Kezer

UNIVERSITY OF PITTSBURGH PRESS

Published by the University of Pittsburgh Press, Pittsburgh, Pa., 15260

Copyright © 2015, University of Pittsburgh Press

All rights reserved

Manufactured in the United States of America

Printed on acid-free paper

10 9 8 7 6 5 4 3 2 1

Library of Congress Cataloging-in-Publication Data

Names: Kezer, Zeynep.

Title: *Building Modern Turkey: State, Space, and Ideology in the Early Republic* / Zeynep Kezer.

Description: Pittsburgh, Pa. : University of Pittsburgh Press, 2015. |

Series: Culture and Politics of the Built Environment | Includes bibliographical references and index.

Identifiers: LCCN 2015037814 | ISBN 9780822963905 (paperback : acid-free paper)

Subjects: LCSH: Architecture and state—Turkey—History—20th century. | Architecture and society—Turkey—History—20th century. | Space (Architecture)—Political aspects—Turkey—History—20th century. | Space (Architecture)—Social aspects—Turkey—History—20th century. | Nationalism and architecture—Turkey—History—20th century. | Nation-state—Social aspects—Turkey—History—20th century. | Ideology—Political aspects—Turkey—History—20th century. | Social change—Turkey—History—20th century. | Cultural pluralism—Turkey—History—20th century. | Turkey—Politics and government—1918–1960. | BISAC: ARCHITECTURE / History / Modern (late 19th century to 1945). | HISTORY / Asia / Southeast Asia.

Classification: LCC NA1368 .K49 2015 | DDC 720.1/03—dc23

LC record available at http://lccn.loc.gov/2015037814

FOR MY PARENTS,

AYDIN AND GÜLER KEZER

CONTENTS

ACKNOWLEDGMENTS

This book has evolved over the course of several years with countless contributions from mentors, colleagues, archivists and librarians, and friends and family who, directly or indirectly, lent their generous support. I would like to express my immense gratitude to one and all for being there and making it happen.

At Berkeley, my mentor extraordinaire Dell Upton forever transformed my understanding of society, space, and culture; and Nezar Alsayyad, with his boundless energy, always challenged me to do more and better. Ken Jowitt, at the Political Science Department, welcomed me to his "submarine"—as an architecture student, I was a strange bird in his seminars. A supporter since my sophomore year in college, Sibel Bozdoğan continuously helped shape and improve this project as an adviser at large in Cambridge and Ankara. I was also blessed with a close-knit group of fellow graduate students, now academics scattered around the globe, whose intellect and friendship I treasure in equal measure. I am grateful to the members of my first writing group, Swati Chattopadhyay, William Littmann, and especially Dianne Harris, who later encouraged me to submit to the Politics, Culture, and the Built Environment Series, and to Jessica Sewell, Arijit Sen, Marie-Alice L'Heureux, Greg Castillo, Rebecca Ginsburg, and Marta Gutman, who over the years shared their resources, enthusiasm, and insights. Sibel Zandi-Sayek, a friend since undergraduate years, deserves a special note of appreciation for the endless hours spent on Skype and e-mail patiently going over numerous drafts with me. In later years, as I moved to other institutions, I benefited from the support of new mentors and colleagues, in particular, Derek Gregory and Sherry McKay at the University of British Columbia; Jeff Day, Patricia Morgado, and Mark Hinchman at the University of Nebraska–Lincoln; and finally Andrew Ballantyne at Newcastle University. Along the way I was fortunate to meet Elizabeth Byrne, Ayhan Aktar, Anne MacLachlan, the late Sarkis Seropian, Rıfat Bali, Zeynep Bagana Önen, and Ruth Thomasian, whose wise input at crucial moments proved indispensible.

Universities, funding agencies, archives, and libraries on three continents provided the vital institutional support and resources to conduct research and to write about it. Funds for this project, as it expanded in scope, came from various grants small and large at the University of California at Berkeley, the Killam Trust and Cecil and Ida Green Fellowship at the University of British Columbia, the Maude Hammond Fling Fellowship at the University of Nebraska, the Getty Foundation, the British Academy, Newcastle University, and the Institute of Turkish Studies. Libraries at Berkeley and Harvard, the Turkish Historical Society (Türk Tarih Kurumu), The History Foundation (Tarih Vakfı), The Turkish Ministry of Public Works, the Grand National Assembly of Turkey, the National Library of Turkey, the British Library, the Archives of the Turkish Republic (Başbakanlık Cumhuriyet Arşivi), VEKAM (Vehbi Koç ve Ankara Araştırmaları Merkezi), Project SAVE, the Pious Foundations Administration (Vakıflar Genel Müdürlüğü), the General Directorate of Religious Affairs (Diyanet İşleri Başkanlığı), SALT archives and collections in Istanbul, Architektur Museum at Berlin Technical University, and the National Archives at Kew, have provided me with invaluable materials. I hereby thank their thoughtful and generous staff. At the University of Pittsburgh Press, Peter Kracht and Abby Collier patiently walked me through this complicated process.

This book is dedicated to my parents, who selflessly invested in our education: My father Aydın Kezer did not live to see me realize his dream of becoming a historian, but, in my mind, I still imagine discussions with him about my work. Güler Kezer, my mother and earliest role model, who instilled in me the love of learning, continues to teach me something new every day. I am also grateful to my brother Sinan, my first and truest sparring partner, for always cheering me on. Last but not least, I turn to Stephan Heilmayr, who has endured my ups and downs, lived through my trials and tribulations, and offered me logistical and emotional support throughout: I can't thank you enough for being an unstinting life partner.

NOTES ON
NAMES, PRONUNCIATION,
AND SOURCES

In Turkey last names were introduced only after 1934 as part of republican reforms, designed, among other things, to keep more accurate records on the population. Although this book covers events that started prior to the adoption of last names, I have chosen to refer to all characters with their last names and without the parentheses that are used in Turkish publications to indicate that the last name was taken after the event described. One exception is Mustafa Kemal Atatürk, whom I refer to by both his last name and his first and middle names.

The Turkish alphabet has several letters with diacriticals, and some other letters differ significantly from their English pronunciation. Below is a brief guide:

C, c	like *j* in English
Ç, ç	like *ch* in English
Ğ, ğ	is a soft *g*, that is like the *gh* in throu*gh*
I, ı	pronounced like the *e* in summ*e*r
İ, i	pronounced like the *i* in *i*t
Ö, ö	like *ö* in German, often transcribed as *oe* in English
Ş, ş	like *sh* in Engli*sh*
Ü, ü	like *ü* in German, often transcribed as *ue* in English

The following information is a guide to the archival sources:

Resmi Gazete, Official Bulletin of the State: Laws become effective only after they are published in *Resmi Gazete*. Wherever there is a reference to a law enacted, I have used the Turkish notation for the publication: Çiftçiyi

Topraklandırma Kanunu [name of law], *Resmi Gazete* [name of publication], no. 6032 [issue number], June 15, 1945 [date of publication], article no. 4753 [number of the law].

TBMM Zabıt Ceridesi (Minutes of the Grand National Assembly): This is a multivolume collection of the minutes of the debates in the Grand National Assembly. The key for locating content is: *TBMM Zabıt Ceridesi* [name of publication], Devre VI [number of term], Cilt 17 [volume number], İçtima 45 [meeting number], p132 [page number] (April 28, 1941) [date of meeting].

Başbakanlık Cumhuriyet Arşivi (Archives of the Republic): There does not seem to be a standard way of referring to the holdings of the Archives of the Republic (Başbakanlık Cumhuriyet Arşivi, BCA in the endnotes). I have adopted the notation used in publications of the School of Political Science at Ankara University: BCA: [archive name] 30. . 10.0.0 [source of holdings (*fon*, in Turkish)]/ 139.997. .4. [location] / 13341 [file number].

BUILDING
MODERN TURKEY

INTRODUCTION

AMBIVALENCES
AND
ANXIETIES

The Turkish History Exhibition was inaugurated by Mustafa Kemal Atatürk, the founder and first president of the Republic of Turkey, on October 20, 1937, at the Dolmabahçe Palace in Istanbul.[1] His larger-than-life green marble bust greeted visitors at the entrance, positioned in an alcove as the centerpiece of the exhibition's introductory tableau. Below him, on the ground, lay a giant map of Eurasia, with a series of concentric circles emanating from Central Asia. According to the newly minted Turkish History Thesis, this was where the Turkish people had originated and spread out in successive waves to the rest of the world, bringing civilization to the new lands wherein they eventually settled. Atatürk's words, pronounced when he first embarked on the ambitious project of producing a "national history" in 1931, framed this map: "*writing* history is just as important as *making* history: if the writers are not faithful to the makers, then the immutable truth will be altered in ways that can confound mankind."[2] Using maps, photographs, drawings, and artifacts from archaeological excavations throughout the country, the exhibition was intended to serve as a material embodiment of the History Thesis, which placed the "Turkish race" at the forefront of world historical development through the ages.[3] Held in conjunction with the much lauded Turkish History Congress, it was ephemeral—lasting only a few days—and had relatively few visitors, but the exhibition's central themes directly fed into educational curricula, civic rituals, and public policy, which vastly augmented its effect.[4] As such, it was part of a much larger discursive project to generate and disseminate a foundation myth, instilling a proud sense of shared history and common destiny as a uni-

FIGURE I.1. THE ENTRANCE OF THE EXHIBITION, ORGANIZED IN TANDEM WITH THE CONFERENCE, FEA-
TURING AN ATATÜRK BUST ATOP THE MAP OF EURASIA WITH THE CONCENTRIC WAVES REPRESENTING THE
WESTBOUND SPREAD OF TURKIC PEOPLES. COURTESY OF THE TURKISH HISTORICAL SOCIETY LIBRARY.

fied nation in a population that had been so profoundly traumatized and
displaced by endless years of war.

Indeed, the last few decades of the Ottoman Empire were a period of
accelerated unraveling under mounting pressures from various internal
and external factors. Growing integration with the networks of imperial
capitalism had transformed the empire's geography and its social and economic structures.[5] Having expanded by conquest and the accommodative
incorporation of diverse peoples and their customs and laws, the empire
historically comprised an inherently pluralistic society, though with in-
built asymmetries in its social structures, that historically had favored its
Muslim populations.[6] Over the course of the nineteenth century, however,
whereas many entrepreneurial non-Muslims who engaged in commerce
and new professions saw their financial fortunes rise, Muslims, despite
their privileged status, saw theirs ebb. Although the actual fluctuations
in wealth and status were more complicated and varied by region, these
shifts reinforced mutually held negative stereotypes, contributing to rising
tensions between the empire's constituent millets (ethnoreligious com-

munities). Increased contact, through conflict or collaboration, with the West also facilitated the influx of Enlightenment ideas. Nascent notions of individual rights, citizenship, and national identity were taken up by the empire's diverse populations and reinterpreted as needed to legitimize new kinds of political activities and demands.[7] Such demands—including secession—were aided and abetted by nineteenth-century imperial powers all of which had designs on Ottoman territories and assets: Great Britain, France, and Russia sought to partition and control certain strategic regions through client states, while Germany was after retaining the empire largely intact but bringing it under its sphere of influence.[8] The confluence of these demands and designs made for a very volatile environment, with wars on several fronts and insurrections in many regions (especially where the central authority's reach was weak), leading to great loss of life, assets, and territory in the waning years of the nineteenth century.

Of all successive wars, defeat in the Balkan War (1912–1913) proved to be a watershed moment because it unequivocally spelled the end of Ottoman presence in Europe, truncating a particular geographic imagination, long cultivated in the minds of the empire's ruling class, of an imperial domain straddling across Anatolia and Rumelia with Istanbul ensconced in its middle.[9] As the first Ottoman foothold in Europe, conquered between the fourteenth and fifteenth centuries, the Balkan Peninsula had been as integral to the empire as its Anatolian half, with which it shared identical governmental, institutional, and social structures. The peninsula was home to the empire's oldest and most prosperous provinces, from which a substantial portion of its military and bureaucratic elite was recruited. The Ottomans had been losing ground in the region since the early nineteenth century, but the Balkans had continued to have a large Muslim population that had remained loyal to Istanbul. Following the Balkan defeat, the ongoing flow of Muslim (both Turcophone and non-Turcophone) refugees escaping ethnoreligious violence mainly from pro-Slavic and Christian forces in regions surrounding the Ottoman Empire peaked.[10] A massive influx of uprooted and dejected people into major Anatolian cities stretched to the breaking point the ability of local authorities to cope.[11] Realizing how real and close to home the threat of disintegration was, Ottoman politicians and intellectuals began to seek explanations—as well as scapegoats—for the empire's misfortunes. It was at this juncture that a particularly zealous faction within the newly formed Congress of Union and Progress (CUP) staged a coup to take over the government and effectively established a dictatorship.[12] Shocked by the loss of their homelands, CUP leaders had become ideologically radicalized. They espoused a highly polarized version of nationalism with strong anti-non-Muslim tendencies, which now they fully expected to translate into policy.[13] The CUP takeover foreclosed all possibilities for Ottomanism, a more liberal ideology calling for a reformed and equalized pluralistic society. Since the CUP's steering cadres had, from their earlier education onward, cultivated close ties to Germany (both military and educational cooperation schemes), the coup also brought the empire into closer alliance with the Axis powers (Germany and the Austro-Hungarian Empire) that were then just in the making.

The CUP's decision to enter the First World War on the side of the Axis powers—with the not-so-hidden agenda of recovering lost lands—turned out to be an unmitigated disaster and precipitated the empire's collapse. Unlike previous conflicts, the Ottomans had to fight this war on several distant fronts at once.[14] Considerably weakened by defeats in preceding wars, the Ottoman army suffered very heavy casualties and experienced mass desertions that not only undermined the morale but also wreaked havoc in the countryside as runaway soldiers turned into bandits and terrorized local populations. Moreover, because the army recruited mainly from the Anatolian peasantry, the absence of this large workforce from the fields severely affected food supplies. Moving armies also helped to spread epidemics—especially cholera and typhus in the summer—thus further contributing to mass civilian deaths. Most important, the First World War gave the CUP leaders an opening to implement some of their most radical ideas regarding population policy. Already before the war, claiming security concerns, they had purged thousands of Orthodox Greeks residing in the Aegean region of Greece.[15] In 1915, using the war and the activities of Armenian nationalists as a pretext, the CUP government ordered the mass deportation of Anatolian Armenians.[16] With the exception of those in Istanbul, all Armenians were exiled to the desert areas of what is modern-day Syria, Lebanon, Palestine, and Iraq in a process that decimated at least 40 percent of their population who died at the hands of CUP officials and marauding bandits as well as from exposure, disease, and starvation.[17] In sum, the Ottoman population endured a 2.5 percent net decrease, something no other First World War participant experienced.[18]

Following the 1918 Armistice, the Ottoman Empire came under extensive occupation by the Allies and effectively lost its sovereignty. In this state of post-occupation confusion, Mustafa Kemal Atatürk, the emergent leader of the nationalist liberation movement (Kuva-i Milliye) managed to pull together a coalition of diverse constituencies, which, despite profound differences of opinion and allegiance, were unified in their opposition to the foreign takeover of Anatolia. Meanwhile, although its leadership was unceremoniously deposed, the CUP's rank and file had remained in place and several of them—including secret operatives from Teşkilat-ı Mahsusa who had been instrumental in executing some of the most ruthless policies during the First World War—also joined Mustafa Kemal's forces.[19] It was this coalition—comprising, in addition to the military-bureaucratic cadre close to Mustafa Kemal at the helm, local notables whose organizations had a more limited geographic outlook, religious leaders whose primary allegiance was to Islam the Sultan-Caliph, and former CUP operatives— that rallied people to fight one last war against post–First World War occupation. The best-known battles of the Turkish War of Independence were fought on the Western front against the Greek army—which, notably, was pursuing its own nationalist vision of unifying the Aegean under a Hellenic flag—but there were also violent guerilla-style wars in eastern and southeastern Turkey to liberate these regions from French occupation. In the end, taking advantage of the vulnerabilities of the Greek army, the war weariness of the Allies, and the postrevolutionary about-face in Russia, the nationalists prevailed, reclaiming the territory that became modern Turkey.

Thereafter, Mustafa Kemal and the military-bureaucratic cadre around him decided that in order to thrive in the post–First World War context, it was imperative to reinvent Turkey as a modern nation-state, rather than returning to Istanbul and restoring the old imperial order. In 1923 they relocated the capital to Ankara, which had been their wartime base of operations, and proclaimed a republic. The challenges of such a comprehensive reinvention were multifarious. On the home front, this was a profound change, which meant not only the wholesale importation of a new form of government with its laws and institutions but also the rejection of the Ottoman legacy that had shaped this land and its people for more than six centuries.[20] It entailed categorically repudiating—rather than repairing—the already damaged tapestry of ethnic and religious communitarian structures that had historically constituted the empire's social fabric. A pluralistic society that accommodated differences in linguistic, ethnic, and religious affiliation and even a range of legal statuses for residency and citizenship was anathema to the nationalist vision of a modern state with a homogeneous population, which identified as Turkish to the exclusion of all other ethnoreligious identities, and was subject to uniform laws.[21] On the international front, it required reestablishing the new state as a recognized peer among other nation-states at a time when such recognition was accorded begrudgingly by the Great Powers (especially the winners of the First World War) that dominated the diplomatic arena.[22] In the eyes of modern Turkey's founding fathers, this also necessitated stitching Turkey more firmly to modern Western traditions, albeit at the expense of their own. Having internalized Orientalist criticisms of the Ottoman state and culture, they sought to introduce Westernizing reforms that would affect the day-to-day lives of the citizenry on an unprecedented scale. Finally, for the long term, to ensure the new order's durability, it called for creating and maintaining a standard legal, institutional, and physical infrastructure regulating relations among citizens and between citizens and the state, thereby sustaining the reproduction of society as a nation.[23]

Inaugurated just a year before the end of Mustafa Kemal's fifteen-year-long rule as the founding president of the republic (as if a bookend to an intense period of transformations), the History Exhibition summarized the official interpretation of these events, the lessons to be drawn from them, and repositioned Turkey historically vis-à-vis the larger world around it. Exhibitions such as this were a favored medium for Turkey's leaders to communicate how they saw themselves and wanted to be seen by others. Borrowing from the well-worn late nineteenth- to early twentieth-century repertoire of modernizing states, Early Republican exhibitions sought to use the persuasiveness of physical objects and images to educate a broader citizenry and entice them to participate willingly in advancing that state's agenda.[24] At the same time, however, contextualized and examined as material artifacts, they also revealed, at their seams, the tensions inherent in formulating and disseminating the official foundation narrative and the difficulty of keeping at bay alternative narratives and factual challenges that could disrupt it. Seen in that light, the exhibition encapsulated Turkey's leaders' most consuming anxieties outlined above: achieving and preserving national integration, territorial sovereignty, and recognition as a peer within the then exclusive international system of states.

The exhibition displayed two distinctive yet interrelated strategies to frame the modern nation-state building project as inevitable and to preemptively discredit challenges that could undermine this narrative. First, the republican section of the exhibition, which, despite spanning barely fourteen years, took up the largest amount of space at the center, was presented as a comparison that sharply contrasted the failures of the Ottoman Empire with the accomplishments and vision of the Kemalist regime. Large posters and glass cases flanking the two sides of the U-shaped alcove proudly displayed the various areas of state intervention successfully pursued by the republican government including justice, economy, customs and tariffs, agriculture, industry, health, arts, education, architecture, and urbanism. Some of these exhibits were designed as two-part displays in a manner akin to "before and after" comparisons commonly seen in advertising. Others, replete with graphs and pictures, proudly displayed the country's growing industrial production, improved educational fa-

FIGURE I.2. A COMPARATIVE IMAGE OF BEFORE AND AFTER FROM THE REPUBLICAN SECTION OF THE EX-
HIBITION FEATURING THE IMPROVEMENTS IN THE JUDICIARY. IN THE EARLY YEARS OF THE REPUBLIC, THIS
VISUAL TROPE OF PITTING THE OTTOMAN AGAINST THE REPUBLICAN TO POSIT THE SUPERIORITY OF THE
LATTER PROLIFERATED IN ALL TYPES OF MEDIA CONTROLLED BY THE STATE. COURTESY OF THE TURKISH
HISTORICAL SOCIETY LIBRARY.

cilities, expanding rail network, and better health care, all of which were
the work of the new regime. Ironically this binary framing, which had
been borrowed from Orientalist discourses and internalized and rein-
strumentalized by the Kemalists, had now become a ubiquitous narrative
device to validate their visions and policies as unprecedented, yet necessary, measures to move Turkey forward and away from past mistakes that
had gotten in the way of its progress.[25] Moreover, it conveniently glossed
over more than a century of Ottoman reforms that had effectively laid the

FIGURE I.3. A SCENE FROM THE CONFERENCE. HASAN CEMIL ÇAMBEL DELIVERS HIS REMARKS. BEHIND HIM IS AN EARLY USE OF THE HITITE SUN AS A LOGO, A PRACTICE THAT CONTINUES TO BE VERY COMMON AMONG VARIOUS PUBLIC AND PRIVATE ORGANIZATIONS. COURTESY OF THE TURKISH HISTORICAL SOCIETY LIBRARY.

ground work for many of the changes implemented under the republic, thus attributing to the republican leadership all the credit for the country's accelerated modernization.

Second, although it appeared to be all-encompassing, the exhibition was, in fact, quite selective about the cultures and connections it featured and how it ordered them. The displays included several ancient civilizations of the broader region—such as Sumeria, Egypt, and classical Greece, co-opting some cultures with which links were at best dubious, as part of modern Turkey's heritage. But it excluded other local contemporary cultures—such as Anatolian Greeks, Armenians, Arabs, and Kurds—who made up the empire's Anatolian population. In order to bolster Turkey's claims to an undeniable place within the genealogy of modern European history, the exhibition dated the presence of the "Turkish race" in Anatolia to the Neolithic period and portrayed it as being related to the region's ancient civilizations to which European nations also traced their cultural ancestry—albeit through similarly fictive processes of cultural appropriation.[26] For instance, the use of the newly excavated Hittite Sun statue as the logo for the Second History Congress, which the exhibition accompanied, was especially telling. The logo presented as a foregone conclusion the shared and uninterrupted lineage between Hittites, an Anatolian civilization from more than three millennia ago, and contemporary Turks. It implied that by virtue of thus antedating other local ethnic groups, whose long-standing presence was known to all but was carefully edited out of the narrative, the exclusivity of Turkish claims to this indivisible territory was justified beyond a doubt.

Despite its careful scripting, the exhibition also lay bare the ambivalences of the new regime and its leaders and their inability to seal the past hermetically. As most ironically epitomized by the venue chosen for the exhibition, Dolmabahçe Palace, rather than, say, a modern republican structure in Ankara, the Kemalist narrative was far from consistent in its historiographic selectivity and the polarization it promoted. Far more dazzling than anything on display, the palace's profusely decorated Ceremonial Hall, with its 36-meter (118-foot)-high domed ceiling and 4.5-ton crystal chandelier—a gift from Queen Victoria—hovering right at the center of the section dedicated to the republic, threatened to undercut any assertions about the purported superiority of Kemalist achievements over Ottoman failures. Such a choice would not have been so noteworthy had the Kemalists not maligned Istanbul and repudiated the legacy of the Ottoman Empire so categorically. But as the last seat of the Sultans, designed and built in the mid-nineteenth century by Garabet and Nigogos Balyan of the long-serving Armenian family of imperial architects, Dolmabahçe was a quintessential part of Turkey's Ottoman past. And it was, by the same token, an embodiment of the foreign affectation, pluralistic constitution, and profligacy for which Kemalists condemned their Ottoman predecessors.

The anxieties and ambivalences embedded in the materiality of the 1937 exhibition also lie at the heart of this book. In retrospect, even when taken on its own terms, the exhibition may be read as symptomatic of the growing cognitive dissonance between the promise of the republic and what it delivered. The centerpiece of the republican section, featuring a large photograph of the inaugural meeting of the Grand National Assembly in April 1920, expressly celebrated democratic self-governance as the culmination, in Atatürk's words, of the "nation's centuries-long quest for self-governance and a living symbol of it"[27] Presented as achieved, this was a goal that eluded the Turkish citizenry. The 1920s and 1930s were characterized by a fierce rivalry among members of the leadership cadre jockeying for power, occasional outbursts of violence and the dissolution of wartime alliances with tribal and religious leaders, who now resented the

FIGURE I.4. THE TWO-PAGE SPREAD FROM *LA TURQUIE KAMALISTE*, THE GOVERNMENT'S MULTILINGUAL PROPAGANDA PUBLICATION, DEPICTING THE EXHIBITION'S CENTRAL SECTION AT THE CEREMONIAL HALL OF DOLMABAHÇE PALACE. NOTE THE LARGE CHANDELIER, A GIFT FROM QUEEN VICTORIA, AND THE ELABORATE DETAILING OF THE MID-NINETEENTH-CENTURY OTTOMAN INTERIOR, A BACKGROUND AGAINST WHICH THE EXHIBITION PALES. COURTESY OF THE TURKISH HISTORICAL SOCIETY LIBRARY.

elimination of their power base by the expanding central authority, and growing resentment and alienation among the population at large whose voices almost never trickled up. The increasingly authoritarian regime that emerged out of this process brooked no dissent, neither in politics nor in historiography, and was ruthless in squashing both. In tandem with the narrowing political horizon, starting from the late 1920s, when attempts to produce a standardized version of Turkish history—especially for use in textbooks—gained momentum, scholars who called for a more critical evidence-based historiography found themselves increasingly silenced by their more ideologically driven counterparts who ultimately put their stamp on the Turkish History Thesis.[28] By the time of this exhibition, what

had once been a fluid debate about the shape of the past and the arc of the future was fixed, preemptively foreclosing alternate paths and the possibility of discussing them in an open scholarly environment—or, for that matter, in a political forum.

Building Modern Turkey portrays Turkey's transition from a pluralistic (multiethnic, multireligious) empire to a modern unitary nation-state as a fitful twofold process that simultaneously unleashed creative and destructive forces. It juxtaposes the drive to put in place the physical infrastructure and sociospatial practices of a new cultural and political order with the urge to dismantle the vestiges of its predecessor and also reveals the inextricable—if hitherto overlooked—interdependence between the two. The Turkish experience also provides a good case study for exploring the spatiality of nation-state building processes, which unfold at different and interdependent scales from that of the individual self to that of larger geopolitical configurations. The fine-grained analysis of specific sites and spatial practices provided here illuminates the concrete and performative dimensions of shoring up a particular political regime, instilling in the population a sense of membership in and allegiance to the nation above all competing loyalties, and ensuring the longevity of a particular social and political order.

This book consists of three main sections that correspond to the concerns outlined above. The first of these, "Forging a New Identity," examines how the formative processes of the new state played out spatially. The first chapter, "Political Capital," focuses on the making of Ankara, which was, by the nationalists' own admission, the crucible in which they sought to forge a new political identity and a modern way of life. But by the same token, contentions over the form, use, accessibility, and ownership of the new capital's physical spaces became symptomatic of broader frictions resulting in the emergence of an authoritarian politics and the formation of an exclusive political and cultural elite that characterized modern Turkey for decades to come. "Theaters of Diplomacy," the second chapter, examines the challenges Turkey faced in gaining recognition as a peer within the international system of states. Moving between scales from Ankara's embassy row to the broader eastern Mediterranean region, it traces hitherto overlooked links between the formation of regional spheres of influence in the unstable geopolitical climate of the interwar years and Turkey's preference for German and (to a lesser extent) Russian models of modernization.

The second section, "Erasures in the Land," explores how the republican leadership sought to take apart the physical and figurative scaffolding that sustained the Ottoman society's historically pluralistic constitution so as to realign people's collective allegiances around a unitary Turkish nation. Despite their great reliance on Islam's existing networks to mobilize the population for the War of Independence, Turkey's leaders regarded religion as a rival to nationalism. Hence "Dismantling the Landscapes of Islam," the book's third chapter, examines the outlawing of the public expression of religious identities, the closure and demolition of various religious enclaves, and the appropriation of assets pertaining to religious organizations, while funneling their revenues to the preferred projects of the cash-strapped republic. The following chapter, "Of Forgotten People and Forgotten Places," investigates how, as if to nationalize Turkey's history and geography, the country's dwindling non-Muslim citizens were marginalized in the public sphere, their properties appropriated, and the vestiges of their existence deliberately eradicated.

While they jettisoned the constitutive institutions of the Ottoman society, Turkey's leaders also sought to replace them with modern ones to ensure the longevity of the state they were building. The third and final section, "An Imaginable Community," discusses how indispensable the creation of a tangible network of sites and services designed to sustain the social reproduction of a homogeneous polity was to forging an "imagined" national community. The fifth chapter, "Nationalizing Space," is dedicated to the efforts to create a material culture closely identified with the new state through the expansion of infrastructural projects designed to shape the daily lives of the citizenry. Through a study of some of the most representative republican institutions, "Manufacturing Turkish Citizens," the book's last chapter, examines how Turkey's leaders deployed a range of prescriptive sociospatial practices to inculcate the masses with a sense of territorial attachment, a shared notion of spatial order, and the habits of body and mind to sustain and transmit these to future generations.

PART I

FORGING A

NEW IDENTITY

CHAPTER 1

POLITICAL CAPITAL

n a laudatory article that appeared in the government-issued multilingual propaganda publication *La Turquie Kamaliste*, an American journalist who visited Turkey's new capital in the late 1930s observed:

> Ankara is a city built by the people of a living generation—by Atatürk and his followers. They wanted and they have a capital, an absolutely new city which would symbolize the breakaway from the old and which would demonstrate to themselves and to their visitors what can be done in a hitherto backward Turkey. . . . It isn't just this giant city that makes us feel that this is Atatürk's city. Ankara embodies the spirit of the new Turkey about which we have read so much but find hard put to find in Istanbul.[1]

Indeed the founding fathers of the republic considered building a new capital in Ankara to be integral to their twin goals of modernizing the country and forging a new political order. They fervently believed that producing a new built environment that physically and metaphorically stood apart from that of its Ottoman predecessor and provided a model site for enacting the modern way of life and reaffirming the new cultural values would lend their revolution a tangibility that discourse alone could not.[2] Beyond a mere change of address for the seat of power, building a new capital provided an extraordinary opportunity for inscribing the structural transformation of the state into the physical landscape. Therefore, although this gargantuan enterprise threatened to drain Turkey's already scarce human and material resources, the nationalists seized on its cathartic quality. If starting from scratch entailed years of severe hardship, it also afforded them a unique chance to articulate a new beginning.

Le Ministère des Travaux Publics.

The Ministrey of Public Works

Das Ministerium für Öffentliche Arbeiten

Ankara is a city of the future. Istanbul is a city of the past. In the latter the visitor thinks in terms of Ottoman rulers, mosques, and history books. The average visitor who has spent a few days rushing from Aya Sophia to the Great Walls and quickly around the old Hippodrome goes home to tell the folks about Turkey. He is no better equipped than the stay-at-homes who get their ideas out of novels about sultans. For in Istanbul he has probably eaten Russian food, got his views on the government from a Greek porter, been guided by an Armenian courier and concentrated exclusively on the relics of

Istanbul est une ville du Passé

Istanbul is a city of the past

Istanbul - die Stadt der Vergangenheit

FIGURE 1.1. A PAGE FROM THE ARTICLE "ANKARA-ISTANBUL" COMPARING THE TWO CITIES. THE ARTICLE IS GENEROUSLY ILLUSTRATED, BUT ONLY THREE OF THE TWENTY-SIX ILLUSTRATIONS PERTAIN TO ISTANBUL. THE TOP IMAGE IS FROM ANKARA AND FEATURES TWO OF THE MINISTRIES IN THE GOVERNMENT QUARTER, DESIGNED BY AUSTRIAN ARCHITECT CLEMENS HOLZMEISTER. BELOW IS THE RECOGNIZABLE SILHOUETTE OF ISTANBUL'S HISTORIC PENINSULA. COURTESY OF THE TURKISH HISTORICAL SOCIETY LIBRARY.

The making of Ankara was riddled with challenges: Turkey's new leaders lacked the social or physical planning expertise needed to define or implement such a complex and comprehensive undertaking. Their widely divergent ideas about a modern capital that could measure up to its Western counterparts were based on fragmented recollections of personal visits to European capitals rather than a systematic understanding of the structure and organization of these cities, their historical development, or their problems. They were also under tremendous pressure to build quickly, as Ankara had neither sufficient office space to accommodate basic government functions nor enough housing for the unprecedented influx of people whose arrival pushed the population from 20,000 in 1920 to 74,000 in 1927 and to 125,000 in 1935.[3] Furthermore, the competing needs and interests of the local population and the incoming groups pulled the process in different and often incompatible directions. Consequently, initial planning and construction efforts were largely uncoordinated and consisted of sporadic attempts to solve discrete problems. As Geoffrey Knox, the chargé d'affaires for the British embassy, put it, urban expansion was rapid and haphazard:

> Every effort is being exerted with a fine disregard for expediency—even of possibility—to make of Angora the strategic, economic, social as well as the political center of the country. . . . Banks spring up like mushrooms on an ever larger and imposing scale, but all with an equally imponderable capital. Houses, shops and villas are built in every direction with no coherent plan in a wave of optimistic speculation. New roads are traced and abandoned after a spell of feverish and expensive work in order to seek another alignment suitable to some man of influence, or, if they reach completion, subside in a few days under the stress of modern traffic. The municipality undeterred by chronic bankruptcy, goes from one grandiose project to another, each more wasteful, incoherent and inept than the last.[4]

Ankara's built environment provides a fertile ground for examining the untidy process by which republican ideals of a modern urban life and a new political culture were translated into action—and not least because so much had been invested in it symbolically, materially, and politically. Probing the discrepancies between the verbal and visual rhetoric used to promote the making of Ankara and actual events on the ground reveals how expediently malleable the nature of modernization discourses and practices were under the republican regime. Similarly, examining the still visible traces of tentative beginnings and altered or abandoned schemes in the city's physical fabric reveals evidence of manifest resistances, rival interventions, and conflicting intentions. In short, when Ankara and its representations are seen through this forensic lens, what was discarded becomes as informative as what was implemented and what was highlighted becomes as telling as what was downplayed.

This chapter focuses on two sites that are especially symptomatic of the divergent forces that shaped both the physical form of Turkey's new capital and its form of government. The first of these is the Citadel and its immediate vicinity, which constituted the town of Ankara until the arrival of the nationalists to set up the wartime headquarters for the post–First World War struggle for national liberation. Although the nationalist leadership invoked the imperative to modernize as the primary driver of their decision to relocate and purge all social, institutional, and spatial vestiges of the Ottoman Empire, the pliable logic by which they physically and rhetorically repositioned the existing town betrayed other more pragmatic—and often self-serving—calculations. The second site is the North-South axis, which became Ankara's main artery, radically transforming the town's morphology. Although the artery was to be punctuated with a sequence of memorials replicating the milestones of Turkey's journey from its grassroots independence struggle to democracy, halfway into the implementation the Presidential Palace replaced the Grand National Assembly as the culmination of that narrative. Far from being accidental, this shift paralleled changes in the political regime, which was fast veering toward authoritarianism. I argue that the intertwined stories of these two sites, taken together, hold clues to broader questions about the nature of political authority in the modern Turkish state and the fraught relationship between the country's ascendant Westernized elites and its population at large.

JUSTIFYING THE MOVE

In the early years of the republic, the nationalist intelligentsia used two complementary tropes to justify the decision to relocate the capital in Ankara. The first of these was a logical extension of the ubiquitous and overarching binary discourse that pitted the Ottoman against the republican order to posit the virtuous achievements of the latter over the failures of the former. Using Ankara and Istanbul—two actual places—to illustrate the differences imparted the comparisons a degree of concreteness that sheer words could not attain. In this ever-expanding verbal visual repertoire of contrasts, Ankara became the embodiment of patriotism and progress, whereas Istanbul was assigned the negative mirror image of these qualities, perfidy and obscurantism. The second trope was the equally persistent myth that Ankara had, miraculously, been built from scratch by the idealist founding fathers of the republic. The home base of the nationalist revolution was now an exemplary capital that was transforming Anatolia's barren plains. Both tropes were widely disseminated through all the means available to the government, in textbooks, newspapers, traveling movie screenings and exhibitions, songs, posters, and speeches. Both masked inconvenient incongruities and pragmatic considerations that would otherwise undercut the image of unmitigated idealism carefully maintained by the republican elite.

In their efforts to validate their actions, the nationalists indiscriminately targeted every aspect of Istanbul and, by implication, the Ottoman legacy it represented. They were critical of the city's location, tucked in the northwestern corner of the country, too far away to hear people's concerns or attend to them in times of need. Yet another cause for concern was the leverage European states had gained in Ottoman politics, mostly through liaisons cultivated with powerful palace officials and bureaucrats since the eighteenth century. They also had substantial reservations about Istanbul's susceptibility to unchecked foreign influence because it was a major port city with a cosmopolitan population. In particular, they regarded the city's predominantly non-Muslim merchants as agents of imperial capitalism whose ventures with European merchants and manufacturers had been detrimental to the national economy and industry. The nationalists were aware that these networks had not necessarily dissolved following the collapse of the Ottoman Empire and remained a serious threat to achieving full sovereignty. Summarizing these concerns in debates at the Grand National Assembly, which led to the proclamation of Ankara as capital, Representative Besim (Atalay) passionately argued that "places like Basra or Erzurum could not be responsibly governed from such a distance.[5] Istanbul, as he put it, was more like a colonial capital "like Congo, like Calcutta, like the colonial capitals of Indochina" rather than a self-selected capital.[6] Finally, the nationalists saw the Ottoman administration as a tenacious roadblock to Turkey's embrace of modernity, and Istanbul itself as the symbol of that stagnation. Not only had the Istanbul government "surrounded itself with a Great Wall of China" cutting itself off from the rest of the country, posited the semiofficial daily *Hakimiyet-i Milliye*, but it had also managed to "isolate Anatolia and the people of Anatolia from the rest of the planet, from the Enlightenment of the civilized world until now."[7]

Therefore, the nationalists reasoned, the relocation of the capital and returning to the "bosom of the nation" (*sine-i millet*) was a vital course correction to safeguard the country's future and protect it from infringements on national sovereignty.[8] Their conviction that there was an active and mutually reinforcing relationship between state, space, and the formation of a new and modern national identity crystallized during the negotiations for funding Ankara's construction at the GNA.[9] Despite the disproportionate investment it would require, they argued that "building a government seat worthy of an advanced state, by outfitting it with the necessary infrastructure, sanitary and scientific dwellings, and other essentials of civilization is one of the most vital duties of our government as authorized and sanctioned by the Grand National Assembly."[10] The making of Ankara was frequently equated with Turkey's efforts to "join civilized nations marching forward on the path of progress,"[11] which was bringing the country in line with Western civilization and, in the republican imaginary, figuratively moving it closer to Europe. In an article that celebrated this very metaphoric proximity, the popular weekly *Yedigün* declared: The construction of Ankara has effectively transformed the map of Europe. We can now claim that Europe starts in Ankara. Was this not the purpose of our revolution?[12]

Nevertheless, becoming modern on these terms also implied an inherent subjugation to Western hegemony, which Turkish nationalists had aimed to break in the first place.[13] Constructing an "other" that could be pushed back to a permanent state of anteriority was a theme borrowed from post-Enlightenment notions of history and progress. It had been very effectively deployed by European powers to legitimize capitalist expansion and colonialism that had also been so detrimental to Ottoman interests. These (now extensively criticized) schemes were predicated on an essentialist divide between the West and the rest, implying that not only past societies but also all living ones could be located within a one-way timeline, the trajectory of which was determined by Western civilization.[14] Perceived distinctions between Western and non-Western cultures were thus construed as spatial and temporal distances, relegating the latter to the periphery and to a perpetual state of arrested development.[15] By polarizing Ankara and Istanbul, and mapping their differences in terms of an insurmountable chasm in time and space, Turkey's leaders now appeared to have appropriated the same rhetoric. This was tantamount to disavowing their own social, cultural, and, at times, political loyalties and engaging in an oppositional relationship with the very people they sought to liberate. It was also uncannily similar to the relationship between the colonizer and the colonized they so overtly denounced. In other words, propelled by a genuine desire to claim a more favorable place for Turkey in a world that was ostensibly ordered and dominated by Western interests, rather than challenging the divide between West and the rest the nationalists found themselves co-opting it.

Explicating this apparent paradox, Partha Chatterjee points at the parallels between the tenets and workings of imperialism and nationalist thought in non-Western societies and suggests that, indeed, nationalism perpetuates the legacies of both Orientalism and Eurocentrism.[16] Despite such fundamental similarities, however, as Chatterjee also recognizes, non-Western nationalist discourses are not simple localized replications of their more dominant Orientalist counterparts. Non-Western nationalists are often painfully aware of their tenuous position as "Easterners" in the West, and "Westerners" in the East, but never quite at home. This in-between place at the interstices of their dual and conflicted identities is precisely the platform whence they have to embark on a cautiously calculated yet volatile discourse, simultaneously reaffirming and refuting the epistemic and moral dominance of the West. In the process, they have to be and are very selective about what to adopt from the West and their choices are inescapably informed by the exigencies of their local political contexts. At the same time, from a historian's perspective, tracing their wobbles and swivels can be quite illuminating.

The obvious inconsistencies it engendered notwithstanding, the rationale for the polarizing rhetoric used to justify the move to Ankara snaps into focus when evaluated against the tense background of political and practical anxieties the nationalist leadership felt about the form of government and the seat of power in Turkey. In the first place, they had significant security concerns. Turkey's ability to monitor and protect the Turkish Straits had been curtailed by the Lausanne Treaty, which stipulated this to be a demilitarized zone overseen by an international commission. With virtually no control over the flow of maritime traffic across this strategic waterway, in the unstable geopolitical climate of the interwar years, Turkey's leaders could not risk keeping the capital in Istanbul. Second, Istanbul was the stronghold of domestic opposition against the nationalists' still tenuous hold on power. Istanbul's liberal intellectuals were critical of the concentration of power in the hands of Atatürk and his supporters and their apparent lack of accountability. The city's conservative intelligentsia objected to the radical change in the form of government, categorically rejecting the idea of instituting a republic. Most dangerously, parallel differences of opinion had also surfaced within the ranks of the nationalists.[17] A potential alliance between them and the regime's critics in Istanbul would further compromise the uncertain hold on power Atatürk and his supporters had. By staying in Ankara, they preempted an imminent power struggle, which likely would erode their authority in the long run even if they were to win in the first instance.[18] In other words, the nationalists needed a place, a platform from which to fend off challenges to the nation's

FIGURE 1.2. AERIAL VIEW OF ULUS FEATURING THE CITY'S GROWTH CIRCA 1930 (1—GRAND NATIONAL ASSEMBLY, 2—COURT OF FINANCIAL APPEALS, 3—MAKESHIFT FIRST BUILDING OF THE GRAND NATIONAL ASSEMBLY, ORIGINALLY, UNION AND PROGRESS PARTY CLUB, 4—ULUS ATATÜRK MONUMENT, 5— MINISTRY OF FINANCE AND TREASURY, 6—MINISTRY OF EDUCATION, 7—PARK (MILLET BAHÇESI), 8—ANKARA PALAS HOTEL, 9—THREE CITY BLOCKS OF HOUSING CONSTRUCTED BY THE PIOUS FOUNDATIONS ADMINISTRA-TION, INCLUDING A MULTISTORY PERIPHERY BLOCK CONTAINING A THEATER, 10—CENTRAL BANK, 11—BANK OF AGRICULTURE). COURTESY OF THE LIBRARY AT THE MINISTRY OF PUBLIC WORKS.

sovereignty and their legitimacy as the self-appointed agents of modernization in Turkey, and Ankara provided just that in practice and in theory.

AN INVISIBLE ANKARA

The second trope presented Ankara as a contemporary miracle, a modern capital built from scratch, through republican ingenuity and determination. Propaganda publications publicized the city's new public and institutional structures, its wide and straight avenues lined with saplings, its proud monuments and verdant parks. Ankara's happy residents also appeared in these places: students in modern schools, riding horses or playing tennis, enjoying a leisurely afternoon on Atatürk's model farm, or parading in the stadium in celebration of the nation's enormous achievements within such a short time. The notion that Ankara was built miraculously from scratch was consolidated in textbooks, and schoolchildren memorized the verses of the "Ankara March":

> Ankara Ankara, handsome Ankara
> Every wretched soul counts on you for support
> And you are all they need Ankara
> May insurgent heads rising up against you be subdued
> May with you Turkish might overcome all odds
> The first city forged out of nothing you are
> May your stones and your grounds live long Ankara![19]

In contrast to these depictions, which featured it devoid of context—standing alone amid a rugged and barren landscape or juxtaposed with Ankara's memorable landmarks—the Citadel was home to several densely packed neighborhoods both inside its walls and on its foothills. The se-

FIGURE 1.3. *ULUS* NEWSPAPER CLIPPING ABOUT EQUESTRIAN RACES HELD IN ANKARA. EQUESTRIANISM, A FAVORITE MIXED-GENDER ACTIVITY OF TURKEY'S NEW MILITARY-BUREAUCRATIC ELITE WAS OFTEN FEATURED IN THE PAGES OF CONTEMPORARY NEWSPAPERS.

FIGURE 1.4. THE HISTORIC TOWN OF ANKARA, CAREFULLY EDITED OUT OF REPUBLICAN REPRESENTATIONS OF THE CITY. LEFT: ANKARA POSTER BY RENOWNED POSTER ARTIST İHAP HULUSI; CENTER: COVER OF A CHILDREN'S BOOK (FOR AN ELEMENTRARY SCHOOL AUDIENCE); RIGHT: ANKARA PALAS LOGO FROM LETTERHEAD—ANKARA PALAS, SITUATED ACROSS FROM THE GRAND NATIONAL ASSEMBLY, SERVED AS A SEMI-OFFICIAL HOTEL FOR MOSTLY OFFICIAL GUESTS. IT WAS ALSO A POPULAR VENUE FOR STATE-SPONSORED BALLS, RECEPTIONS, AND OTHER SOCIAL EVENTS. THESE THREE IMAGES DEPICT IMPOSSIBLE VIEWS. THE CITADEL COULD NOT HAVE BEEN SEEN AS IT IS REPRESENTED IN JUXTAPOSITION WITH EITHER THE NATION (ULUS) MONUMENT OR ANKARA PALAS. IMAGES ON THE LEFT AND RIGHT ARE FROM THE COLLECTION OF BURÇAK EVREN.

lective omission of the built fabric in and around the Citadel highlighted its monumental qualities while downplaying the lives and livelihoods it engendered. Although it is common to take some artistic license streamlining images, stylizing objects, simplifying or eliminating details, and conjecturing impossible views especially in logos and posters, this imagery, which rendered Ankara's existing urban fabric invisible, was paralleled by political maneuvers that also kept its inhabitants out of relevant decision-making processes about their town's prospects. A brief detour in time will help to identify the genesis of these profound fractures, which eventually informed the way Ankara was conceptualized and experienced by different constituencies in the early years of the republic.

By 1919 when the nationalists arrived, Ankara, once a prosperous town in central Anatolia, had fallen on hard times. Throughout the 1800s, the town's once world-renowned mohair industry had nearly collapsed as mass-produced cheap European fabrics flooded the Ottoman market, and British entrepreneurs succeeded in breeding Ankara's rare and epony-

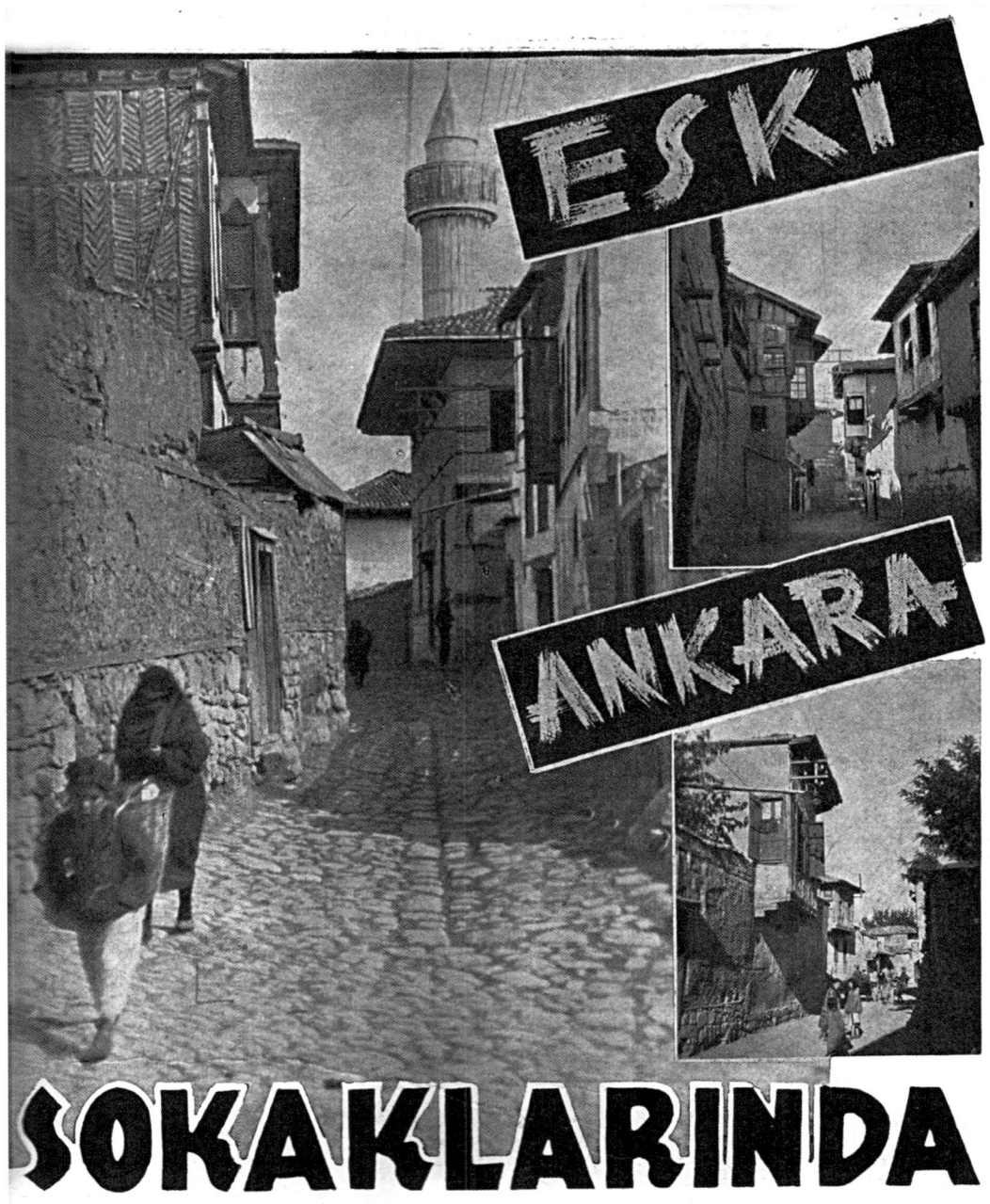

FIGURE 1.5. OTTOMAN ANKARA WITH ITS TIGHT, NARROW, MEANDERING STREETS AND COMPACT URBAN FABRIC DEPICTED TO SHOW WHAT REQUIRED MODERNIZATION. COURTESY OF VEKAM, VEHBİ KOÇ AND ANKARA RESEARCH CENTER.

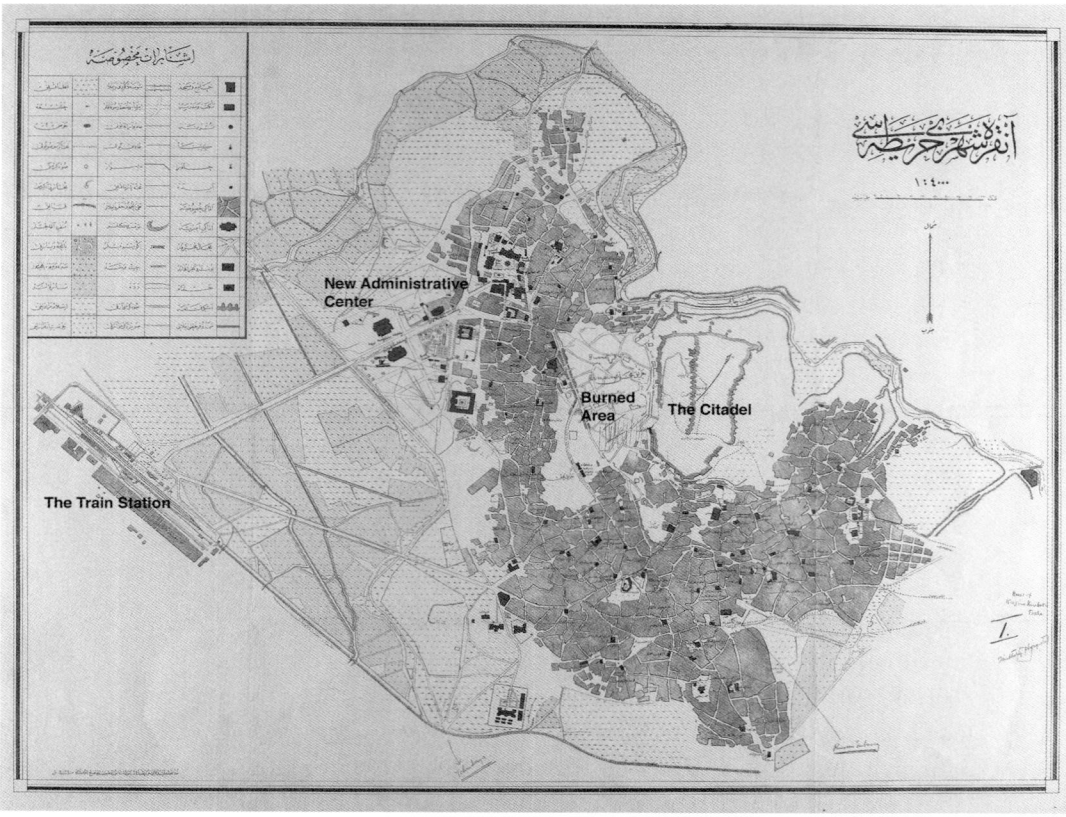

FIGURE 1.6. MAP OF ANKARA 1924. COURTESY OF VEKAM, VEHBİ KOÇ AND ANKARA RESEARCH CENTER.

mous goat in South Africa.[20] Ankara's prospects had improved somewhat toward the end of the century. As part of Ottoman administrative reforms, it had become a provincial capital. The ensuing construction of government offices, the opening of some modern institutions, including new schools, and the improvement of intercity transportation and communications gave it a regional advantage. Most important, the inauguration of rail service in 1893 converted Ankara into an important break-in-bulk point for Central Anatolia. These developments spurred the emergence of a new commercial-administrative area to the west of the Citadel, toward the station, thus breaking open Ankara's self-contained and rather insular form. While artisanal trades, purveyors of agricultural goods and traditional consumer items (foodstuffs, fabrics, household items) remained in the old commercial center by the southern gate of the Citadel, newer types of business engaged in import-export brokerage, warehousing, and sales of foreign goods began to define the new center to the west.[21] The construction of the new Ottoman institutions in this area further cemented the trend. Nevertheless, successive wars, bad harvests, and fires continued to take a toll, and these developments and expansions were not enough to counter Ankara's streak of bad fortune.[22]

In the post–First World War years, following the arrival of Atatürk and his supporters in Ankara to stage the War of Independence, Ankara assumed "a magnetic aura," especially in the eyes of those who stayed in Istanbul and longed to join them.[23] "Ankara, the ideal" wrote Yakup Kadri Karaosmanoğlu, "loomed in their imagination like a promised destination as if shrouded in mystery."[24] The striking view of the Citadel perched on a promontory hovering over the vast Central Anatolian plains was the most indelible image etched in the minds of the nationalists who contemplated Ankara for the first time as they made their way to the city from the train station. Circulating widely in banknotes, commemorative medals, posters, school textbooks, and the commercial logos of Ankara's prominent new businesses, this memorable image became closely identified with official foundation narratives. The solitary depictions of the Citadel became as familiar as images of modern Ankara, and together they served as proof positive of the magnitude of the transformations under the republic.

However, the romance with the idea of Ankara as a mythical place faded quickly once the decision was made to stay there permanently. Although they publicly declared that they took pride in renouncing Istanbul's urban comforts and pledged to "wear Ankara's dust and dirt on their sweaty foreheads as a badge of honor," in private, many members of the military-bureaucratic cadre balked at moving their families to the new capital, which lacked adequate roads, infrastructure, and housing.[25] Ankara's natives, meanwhile, found the sudden influx of strangers rather disruptive and referred to the "clean-shaven, shirt-wearing" newcomers as "yaban" (stranger), and were reserved, if not apprehensive, in their interactions with them. The nationalists and Ankara's natives had little, if any, cultural affinity with one another. The nationalists sought recognition for what they viewed as their superior skills and more refined tastes as well as an appreciation of the heroic mission they had embarked upon. But such distinctions carried little meaning for their local counterparts. As Vala Nureddin wrote of this wary first encounter: "One could distinguish the newcomers from the locals anywhere, anytime. The two crowds stood apart like oil and vinegar. On the one hand, the newcomers wanted to rise to the top like oil. On the other, the natives were as sour as vinegar toward them."[26]

Both sides held off on acting on their disagreements because they considered the arrangement temporary. After the War of Independence, however, tensions that had been festering beneath the surface began to crop up. The locals had mixed feelings about the nationalist bid for power and the decision to stay in Ankara. As the denizens of a small and impoverished town, they were proud of their contribution to winning the war and hoped to benefit from the change, but they also knew that, as a consequence, their town was no longer theirs alone.

THE POLITICS OF PLANNING THE CAPITAL

Nationalists' ambitions to build a model city were tempered by manifold challenges on the ground. They lacked the necessary planning and architectural expertise and were short of funds and workforce—especially qualified tradesmen—to complete such an undertaking. Critically, although after large fires in Ottoman cities, partial plans for burned-out districts had been carried out before, master-planning a complete city was uncharted territory.[27] In their search for solutions, the nationalists turned to foreign specialists. The first master plan for Ankara was commissioned to Carl Lörcher, a German planner who had previously worked for the Ottoman government in Istanbul.[28] Lörcher's initial proposal, dated 1925, concentrated on the city's existing core in the North though it also recognized incipient trends toward a southbound expansion in a two-part plan. In the north, around Ulus, he used the Citadel as a reference point for organizing the city's layout. He charted a web of baroque-inspired avenues, flanked by perimeter blocks reminiscent of Central European cities, stretching like spokes between the Citadel and the train station, which he designated as Ankara's main portal. He proposed a number of cultural and recreational amenities for Ulus, in addition to the official buildings already in place or in progress in the area—such as the original makeshift Grand National Assembly, which had since become the headquarters of the ruling Republican People's Party (RPP), and the nearby new Assembly, for which ground had been broken even prior to Lörcher's proposal.

It proved more difficult to integrate the inexorable trend toward southbound expansion coherently with Ankara's existing urban form and the radial geometry Lörcher had introduced to position the Citadel as a central reference point for the capitals' future development. The push for southbound expansion had predated Lörcher's proposal by a few years, having started in 1921 when Ankara's notables presented him with a vineyard estate on the Çankaya Hills and gained momentum as the republican elite rushed to take residence in similar estates near Atatürk's. During the last year of the War of Independence, heavy machinery, which

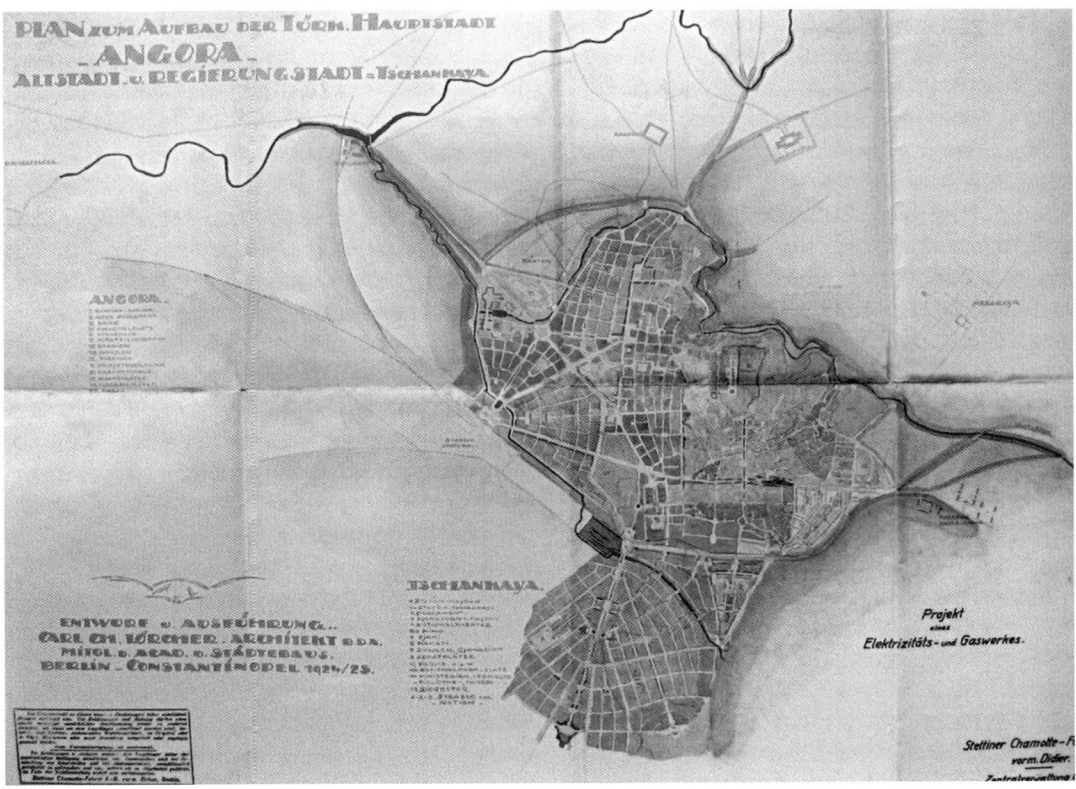

FIGURE 1.7. THE LÖRCHER PLAN FOR ANKARA. THE MAP REVEALS THE TENSIONS BETWEEN A PATTERN WITH SPOKES RADIATING FROM THE TRAIN STATION TO THE WEST, AND THE SOUTHBOUND PRESSURES FOR FUTURE DEVELOPMENT, WHICH EVENTUALLY PREVAILED. COURTESY PERA MÜZESI VE İSTANBUL ARAŞTIRMALARI ENSTITÜSÜ.

had been assigned to the construction of the Ankara–Sivas railroad, was diverted to stabilize the road connecting the vineyard estate to the Assembly Building, four miles to the north.[29] The distance between Ankara's historic core and the new development centered around Çankaya posed a challenge for any planner, considering there was neither the population nor the building density to sustain this peculiar growth pattern as a congruent urban whole. To tie the two together, Lörcher tried to formalize the path between the two parts of the city as a wide tree-lined boulevard. He also proposed a series of activity nodes along the way, the most prominent of which was the Government Quarter, a civic and political hub located halfway between Ulus and Çankaya. The uneasy shape of this conceptual splicing is evident in the way the density of buildings and suggested uses drop around halfway between the existing northern hub

31

FIGURE 1.8. A LOOK TOWARD THE NORTH AT ANKARA'S MAIN NORTH–SOUTH AXIS. THE MAIN ANKARA BRANCH OFFICE OF THE OTTOMAN BANK OCCUPIES THE TRIANGULAR LOT. TO ITS RIGHT IS THE MULTIUSE APARTMENT BUILDING DESIGNED BY MIMAR KEMALEDDIN. THE BUILDING, WHICH ALSO HOUSES A THEATER, WAS FUNDED BY THE PIOUS FOUNDATIONS ADMINISTRATION. TO ITS RIGHT IS THE HEADQUARTERS OF ZIRAAT (AGRICULTURE) BANK, THE LARGEST STATE-OWNED BANK. FURTHER UPHILL IN THE DISTANCE, THE ORTHAGONAL FORMS OF THE CENTRAL BANK, BY CLEMENS HOLZMEISTER, CAN BE DISCERNED. INTENDED AS PERIMETER BLOCKS, THESE BUILDINGS WERE RELATIVELY SMALL IN SIZE, WITH TOO MANY GAPS BETWEEN THEM TO DEFINE THE STREET'S EDGE.

and the new Government Quarter, where the boulevard looks almost like an isthmus connecting the two parts of the plan.

Nevertheless, Lörcher's plan was only partially implemented. Some of his proposed radial boulevards were built and some of the new capital's earliest landmarks, including new administrative buildings (the new Assembly, the Ministry of Foreign Affairs), banks (Ziraat Bankası, İş Bankası, Osmanlı Bankası), residential structures (Evkaf Apartments), cultural institutions (Ethnography Museum, Turkish Hearths Association), and recreational facilities (Ankara Palas, Millet Bahçesi) were positioned according to its precepts. These structures designed in the Ottoman revivalist style were the work of architects recruited from the Istanbul Fine Arts Academy (Giulio Mongieri) or defunct Ottoman agencies (Kemaleddin Bey, Vedat Tek, Arif Hikmet Koyunoğlu). Their architecture combined distinctly modern building programs with a beaux arts–style compositional sensibility and Ottoman-inspired decorative features, which conferred on them a recognizable character. Although they were fitting choices in terms of their massing and the street definition they provided, these mostly institutional structures were not enough to fill up the large gaps in the landscape; their intricate detailing prolonged their construction and increased their costs.

More important, the ruling elite's priorities had changed, jettisoning Lörcher's vision of a dense streetscape reminiscent of European boulevards and a pattern of growth centered around Ankara's historic core. Instead, emphasis was placed on the southern portion of his plan—specifically his proposal for 150 hectares of land that had been appropriated by the Assembly without any expert input, which blindsided Lörcher.[30] With this momentous recalibration of the direction of future growth, urban development effectively leapfrogged toward Çankaya, sidelining the historic core to the north. The government's ambivalent embrace of Lörcher's plan added to the chaos created by unchecked speculative construction, mainly of rental units, filling the empty lots in Ankara's older neighborhoods and an unbridled competition for acquiring land in the south, driving real estate prices beyond the range of all but the wealthiest. Many of these interventions were uncoordinated and consisted of sporadic attempts to solve discreet problems rather than comprehensive, long-range planning efforts. But they had began to concretize Ankara's incipient growth trends.

To rein in these haphazard developments and respond to increasing complaints, in 1928 the government organized a competition and selected Herman Jansen, a professor from Berlin Technical University, to draw up a new master plan for Ankara.[31] Jansen retained many of Lörcher's ideas—especially for the newer parts of town and the layout of major streets. Lörcher and, later, Jansen introduced a vocabulary of urbanism that differed significantly from Ankara's established settlement patterns. Both prescribed a change in scale and new paths of movement through the city. First, whereas prerepublican Ankara had narrow and irregular streets, the newly planned parts of the city had a regular geometry, bigger lots, and wider streets. Rather than conforming to the topography, the new layout imposed a comprehensive preconceived pattern of paths and nodes that highlighted the monuments of the new capital.

Second, Jansen also instituted the concept of zoning: he grouped similar land uses together and proposed wide greenbelts as buffers between them.[32] These ideas were antithetical to the spatial logic of the existing city. Jansen sought to override this conspicuous incompatibility by subordinating the Citadel and its environs to his scheme and assigning them a single land use. However, unlike the single-use zones around them, the Citadel

FIGURE 1.9. JANSEN'S ZONING FOR ANKARA 1932 (*ARBEITER-VIERTERL*: WORKERS' DISTRICT; *INDUSTRIE*: IN-DUSTRY; *HOİCHSCHULİ VIERTEL*: UNIVERSITY DISTRICT; *REGIERUNGS VIERTEL*: GOVERNMENT QUARTER; *LANDHAUS VIERTEL*: COUNTRY HOUSES; *WOHN-RESERVE*: FUTURE RESIDENTIAL DEVELOPMENT AREA). THE CITADEL APPEARS IN BLACK, AND ANKARA'S EXISTING FABRIC PRIOR TO ITS NEW ROLE AS CAPITAL IS MARKED "ALTSTADT," OLD TOWN. ARCHITEKTURMUSEUM TU BERLIN, INV. NR. 22598.

and its environs comprised a fully functional city, integrating multiple uses in a compact area. Religious buildings, commercial structures, small workshops, and neighborhood stores intermingled with residential uses without clear demarcations. Jansen's decision to reduce this area to just another single-function zone implied that he had assigned the existing city as a whole the exclusive function of "being historic." Indeed, in his zoning map, the existing core of the city was labeled Altstadt, Old Town.

Jansen sought to buffer "Old Ankara" away from the "New Ankara" with greenbelts because he believed that old quarters, which imparted to each city a unique character, had to be protected and wanted to prevent speculation, which had torn the historic fabric of European cities in the late nineteenth century.[33] He also recognized how central the image of the "Old Ankara" and, especially, that of the Citadel (albeit in its pared down form) was to republican foundation myths and sought to preserve it as a vessel for the nation's collective memory. However, the circulation pattern he proposed, rather than protecting the "Old Ankara," effectively severed it from the rest of the growing capital, isolating it as though it were an island. Designating "Old Ankara" as a picturesque still-life or a revered— but hollowed out—monument belied its vitality as an active urban environment housing more than half of the city's population and commercial establishments.

Nonetheless, these measures turned the "Old Ankara," with its unmistakably premodern spatial order, into the perfect foil to set off the modernity of the new. Standing prominently and as a constant backdrop to the feverish construction activity, the once inspirational Citadel and its environs slipped into the role of republican Ankara's underdeveloped other more readily—if not entirely intentionally—than Ottoman Istanbul. In other words, despite passionate claims to the contrary, the elites' practice of insulating themselves from the population at large had resurfaced in the new capital, keeping the republican leaders just as distant from the "bosom of the nation" as the Ottoman administrators they had once so severely criticized.

It is noteworthy that the founding fathers' professed commitment to modernization conveniently dovetailed with their less lofty pursuit of private interests. They were unwilling to retrofit existing districts, arguing that it would be costly or would not satisfactorily showcase the republic's achievements. Çankaya was sparsely built, located farther away and uphill from the densely populated older quarters. Providing it with infrastructure would clearly imply higher total and per capita costs. But the republican leaders, who stood to benefit from this southbound development, raised no objections to the expenses that would be incurred to

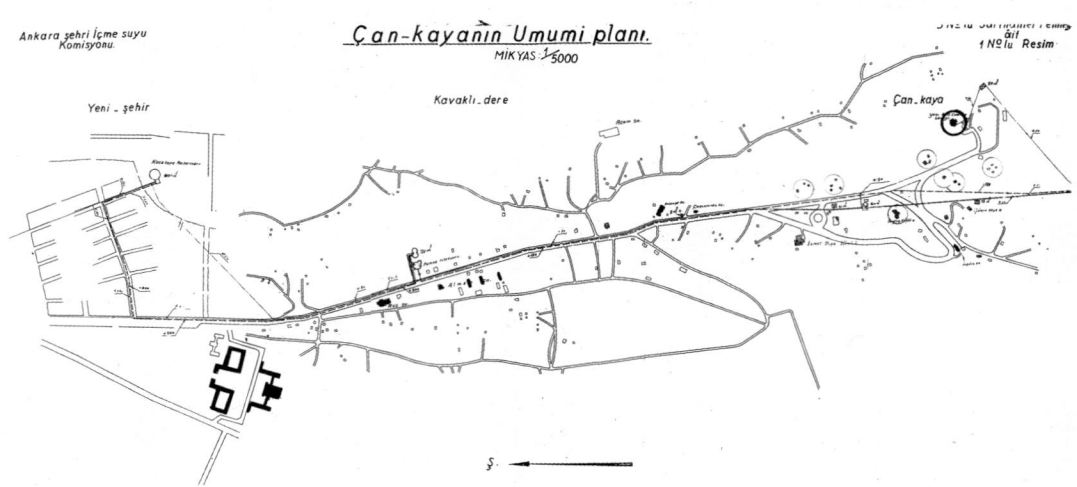

FIGURE 1.10. WATER UTILITY PROVISION MAP OF ÇANKAYA, INDICATING WATER PROVISION BY ADDRESS. IN ADDITION TO THE PRESIDENTIAL RESIDENCE (DARK CIRLCE, TOP RIGHT) AND EMBASSIES, SEVERAL HOMES OWNED BY THE REPUBLICAN ELITE ARE LISTED. WHILE ÇANKAYA WAS UPHILL AND ABOUT TWO MILES FROM ANKARA'S CENTER, THE PROVISION OF UTILITIES IN THIS AREA WAS GIVEN PRIORITY.

accomplish such an expansion. Consequently, water, electricity, gas, and telephone lines arrived several decades later in the older neighborhoods than in their newer counterparts. Furthermore, Ankara's new elite used their political capital to exclude the locals from decision-making processes through procedures ostensibly aimed at streamlining the implementation of projects to meet the new capital's pressing needs. Notably, the locals' exclusion from the city's verbal and visual representations and the introduction of the myth that Ankara was built from scratch by the founders of the republic occurred at the same time. Thus, the Citadel, which had once been a widely shared symbol of hope and freedom, continued to conjure up romanticized memories of the War of Independence for the new elite, but for the locals, it increasingly became the zone of their confinement and invisibility.

A THWARTED IDEAL

During his brief posting in Turkey, General Charles H. Sherrill, the American ambassador, enthusiastically recognized the direction of Ankara's future development. "Ankara is remarkably similar to the seat of our own government in Washington D.C.," he wrote. "The large tree-lined avenue between the new government quarter and the old town is reminiscent of the Mall in Washington with a similarly gentle slope leading up to the Capitol Hill."[34] Albeit far more modest in scale and ambition than its American counterpart, Ankara's Government Quarter was similarly structured around a central axis, a pedestrian promenade that would eventually be flanked by the most important institutional buildings of the new state. As with the Capitol in Washington, the crowning element of the design was the new Grand National Assembly Complex, which was to be built on the highest point of the slope, marking the terminus of the promenade, and the pinnacle of the proposed design.[35] The layout of the streets fanning out symmetrically on either side of the axis, echoing the geometry of the Government Quarter, augmented the visibility of this administrative core and emphasized its processional character.

Although Sherrill seems not to have noticed, interventions that rapidly and profoundly changed the plan's spatial hierarchies were already in progress during his tenure. By the time his book went to press, the existence of a major axis culminating at the Assembly was hardly noticeable at the pedestrian level. According to the new configuration, the avenue bordering the eastern edge of the Government Quarter replaced the promenade as the plan's dominant axis, terminating, instead, some three kilometers to the south, at the gates of the Presidential Palace in Çankaya. Repositioning the central axis of an otherwise strictly symmetrical design had a lasting effect on the entirety of Ankara's urban form.[36] It effectively undercut the Assembly's prominent position within the city's physical layout and trumped its primacy within the new capital's political and symbolic landscape.

The space straddling the gap between the new and discarded axes precisely at the heart of Ankara may best be characterized as an anamorphic site: imperceptible at close range, the extent of its effect coming into focus only when seen from above and examined within the larger context of Ankara's urban form. In paintings, as a relational phenomenon that is inherently destabilizing, anamorphism reveals the coexistence of two incommensurate views on the same canvas, putting into question the validity of both.[37] When it occurs in the built environment, as it did in this case, anamorphosis opens up the possibility of imagining other ways of using space, mediating interactions, or ordering society. Hence beyond revealing the shape of abandoned designs, the juxtaposition of "what is" and "what might have been" at Ankara's Government Quarters offers a rare glimpse into the existence, in the formative stages of the republic, of alternative political visions and foundation myths that were similarly cast off.

Ankara's master plan was intended to fuse—quite literally—symbolic

FIGURE 1.11. (LEFT) AERIAL VIEW OF KIZILAY, RE-VEALING THE POINT AT WHICH THE AXIS VEERS TOWARD ÇANKAYA, BYPASSING THE GOVERN-MENT QUARTER. (BELOW) JANSEN'S REVISED DRAWINGS FOR THE PIVOTAL POINT WHERE THE BOULEVARD WAS ORIGINALLY MEANT TO BIFURCATE SYMMETRICALLY. DRAWN IN OCTO-BER 1930, THIS MODIFICATION AT THE SQUARE, TO THE LEFT OF THE DRAWING, REROUTES ONE MAIN BOULEVARD TOWARD ÇANKAYA. ARCHITEKTURMUSEUM TU BERLIN, INV. NR. 22975.

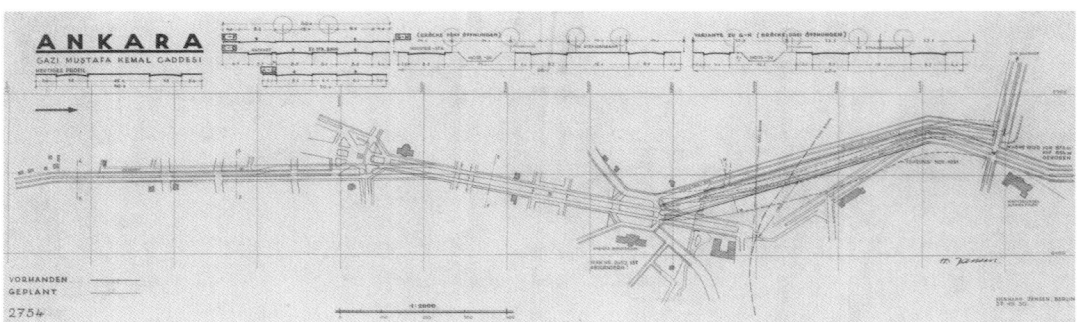

narrative with physical form. The names chosen for the city's major streets and squares were explicitly linked to the milestone events of the recent past, thereby stitching national foundation myths to the new capital's built environment. Without a doubt the most prominent of these narra-tive sequences was the one embodied by the new North-South axis, which appears as (Strasse der Nation/Nation Boulevard) in Lörcher's plans. The two-mile stretch from the makeshift first building of the Grand National Assembly to its future site on the southern tip of the Government Quarter

FIGURE 1.12. A VIEW TOWARD THE STATION FROM ULUS (NATION) SQUARE, ANCHORED BY ATATÜRK'S EQUESTRIAN MONUMENT, FEATURING BELOW ARCHETYPICAL CITIZENS CONTRIBUTING TO THE WAR EFFORT. THE STATUE FACES WEST, TOWARD THE TRAIN STATION IN THE DISTANCE. TO THE RIGHT IS THE FIRST BUILDING OF THE GRAND NATIONAL ASSEMBLY AND THE COURT OF FINANCIAL APPEALS. TO THE LEFT THE DOMES OF ANKARA PALAS HOTEL CAN BE SEEN.

would be marked at major intersections by a series of monuments, commemorating the successive stages of Turkey's resurgence following the collapse of the Ottoman Empire at the end of the First World War.

Moving from North to South, the first of these monuments was the National Sovereignty Memorial, Turkey's version of the "Monument to the Unknown Soldier." The monument's location just outside the first Assembly, which in 1920 had brought together diverse representatives with the collaboration of myriad local organizations to form a government in exile, clearly linked the building with the grassroots mobilization that had been necessary to fight the War of Independence. Designed by German sculptor Heinrich Krippel and inaugurated in 1926, the tableau commemorated the unknown and unsung men, women, and children who contributed to the war effort under Atatürk's leadership. For a town that had sent thousands of souls off to the front over the course of the War of Independence, the imagery was painfully familiar. Although the art of figurative sculpture and the use of public monuments were relatively new in Turkey, everyone could identify with the characters of this tableau.

The second monument along the axis was to be a Triumphal Arch, celebrating the victory in the final battle of the War of Independence. At the convergence of the first set of diagonal streets that embraced the Government Quarter, the arch was to be a gateway between the old and the new parts of the city. On either side of Millet Boulevard, at the abutments of the arch, Lörcher proposed two symmetrically laid parks, which would be further animated by the presence around them of modern cultural and recreational facilities such as a theater, a cinema, cafés, and restaurants.[38] This looked to be precisely the kind of model public outdoor space for acting out the type of urban activities so widely publicized in propaganda publications.

Further to the south, Millet Boulevard bifurcated at the tip of the triangular superblock comprising the Government Quarter, at Republic Square. Lörcher proposed an obelisk to anchor this point with a prominent vertical gesture. This marked the transition from vehicular to pedestrian traffic, while retaining the focus on the main axis, which continued on, flanked "by some of the finest buildings the republic has to offer."[39] The Prime Ministry, Ministries of Justice, Education, Public Works, and the High Court of Appeals would frame this walkway, which gradually rose uphill and widened to become the courtyard of the Ministry of Interior, terminating at the forecourt of the future Assembly Complex. The Assembly's large ceremonial forecourt would provide a sense of arrival, a place from which one could contemplate sweeping views of the capital in the making. Within the succession of commemorative landmarks, the Assembly would be both the formal culmination of Ankara's master plan and the climax of the symbolic narrative embodied by that plan, celebrating Turkey's long journey to become a modern parliamentary democracy.

But then, as construction progressed, two particular modifications were made that had profound implications for Ankara's urban form and the symbolic narrative it was meant to embody. The first of these was the scrapping of the Triumphal Arch and replacement with the Victory Monument, designed by Italian sculptor Pietro Canonica. Inaugurated in 1927, the monument featured Atatürk in his field marshal uniform, a rank he had acquired for his decisive success as a military commander at Dumlupınar. This change had formal and symbolic implications. The arch had honored the old and the new parts of the city equally. It traversed the boulevard bridging between the twin parks on either side, and by virtue of its form, it emphasized the experience of passage for vehicles and pedes-

FIGURE 1.13. VICTORY SQUARE, WITH CANONICA'S ATATÜRK MONUMENT IN THE MIDDLE. THE OFFICERS'
CLUB, WHICH IN LATER YEARS WILL EXPAND TO BOTH SIDES OF THE PARK, OVERLOOKS THE GREEN SPACE.
COURTESY OF BURÇAK EVREN.

trians alike. Canonica's design did not afford a comparable participatory
dimension that involved passersby. Rather, it presented Atatürk's bronze
likeness as its single focal point, a celebration that downplayed in its iconography the popular sacrifice that had made victory possible. Such a shift
could be dismissed as a minor adjustment were it not succeeded, in short
order, by the change of Millet Boulevard's name into Atatürk Boulevard.[40]
Furthermore, the construction of an Officers' Club on the east side of the
boulevard, overlooking one of the twin parks, militarized the space, for-
saking Lörcher's initial vision of creating a cultural hub that would serve
as an outdoor civic enclave at the center of the city.

The second and even more dramatic change was the rerouting of the
boulevard's North-South axis that had originally been designed to cul-
minate at the Assembly. The axis now veered toward the southeast, continuing up the hill to terminate at the gates of the Presidential Palace in
Çankaya. This move threw a carefully worked out symmetrical design
off kilter, eliminating the Republic Square and its obelisk altogether. But
more important, it undercut the Assembly's prominence within the city's

FIGURE 1.14. ATATÜRK'S RESIDENCE IN ÇANKAYA, DESIGNED BY CLEMENS HOLZMEISTER, WAS THE NEW TERMINUS OF ANKARA'S NORTH-SOUTH AXIS. IN THE FOREGROUND, THE VINEYARD HOUSE, THE INITIAL PROPERTY TO WHICH HE MOVED SHORTLY AFTER HIS ARRIVAL IN ANKARA. COURTESY OF THE TURKISH HISTORICAL SOCIETY LIBRARY.

physical and symbolic landscape. Thereafter the Presidential Palace became the crowning element in the layout of the capital and the narrative it was to engender.[41]

In this tortured process Jansen also found himself having to compete professionally with Clemens Holzmeister, an Austrian architect who, thanks to the large number of commissions he received, had almost become a de facto shadow planner for the city. Holzmeister was arguably more gifted in expressing his architectural vision, and significantly, his political inclinations were closer to those of the increasingly powerful authoritarian contingent within the republican administration.[42] Holzmeister had initially been retained to design the new Presidential Palace in Çankaya but was subsequently asked to design various buildings for the government and the military, including the Officers' Club by the Victory Monument, the Headquarters of the Army Joint Chiefs of Staff, and the Ministry of Defense, on lots adjacent to the triangular superblock of the Government Quarter, which Jansen considered to be violations of his master plan.[43] Holzmeister prevailed over Jansen's objections in shaping the Government Quarter because he also was appointed to design the Ministry of Public Works and the High Court of Appeals.[44] Designed in a formal stripped-down neoclassical style, Holzmeister's government

FIGURE 1.15. THE SECURITY MONUMENT COMMEMORATING THE STATE'S SECURITY FORCES (POLICE, GENDARME, AND MILITARY) WITH THE LARGE MASS OF CLEMENS HOLZMEISTER'S MINISTRY OF THE INTERIOR TAKING SHAPE IN THE BACKGROUND. THE MONUMENT'S PLATFORM AND THE MINISTRY EFFECTIVELY DESTROYED THE ORIGINAL VISTA PROPOSED BY BOTH LÖRCHER AND JANSEN. ALSO, IN THIS IMAGE, THE MINISTRY'S SILHOUETTE BLENDS WITH THE HEADQUARTERS OF THE JOINT CHIEFS OF STAFF, WHICH WERE ALSO DESIGNED BY HOLZMEISTER. THE ATROPHIED BOULEVARD ABUTTING THE WESTERN EDGE OF THE GOVERNMENT QUARTER (NOT DEPICTED) BECAME AN INCREASINGLY MILITARIZED ZONE WITH A RANGE OF BUILDINGS THAT BELONGED TO THE MINISTRY OF DEFENSE AND VARIOUS FORCES. COURTESY OF THE TURKISH HISTORICAL SOCIETY LIBRARY.

buildings were inward-looking masses that projected a sense of impenetrability. Holzmeister's most incompatible—and subversive—intervention was his design for the Ministry of Interior, which effectively cut the pedestrian axis off before it ever reached the site of the new Assembly. His spatial coup was completed with the installation of the Security Monument, inaugurated on the twelfth anniversary of the Republic of Turkey. Replacing the proposed obelisk at the northern end of the Government Quarter, amid what would have been Republic Square, the Security Monument honored the Police and Gendarme corps, rather than celebrating national unity as had initially been proposed. With its wall-like wide base running above eye level, the monument all but blocked the view toward the Assembly, the construction of which had already been postponed.

The disintegration of the plans for the Government Quarters affected Ankara's overall urban form and its long-term patterns of growth. As a result of the shift in the axis, Milli Müdafaa (National Defense) Avenue, which formed the western edge of the site lost importance and atrophied. In contrast, Atatürk Boulevard, which defined the eastern edge, flourished. New housing development leaped further south toward the Kavaklıdere-Çankaya Hills, and a residential corridor dotted with ostentatious villas on the way to the Presidential Palace emerged. Widely criticized as expressions of the unbridled greed and the unrefined tastes of the republican elite, the mishmash of styles displayed along the boulevard—ranging from the highly ornate Ottoman revivalist to the abstract geometric compositions of Central European modern, locally dubbed "kübik stil"—may well be interpreted as often conflicted attempts to define the new Turkey's "high culture" within the domain of residential architecture.[45] After the shift, the urgency to complete the Government Quarter lost steam. Although some ministerial buildings were constructed to meet the pressing need for office space, glaring gaps remained on the site for decades and the axis turned into a service road between office buildings rather than the ceremonial passage it was envisioned to be. In the 1960s a new westbound artery was built through the Government Quarter, severing the already weakened connection between the Grand National Assembly and the rest of the Government Quarter. Today, the Assembly building stands alone over a large but insular plot of land, and the pedestrian walkway is all but gone.[46]

STAGING POWER

The incompatibilities between Holzmeister's commissions and the plans of Lörcher and later Jansen had remarkable parallels with the larger disputes over the country's political order. These disputes had their own highly codified—if jarring—manifestations, which were equally consequential in shaping the new capital. Though they were united by their desire to fight off post–First World War occupation, the groups comprising the nationalist coalition did not necessarily share a common vision of government. Their differences even compromised their ability to present a unified front at critical times during the War of Independence. To this day, official histories present the proclamation of the republic and Atatürk's ascendancy as the country's founding president as a smooth transition from the wartime conditions of emergency. Nonetheless, the decade after the war was fraught with infighting among various contending factions. On the one hand were those who espoused a liberal definition of the state with a parliamentary democracy predicated on popular support. On the other hand were the military-bureaucratic cadres who had strong Jacobin tendencies and were anxious to "catch up with Western civilization."[47] They envisioned creating a modern unitary nation-state, if necessary through authoritarian policies. The leader of this latter faction was Atatürk, who proved to be as uncannily gifted a tactician in the political arena as on the battleground, neutralizing both the liberals in the first camp and those whose own personal ambitions posed a challenge to his leadership.

Wartime alliances were weakening outside Ankara as well, and the population at large was growing restless. Especially in eastern and southeastern Turkey, the administration's decision to continue the centralizing policies initiated by Ottoman administrators with renewed zeal met with frequent and often violent resistance in the largely Kurdish eastern provinces. The Kurds, who had mostly collaborated with the nationalists during the War of Independence, were taken aback by the new assimilationist policies for suppressing their distinct identity and culture. Small ongoing skirmishes occasionally flared up, most notably with the 1926 Şeyh Said Rebellion, which lasted several months and brought the government down, before being suppressed through the use of extraordinary military measures.[48] Meanwhile, the republican administration's economic policies were cause for discontent especially (but not exclusively) in the historically more prosperous coastal regions and western provinces. After the onset of the Great Depression, things took a distinct turn for the worse as the financial situation deteriorated. The constant instability and violence in the east and the growing support for incipient rival political movements in the west gave the Ankara government the pretext to clamp down on the public sphere, introducing martial law in several eastern provinces and, across the country, outlawing all sorts of activities that it perceived as a threat to its grip on power. The press was brought under even closer scrutiny, and various civic organizations, including those with sympathetic causes, were closed down.[49] The circle of power in Ankara narrowed concomitantly. Atatürk assumed tighter control while the Assembly was further drained of its already reduced importance. As Geoffrey Knox, the British chargé d'affaires in Ankara described the situation in a letter to the Foreign Office:

> In constitutional theory Turkey is a republic, in which the sovereignty of the people is expressed in an elected Assembly, which itself nominates for the term of its own life a President of the Republic, in whom are vested very lim-

ited powers. The reality is less simple. The National Assembly is composed almost entirely of nominees of the People's party, major projects of policy are dealt with in the first instance by the party committee, the real debating body, which proceeds in secret. . . . The initiation of these policies rest with a body even more powerful than the party committee—the private Cabinet of Chankaya [*sic*]. This consists of the President of the Republic himself and his own immediate circle, and meets . . . at the President's house. . . . The official Cabinet, I am inclined to believe, carries less weight. . . . With reservation it is, I think, safe to say, that in all major matters the Government of the country lies essentially in the hands of the President and the *inner conclave*.[50] (emphasis added)

This kind of highly personalized politics predicated on Atatürk's persona—as opposed to one that fits within a well-defined constitutional framework—had its own spatiality; in fact, it achieved its effect precisely through judicious and high-profile spatial practices that were just as influential in shaping Turkey's new capital. Like a theatrical presentation that pans out only if the actors and the audience bond, in Ankara the production—and maintenance—of charismatic authority was contingent as much on the leader's performance as on the followers' acknowledgment. It came to life through people, in their bodies, words, and actions, and in spaces that facilitated such transactions. Atatürk had a solid grasp of the possibilities that Ankara's scant social venues offered and used them to his advantage to augment the influence of his presence and the visibility of his actions. In turn, a willing audience, whose members surrendered their autonomy in exchange for the perks of their positions, helped him further cement his authority. In so doing, Atatürk and his entourage creatively expanded the repertoire and stages of political action and public personhood in Turkey. Through their example, they also set the precedents for the power performances that were thereafter imitated—albeit with mixed success—by others who assumed the role of leadership in Turkey.[51] No account of Ankara's early days as capital would be complete without acknowledging the centrality of this theatrical production of power and its legacy on Turkish political culture.

By all accounts, Atatürk's vineyard residence in Çankaya was the center of Ankara's social and political life and the prime stage for performance of his personalized style of politics. In the early 1920s Ankara was still a provincial town with little to offer in the way of cultural or recreational attractions. For the republican elite, most of whom had been transplanted from Istanbul, attending soirées at Çankaya was a bright spot in an otherwise dull social calendar. Atatürk had a long history of nightly gatherings with his closest coterie of friends that dated back to military school when, like so many military students of his generation, he gathered with his cohorts for dinner to eat, drink, and discuss important political matters—especially their plans to "save the Empire" from its imminent collapse.[52] In peacetime the practice continued, became more lavish, and expanded to include an ever-changing list of nightly guests. He also extended invitations to experts or scholars if, in the course of the evening, he planned to consult them in their area of specialization, such as language and literature, music, culture, history, and economics. At other times, he commandeered, on the spur of the moment, musicians, singers, and poets "to perform their art" for the evening's audience.[53]

The dual character of the Presidential Palace as both a residence and office was especially conducive to the kind of personalized politics centered around a charismatic leader, which, in turn, rendered it a heterotopic site within Ankara's political landscape.[54] Unlike the Assembly or a government office, entering the residence—or specific rooms within it— depended on receiving a formal invitation even if that is where the public's business is conducted. The ambiguity enabled Atatürk to modulate the thresholds between the private and the public as he saw fit, filtering desirable visitors from the rest. Once they passed through the carefully guarded gates of the Presidential Residence, the guests had to put their faith in established procedures and legal or bureaucratic conventions on hold and submit themselves to an alternate set of rules and rituals the sole arbiter of which was Atatürk. They were expected to partake in the rituals of servility, including the nightly poker and pool games in which Atatürk's preordained wins served as reaffirmations of his absolute power over his guests, and his return of the evening's earnings to the losers as signs of his magnanimity.[55] He could, on a whim, subject guests to random tests in front of others and impose strange and unusual penalties when dissatisfied with the answers. He was known to dismiss guests for not dressing properly, scoff at his office personnel about their table manners, and place impossible demands on his waitstaff.[56] Cabinet officials, members of parliament, and high-level bureaucrats were routinely summoned to Çankaya, sometimes on a whim. The United States ambassador John Grew recalled that when the order came, other engagements, no matter how important, had to be broken:

> Just before dinner, Rouschen Eshref [sic] was called to the telephone and said that the Gazi had summoned him immediately. Alice and I both told him just what we thought of such arbitrariness, which would not be found in any other country, and that the diplomats were far from pleased with this practice

of deputies upsetting dinner arrangements at the last minute. I said that the President of the United States would never expect a guest to break a dinner engagement at such short notice. . . . He took our remarks perfectly well, but said that Turkey was run by a small group of about a dozen men of which he was one, that the Gazi slept most of the day and that he generally desired to begin work in the evening; there was no way of getting out of it when summoned.[57]

As clear instances of Atatürk's ability to commandeer people's personal time and attention, such demands were not unusual. They were essential to the generation and upkeep of charismatic authority, as was the ability to perform and elicit from others actions that directly contradicted commonly established rules of politics, diplomacy, or civility. The Presidential Palace was the indispensable site where these transactions unfolded and where political fortunes were made and unmade. It was the stage on which every gesture or statement was larger than life and always subject to endless speculation.[58]

Foreign observers of this multilayered entourage were often critical of Atatürk's "policy to employ only second-class men" because, they noted, it undermined the effectiveness of the reforms he wanted to implement, and yet mediocrity was precisely the quality he sought in the members of this exclusive group.[59] It was not that he was unable to recognize the weaknesses, lack of imagination, or limited skills of his entourage. In fact, on the rare candid occasion, he admitted that in having eliminated some of the more accomplished members of his circle to undercut possible challenges, he had become rather lonely at the top.[60] But as an ambitious leader who did not like competition, Atatürk had chosen to place powerless men in positions of power. Through these men, most of whom had neither the competence nor the confidence to hold those appointments on their own, and who were, therefore, beholden to him, Atatürk was able to accumulate even more power in his hands. What foreign observers overlooked, however, was the existence of a uniquely symbiotic relationship between Atatürk and his entourage. Whereas the social and political positions of the members of this inner conclave were defined by their proximity to the leader, it was their faithful and spectacular subservience that reinforced the visibility of Atatürk's charismatic power.

This symbiotic relationship also shaped Ankara's elite residential landscape because everybody who was somebody or aspired to be somebody wanted to live close to the Presidential Palace so as to accumulate political capital through proximity. The rush to purchase land on the vineyards along the boulevard drove up real estate prices at an unprecedented rate.[61] Personal calculations were never too far from the political, and the repub-

FIGURE 1.16. KAVAKLIDERE-ÇANKAYA DISTRICT WAS THE NEW POPULAR RESIDENTIAL DISTRICT NEAR THE PRESIDENTIAL RESIDENCE. FEATURED HERE IS FUAT BULCA'S MODERN NEW HOME, DESIGNED BY ERNST EGLI, OVERLOOKING THE PLAINS BELOW. BULCA, A HIGH-RANKING ARMY OFFICER, WAS A CLASSMATE OF ATATÜRK IN MILITARY SCHOOL. DURING THE EARLY YEARS OF THE REPUBLIC, HE ALSO SERVED AS THE CHAIR OF THE TURKISH AVIATION SOCIETY, THE HEADQUARTERS OF WHICH WAS ALSO DESIGNED BY EGLI. COURTESY OF THE TURKISH HISTORICAL SOCIETY LIBRARY.

lican elite were able to use their influence to alter the official plan to maximize their financial gains through various private construction and real estate deals into which both they and their friends and families entered. As they spurred speculative land transactions in and around Çankaya, they also managed to divert infrastructural investment and other scarce resources in that direction, leaving the Citadel and its environs to fate. This pattern of development, which also left large gaps in the city's footprint especially in the first few decades, laid bare how the very revolutionaries who passionately critiqued the Ottoman brass for insulating itself from the rest of the population were brazenly building their own enclaves to keep their distance from the ordinary folk with no access to political power.

As Ankara's primary site for politics and policy, Atatürk's residence had, therefore, supplanted the Assembly, co-opting its functions and decisively subverting the formal and symbolic idealism of the plan proposed by Lörcher, and later by Jansen. Using the Çankaya residence might initially have been a matter of expediency because of the widespread lack of adequate spaces for meeting in the city. There was no specific decision to table the construction of a new Assembly, but considering that all important decisions were made by one person surrounded by a close coterie of supporters at an office that doubled as a residence, nobody pushed for its completion either. By the same token, it is entirely understandable how the design and implementation of the Presidential Palace in Çankaya to accommodate its expanded functions could gain priority. Eventually a competition was organized for the design of a new Assembly Building in 1942, and, ironically, the winner was Clemens Holzmeister. In yet another ironic twist, the new building was inaugurated only after the 1960 military coup and was used as the seat of a special legislative assembly, resuming normal parliamentary functions in 1961. By then whatever was left of the pedestrian portion of the North-South axis was already fast disintegrating.

Although Çankaya was his primary base, Atatürk frequently ventured out to Ankara's prominent public venues, which brought them into the repertoire of political spectacle and further amplified his ability to project power by manipulating the gradients between the public and the private, just as he was doing at the Presidential Palace. To facilitate his spectacular jaunts through town, several public buildings in Ankara—including the Turkish Hearths Association (later Ankara People's House), the Faculty of Language, History, and Geography, and the new train station—were designed with dedicated rooms, equipped to provide him space to work, receive visitors, and rest if necessary.[62] These private accommodations, located, unusually, in public buildings, worked as if they were extensions of the Presidential Palace, with comparable constraints on behavior and patterns of exclusion, suggesting, not so subtly, that Ankara as a whole was under Atatürk's gaze. Outdoor spaces most closely associated with the modern lifestyle fervently promoted in republican media, such as the city's main arteries, the stadium and parade grounds, Atatürk's model farm facilities, were under strict vigilance. Atatürk always traveled with a large entourage, and his motorcades going up and down his namesake boulevard claimed the entire length of this strip for state protocol. During state visits or commemorative celebrations people lined up along the route and cheered their leader enthusiastically, waving flags and banners. Ankara's officious and ironfisted mayor-governor Nevzat Tandoğan ensured that those who did not conform to the image of a modern citizen—peasants, beggars, loiterers—were kept off the main arteries, especially the boulevard.[63] Ostensibly implemented as security measures, these tactics under-cut the possibility of experiencing the boulevard as an authentic public space, turning it instead into a simulation thereof.

These urban spectacles are also notable because they reveal how Atatürk appropriated Ottoman displays of authority and infused them with new meaning. Despite his explicit pronouncements about rejecting all Otto-man precedents, much of the pomp and circumstance outlined above was remarkably similar to the mid-nineteenth-century practice of cheering the Sultan on his way to the Friday prayer. This itself was an imported tradition that was closely linked to the formation of modern nation-states and their emerging ceremonial practices.[64] Atatürk took advantage of the familiarity of this format, which he retained, but he secularized the prac-tice by choosing sites of national, rather than religious, communion as the destination of these excursions. Moreover, not unlike his Ottoman prede-cessors—and ironically like the much reviled Abdülhamid II—he retained the conviction that this type of direct and seemingly interactive practice, which projected a sense of participation without really delivering it, would help them continue to avoid "inconvenient intermediaries like political parties and the parliament."[65]

The story of Ankara's urban development has long been viewed as a failure to implement the plan and to control growth, due to corruption and the lack of means and experience. This characterization, although not wholly untrue, reduces a complex process to a product, thus flattening a multilayered narrative of visions, frictions, and resistances that informed the making of Turkey's capital and its political order. Most important, it consistently deflects attention from political will to the petty calculations of individuals in undermining the plan—preserving the leader's immu-nity. This approach obscures how the city's spaces served as a stage for politics by other means. Individual infractions, mainly in the form of per-mit violations, land speculation, and shady property deals, chipped away at the plan in a piecemeal fashion—although taken together they played a substantial part in undermining the integrity of the plan. Political inter-ventions, in contrast, subverted the overarching organizational principles of Ankara's urban form and, consequently, the carefully scripted symbolic meanings attached to it. These rival patterns of development were not pre-planned or coherent. Rather, they evolved little by little around Atatürk's charismatic presence and were advanced by the personal ambitions of the republican oligarchy. They were however, equally representative of the character of the new state, as a materialization of its realpolitik. Reincor-porating the political dimension casts light on the otherwise impercep-tible links between seemingly discrete interventions at strategic points of the plan and re-creates the context within which particular forms of private transgression were possible and meaningful. Rather than mere signs of failure or incompetent town planning, Ankara's distorted spaces, misaligned structures, and erased paths can be interpreted as the physical clues that illuminate the conflicted process of building a modern state in Turkey. Acknowledging this fluid spatiality as historic evidence reveals the state to be "an ongoing dynamic, a changing set of aims, as it engages other social forces" rather than a fixed ideological entity.[66]

CHAPTER 2

THEATERS OF
DIPLOMACY

After relocating the capital, the Kemalists hoped that, like the state's own bureaucracy, the corps diplomatique would also follow them from Istanbul to Ankara. Much to their disappointment, however, this did not turn out to be the case. Foreign missions were unwilling to leave Istanbul, a large, diverse, and cosmopolitan city of renowned beauty that offered a wide range of urban amenities. As the British foreign secretary Austen Chamberlain put it in a letter to Lord Crewe, Britain's ambassador in Paris: "His Majesty's Government cannot ask a diplomat of ambassadorial rank . . . to submit to the conditions of residence in a dirty little mountain village in the center of Anatolia . . . or condemn [him] to a painful and inglorious exile in the latter town . . . [such a diplomat] ought not be exiled to the squalor and fleas of Angora as his permanent residence. . . . Since Turkey remains in Europe, let us get what little advantage we can out of her presence there."[1] Britain not only refused to move its own embassy but also quite successfully lobbied its Allies from the First World War to do the same. Foreign governments, which, at least initially, perceived Ankara's long-term prospects as capital to be uncertain, were generally disinclined to make the investment necessary to relocate their embassies. This state of affairs left Turkey's leaders in an untenable predicament. They either had to accept the retention of embassies in Istanbul, which implicitly would diminish Ankara's status as their chosen seat of government, or agree to the opening of legations in Ankara, demoting the level at which diplomatic transactions would take place. The outcome in both cases was tantamount to Turkey's losing its bid for recognition as a peer nation-state by major world powers.

Truth be told, Britain's overzealous multilateral diplomatic offensive

FIGURE 2.1. GERMAN EMBASSY IN ISTANBUL (TOP), WINTER QUARTERS (MIDDLE) IN PERA OVERLOOKING THE GOLDEN HORN AND BOSPHORUS, AND SUMMER QUARTERS (BOTTOM) ON THE BOSPHORUS.

had more to do with unsettled scores at the end of the Lausanne Treaty than with the inconvenience of moving diplomatic missions to Ankara. The treaty brought an end to armed conflict and recognized Turkey's right to exist but did not settle its dispute with Britain over the control of the oil-rich provinces of Musul and Kirkuk. The issue caused such an impasse at the peace conference that at the urging of the other participants, the two countries agreed to conduct bilateral talks to determine the shape of Turkey's southeastern border with British-controlled Iraq. This arrangement effectively provided an opening for Britain to use the relocation of its embassy and those of its First World War Allies as leverage against Turkey in the resolution of the Musul-Kirkuk question.

To counter Britain's actions, Turkey turned to its former First World War partner Germany and forged a new alliance with the Soviet Union.

Both countries, which had similarly been marginalized in the international arena in the aftermath of the war, opened embassies in Ankara early and cultivated close relations with Turkey. Despite past acrimonies, Turkey, Germany, and the Soviet Union formed an alternative and mutually beneficial political block in Eastern and Central Europe that afforded its partners the influence over international affairs they individually lacked. Moreover, Germany and the Soviet Union took advantage of the absence of competition from Britain and its allies to assume an important role in shaping Turkey's postwar reconstruction and modernization. These contacts enabled the Soviet Union and especially Germany to have a broad and lasting influence over the physical forms and practical conventions of Turkish modern. In turn, Turkey, in particular Ankara, served as an indispensable outlet for showcasing the cultural and industrial achievements of its allies, mediating their redemption in the international arena.

Turkey's experience provides a relevant case in point for understanding the hitherto overlooked spatial dimension of international relations. Gaining acceptance on a par with other sovereign nation-states on the world stage and securing the recognition of its international borders were the defining foreign policy concerns for Turkey's leaders, and remarkably, the making of Ankara became instrumental in the negotiation of both. Consequently, this chapter examines the interdependence between the different spatial scales at which international politics operated. It demonstrates how, on the one hand, questions of regional geopolitics informed diplomatic maneuvers at the urban scale. On the other hand, it shows how spatial tactics exercised in small face-to-face encounters with foreign officials could influence policies implemented at the national scale.

RELOCATION AND ITS GEOPOLITICAL CONTEXT

The staunchest resistance to moving embassies to Turkey's new capital came from Britain. British officials were vocal in their protestations of Ankara's harsh climate and rudimentary conditions of life; but what really triggered such a strong reaction were Britain's unfulfilled geopolitical ambitions by the end of the Lausanne Treaty. Britain had long tried to sever Turkey from Europe, confine it exclusively to Asia Minor, and take control of the Turkish Straits.[2] The First World War came close to delivering this objective. With the core lands of the empire partitioned between the Allies, prominent British politicians, including Lord Curzon, foreign secretary and chief negotiator at Lausanne, speculated that the capital of the state to eventually emerge in Turkey would be in an Anatolian town, such as Bursa, Konya, or even Ankara. Meanwhile, Istanbul, he argued, would ideally be left to British supervision.[3] Turkey's success in the War of Independence thwarted this vision, but the Lausanne Treaty brought an ambiguous solution that was to the satisfaction of neither Turkey nor Britain. Turkey reclaimed Thrace and northwestern Anatolia from Allied occupation, but the Straits and the Marmara Sea were declared a demilitarized zone open to the unlimited commercial and military navigation of nonriparian powers. Because the authority to enforce rules, supervise the traffic, and monitor activities in the Straits rested with the International Straits Commission, Turkey's ability to exercise sovereignty over this highly strategic waterway running through its midst was severely curtailed.[4] These conditions increased Istanbul's vulnerability and provided further justification for the Kemalists' decision to relocate the capital to a physically impregnable location like Ankara. The British, for their part, were quite irritated that the Turks had managed to hold on to the territory around the Straits but moved their capital away from Istanbul. Britain had long exerted significant influence over the empire's affairs through carefully cultivated connections with Ottoman dignitaries. By relocating the capital, the Kemalists had effectively dislodged this elaborate circuitry of power, prompting retaliatory action from Britain.

An equally contentious reason at stake was the southeastern border at Musul and Kirkuk—two provinces that were included in the original Misak-ı Milli, which Turkey claimed had come under British occupation illegally at the end of the First World War.[5] The oil-rich region's fate had come up at Lausanne and had brought the conference to a deadlock several times.[6] Finally, at the insistence of other governments at the conference, Turkey and Britain had agreed to resolve the issue through bilateral negotiations within five years following the conference. The dispute was eventually taken before the League of Nations, where Britain was the dominant power, and was resolved in that country's favor in 1926. For the three intervening years between 1923 and 1926, Turco-British relations were characterized by hostility as both governments looked for ways to prevail over each other.[7]

Within this context, British officials deftly used the recognition of Ankara as the perfect trump card against Turkey.[8] They first lobbied Britain's former First World War allies to dissuade Turkish leaders from relocating the capital to Ankara—though the Turks pressed on with their decision. Next, they began a relentless campaign to stop France, Italy, Japan, and the United States from opening embassies in Ankara and, after intense pressure, convinced them to retain their ambassadors in Istanbul and to appoint minor envoys to Ankara to facilitate their dealings with the Turkish government.[9] Because doubts about Ankara's longevity and the stability of the Kemalist regime persisted, the former Allies considered it prudent to refrain from rushing into an expensive move. Although they were motivated more by pragmatism than by an actual ongoing conflict with Turkey, they clearly recognized the advantages of taking such a position. Their reticence to relocate gave them leverage over the Turkish government and left Britain in their debt because their unified stance augmented the effect of the boycott on Ankara. In sum, while selecting the national capital would ordinarily have been a matter of domestic policy, the persistence of a dispute with a major world power dragged the issue into the international arena, where Britain had the upper hand and Turkey was a relatively marginal player.

The refusal of modern Western states to recognize Ankara and their decision to diminish their level of diplomatic contacts constituted tremendous setbacks for Turkey's standing, for this meant, in no uncertain terms, that foreign governments did not regard Turkey as their peer. Nothing could be a worse blow for the republican leadership, who considered Ankara central to the modern identity they wanted to inaugurate for Turkey and their desire to gain international respect and recognition for this formidable feat. To counter the dismal consequences of this standoff, they resorted to two strategies. In the first place, they gradually restricted the channels of regular contact with states that refused to relocate their embassies, thereby isolating them from relevant political developments in the country. Second, they offered land and tax incentives to foreign governments that agreed to relocate their embassies to Ankara.

In the first instance, at the end of the War of Independence, the Turkish government appointed Adnan Adıvar, a highly respected official who also had Mustafa Kemal's ear, to oversee the orderly withdrawal of foreign troops from northeastern Turkey and maintain routine communications with the diplomatic missions in Istanbul.[10] After Ankara became the capital, the government retained him as its liaison in Istanbul until the corps diplomatique completed its relocation. However, when this goodwill gesture intended to ease the migration of diplomatic missions backfired by becoming a disincentive for them to move, Adıvar was summarily replaced with Nusret Bey, an official of lower rank, limited experience, and far less clout within the government circles.[11] With Adıvar's departure, the already inadequate communications with Ankara further deteriorated, leaving the foreign missions in Istanbul out of touch not only with the Turkish government but also with one another as they lacked the logistical support normally provided by a host state to the corps diplomatique stationed in its capital.[12] The Turkish government pointedly ignored the existence of diplomatic missions in Istanbul and divulged little information about developments that could have been of potential interest to their governments. In a most bitter account of the frustration experienced by the diplomats who found themselves caught in this standoff, the British ambassador Ronald Lindsay wrote:[13]

> We, as a mission, are unfortunately suffering a stagnation. . . . We are like a colony of crabs in low tide stuck in the dry and desolate cavities of rocks on the shores of a formerly resplendent sea. Sometimes we organize thé dansants and dinner parties among us. . . . Those of us who have been here for a long time find solace in the memory of the good old days. It has been years since a list of the corps diplomatique that includes our names has been printed. We do not even know each other. Our titles are variegated. Some of us are ambassadors, others ministers, representatives, chargés d'affaires, and some high commissioners. Some of us still appear to be at war with Turkey, others seem to be almost at peace.[14]

Further increasing the effectiveness of the isolation strategy was the deliberate refusal of high-level Turkish officials—such as the prime minister and the president—to meet the ambassadors stationed in Istanbul when they did travel to Ankara within the small window of time defined by their often short visits.[15] Finally, when the Turkish government prepared budget appropriations for fiscal year 1926, it made no provisions for the liaison's office in Istanbul, thus compelling foreign governments to reconsider their positions—since even a politics of hostility required appropriate channels of communication.[16]

The second and more proactive strategy the Turkish government used to allure diplomatic missions to Ankara was to offer land grants and tax breaks for the construction of embassies. In February 1925 a law was passed granting free land for embassy buildings in Ankara.[17] The Ministry of Foreign Affairs officials who promoted the bill acknowledged that, although it would cost the government dearly to provide extensive land grants and tax breaks, this was not too heavy a burden to bear, considering what it could do in normalizing Turkey's political and administrative transactions with other governments and restoring its status in the world.[18] According to the new law, the government would provide twelve thousand square meters for legations, and twenty thousand square meters for embassies free of charge and grant tax exemptions on the importation of necessary construction materials.[19] Diplomatic missions could choose any site in the city and petition the Ministry of Foreign Affairs for the transfer of that property.[20] In Ankara, where rampant land speculation was driving up real estate prices at a "rapid and unaccountable" pace, the free land offer was acknowledged by several diplomats as a beau geste because it meant a significant reduction in moving costs, which had been a major cause for concern.[21] As many of them saw it, even if the prospect of moving to Ankara was still not all that appealing, the offer of free land was.

The gradual migration of diplomatic missions to Ankara started in earnest, once the Istanbul Office of the Ministry of Foreign Affairs was closed. Germany, the Soviet Union, Afghanistan, Albania, Belgium, Czechoslovakia, Egypt, and Poland had already moved their embassies to Ankara by 1926. The embassies of Austria, Bulgaria, Denmark, France, Hungary, Italy, Japan, Iran, Romania, Spain, Sweden, Switzerland, the United States, and Yugoslavia were still in Istanbul. However, after Adıvar's departure, many of them acquired small permanent offices with enough space for a chargé d'affaires and a small staff stationed in Ankara. These satellite offices often included accommodations for their ambassadors who also began to visit Ankara with increasing frequency. Despite their makeshift quality, these modest quarters were an improvement over the railroad cars parked by the old train station, which visiting dignitaries rented at 5 liras a night due to the lack of decent hotels in the city.[22] Nevertheless, this arrangement was far from ideal, as Joseph Grew, the American ambassador complained. Running a divided embassy, with periodic exchanges of staff between Istanbul and Ankara, which required much duplication of effort and hindered continuity, was unsustainable in the long run (see fig. 1.2 for an aerial view of Ulus).[23] Italy, France, and Japan, which, like the United States, had initially sided with Britain, were also seriously reviewing their options.[24] By 1928, the French were breaking rank. As a concerned British ambassador reported to the Foreign Office with concern, his French counterpart, Mr. Chambrun, had expressed a desire to "infuse more *cœur*" in his relations with the Turkish government and had declared to the press that "Angora was the heart of Turkey, and that the French Embassy must forthwith be established there."[25]

There were both political and economic reasons behind this change of heart among European states. Throughout the 1920s, by following a consistently pacifist foreign policy and building multiple political alliances within its region, the Turkish government had come to occupy a respectable position in the Middle East and the Balkans. Turkey's rise as an indisputable regional power was a development that neither Britain nor its Allies could overlook.[26] Moreover, as Turkey showed signs of emerging from its postwar trauma, its government became more stable and rooted in Ankara, and large-scale infrastructural projects got under way, European states began to weigh the cost of their solidarity with Britain against the possibility of using their embassies to make important business deals and taking part in Turkey's potentially lucrative reconstruction process.[27] According to an article published in the British paper, the *Times*, the Turkish government had centralized all of its operations in Ankara, effectively leaving Istanbul out of the loop: "Nor is it only the diplomatic centre of gravity swinging slowly towards Angora. Businessmen are finding that nothing can be done without reference to Angora. Owing to the Government and the Prefect of Constantinople both being nominated by the Cabinet, Angora is able to keep a tight hold upon the administration of the city, and outside Constantinople there are few centres where any big contract could be made without the express or implicit consent of the Government."[28]

With the Musul question resolved in its favor and the embassies of its most influential allies moving to Ankara, Britain's continued resistance not only had lost its strength but also had become counterproductive. France was moving to forge closer relations and to gradually enter into joint ventures with Turkey. Britain could not simply ignore this insofar as the two countries historically had a complex relationship characterized as much by competition as by cooperation. Moreover, within the emerging context of economic relations and geopolitical configurations in Central and Eastern Europe, collaborating with Turkey rather than opposing it was becoming a more effective policy for Britain in maintaining its influence in the Middle East. Hence, a year after France, Britain agreed to build a new embassy in Ankara on property granted by the Turkish government. As George Clerk acknowledged in his annual report for 1929, "so long as her representatives in the capital were lodged in a small and draughty châlet, it is difficult to persuade the Turks that Great Britain took the new republic very seriously."[29]

In sum, the recognition of Turkey's new stature in international politics was inextricably linked to the recognition of its capital. With the relocation of the British embassy, the embassies of all leading world powers had finally moved to Ankara. The process had been slow, strenuous, and costly. Despite having the cards stacked against it, however, the Turkish government had successfully lured foreign missions to its new capital through careful negotiations and by permanently displacing Istanbul's long-standing circuitry of power to the new capital, in the process making it very clear that those who wanted to do business with Turkey could not afford to stay in Istanbul.

GERMANY AND THE SHAPE OF TURKISH MODERNITY

Spurned by the Allies initially, Turkey turned to the Soviet Union and Germany, which had been similarly marginalized in the post–First World

War reconfiguration of world powers. The Soviet Union had entered the war with the Allies but found itself both out of the war and in sudden isolation as a result of the Russian Revolution. Consequently, the new Soviet regime, in its search for new alliances, made an effort to establish good relations with Turkey, despite the long history of hostilities between czarist Russia and the Ottoman Empire. Even before the War of Independence was finalized, in 1921, the two countries signed a Friendship and Fraternity Treaty, and the Soviets appointed an ambassador shortly thereafter.[30] The Soviet delegation rented a modest house close to Ulus, near the Citadel, and maintained very close personal relations with the nationalists. In later years, shared security concerns arising from the demilitarization of the Straits and the opening of the Black Sea to the unrestricted navigation of military and commercial vessels of nonriparian states, as dictated by the Lausanne Treaty, would bring the two countries closer.[31]

Germany, Turkey's former ally in the First World War, was also in a precarious situation. Along with the war, Germany had lost its place on the world stage. It was expected to pay war reparations, but its industries lay fallow and its economy was stagnant. Intent on recovering some of its influence in the Middle East, where in the aftermath of the war Britain had become the dominant player, the German government eagerly moved to rebuild its ties with the neophyte Turkish state. Soon after the proclamation of the republic, Rudolf Nadolny, who, as consul general in Istanbul, had been waiting in the wings since the summer of 1923, was appointed as Germany's new ambassador. Nadolny was a singularly resourceful diplomat who recognized that he could help forge a mutually beneficial relationship between the two countries by channeling German assistance to Turkey's modernization projects, which in turn would generate business and a new visibility for Germany's industries and expertise. As Nadolny would later acknowledge in his memoirs, his posting came at a crucial time for both countries:

> I came to Turkey at the right time: Instead of the Ottoman Empire, a new national Turkey, which had rid itself of the Arab regions, was created and a new order was introduced everywhere. The new capital was the symbol of the new world. The soul of all the progress was Gazi Mustafa Kemal. He had the ambition to Europeanize Turkey, and he preached these ideals to his people. Everywhere, people were gripped by the fever of Europeanization. And I resolved to help Turkey wherever I could in this pursuit. . . . I did have my own priorities: I needed to restore Germany's respectable image, and regroup the local colony of Germans. . . . But I still had time to help the Turks with the establishment of their new state, and by doing that, I also furthered our own interests.[32]

FIGURE 2.2. GERMAN EMBASSY COMPLEX IN ANKARA. COURTESY OF THE TURKISH HISTORICAL SOCIETY LIBRARY.

While German interests in Turkey were mostly economic in nature, the Soviets primarily wanted to build a political alliance with Turkey. According to Nadolny, their distinct goals also made it possible for the two ambassadors to coordinate their efforts in their respective endeavors: "My Russian colleague Jacob Suritz was a very nice man. . . . I immediately became friends with him, and we later made a gentleman's pact that he would only pursue political interests in Turkey, supporting me in my economic endeavors, and in turn I would back him in politics. We both remained faithful to this agreement, which bore rich fruits."[33] At the time, in the absence of other heads of foreign missions, the presence of the German and Soviet ambassadors was all the more prominent. Rudolf Nadolny, his Soviet counterpart, Jacob Suritz, and officials from both embassies frequently kept company with the republican elite and attended dinners and receptions hosted by Turkish dignitaries. It is noteworthy that their willingness to stay and build embassies in Ankara even before offers of

FIGURE 2.3. PAUL VON HINDENBURG'S FAMILY HOME IN NEUDECK.

free land were extended, had a positive effect on their relations with Turkey from the outset.[34]

Rudolf Nadolny hoped to use his embassy as a "vessel to bring the German image back to honor."[35] Site selection was, for him, a strategic decision, and he attended to it personally. He needed a large lot in a visible location that was also easily accessible to the dozens of German businessmen and professionals he expected to bring to Ankara. He turned down a lot chosen earlier by Herr Freitag, the embassy's chargé d'affaires, because at 16,000 square meters (4 acres) it was too small and despite its proximity to Mustafa Kemal's residence in Çankaya, it was hard to reach from the train station. Instead, he opted for a 30,000 square meter (7.5 acre) lot, facing Atatürk Boulevard, which was also quite close to the new Government Quarter and received another 21,000 square meters (5.2 acres) from the government, once the land grants became available.[36] Furthermore, Nadolny convinced the German Ministry of Foreign Affairs to increase its funding for the embassy from 100,000 to 250,000 deutsche mark—a sum the British ambassador criticized for being unduly extravagant.[37]

Built in the style of East Prussian manor houses, the German embassy in Ankara had a distinct resemblance to the family home of then pres-

FIGURE 2.4. KAYSERI AIRCRAFT FACTORY, JUNKERS ASSEMBLY PLANT. COURTESY OF DAVUT GÜLEÇ.

ident of the Weimar Republic, Paul von Hindenburg, in Neudeck.[38] The fenced compound's formal entrance was marked by large wrought-iron gates. A wide cobblestone path led to the embassy building and the two smaller office buildings that flanked it symmetrically. In front of the main entrance of the embassy, the path bifurcated and snaked up to the hillside garden in the back, which resembled an urban park.[39] The main embassy building contained the consular section and sizable reception rooms. Until the completion of the ambassadorial residence, the building also housed temporary quarters for Nadolny and his immediate subordinate, Herr Holstein, on its top floor. The compound included, in addition to the structures necessary to perform its primary diplomatic functions, equestrian training grounds, a small stable, a fish pool, and a winter garden.

Nadolny cleverly used his embassy compound in two important ways to further Turco-German relations. In the first place, the compound in its entirety served as an ideal showcase for displaying Germany's technological strength and architectural sophistication. Nadolny turned the construction process into a veritable spectacle specifically with the interests of the republican elite in mind. He cultivated a large, lush garden and when he had delicate plants specially brought from his former residence in Istanbul, he sent gift specimens to Mustafa Kemal.[40] With water in Ankara in short supply, his efforts to ensure that the embassy had its own supply for the upkeep of its ponds and gardens led to a particularly memorable display of German ingenuity, as technicians of different stripes searched for underground reserves, digging deep wells and unusually intricate tunnels into the bedrock under the embassy.[41] As the sprawling compound, which over time would expand to fourteen buildings, began to take shape, Turkish officials frequently came to Çankaya to check on its progress. Nadolny proudly noted that the German embassy was the premier example of European taste in Ankara, and that, as such, it influenced much of what was built by the aspiring elite as well. "It was thrilling," he observed, "to see how the locals imitated what we built. Everywhere one saw German-style gates, and cobblestone paths to the houses."[42] When the embassy was completed in December 1928, it was inaugurated with a reception attended by Mustafa Kemal himself, who personally praised the ambassador for building a jewel for Ankara.[43]

Second, Nadolny used the embassy as an indispensable base for networking, by converting it into a hub of social, cultural, and commercial exchanges. From very early on, he understood that participating in Ankara's social scene was key to achieving goals in intergovernmental affairs. Consequently, during his nine-year stay, Nadolny always made himself visible and available, and to prevent the disruption of his dealings with Turkish officials, he kept his embassy running in a wooden prefabricated structure erected at the site throughout the construction process.[44] Once the lavish compound was complete, he arranged for exchanges of scholars, sponsored guest lectures, and graciously hosted several receptions and dinner parties.[45] These large gatherings brought together not only the rather sizable resident German community in Ankara but also the corps diplomatique, members of the cabinet and the parliament, and high-level state officials. As such, they provided perfect opportunities for German entrepreneurs to meet the Turkish brass in a seemingly casual way.

As Nadolny would later acknowledge in his memoirs, he hoped that success in a task as challenging as steering the modernization of Turkey would bring credit to Germany and help to restore its reputation on the world stage as a leading industrialized power.[46] Backed by his government, he enthusiastically worked to build a cycle in which more experts begot more materials, techniques, and standards, which opened the doors for further German involvement. Sometimes, he personally introduced Turkish dignitaries to German businessmen and professionals, who offered their advice and services on a wide range of subjects. It was through such introductions that the Philip Holzman Construction Company, which built the German embassy, obtained the contract to build Mustafa Kemal's model farm on the outskirts of the city.[47] Similarly, German engineers, whose work in providing water for the embassy had elicited much admiration, were hired

FIGURE 2.5. THE INFLUENCE OF CENTRAL EUROPEAN VERNACULAR IN SOME OF ANKARA'S RESIDENTIAL ARCHITECTURE. COURTESY OF THE TURKISH HISTORICAL SOCIETY LIBRARY.

to drain the marshes by the train station, which were breeding grounds for the malaria that afflicted the entire town.[48] When a limited urban design competition was organized for the plan of Ankara in 1928, two of the three invited contestants were German, and the selection of the professor Hermann Jansen came as no surprise because he already had a web of contacts in the city.[49] To be sure, Germany's eagerness to do business was a boon for the Turkish leaders who were seeking technical, technological, and financial support, institutional and administrative models, and expert assistance in initiating wholesale reforms to modernize the country. But it was Nadolny's intense lobbying that was instrumental to opening up the much needed job opportunities in Turkey for many qualified researchers, engineers, administrative specialists, military experts, and various other specialists who found themselves unemployed in postwar Germany.

German influence in shaping the physical environment in Turkey was manifest at different levels. Beyond providing the prototypes of sophisticated domestic architecture in the new capital, German cities provided the tangible imagery of modern urbanism upon which republican leaders based their visions for the future of Turkish cities.[50] Germany provided the technology, materials, credit, and expertise for several large projects, including the building of Ankara, and German professionals were at work everywhere in Turkey. It is important to note that at a time when Turkey needed capital for industrial and infrastructure investments and help in paying off its debts, German bankers were more willing to take risks in Turkey than were their British or American counterparts.[51] A comprehensive clearing agreement between Germany and Turkey that allowed for the exchange of industrial products and expertise from the former with raw materials and agricultural goods from the latter further cemented this relationship.[52] In an article published on December 22, 1924, the special correspondent of the *Times* in Ankara wrote at length about this overwhelmingly prevalent German presence:

> It is quite obvious . . . that the new quarter of Angora—the Ausstadt, as the Vali himself described it to me—is to have a highly German flavor, and that the many Germans who are here now will feel more than ever at home.[53] And there is no mistaking the seriousness of the endeavour they are making to capture the Anatolian market. In this hotel the only foreign language that is spoken with accuracy by the guests is German, and one hears more German than anything else in restaurants . . . the fact remains that the Germans are creeping back in ever-increasing numbers and have laid a firm hold upon the contracts or the supply of railway rolling stock, upon the sale of agricultural machinery, and so forth.[54]

The numbers backed such impressions. Trade between Turkey and Germany, which had come to a halt in the immediate aftermath of the First World War, was jumpstarted in 1923. Germany quickly became Turkey's top supplier of industrial products and German exports to Turkey increased from 9.1 million Turkish lira to 31.6 million Turkish lira in 1928.[55] Meanwhile, Britain, which on the eve of the First World War was the largest exporter to the Ottoman Empire and controlled 28 percent of the market, lost its position as its sales dropped to 16 percent of Turkey's imports.[56]

Britain's losses in a market it once dominated were not lost on the British Parliament, press, and business. Intensifying Turco-German relations were also beginning to raise security concerns among British diplomats, who observed that despite Germany's mandatory post–First World War demilitarization, former army and navy officials were "acting clandestinely as military advisers in such fortified zones as Smyrna."[57] As early as 1925, members of the opposition began to criticize Britain's official policy regarding Turkey. In a House of Commons session on December 22, 1925, Sir Fred

Wise and Captain W. Benn questioned the undersecretary to the Foreign Office, G. Locker-Sampson, stating that the government's unwillingness to move the embassy was putting Britain at a disadvantage.[58] Locker-Sampson defended the government's position, stating that in Ankara the general conditions were "not yet adequate as regarded housing or other requirements," and argued that even though the ambassador was stationed in Istanbul, he paid frequent visits to Ankara, and that there was "no reason to suppose that the present arrangements impaired the usefulness of his Majesty's Ambassador at Constantinople."[59] Nevertheless, businessmen who tried to obtain contracts in Turkey opined differently. In a letter written to the editor of the *Times*, Alwyn Parker, a British commercial envoy for British railroad interests, denounced the government's actions as follows: "During the past two years, I have spent many months in Angora, and I can testify to the irreparable harm done to British commercial interests by the cynical neglect of the British Foreign Office in failing to maintain an Ambassador at Angora, while many thousands of pounds are wasted annually by diplomatic establishments at Pera in winter and Bosporus in summer. We shall never recover the ground we lost on this account."[60]

Indeed, the initial ground Germany gained from the absence of competition from Britain and its allies, had a remarkably long-lasting influence. The Germans became involved with Turkey's modernization project at a crucial formative stage and enjoyed the benefits of cooperating with a leadership that was intent on an unprecedented degree of centralization and homogenization across the land. Since the initial components of that infrastructure were laid according to German standards and specifications, the subsequent parts had to conform to it and Turkish technocrats educated by German teachers often saw to it that they did. Hence, long after British and Turkish governments established closer relations, the United States emerged as a new dominant player in the region, and Germany once again became marginalized in the aftermath of the Second World War, the legacy of German experts and technologies persisted in the Turkish cultural landscape. The choices for the material culture of Turkish modern were made at the interstices of two spatial scales that are rarely thought of together—but in the Turkish experience considerations about great geopolitical tensions were never too far from the dinner tables that Nadolny set for Turkish officials and their German counterparts.

ANKARA'S EMBASSY ROW

At the celebrations for the tenth anniversary of the Turkish Republic, the Soviet Union staged a spectacular performance.[61] A delegation headed

FIGURE 2.6. A NEWSPAPER CLIPPING OF RUSSIANS ARRIVING FOR THE TENTH ANNIVERSARY CELEBRATIONS. THE GRAPHICS MAKE THE GEOPOLITICAL SIGNIFICANCE OF THE VISIT CLEAR.

by the minister of war, Marshal Klimenty Voroshilov (a close deputy of Stalin), and a large entourage including the minister of education, Sergei Bubnov, and the cavalry general, Semyon Budenny, sailed into the Istanbul harbor escorted by a squadron of the Red Fleet on October 26, 1933. The Soviet guests were greeted with thundering salutes by an enthusiastic crowd, and their visit generated significant press coverage at home and abroad.[62] This was a remarkable occasion not only because it marked the first time that "members of the Politbureau . . . had ever ventured outside the Soviet Union since it was founded" but also, as *Time* magazine reported, because they were traveling with their wives in "great exception to Stalin's ban against junketing."[63] Upon their arrival in Istanbul, the ladies were whisked away by "the svelte Mme. Suritz," wife of the Soviet ambassador, who had "Paris gowns ready for the dowdy wives from Moscow and an expert modiste on hand to fit them." When the party

FIGURE 2.7. ATATÜRK AT A DINNER WITH OTHER AMBASSADORS AT THE SOVIET EMBASSY. COURTESY OF THE TURKISH HISTORICAL SOCIETY LIBRARY.

continued on to Ankara, "Under Dictator Kemal's critical eye," the ladies "shone at his grand ball like 'Soviet Cinderellas.'"[64] The Soviets also presented Turkey with a gift of several warplanes, which were unveiled and flown as part of the aerial acrobatics displays in Ankara on October 29, Republic Day.[65] The entire affair was recorded and later included in the documentary *Ankara: The Heart of Turkey*, commissioned by the Turkish government and prepared by Sergei Yutkevich and Leo Arnstam, two of Russia's most promising young filmmakers, who had accompanied the Soviet delegation.

Carefully orchestrated by the Soviet ambassador Jacob Suritz, the dramatic events outlined above illuminate the relatively overlooked intersection of the different levels at which international diplomacy operates. While the post–First World War rapprochement between Turkey and the Soviet Union was driven by each country's pressing geopolitical concerns, it was articulated and conveyed to the world at large through painstakingly planned symbolic performances for which public events, such as the anniversary celebrations, provided an ideal stage. Politically and ideologically marginalized in an unfriendly international environment after the revolution, the Soviets were determined to combat what they perceived to be a "hostile encirclement" through regional alliances that West European states could not afford to ignore.[66] To accomplish this, they sent one of their most skillful diplomats to Turkey. Ambassador Suritz came to An-

FIGURE 2.8. THE SOVIET EMBASSY WAS THE FIRST PURPOSE-BUILT EMBASSY COMPOUND AND THE FIRST MODERNIST BUILDING IN ANKARA. COURTESY OF THE TURKISH HISTORICAL SOCIETY LIBRARY.

kara in 1923, following a four-year posting in Afghanistan, during which the ties he was rumored to have established with local tribal leaders had undermined Britain's efforts to bring that country within its sphere of influence.[67] Suritz's appointment was, therefore, no subtle reminder to Britain of Soviet designs to counterweigh British dominance in the region by maintaining a close relationship with Turkey. Jacob Suritz moved quickly into Ankara's diplomatic scene and started work on building a military-political alliance, which, in addition to Turkey, was to include Iran and Afghanistan—strengthening the Soviet Union's sway in West Asia.[68] In return, the Soviet Union lent its weight as Turkey sorted out its differences with Britain and confronted Italy about its rumored intention to annex southwestern Anatolia. Russian support included military aid, and in the aftermath of the Great Depression, it expanded into the economic field with the implementation of a Soviet-style economic development strategy that emphasized state ownership of heavy industry and large-scale enterprises. In sum, despite a long history of animosity between their imperial predecessors, the leaders of the newly formed Soviet and Turkish states chose to look past their old resentments and ongoing reservations and focused on their mutual defense concerns over the security of the Straits and a shared desire to resist the expansion of imperial capitalism.

The significance of the spectacle staged by the Turks and Soviets on the tenth anniversary of the republic snaps into focus against this highly charged geopolitical background. Far from a superficial display of niceties, the Soviet Union's unusually high-profile presence and military gifts were an enactment of its solidarity with Turkey. Similarly, the Soviets' conspicuous use of the Red Fleet to sail down the Black Sea and through the Bosphorus and the Turkish hosts' staging of a dramatic landing in Istanbul were gestures that announced to a broader international audience in no uncertain terms the two countries' will to exercise control over these highly contested strategic waterways.

In turn, beyond reaffirming the strength of their bilateral ties, the Soviets used their presence in Turkey to reach out to a broader international audience and redefine their postrevolutionary image as a modern society, having broken with the past and its trappings. Unlike other European capitals where they had diplomatic representation, Turkey offered the Soviets a friendly platform from which to project a favorable impression. When seen within the context of their intense efforts to garner international respect and recognition, even seemingly frivolous acts—such as providing the "dowdy wives from Moscow" a Cinderella-style makeover—acquire new meaning as calculated moves to present the new face of Russia.

Such preoccupations also appear to have shaped the new Soviet embassy, the first permanent embassy facility to be completed in Ankara. Inaugurated in April 1926, the Soviet embassy was also the first building to introduce a modernist aesthetic in the Turkish capital. Despite the limitations of available construction technologies and the lack of skilled labor, the Soviets had opted for an industrial look. Described as having an "ultramodern appearance" with "soaring porches" resembling the "wings of an airplane," the Soviet embassy was unlike anything else in Ankara.[69] By forgoing allusions to specific historic and regional architectural traditions, the building also intimated a universalism that was in line with the Soviet vision of a global proletarian revolution. This was in striking contrast to the German embassy, which with a replica of president Paul von Hindenburg's manor house invoked the landscapes of the Prussian heartland (see fig. 2.4 earlier in the chapter). Whereas the Germans reminded their European neighbors that despite their temporary marginalization they shared the same geography and cultural traditions, the Soviets announced a break with the bourgeois-aristocratic traditions of the continent. The

FIGURE 2.9. THE BRITISH EMBASSY—ALTHOUGH IT WAS ONE OF THE LAST TO RELOCATE TO ANKARA, IT ACQUIRED A LOT ADJACENT TO THE PRESIDENTIAL PALACE. COURTESY OF THE TURKISH HISTORICAL SOCIETY LIBRARY.

Soviet embassy, a representative export of a short-lived visionary utopianism, was an unmistakable attempt to assert a new revolutionary identity.

By virtue of building large embassy compounds, the Soviet Union and Germany brought Turkey's new capital into the fold of a new kind of international competition for visibility and real estate acquisition, placing Ankara at yet another intersection between gestures at the architectural level and politics on a regional level. Istanbul's isolation from the conduct of international negotiations and business opportunities made it increasingly inconvenient for embassies to remain in the former Ottoman capital. Meanwhile, the Turkish government's offer of free land made it appealing to move. But it was the ability of the German and Soviet governments to take advantage of the absence of other diplomatic missions in Ankara and to reinvent themselves in the international arena that turned embassy construction in Ankara into a bona fide competition. Furthermore, the Turkish government's offer of land brought out the bargain hunter in

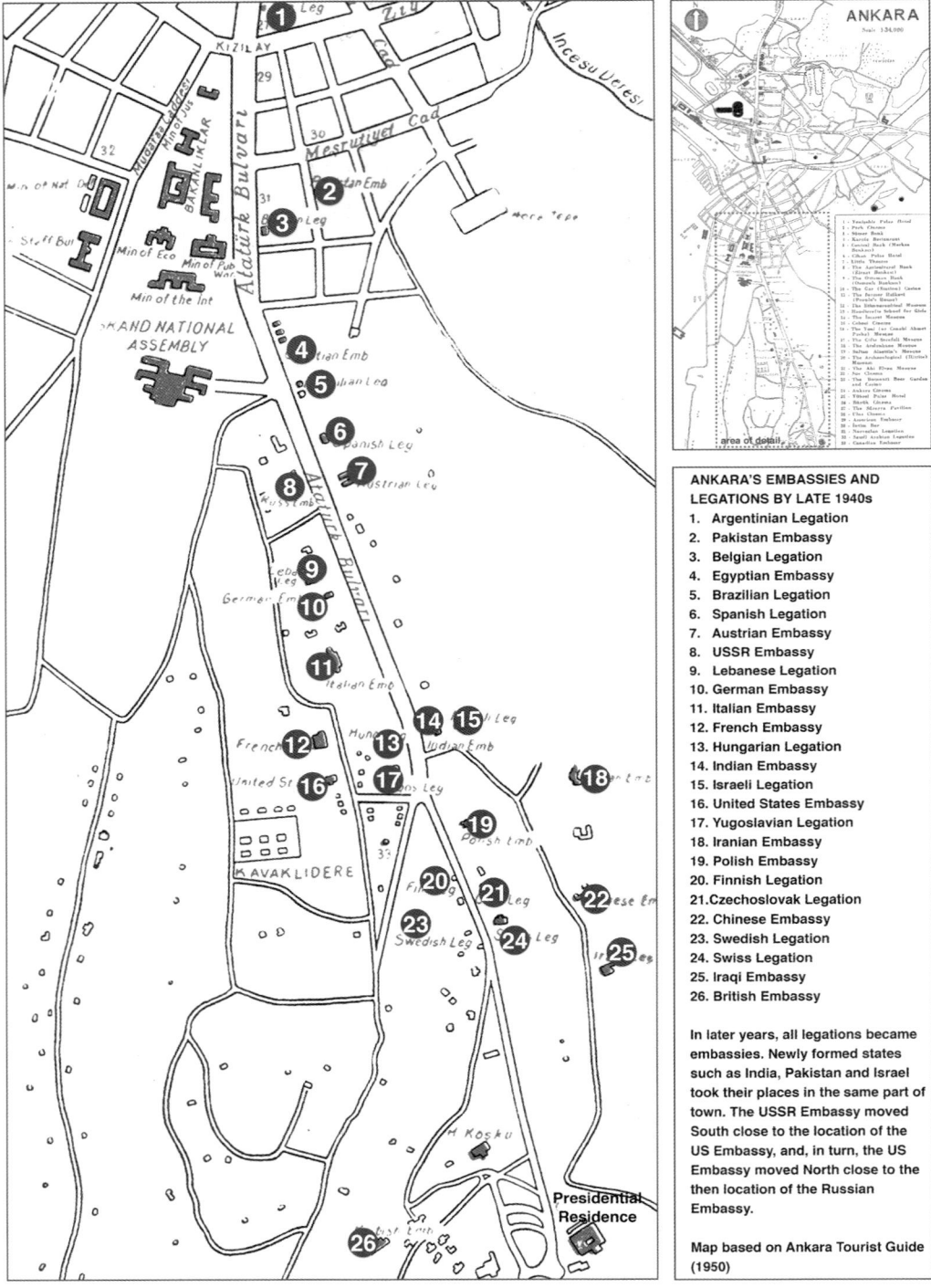

ANKARA'S EMBASSIES AND
LEGATIONS BY LATE 1940s
1. Argentinian Legation
2. Pakistan Embassy
3. Belgian Legation
4. Egyptian Embassy
5. Brazilian Legation
6. Spanish Legation
7. Austrian Embassy
8. USSR Embassy
9. Lebanese Legation
10. German Embassy
11. Italian Embassy
12. French Embassy
13. Hungarian Legation
14. Indian Embassy
15. Israeli Legation
16. United States Embassy
17. Yugoslavian Legation
18. Iranian Embassy
19. Polish Embassy
20. Finnish Legation
21. Czechoslovak Legation
22. Chinese Embassy
23. Swedish Legation
24. Swiss Legation
25. Iraqi Embassy
26. British Embassy

In later years, all legations became
embassies. Newly formed states
such as India, Pakistan and Israel
took their places in the same part of
town. The USSR Embassy moved
South close to the location of the
US Embassy, and, in turn, the US
Embassy moved North close to the
then location of the Russian
Embassy.

Map based on Ankara Tourist Guide
(1950)

FIGURE 2.10. ANKARA'S EMBASSY ROW ALONG THE ATATÜRK BOULEVARD.

every diplomatic mission, and, in turn, their unbridled competition to get the best lots in town for free further reinforced Ankara's position as the permanent seat of government. In early Republican Ankara what determined prestige was one's location relative to Mustafa Kemal, and the sites closest to his Çankaya residence were the most prized ones. Hence, whereas in 1923 the vineyard properties on the Kavaklıdere-Çankaya hills had little appeal for anyone outside Ankara's new elite, by the late 1920s they had become the address of choice for most embassies. Italy, Greece, Yugoslavia, and Poland chose their sites on the sides of Atatürk Boulevard. The lots requested by the Iranian, Swedish, and French embassies were in the same vicinity, on smaller streets off the main road.

In the international arena, embargoes, blockades, or sanctions against a given state work only if all other states abide by these self-imposed restrictions. The sizable—if briefly handicapped—German and Soviet states never joined the British-led rejection of Ankara, thus limiting the effectiveness of Britain's opposition from the outset. What is more, the momentum generated by their large embassy construction projects—and the improved international business opportunities that followed—prompted other governments to do an about-face and break ranks with Britain as it became increasingly clear that they just could not stay out of the competition to assert their presence once their peers were in it. These developments, together with the resolution of the Musul-Kirkuk issue in its favor, finally persuaded the British government to enter the competition and, despite joining the game quite late, lay claim to a very large lot adjacent to the Presidential Palace with a panoramic view of Ankara, befitting its position as the most powerful player in international politics.[70] Despite their initial resistance to moving to Ankara, Britain and its First World War allies could no longer afford not to be there if they wanted to maintain their clout as world powers.

Eventually, the competition for ostentatious structures at the most coveted sites of the new capital took on a life of its own. Ambassadors closely followed what their counterparts were spending on their embassies and petitioned their own governments for additional funding, further upping the ante. As the competition stiffened, the British ambassador Sir George Clerk argued for the importance of building an embassy that was proportionate to Britain's ambitions in the Middle East: "Incidentally I venture to observe that with Italy prepared to spend over £200,000 on building an Embassy in Angora . . . and the intentions of France as now announced by M. de Chambrun, it becomes more than ever politically important for the credits of our more modest building estimates to be granted in the next budget."[71]

Once embassies took possession of their new sites, the size and characteristics of their respective lots became as important a basis for competition as location. Demand for properties with topographical accidents that afforded both views and visibility to the main embassy building was particularly high. Many embassies complained that the size of the lots provided by the government was insufficient for their needs and began to ask for more land under various pretexts.[72] They often framed their requests as readjustments to make up for uneven site conditions. Such claims, if conceded, often triggered further claims by other embassies, which regarded themselves to be of equal or superior importance. In other words, the Turkish government had initially assigned two standard lot sizes based on the level of representation, but the foreign missions demanded sites that were commensurate with what they perceived to be their status in the international matrix of nation-states.

The peculiarities of Ankara's political culture and logistical conditions heightened the rivalry between the represented states. Ankara's protocol, consisting of prominent politicians, high-level bureaucrats, and the corps diplomatique, was smaller in size than protocols in more established European capitals. But there were as many if not more events that brought its members together.[73] The diplomats lived virtually "in each other's pockets," and, according to a British observer, no one among them could give "a big party without inviting all his colleagues."[74] Furthermore, due to the shortage of suitable government buildings, state business often had to be discussed in clubs and private residences."[75] Although official dinners, balls, *thés dansants*, and cocktail parties were primarily social events, they effectively doubled as occasions for negotiating serious issues.[76] For members of the republican elite, partaking in these events was crucial for maintaining their social status and their prospects for advancement. For the diplomats, attendance at such events carried political meanings as well. Their presence was often interpreted as a sign of positive relations between Turkey and the government they represented, and conversely, absences were usually cause for concern

Gatherings that brought diplomats and Turkish officials together mapped out, in the space of ballrooms and banquet tables, the current state of international affairs. Both diplomats and Turkish officials used them to assert the position of their respective governments within the international system of states. Hence, the events Ambassador Nadolny hosted at the German embassy, showcasing his country's accomplishments in the arts and sciences, were also intended to proclaim Germany's bid to reassume its position as a player in world politics. Meanwhile, Mustafa Kemal's dismissal of the Egyptian ambassador for wearing a fez at a Republic Day ball, which caused a serious rift between the two countries, signaled not merely his distaste for a headgear associated with Arab-Islamic culture but, more important, Turkey's determination to sever ties with the East to join the ranks of the West. In the volatile context of the interwar years, after the resolution of the Musul crisis, and especially in the lead-up to the Second World War, Turkish leaders increasingly focused on a politics of balance between key players of the European theater. They rebuilt bridges with Britain while maintaining their working relations with Germany and the Soviet Union. Especially as the regimes of the latter countries appeared to be hardening, Turkey's leaders were careful to avoid being pulled into either orbit. Such repositionings were also conveyed through the highly codified language of diplomatic performance—as in the case of Mustafa Kemal's careful placement of himself between the Russian and British ambassadors at a banquet, publicly announcing the parity between the two as Turkey's friends.[77] In reporting the details of such encounters to the foreign office, ambassador George Clerk wrote that such events "would scarcely warrant recording in an official dispatch, but Angora is not other places."[78] In Ankara, the dual-purpose gatherings of diplomats and officials were always spatial representations of larger geopolitical constellations.

PART II

ERASURES IN
THE LAND

CHAPTER 3

DISMANTLING THE LANDSCAPES OF ISLAM

In late December 1919, after more than seven months of touring Anatolia and attending organizational meetings, the nationalists finally arrived in Ankara on an icy cold morning, where they were greeted by cheering crowds who had gathered just outside town at the Dikmen Hills to welcome them. Thousands of armed seğmen troops, some on foot and others on horseback, and dervishes representing Sufi lodges, all of them in full regalia, accompanied the party for the remainder of their journey to Ankara, and more people joined them along the way.[1] Some were from Ankara, others had traveled from nearby towns to show their support. People cheered the nationalists and their growing entourage as they made their way downhill; town criers walked through major streets announcing their arrival, and sonorous chants of Koranic verses echoed in the air.[2] The nationalists and Ankara's notables and religious leaders who had invited them walked through streets that were decorated with banners featuring Koranic verses and local guilds' standards. They stopped at Ankara's most venerable mosque, the tomb-mosque of Hacı Bayram Veli, and marked the occasion by attending a rousing religious ceremony at the courtyard of the complex.[3]

A few months later, when preparations for the first Grand National Assembly were complete, its inauguration was marked similarly with a quasi-religious ceremony, purposely scheduled to coincide with a Friday prayer, on April 23, 1920. The day began with a public prayer at the Hacı Bayram Mosque. Afterward, the crowd comprising the nationalists, local notables, religious leaders, and newly arrived representatives from around the country marched toward the makeshift Assembly building accompanied by a military escort. Inventively fusing the religious with the military,

FIGURE 3.1. LOCAL SEĞMENS CELEBRATING THE ARRIVAL OF THE NATIONALISTS. COURTESY OF ANKARA MUNICIPAL ARCHIVES.

Sinop representative Hoca Abdullah Efendi carried the Sancak-ı Şerif (Holy Flag) and a box containing strands from Prophet Muhammed's beard, the most valuable relics of Islam kept at Hacı Bayram, raised above his head, guarded by a platoon of soldiers on either side. When the cortege passed through the portal, they were greeted by an even larger crowd. Müezzins and *hafiz*s welcomed them with Koranic verses, their voices blended with the enthusiastic mass as they communed together.[4] To consecrate the inauguration of the Assembly three sheep were sacrificed and their blood was smeared on the foreheads of the nationalist leaders in a recognized ritual act of benediction.[5] The interior arrangement of the building also mixed nationalistic and religious symbolism. The first room by the entrance had been arranged as a small prayer room, and inside the chamber, in addition to the enduring nationalist motto "sovereignty unconditionally belongs to the nation," framed Koranic verses reminded the representatives of their religious duty. Once the representatives arrived in the main chamber, the Koran, the flag, and the box that had been brought from Hacı Bayram were placed by the lectern and the session began with a prayer. The sequence of events left no doubt that, on this auspicious day,

FIGURE 3.2. MUSTAFA KEMAL (ATATÜRK), HIS ENTOURAGE, AND ANKARA'S NOTABLES AND RELIGIOUS LEADERS PRAYING TOGETHER ON THE OPENING DAY OF THE GRAND NATIONAL ASSEMBLY. COURTESY OF ATILIM UNIVERSITY, ANKARA DIGITAL CITY ARCHIVE.

joining the Nationalist Movement was akin to attending a mosque for Friday prayers.

In a move that almost foreshadowed the synchronization of nationwide collective ceremonies of later years, the nationalists also arranged for celebrations of the Assembly's inaugural meeting across a broader geography. Using supportive religious networks, they reached out to more remote congregations and were thus able to assemble a vicarious community of believers to join in from their own local Friday prayers— albeit from a distance. On that auspicious day, in parts of the country that were not under occupation, imams at several mosques included, in their Friday sermons, pledges of solidarity with the nascent nationalist government in Ankara.[6] As the war progressed, important events were observed with rituals that were laced with religious references, fusing faith with nationalistic fervor.

These calculated and spectacular performances with conspicuous religious references were critical for the nationalists' ability to enlist the broader population to join their cause, as were the explicit blessings of trusted local religious leaders for establishing their legitimacy as the leaders of the liberation movement. As a renegade brigade, their activities effectively violated the terms of the 1918 ceasefire, putting the Ottoman government in a difficult position vis-à-vis the Allies. In response,

FIGURE 3.3. A TEMPORARY ARCHWAY NEAR THE ENCLOSURE OF THE FIRST GRAND NATIONAL ASSEMBLY BUILDING. THE STRUCTURE RESEMBLES THE SILHOUETTE OF A MOSQUE QUITE CLOSELY. ARCHWAYS SIMILAR TO THIS WERE WIDELY USED IN THE LAST DECADES OF THE OTTOMAN EMPIRE, DURING THE WAR OF INDE-PENDENCE, AND THE FIRST YEARS OF THE TURKISH REPUBLIC FOR CELEBRATIONS AND COMMEMORATIVE OCCASIONS. IT APPEARS THAT THEY WERE PHASED OUT BY THE LATE 1920S, AT ABOUT THE SAME TIME AS THE MARGINALIZATION OF RELIGION IN PUBLIC LIFE, TO BE REPLACED WITH MORE MODERN LOOKING GATE-WAYS OF MOSTLY ABSTRACT GEOMETRIC CONFIGURATION. COURTESY OF ANKARA MUNICIPAL ARCHIVES.

the Ottoman government declared Atatürk and twenty-two of his close associates to be traitors and, pointedly, obtained from the *şeyhülislam*, the country's highest ranking religious official, a *fetwa* authorizing their capture, dead or alive.[7] Anatolian religious leaders sought to offset the Istanbul fetwa with a counter-fetwa, refuting the suggestion that the nationalists were disputing the sultan-caliph's authority. They argued, to the contrary, that the nationalists' struggle aimed to restore his power and liberate the lands of Islam that were under infidel occupation. More-over, religious leaders, the Orthodox ulema and the heads of Sufi orders alike, had access to expansive social networks that would be indispens-able for mounting the kind of grassroots resistance the nationalists en-visioned.

Using Islam to legitimize and buttress political authority was as old as Turkish presence in Anatolia. From the eleventh century onward, colonizing dervishes had been instrumental in consolidating the newly acquired territories under Seljuk rule by helping to Islamicize the population.[8] In return they had received *vakıf*s (endowments) in the form of tax revenues and land grants for the upkeep of their orders.[9] In this process, *ahi* chambers, professional fraternities founded upon and bounded by religious principles much like medieval European guilds, had also helped.[10] Under Seljuk and later Ottoman rule the myriad local Sufi orders and ahi chambers helped to establish and sustain the patterns of social life in times of peace, and at times of unrest or war they were called upon to rally political and even military support.[11] Rather than a unified, if alternatively canonized, version of Islam, the members of these organizations practiced an amalgamation of Islam with local beliefs and Central Asian traditions with multiple regional variations. This vernacularized Islam did not always conform to the Orthodox Islam espoused by the ruling elites, and at times the differences were the cause of violent confrontations. Nonetheless, official recognition of their contributions in the conquest and pacification of Anatolia had set an early precedent for the imperial patronage of Sufi dervishes, ahis, and the orders they represented.[12] Through this quasi-official arrangement, these diverse enclaves of vernacular Islam continued to maintain a powerful presence among lay people and controlled significant amounts of land in towns as well as the remote rural countryside. This influence over people's collective allegiances was the crucial asset the nationalist leaders wanted to win over.

Consequently, on their way to Ankara, in addition to high-profile congresses in Amasya, Erzurum, and Sivas, where they worked with delegates from around the country to chart a path of action, the nationalists made detours to remote locations, privately met with prominent Sufi leaders and obtained their support. Thus, for instance, at a farm near Kayseri, they spoke with Salih Niyazi Dedebaba, leader of the Bektaşi order, and with Şeyh Çelebi Cemalettin Efendi, a well-respected Alevi leader, both of whom were influential in securing the participation of the Alevis, who composed roughly a quarter of the population at the time.[13] Their visit in Ankara with Bayramizade Mehmet Tayyib Efendi, the fifteenth-generation descendant of Hacı Bayram Veli, founder of the Bayrami order and patron mystic of farmers and small merchants, was part of the same alliance-building effort.[14] Unlike in Istanbul, in a provincial town such as Ankara, the relationship between Orthodox Islam and Sufism was porous, and the leaders of both collaborated to support the nationalists, providing much needed assistance. With the help of Ankara's Sufi leaders and ahis as well as other merchants and tradesmen, Ankara's *müftü* Börekçizade Rıfat Efendi collected sizable donations to finance the war, especially in its initial planning stages.[15] They even extended their hospitality to nationalist leaders by putting up some of them in their own homes. Later, when the incomplete club building of the Congress of Union and Progress (CUP) was chosen as the site of the first Grand National Assembly, Mehmet Tayyib Efendi donated the timber for the roof, which he had originally purchased for the repairs of the Bayrami lodge in Ankara.[16]

The support of local religious leaders was also conspicuous in the Grand National Assembly's composition. Since there was no uniform dress code in the first term of this makeshift National Assembly, the representatives' backgrounds were easy to identify.[17] Twenty-four out of the 115 wore diverse types of turbans and accessories that displayed their affiliations with various religious organizations.[18] Some had even managed to come from regions under occupation. For example, Aydınlı Hoca Esat Efendi wore his turban on his head and attended the meetings with a rifle in his hand and a double string of bullets around his neck. Their visibility in the Assembly inoculated the nationalists against accusations of disloyalty, which seriously jeopardized the validity of their cause. At a time when armed groups claiming to be the caliph's guardians and backed by the Istanbul government and the Allies organized uprisings against the nationalists and threatened to march on Ankara, the presence of prominent religious leaders standing as representatives in the Grand National Assembly was an indispensable counterweight.[19]

Once the war was over, however, there was a sudden change in the nationalists' public approach to religion and religious leaders. On the one hand, in private, Atatürk and many of his closest collaborators, largely influenced by their post-Enlightenment formation, had long harbored an ideological rejection of religion as a source of political authority. This sentiment was compounded when the sultan used his authority as caliph to undercut their efforts to liberate the country from post–First World War occupation. On the other hand, they were aware of the volatility of their alliance with the diverse ulema leaders, Sufi sheikhs, and ahi elders. Their backing had been useful for countering the sultan-caliph and his supporters, but that very process had also revealed Islam's capacity to autonomously draw and organize people or polarize their allegiances. Despite objections from some of his closest supporters, Atatürk was convinced that a new state could not maintain a stable relationship with a constituency that could potentially turn against it in the same explosive manner. Thus what had initially been an invaluable asset was now regarded as a fundamental threat and therefore had to be reined in or eliminated.

Although the implementation was piecemeal, eliminating one strategic footing after another so as to modulate popular reaction, the direction of change toward disestablishing religion was evident. In November 1922, on the eve of the Lausanne peace talks, the sultanate was abolished and Mehmet VI, the last Ottoman ruler, was sent into exile, largely to preempt a ploy of the Allies to include an Ottoman delegation at the negotiations that would undercut the nationalists as a parallel delegation representing the same constituency. The position of caliph was retained and the role was assigned to Abdülmecit Efendi, also from the Ottoman dynasty. But just a few months after the proclamation of the republic, the caliphate was dissolved.[20] The move came in retaliation for the pomp and circumstance favored by Abdülmecit Efendi that ostensibly revealed his imperial designs, which were inherently incompatible with the premises of the republic. But the broader motive was to reduce the institutional scope of religious authority and, by implication, its sway over social and cultural life. Accordingly, the new Office of Religious Affairs (Diyanet İşleri Başkanlığı) was formed as a centralized agency in charge of overseeing exclusively the administration of religious affairs, and the Ankara müftü Rıfat Börekçi was named its director. The move fully bureaucratized religious services, enabling one central authority to prescribe the content of advice and sermons delivered by imams and to keep tabs on their skills and knowledge through regular exams and inspections. Meanwhile, ancillary functions that had historically been under the jurisdiction of the caliph's office according to sharia law, including education, law, and social welfare, were redistributed to various new government agencies.

Islam was extensively stitched into the physical fabric of the country and deeply entangled in the daily rhythms and routines of the people; therefore, reducing its presence in national life unfolded as a correspondingly spatial process. These interventions were manifold: they affected life at different levels and in myriad ways that cannot be inventoried here. Hence, for this chapter, I have selected three types of sites that are most representative of the transformations taking place simultaneously and on multiple scales. First, I focus on the unmaking of vakıfs, pious foundations that comprised a vast institutional network providing spiritual, commercial, and welfare services. Vakıfs were prominent in cities as owners and operators of various public facilities and they also controlled large stretches of land in the countryside through the farms, forests, and waterways that they owned. They were, in short, essential to Ottoman social and economic life. Second, I examine the crackdown on the enclaves of vernacular Islam, which, unlike Orthodox Sunni Islam, would not be brought under the state bureaucracy. Third, I turn to the body as a site of self-expression in the public sphere, concentrating on the imposition of Western-style attire as a strategy to erase visible distinctions among the population heretofore expressed through clothing and accessories.

FAITH, WELFARE, AND URBAN LIFE

What gave Ottoman Istanbul its inimitable silhouette were its imperial *külliye*s, large multifunctional complexes anchored by a sizable mosque, with cascading domes, large and small, almost replicating the topography underneath, and a rhythm that was occasionally punctuated by slender minarets defining the city's skyline. Built to serve the public and thus legitimize the sultan's benevolent rule, a typical külliye comprised, depending on the wishes of its patron, some combination of educational facilities, such as libraries, medreses,[21] elementary schools, observatories as well as a range of charitable functions including soup kitchens, baths, overnight accommodations for travelers, and hospitals (see fig. 1.1).[22] Several Ottoman cities, former capitals Bursa and Edirne and provincial seats such as Manisa and Amasya, where Ottoman crown princes resided as part of their training to become statesmen, boasted of külliye complexes in highly visible locations, often structuring the central section of the city, imparting to it a recognizable character as well. The Ottomans had inherited and enhanced this city-building strategy from the Seljuks, who used imarets, similar—if more modest—multifunctional complexes comprising a mix of religious and social services to animate towns that came under their rule. To this day, Seljuk imaret complexes remain as memorable presences in cities like Konya, Kayseri, Sivas, and Erzurum.

Underpinning the provision of these charitable services was the vakıf (pious foundation) system.[23] Although the most famous and largest vakıfs were established by sultans, one did not have to be a ruler to establish a vakıf and endow it with whatever modest worldly wealth one had. In Istanbul and other provinces, members of the royal family and ranking officers of the imperial bureaucracy were also active in establishing vakıfs. The sultan could also set aside land as vakıf to support a certain activity. Hence, for instance, some of Anatolia's earliest vakıfs were granted by Seljuk rulers during the initial stages of Turkish settlement to colonizing dervishes and the Sufi orders to which they belonged in order to support their peaceful conversion of local, mostly Christian, populations into Islam. Since such acts of charity were considered to be signs of religious virtue, benevolent elders in towns and even remote villages also founded vakıfs, albeit smaller in scale but often providing similar services for the welfare of the community around them. These were contingent on the will—and the whim—of the benefactor and the resources he or she commanded, so there was great variation in both the type of charity and the breadth of coverage. Vakıf property, generally known as *mevkuf*, consisted of *hayrat*, charitable services and the sites where they were administered, and *akarat*, real estate and other assets to fund these functions. Hayrat typically included the provision of welfare, such as the construction and upkeep of mosques, schools, hospitals, libraries, aqueducts, burial grounds, public baths and latrines, and so on. In turn, akarat customarily consisted of commercial structures such as *han*s, bazaars, *arastas*, and *bedestens*. On the outskirts of towns, in the countryside, and in villages, income generated by farms, livestock, orchards, and forests could also be earmarked as akarat to support vakıfs. Sometimes, the tax revenues of an entire village could be deemed as an endowment.[24] The vakıf arrangement could also connect remote geographies: the hayrat services and the akarat that supported it could be miles apart from each other or the akarat supporting one hayrat could be distributed across a wide terrain.[25]

In Ottoman towns vakıfs typically provided many basic urban services that today have become the duties of a modern municipal administration. As multifunctional complexes comprising a range of social and religious services, they were also effective in promoting urban development in Anatolia and Rumelia.[26] Consequently, they were tightly woven into the routines of daily life: they offered work and places to work, they gave shelter to the poor and food to the needy, they tended to the sick and educated the young. Since most local merchants and tradesmen rented their workspaces in akarat property, vakıfs were central to the commercial life of a given locality. Motivated by faith and brought to life by individuals, each vakıf had a very specific set of causes it supported with its own sources of revenue, it had its own board of trustees and idiosyncratic bylaws. Under Ottoman rule the urban landscape as defined by vakıf jurisdictions constituted a piecemeal mosaic of variegated sites and services. They were uneven in distribution, sometimes their coverage overlapped, and at other times it was discontinuous. By the time the Turkish Republic was established, there were about 30,000 vakıfs in Turkey of various sizes, with varying degrees of autonomy, and affiliated with diverse networks of faith, orthodox and heterodox.[27]

This complex tapestry of intricately woven social, commercial, and religious activities was anathema to the republican vision of the new Turkey, the modern life, and reforms the nationalists wanted to institute. In the first place, perpetually sacrosanct and immune under the protection of Islamic law, vakıfs were, to a large extent, opaque to the surveying and standardizing eye of the modern state. Their intrinsic autonomy, originally intended to shelter them from changing political winds and allow them to continue performing their designated functions unperturbed, also generally shielded them from scrutiny. Channeling vakıf revenues for private use or setting up family vakıfs to bypass strict Ottoman restrictions against intergenerational property transfer was not uncommon, and such abuses were criticized as early as the seventeenth century.[28] Moreover, because they were largely tax-exempt, establishing vakıfs as a front had become rampant among provincial notables, at great cost to the imperial treasury.[29] In the early nineteenth century, reformist Ottoman bureaucrats had, as part of their modernization efforts, attempted to bring vakıfs under the central authority of a ministry and, among other things, to regulate the use of their extensive assets.[30] Despite making some inroads, however, their ability to permeate and centralize such an unwieldy and diverse variety of institutions with limited state penetration was, at best, limited.

Second, the nationalists were deeply suspicious of vakıfs' financial and logistical support for a wide range of religious and welfare services, which in turn bound together their followers and thus claimed their communal allegiances. Theirs was an unwieldy aggregate of civilian networks with their own respective internal structures of authority that lay outside the state's purview and, when needed, could be mobilized independently. Ironically, these were the same networks the nationalists had tapped into when they had tried to rally support across Anatolia for their war effort. Nonetheless, they were haunted by the possibility that these organizations could turn against them. Afterall, the Orthodox ulema already had a history of opposing modernizing reforms, which they regarded as a threat to their authority, and vernacular Islam's relations with the central authority had almost always been volatile.[31] Jealously protective of their own—rather tenuous—hold on power and leery of other loyalties that could rival nationalism, which they sought to instill exclusively in the population, Turkey's new leaders were intent on keeping under check what they saw as Islam's constitutive role in society. Hence, to preempt obstruction, republican leaders tried to curtail the remit of religious leaders, thus starving them of their resources and audiences. Interventions were two-pronged—on the one hand they tried to subordinate the vakıf institution, and on the other they tried to close down the enclaves of heterodox communion.

Unlike their Ottoman predecessors, who had merely tried to reform the vakıf system, republican leaders' overriding goal was to dismantle the legal framework (sharia) that underpinned it, rendering the vakıf system very vulnerable. Their first and strategically most consequential move in this direction was to decapitate the Orthodox Islamic hierarchy with the abolition of the caliphate in 1924 and to invalidate the sharia's jurisdiction. In 1926, the new Turkish Civil Code (Medeni Kanun) redefined the concept of vakıf by secularizing it, removed its perpetual immunities, and effectively reduced the creation of new vakıfs to almost nil.[32] In 1928, the new Endowments Law further centralized the administrative and fiscal functions of all vakıfs nationwide under the auspices of the newly formed General Directorate of Vakıfs. Thereby, the Vakıf administration lost its seat in the cabinet, which it had held since the 1839 reforms, and the leverage that came with it. It was demoted into an agency directly under the prime minister's office.[33] The Endowments Law also dictated the transfer of all vakıf property and liquid assets to the Treasury if the original mission of the vakıf was no longer valid or if there were no further surviving regent-heirs. Deciding which vakıfs were expired and what properties and assets were ripe for transfer to the Treasury was the prerogative of government bureaucrats.

These legal arrangements laid the groundwork for a massive transfer of property and revenues from vakıfs for use in the realization of the cash-strapped republican government's preferred projects. The magnitude of this move snaps into focus when we consider that vakıf hayrat and the akarat combined comprised a substantial portion of the religious, charitable, and commercial buildings in towns across the country. For instance, in Istanbul, on the eve of the republic, a quarter of all public spaces (buildings and other property such as cemeteries) belonged to vakıfs. In addition, in the late nineteenth century as much as one-third of all arable land in the Anatolian and Rumelian core lands of the empire were also vakıf property.[34]

Arguably one of the most prominent uses of vakıf resources was in the making of the new capital in Ankara. The special legislation that established the Ankara Planning Office as an agency reporting directly to the prime minister also gave it powers to expropriate, at no cost, any vakıf property (with or without buildings on it) that it deemed necessary for its projects.[35] The earliest vakıf concessions in Ankara were taken from the Kızıl Bey Vakıf, which between 1926 and 1935 was gradually forced to give up all of its property for the construction of the capital's first government buildings and institutional structures. These included the sites for the Grand National Assembly Building, subsidized rental apartments for members of the Assembly, the headquarters of the semiofficial Anatolian News Agency, the headquarters of the Central Bank and Bank of Agriculture, Ankara's first theater, and Ankara Palas, the city's first European-style hotel and ballroom, among others. The mausoleum of Kızıl Bey itself was razed when paving the road in front of the Grand National Assembly and Ankara's first memorial, and the National Sovereignty monument was erected just a few yards away from the site of Kızıl Bey's mausoleum. Similarly, Numune Hastahanesi (Ankara's first modern hospital), Doğumevi (Birth Clinic), the city's first two modern high schools, the headquarters of the Turkish Hearths Association, and the Museum of Ethnography were erected on one of the most sacred sites in Ankara, the Namazgah Hill, which was the site of a former vakıf-administered cemetery and an open-air prayer place. Under the provisions of the 1928 Endowments Law, the General Directorate of the Vakıfs was also required to finance the construction costs from the revenues diverted from vakıfs around the country.[36] Consequently, more than 8.5 million Turkish lira were spent funding construction projects in Ankara, and another 1,967,886 lira were used in sponsoring the activities of the new republic's cultural institutions.[37] Although initially much of the financial support obtained from the General Directorate of Vakıfs was classified as debts, laws were passed with a certain regularity and predictability to "forgive the mutual debt that may exist between government agencies and vakıfs."[38] Ironically, although the making of Ankara purportedly represented a full departure from Istanbul, the new capital's most distinctive landmarks, like those of its Ottoman predecessor, were built on vakıf land and with vakıf money.

In later years, legal arrangements culminating in the passage of the Municipalities Law expanded the process of chipping away at the cultural landscape formed by and around vakıf properties nationwide at a steady—albeit slower—rate.[39] Although from the second half of the nineteenth century onward, modern local governments had begun forming under Ottoman rule and were providing public services alongside various vakıfs and private enterprises in various configurations, the new law standardized the rights and duties of municipalities and gave them exclusive oversight over the provision of services such as city water, burials, and cemeteries.[40] It also transferred to municipalities control over existing public infrastructure, such as vakıf-owned public water infrastructure and cemeteries. Last but not least, the right to expropriate vakıf property at no cost, which had first started in Ankara, was extended to other cities as well. Armed with such broad-ranging powers, municipalities played an important role in undermining the vakıfs' institutional structure and integrity as urban places. A very common municipal request was for road construction. Although most of these requests were for relatively modest square footage, they often broke up vital spatial relationships between closely clustered buildings.[41] Vakıf cemeteries, many of which were scattered through towns, often within the precinct of a complex, were similarly vulnerable to takeovers. The law directed municipalities, for public health reasons, to relocate cemeteries outside settled areas. Vakıf cemeteries, deemed old and disused—a classification that was itself open to interpretation—could thus be decommissioned, parceled, and sold off or slated for other uses by the municipality in accordance with its own urban development plans.[42] Similar authority to make real estate transactions also applied to other unbuilt vakıf property with even fewer obstacles.[43]

The state sometimes took part in the redistribution of vakıf holdings more directly. At the urban level, it handed out buildings, revenue-generating assets, or land to government agencies or charities that it approved of and could more easily control. For instance, in 1926, in Istanbul, the Imperial Bezm-i Alem Vakıf, which operated the Gureba Hospital and the large cemetery nearby, was ordered to surrender plots for use by the Turkish Red Crescent and newly formed Turkish Aviation Society—charities with strong government ties that were autonomous on paper only.[44] The same vakıf was also asked in 1934 to finance the construction of educational facilities for the school of medicine that would be adjacent to the hospital, a demand that the General Directorate of Vakıfs had to decline for lack of sufficient revenue in the midst of a global financial crisis.[45] On a larger regional scale, the government also took over vakıf farms, olive orchards, forests, and water springs—that is, revenue-generating assets. Some of these were sold at reasonable prices to local populations or to incoming Muslim immigrants who were settling in various locations in Turkey.[46] Olive orchards and forests were severed from their vakıf origins, under the rubric of scientific management, and gradually subsumed under government agencies reporting to the prime minister's office.[47]

The inventory of predatory takeovers of vakıf assets was varied and often multipronged, but what they shared in common was the effect of severing the critical interdependence that existed between hayrats and akarats, which had historically afforded vakıfs their autonomy. Under the new regime, the relegation of certain services that the hayrat had provided made the akarat "superfluous," and the confiscation of akarat, in turn, atrophied the hayrat, which depended on the revenue. Both developments could lead to the expiration of a vakıf, which rendered even more of its assets open to appropriation by various parties, prompting a process by which a cluster of formerly related structures disintegrated unevenly, losing their coherence. For instance, following the abolition of the caliphate and passage of the Unification of Education Law, which wrested control of education from the caliph's office and assigned it instead to the newly formed Ministry of Education, schools that pertained to vakıfs were closed down. Although the reuse of school buildings was permitted if they were far enough away from sites of ritual and communion, because many of them were in integrated cheek-by-jowl facilities, over time many of these structures fell into disuse and deteriorated. Abandoned vakıf buildings were at times turned into museums, especially medreses, which—rather than preserving the nation's heritage, as advertised—were used for keeping ritual accessories and equipment outside the reach of peoples whose culture was very much alive. Other buildings were converted into storehouses by the military or into archives by bureaucrats in various cities.[48] Sometimes they were appropriated as homes by poor squatters or by petty criminals for shady transactions. Ostensibly to simplify their administration by consolidating smaller properties into larger single akarat that produced more reliable, increased revenue, many properties were put on the market. But during the austere years of the early republic, the population did not have sufficient accumulated capital, few were interested in properties advertised for sale or rent by the General Directorate of Vakıfs, and many of these structures were left to deteriorate. Decrying the blighted conditions of medreses in Bursa, during the 1941 budget negotiations, Abdülhak Fırat, a representative at the Grand National Assembly, noted:

> It looks like we separated out buildings that look the same and are part of the same whole and handed them to the demolition crew. I visited Bursa's medreses several times, the mosques are still standing but the medreses are in a state of utter disrepair. They have turned into filthy nuisances, in full contrast to their mosques. . . . We need to devise a solution for this disgraceful situation and save at least those with architectural landmark qualities. Consider, for instance, the medrese of the Yıldırım Mosque, where immigrants have been installed. These people have removed the building's tiles and taken its windows and we cannot ever replace them. The building is filled with dirt and debris, it breaks my heart to watch it from afar, let alone go near it.[49]

Some members of parliament like Abdülhak Fırat and officials at the General Directorate of Vakıfs tried to mitigate the rapid disintegration of vakıf complexes in what was ultimately an uphill battle. They protested that dismantling components of külliyes and granting individual buildings to different agencies with different priorities disrupted their integrity and made their preservation as landmarks very difficult. Hasty remodeling and repurposing, they argued, damaged the fine craftsmanship for which many of these buildings were known. Sometimes vakıf officials stalled the process, delaying the surrender of assets,[50] complained to the cabinet about unlawful occupations,[51] and refused to hand in their revenues.[52] Nonetheless, most of their objections fell on deaf ears. In fact, many of these takeovers were calculated attacks on the vakıf system, some even carefully timed so nobody had the time or the opportunity to stop the confisca-

FIGURE 3.4. BURSA YILDIRIM MEDRESE IN THE 1930S, THE DILAPIDATED STATE OF WHICH WAS BROUGHT UP DURING PARLIAMENTARY DISCUSSIONS. COURTESY OF TURKISH MINISTRY OF EDUCATION, EDUCATIONAL INSTRUMENTS AND PUBLICATIONS OFFICE.

tion or demolition.[53] Vakıf officials brought lawsuits, but these languished in courts awaiting resolution, while other players opportunistically took advantage of the ongoing uncertainty. In one notable instance, which juxtaposed equally unlawful trespasses by those on opposite ends of the social pyramid, the Planning Office, the Treasury, and the General Directorate of Vakıfs were caught in a protracted dispute over the ownership of a vakıf cemetery, but the site itself was simultaneously occupied by Ankara's cheap migrant workers, who built themselves ramshackle huts (*gecekondu*) to live in, and used for equestrian training by the city's new elite.

The layering of the institutions of the new state on existing sacred or vakıf property and the forced financing of these projects by the vakıfs deserves our attention on a number of levels. In the first place as a strategy that brought about the attrition of a particular system of social support in favor of the creation of another under a new state structure, the dismantling of vakıfs was tantamount to a full rearrangement of fundamental social bonds. Second, it implied the remapping of the urban space in terms

95

of the configuration of its sites and services. With rather unprecedented radical measures that ruled and restricted sociospatial practices, the republican leaders were trying to transform what urban and being urban meant for the polity.

BANISHING THE PRACTICES OF VERNACULAR ISLAM

In their relentless pursuit to eliminate the influence of rival communal allegiances, republican leaders were especially concerned about vernacular Islam's popular sway. More than a quarter of the population subscribed to indigenous versions of Islam and a substantial number of them lived in regions where state penetration was relatively tenuous. Especially those in the east had ethnic (Kurdish) and tribal allegiances that when superimposed with religious difference further reified cleavages that seriously undermined republican efforts at internal pacification and national integration. Practitioners of vernacular Islam had long maintained a distance from the organized hierarchical structures of Sunni orthodoxy, which had historically enjoyed the backing of the Ottoman state. They preferred a more autonomous constitution, formed alliances as needed, and some even had a history of violent frictions with central authority, which distrusted them and sometimes ruthlessly punished them.

The flare-up that triggered radical government interventions against vernacular religion's strongholds came with the Şeyh Said Uprising in southeastern Turkey. The insurrection, led by a coalition of Kurdish tribes and local *tarikat*s (Sufi orders), was very violent, spread to several provinces, and lasted many weeks. It brought the cabinet down and was finally subdued when very strict civil and military measures were implemented by the new prime minister. In August 1925, the Independence Tribunal, an extraordinary wartime court known for its opaque proceedings and its powers to summarily judge and execute people, was revived to prosecute the insurgents. The court also ruled to close down all gathering and meditation places that belonged to Sufi orders in eastern and southeastern Turkey. According to the tribunal, these had become "fountains of evil and conspiracy" that were taking advantage of their long-standing credibility in the public eye to incite people against the authority of the state.[54] To expedite the process and prevent further outbursts of violence, gendarme troops were sent to aid provincial governors and local officials, who were repeatedly admonished for the slightest delays or inefficiencies, and were themselves threatened with prosecution if they failed to comply immediately. In September 1925, using the Şeyh Said Uprising as a pretext, the government expanded the tribunal's ruling nationally. With immediate effect and without any exceptions, all congregational spaces and sacred sites that belonged to tarikats were closed, all of their activities banned, and all offices pertaining to these organizations eliminated.[55] Thereafter, with the exception of homes that tarikat leaders inhabited, in which they were permitted to live out the rest of their lives, all vakıf properties of every tarikat had to be ceded to the relevant government agencies. The use of mosques for other devotional activities of a tarikat was also forbidden.

Sufi practices, which had thus been brought to an abrupt halt, were inextricably intertwined with Turkish presence in Anatolia and the Balkans. Colonizing dervishes, whose agency was as important as military incursions in securing a foothold in the region for Turkic dynasties, had enticed local populations through peaceful conversion, cleverly offering a blend of Anatolian, Christian, Islamic, and Central Asian cosmologies around which they could come together. *Tekke*s (dervish lodges) and *türbe*s (mausoleums) were especially important enclaves for the amalgamation of these diverse strands. For instance, the veneration of saints at their gravesites was a tradition that predated Turks, but one that they readily incorporated into their social and spiritual practices, because they too had brought similar ideas from Central Asia and Iran about honoring the burial sites of saints and martyrs, even though such rituals were strictly forbidden in Islam. Colonizing dervishes who built Anatolia's earliest türbes to honor their leaders cannily situated them in locations that already had sacred meanings for the locals. This kind of layering reinforced the continuity of local mystical geographies, while providing an expedient opportunity for local converts to mitigate the spiritual transition by incorporating aspects of their former belief systems with the religion of their conqueror.[56]

The türbe was typically the anchor of a cluster of religious-social functions and facilities that, like those of Orthodox Islam, were under the protection of the vakıf system. Tekkes, the sites of devotional practices were situated nearby the türbes of the founding dervishes of a given tarikat. The followers of Sufi orders considered their leaders to be the spiritual descendants of Muhammed and believed that their affiliation with the leaders honored the prophet himself. Their tombs were further integrated into the space of worship through highly formalized transcendental rituals in which the saints were brought to life symbolically.[57] Tekke precincts varied in size and contents but, in addition to spaces designated for devotional performances, many contained rooms for the recital of literary texts, which were also highly ritualized acts, and workshops for arts and crafts such as calligraphy, manuscript illumination and illustration, wood inlay and carving, and so on.[58] Many tekkes were also affiliated with educational institutions (*zaviye*) and offered religious teachings at different levels.

FIGURE 3.5. INTERIOR OF MEVLANA CELALEDDIN RUMI'S TOMB (TÜRBE) WITH HIS SARCOPHAGUS. THE MAU-SOLEUM WAS CONVERTED INTO A MUSEUM IN 1927, AND FOR SEVERAL DECADES WAS OFF LIMITS TO RITUAL USES. COURTESY OF TURKISH MINISTRY OF CULTURE AND TOURISM, KONYA MUSEUM.

Formal membership in a tarikat was a serious commitment; initiation rites were strenuous and relevant duties required almost full-time attention and physical strength. The devotees were under the constant supervision of their elders and the hierarchical constitution of the order was strictly observed at all times. Although such severe conditions made *tarikat*s a rather exclusive form of association, less demanding forms of affiliation, which rendered the precinct of the tekke more accessible to the ordinary people, were also possible. Sufi orders also had close connections to ahi chambers.[59] In fact, it was through these loosely structured informal activities of a more collective nature that tarikats gained a very strong grip on the social life of the communities that surrounded them.

Holidays, Ramadan, and other religious festivals were especially important occasions that brought the dervishes and the members of the broader congregation together to take part in commemorative rituals performed by the side of these tombs. These rituals were performed with a great deal of pomp and ceremony. The dervishes adhered strictly to the codes of hierarchy among themselves, but they mixed and mingled with the public, chanting their *salavat*s (ritual prayers and hymns) together and sharing the incense that was dispensed customarily.[60] These sites were etched in people's collective memories not solely as they came to life in communal devotional rites but also at a more personal level. Important milestones of one's life such as circumcisions, births, and marriages also constituted reasons for visiting the saintly ancestors and paying homage to their legacy. Many tekkes and türbes were also pilgrimage sites at the local or more regional level, and people came to visit them from afar to contemplate their relics or ask for a saint's intervention in resolving material or spiritual problems. Others were said to have thaumaturgic properties and became sanctuaries for ailing patients. The sheiks (leaders) of the tarikats associated with these tekkes were seen as authorities with the key to dispensing sacred wisdom, which in turn vested them with considerable local power.

The closure of tekkes and türbes officially marked the end of such communal practices and ruptured the fabric of everyday life in many localities. It meant that mausoleums people visited to pay homage to ancestors, shrines where they made wishes, lodges where they congregated and communed, zaviyes where they studied—in short, numerous tangible nodes of social life—were sealed away from everyday use.[61] Given the rich repertoire of interactions with the sacred, ranging from the most painfully private to the most commonly shared, such nodes had, in some way, touched almost everyone's life in a given locality. The existence of such deep and variegated communal ties heightened the effect of the closure of vernacular Islam's sites and services and made them conspicuous acts of severance that disrupted, radically modified, and, at times, completely abolished long-standing social spheres and spatial practices. There were thousands of türbes, tekkes, zaviyes, shrines, and other sites of communion scattered throughout the country and these were both visually and socially prominent enclaves of collective life.[62] In Istanbul alone, in the early 1920s, there were approximately 250 tekkes (dervish lodges).[63] During the First World War approximately sixty thousand males, that is, one in every four men in the city, were affiliated with a tekke in some capacity and typically visited one at least once a week.[64] Ankara, with its much smaller population of about twenty thousand, had eleven tekkes and seventeen türbes listed in the official city almanac of 1325/1907.[65] Thirteen of these were regional pilgrimage sites at which saints were believed to have thaumaturgic or wish-granting powers. In provincial towns, these enclaves were likely to enjoy even higher visibility for there were few other alternatives for sociability, and the tight-knit Muslim elites of such towns often had very close ties to these organizations.[66]

The government justified the decision to close tekkes and türbes, stating that "unsuspecting innocent citizens" were lured by self-appointed religious leaders to hotbeds of subversive political activity under the guise of religious and cultural functions.[67] In his public addresses, Atatürk chastised tarikat activities for being divisive and obstructing the nation's manifest path toward modernization. Urging the heads of tarikats to close their tekkes immediately, he asserted "May it be understood by all that the Turkish Republic is no place for sheiks, their disciples and sympathizers."[68] If the ultimate purpose of a tarikat was the procurement of worldly and spiritual happiness for its followers, from then on the "truest tarikat" (path) had to be that of modern civilization, "because in this age of science and rational thinking, it is unacceptable to be so naive as to seek these elements in the so-called wisdom of a sheik."[69]

The closures were conducted under the supervision of local commissions consisting of administrative officers and representatives from the Pious Foundations (vakıfs) Administration.[70] The members of these commissions were to visit every single known site, inspect the interiors, itemize their contents, and produce several copies of the inventories for archival purposes. Moreover, they were to assess the value of every object and select those of artistic or historical value. "Valuables" were to be sent to storage for exhibition in museums and the rest were to be discarded. Upon departure, they were to close up the doors with a bright red seal, forbidding trespass—let alone use—under any circumstances.[71] Where possible, facilities were then to be transferred for use to other government agencies or sold as needed. The implementation of the process, however, was not smooth: the inventories were far from accurate and some were never filed, instructions lacked clarity about who would oversee the sales or benefit from their proceeds, sorting and archiving were done haphazardly, portable valuables (rugs, woodwork, and other crafts) disappeared, and although underreported, there were unauthorized takeovers and demolitions by overenthusiastic local officials. Regardless of the irregularities behind the scenes, in the end, as far as ordinary people who participated in and benefited from the activities of these socioreligious enclaves were concerned, tekkes, zaviyes, and türbes were off-limits.

Neither religious activities nor allegiances could be obliterated with the closure of sacred sites and the confiscation of their assets, though. These were pushed toward the margins of visibility and, at times, severely penalized but continued to exist clandestinely even in Ankara where state surveillance was at its most powerful.[72] Forbidden sites were open to

FIGURE 3.6. FORMER VAKIF FACILITIES—SUCH AS MEDRESES, MAUSOLEUMS, EVEN MOSQUES THAT WERE DEEMED UNDERUSED—WERE CONVERTED INTO MUSEUMS OR STORAGE FACILITIES FOR MUSEUMS. THE IMAGE, TAKEN FROM REMZI OĞUZ ARIK'S BOOK ABOUT MUSEUM DEVELOPMENT FEATURES SEVERAL SUCH CONVERSIONS ACROSS THE COUNTRY. FEATURED HERE IS THE SITE OF A DISUSED MOSQUE, CONVERTED INTO THE DENİZLİ MUSEUM AND STORAGE FACILITY UNDER THE MANAGEMENT OF THE MINISTRY OF CULTURE. COURTESY OF TURKISH MINISTRY OF EDUCATION, EDUCATIONAL INSTRUMENTS AND PUBLICATIONS OFFICE.

constant surreptitious forays despite strict restrictions on the public performance of religious rites. In Ankara's Hacı Bayram Veli Türbe, when night fell skittish flocks of believers gathered at the sealed entrance and quietly prayed together.[73] Ironically, the silent mumbling of prayers often included voices of the republican elite too. Lipstick-wearing women, "elegantly dressed in fur coats and high heels," sometimes even accompanied by their suit-wearing spouses, joined the "superstitious" natives in making wishes and lighting candles. Policing a pilgrimage site like Hacı Bayram did not help: as if to defy the administration, for every crackdown, more people found ways of sneaking in and leaving cryptic carvings to evidence their visits in the dark. The street signs that changed the name of the district disappeared frequently, the seals were broken, and locks were cut. Moreover, prosecution was rendered impossible by the deliberate silence of the people who chose to represent these events as the mysterious vengeance of Islamic saints.[74] The provision allowing the *tarikat*'s leader to remain in the residential section of the *tekke* was a widely exploited loophole. Üsküdar's famous Özbekler Tekkesi, for example, continued to be the community's focus even during the strictest years of the prohibition, hosting events and dinners that brought together its followers.[75] Gatherings and the performance of rituals also moved to other spaces as needed. Outside of working hours mundane commercial spaces—local shops, reading rooms (*kıraathane*), or coffeeshops (*kahvehane*)—doubled as sites of communion as did private homes and backyards.[76]

Tarikats, on the one hand, were vulnerable, because they had been weakened by the seizure of their properties and diversion of their revenues—a process that had started under Ottoman reforms but gained new momentum under the republic.[77] Many of their premises, even before their closures, were in a state of disrepair. On the other hand, they were resilient: they could retreat into survival mode and continue to perform their communions clandestinely in more modest settings until the opportunity to return to the public sphere would arise again.[78]

EXPRESSION OF THE SELF IN PUBLIC

On December 6, 1934, the cover page of the weekly *Ankara Haftası* featured a cartoon titled "The Departure of the Stork."[79] The caption reads "They flew they flew, Ağa, Hafız, Bey Beyefendi, Paşa, Hanım, Hanımefendi, Molla, Hacı, flew away." The reference here is to a popular children's game where a designated lead player randomly yells out the name of a familiar object, an animal, or a person, trying to fool the others about whether it flies or not. In this cartoon, things that normally do not fly are carried away by a migrating bird, implying their disappearance from the public sphere. But while it is the costumes that are being carried away, the caption refers to the people who would be wearing them in public, revealing the tacit assumptions in the minds of both the cartoonist and his audience about the virtual interchangeability between the costumes and the people who wear them. This cartoon appeared three days after the passage of a law that proscribed wearing certain kinds of attire in public. Clergy, regardless of their religion and sect, were banned from wearing their professional garb outside the precincts of their respective temples and beyond the designated hours of office. Members of civic organizations, such as sports clubs and scouts troops, could wear only the uni-

Karikatür: Leylek gidişi.

— Uçtu uçtu, Ağa, Hafız, Bey Beyefendi, Paşa, Hanım, Hanımefendi, Molla, Hacı uçtu!

FIGURE 3.7. A CARTOON ANNOUNCING SARTORIAL REFORMS WITH THE CAPTION: "THEY FLEW THEY FLEW, AGA (LANDLORD), HAFIZ (RECITER OF KORAN), BEYEFENDI, PASA (PASHA/OTTOMAN GENERAL), HANIM (MADAM), HANIMEFENDI (MADAM), MOLLA (ISLAMIC RELIGIOUS OFFICIAL), HACI (PILGRIM), THEY FLEW AWAY!" THE STORK IS FLYING AWAY WITH VARIOUS ITEMS OF CLOTHING AND ACCESSORIES ASSOCIATED WITH ARCHETYPAL CHARACTERS OF OTTOMAN SOCIETY (FROM LEFT TO RIGHT): THE AĞA, A RURAL LAND-OWNER AND NOTABLE, WITH HIS BROAD ŞALVAR PANTS, VEST, AND TURBAN-LIKE HEADGEAR; THE PAŞA, AN OTTOMAN ARMY GENERAL WITH HIS FEZ, HIS UNIFORM WITH EPAULETTES AND DECORATIONS, ANKLE-HIGH BOOTS, AND A CROP; THE BEY/BEYEFENDI, AN URBANE GENTLEMAN WITH HIS TAILORED SUIT, FINE-FITTING SHOES, AND TASSELED FEZ; THE MOLLA, A RELIGIOUS LEADER WITH HIS LONG CLOAK, TURBAN, AND ROSA-RY; THE HANIM/HANIMEFENDI, AN URBANE LADY WITH HER VEIL, LONG DRESS, AND HIGH-HEELED SHOES.

forms and accessories described and permitted in their legally registered charters. Exemptions could be obtained only by special arrangement—temporarily and for special occasions. These restrictions applied even to foreign nationals who were not allowed to wear clothing that displayed their allegiances to political, religious, or military organizations of their home countries. Diplomats or visiting foreign military officials had to abide by international conventions.[80]

This was the last major piece of legislation in a series of laws and ordinances regulating individual appearances in public spaces. The process started at about the same time as the crackdown and closure of tekkes and türbes following the Şeyh Said Uprising. In late August 1925, during a trip to Kastamonu and Inebolu, coastal towns by the Black Sea known for their religious conservatism, Atatürk intimated the impending changes. Pointing at a man in the audience, he expressed his disdain for what people commonly wore in public: "Look, for instance, at him seated in the crowd! He is wearing a fez on his head, wrapped in a green cloth, and a peasant shirt on his back. But then his jacket is like mine. . . . Now what is *this* outfit? Does a civilized person wear such a strange ensemble allowing himself to become the laughing stock of the whole world?" (emphasis added).[81] One could not simultaneously claim to be a part of modern civilization and exhibit an appearance that flew in the face of such claims, Atatürk believed.[82] Thereafter, he declared, starting with state employees, the clothes of the entire nation were going to be revised to match internationally recognized standard, scientific, sanitary, and practical needs.[83] Soon after this Black Sea trip, with an order issued on September 2, 1925, all civil servants were required to wear Western-style clothes and hats both in the workplace and outside.[84] On November 25, 1925, the Hat Law, which outlawed wearing any headgear other than European-style hats and caps by anyone holding an official title (local or national), declared the hat as the national headgear. The republican administration was so keen on replacing the fez—ironically an import from Morocco imposed as part of Mahmud II's reforms—in the workplace in short order that it imported a large shipment of hats from Italy and sold them to civil servants at 50 Turkish lira each. At the time, this was equal to approximately twice the monthly salary of an average civil servant, so special credit and financial aid programs were established to ensure that hats could be purchased and worn.[85] Government subsidies of this kind, to help establish the prototype of the modern ideal republican citizen in the public eye, were not uncommon at the time.[86]

Although couched in a terminology of simulation of and eventual integration with the West, the Hat Law was part and parcel of an ambitious social engineering project of corporatist homogenization. Insofar as they affected the individual's body and how one groomed it, legal restrictions on clothing and accessories signaled state permeation into ever-increasing and unprecedented aspects of the private lives of its citizens. Moreover, such restrictions were symptomatic of an unprecedented will to dictate the norms and forms of self-expression in the public sphere, especially as they pertained to religious affiliation and communal allegiances. This was a fundamental shift in the interface between the private and public spheres, which also revealed the republican leaders' willingness to deploy the state's coercive resources to regulate that interface by imposing severe punishments on those who flouted it. As some opponents of the law pointed out during the debate at the Grand National Assembly, these restrictions were incompatible with the basic freedoms of creed, thought, and the autonomy of conscience guaranteed by the constitution, but their objections were overridden.[87] Meanwhile, by arguing that individual freedoms could not be so unlimited as to cater to the whim of reactionary Islam, proponents of the law, such as the minister of justice, Mahmut Esat Bozkurt, revealed in no unmistakable terms that these restrictions were about driving religion out of the public sphere.[88]

This last claim gains validity in light of the fact that, in the Ottoman public sphere, clothes were not simply a matter of fashion or personal taste. Rather, they were bearers of broader messages about one's communal affiliations. This was especially true of the members of the various tarikats. For them religious garb was about distinction, it was not simply worn but had to be attained. The basic costumes of these orders were similar, but they varied in details and accessories. Not surprisingly, headdresses were particularly prominent features that helped to distinguish one order from another and the ranks within each order.[89] The orders had strict regulations about the rites of passage necessary for the achievement of a certain rank and the right to bear the corresponding accessories. The devotee was invested with these in solemn ceremonies after the completion of a series of rites under the supervision of an elder from the same order. Manuscripts describing the nuances of the costumes and accessories as well as their meanings were available as guides for the presentation of the self. Furthermore, treatises were written about the posturing and grooming of the body, the mustache and the beard, with specific significances attached to each one of them.[90] Also, members of ahi chambers, who were typically recruited as prepubescent males from merchant and artisan families, wore distinctive costumes that displayed their place within the organization's rigid hierarchical structure. As with tarikats, membership required enduring resolve, commitment to the craft, and approval from the masters, and advances to the next level were marked by solemn rites of passage. Ahi practices and traditions were profoundly steeped in Sufi mysticism but were distinct from tarikats in that ahi members were also practicing professionals who played an active role in civic matters that affected their

FIGURE 3.8. MEMBERS OF THE BEKTAŞI ORDER OUTSIDE THEIR LODGE WITH THEIR LEADER, SALIH NIYAZI DEDEBABA, WEARING THEIR DISTINCTIVE GARB AND ACCESSORIES IN THE EARLY 1920S. SALIH NIYAZI DEDEBABA, WHO HAD BEEN A GREAT SUPPORTER OF THE NATIONALISTS DURING THE WAR OF INDEPEN-DENCE, LEFT TURKEY FOR HIS NATIVE ALBANIA FOLLOWING THE CLOSURE OF HIS LODGE AND THE PRO-SCRIPTION OF HIS ORDER'S ACTIVITIES.

local communities.[91] Relatively more subdued in their choice of garb than their counterparts in *tarikat*s, ahis avoided flamboyant colors, and instead of a dervish cloak (*hirka*) they wore dark broad-cut and draped black şalvar pants and around their waists they wore specially made, distinctive thick sashes, called *sed*. In earlier times, in towns where ahis undertook the maintenance of public order, they were known as *seyfi* and held a special license to carry knives and swords in public. In addition, each ahi chamber had a distinctive standard called *sancak*, and a small band consisting of drums and horns with which they paraded on holidays—as they had done on the day the nationalists arrived in Ankara to set up the nationalist government in exile.[92] In short, in the Ottoman town, what one wore and how one carried themselves in public were an expression of the self, primarily as part of his devotion to a particular path and the community of its followers as distinct from others who shared the same public space, and *this* was the message the state intended to intercept.

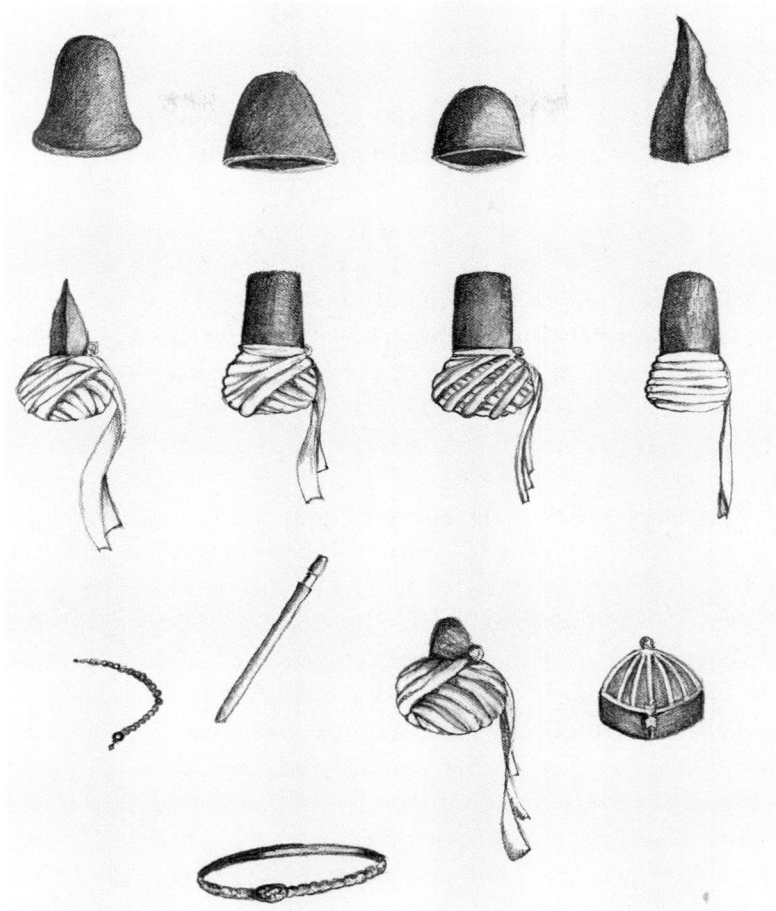

FIGURE 3.9. MISCELLANEOUS RITUAL HEADDRESSES AND ACCESSORIES WORN BY THE MEMBERS OF THE MEV-LEVI ORDER THAT DISTINGUISHED THEIR RANK WITHIN THEIR ORDER AND REVEALED THEIR ALLEGIANCES AND STATUS WITHIN THE BROADER COMMUNITY. FROM TOP ROW TO BOTTOM, LEFT TO RIGHT: (1) *DAL SİKKE*; (2) *SEYFİ KÜLAH*, SIDE VIEW; (3) *ARAKKİYE*, SIDE VIEW (4) *SEYFİ KÜLAH*, FRONT VIEW (5) *CÜNEYD-İ DESTAR*; (6) *ŞEKER AVİZE DESTAR* (WRAPPED *DESTAR*); (7); *ŞEKER AVİZE KAFES-İ DESTAR* (*DESTAR* WRAPPED IN A LATTICE PATTERN); (8) *DOLAMA DESTAR* (SIMPLE WRAPPED *DESTAR*); (9) *HABBE*, SEMIPRECIOUS STONE ACCESSORY ATTACHED TO A SILVER OR NICKEL CHAIN, WORN USUALLY ON THE SHOULDER OR THE CHEST; (10) *HİZMET*, MEANING SERVICE, ACCESSORY SYMBOLIZING THE DERVISH'S FORMAL TRAINING IN THE TWO KITCHENS OF THE MEVLEVI ORDER WHERE THE PRODUCTION AND CONSUMPTION OF FOOD WERE AN IMPORTANT PART OF THE RITUAL PRACTICES; (11) *ÖRFİ DESTAR* (*SIKKER* WRAPPED IN MELONLIKE SHAPE; (12) *SİKKE-I DÜVAZDEH-KÜNGÜRE* (CAP OF SHAMS, A CLOSE FRIEND OF MEVLANA CELALEDDIN RUMİ, AND A FOUND-ING FATHER OF THE ORDER; (13) *KEMER*, BELT WITH ORNAMENTAL BUCKLE AND SEMIPRECIOUS STONES; (14) *ELİF-İ NEMED*, CUMMERBUND. DRAWINGS BY THE AUTHOR BASED ON SKETCHES IN ABDÜLBAKI GÖLPINARLI'S *MEVLANA'DAN* SONRA MEVLEVİLİK (ISTANBUL: İNKILÂP KİTABEVİ, 1953).

Religious garb and accessories, properly decoded, conferred status on their wearers, which republican leaders regarded with suspicion. It undermined their efforts to convert religious office into a centrally administered professional bureaucracy with the exclusive right to publicly don uniforms that identified them as such and sanctioned them to administer religious services only. Expressing his consternation at the persistence of the allegiances that certain items of clothing could invoke, Atatürk noted: "The republic of Turkey already has an Office of Religious Affairs and properly trained civil servants charged with administering the necessary services. However, it has come to my attention that certain individuals continue to wear religious garb and pretend to guide the people as though *they* were their leaders thus posing a serious obstacle against *our* contact with the people. I would like to ask them, who gave them this appointment, where did they obtain this position?"[93]

Subsequent policies further reinforced the restrictions over clothing and accessories. In addition to passing the Hat Law, an important amendment was made to Articles 130 and 131 of the Turkish Criminal Law. According to the Grand National Assembly's Justice Commission in charge of reviewing these amendments, certain individuals "insisted on the bad habit of wearing in public turbans and other items of clothing related to religious office," causing widespread confusion among the public because "it [is] difficult to tell them apart" from government-appointed religious officials. The report also mentioned that the presence of such impostors "undercut the authority of the authorized personnel."[94] With these new arrangements, wearers of religious garb were also required to carry government-issued permits at all times. Moreover, people wearing unauthorized attire that vested them with "an authority they only pretended to have" were apprehended and could be sentenced from three months to a year in prison.

The outlawing of religious attire and the enforcement of uniform headgear met with popular discontent within the space of a month. Whether stirred by religious leaders who had vested interests or by locals who simply did not want to give up traditional headgear for practical reasons, and whether controversial in tone or civil, these moves were seen mainly as reactionary feats by the government and were relentlessly prosecuted and, at times, violently suppressed.[95] Although press censorship prevented any publicized coverage of these incidents, memoirs, diplomatic correspondence, and contemporary court documents that were made public in later years suggest there was widespread discontent with the government crackdown on the expression of religious allegiances. For example in Kayseri, Malatya, and Maraş at the urging of their religious leaders protestors marched in the streets denouncing the requirement to wear a hat.

Rumors that women would also be made to shed their traditional veils or that the possession of a Koran could also be outlawed further exacerbated the situation.[96] Although these demonstrations were relatively peaceful, coming on the heels of the Şeyh Said Uprising, which took months to quell, they elicited a very severe response. Many were detained and others were referred to the Independence Tribunal, which was equipped with extraordinary powers including that to process a death sentence without the formal approval of the Grand National Assembly as required by the constitution.

There were also some larger and more violent protests, notably those that took place in Erzurum and Rize. In Erzurum, after Friday prayers on November 24, 1925, under the leadership of their sheikh, the locals petitioned the governor to allow them to continue wearing wool hats that were better suited to Erzurum's cold winters.[97] But when the governor refused, thousands of men and women came out onto the streets, denouncing the governor as an infidel. The gendarmes fired on the crowd, killing about two dozen protesters. The local military tried about a hundred of these demonstrators and one month of martial law was imposed on the province. In the coastal town of Rize, on the Black Sea, as many as a thousand protestors, convinced by local notables that the government in Ankara had fallen, took to the streets.[98] The disturbances escalated quickly, engulfing neighboring towns. It took ten days and bombing of the coast by warships to reinstate order in the region. Especially in the case of the Şeyh Said Uprising and the Rize, a sense of religious transgression was neither the only reason nor the main one for people to rebel, but just as the republican leaders fretted, it galvanized large numbers to take action. As the number of cases grew, the Independence Tribunal, which had been moving from town to town between late November and mid-December 1925, relocated to Ankara, as did the defendants and their files. With the exception of a few who were acquitted, those accused of "leading popular unrest against the government and inciting the people against the new headgear" were either executed, given long prison sentences, or expatriated.[99]

As with the processions that jumpstarted the Nationalist Movement, these trials and executions were also conducted as public spectacles—the irony was unlikely to have been lost on those who witnessed such a rapid swiveling away from religion. These men were on trial for precisely the same reasons that had made them respectable in their own communities. Their detention, indictment, and the public display of their fate was obviously intended to serve as an object lesson in obedience and conformity to the population at large.[100] Not only were their identities highly publicized through their pictures plastered across the covers of the dailies, but their fall from grace was made into a spectacle at the heart of town in Ankara.[101] Every day, on their way to court, they were paraded through the streets in handcuffs and wearing their newly acquired hats. At the end, their executions too were public affairs: conducted at dawn, just before crowds filled the streets to find lifeless bodies dangling off of gallows at major squares in Ankara, Erzurum, Rize, and elsewhere.[102]

The expression of alternative allegiances through items of clothing posed a threat to the integrity of the state because it implied the splintering of the polity along sectarian lines and was therefore unacceptable. Ironically while they meant to redefine public appearance and personal grooming as matters of private taste, the leaders of the republic simultaneously converted them into issues of public policy in an unprecedented manner. Far beyond a mere matter of appearances, these were symptoms of the dismantling of an entire system of meanings, a medium of communication where at least a rudimentary recognition of the coding was essential for one's orientation in the urban landscape. For transient as such presences were, they were integral to the perception and understanding of one's self and of others in the urban environment, and the constitution of mental maps of the sociospatial patterns of the city relied as much on them as on fixed features of the built environment. Thus what made the identification of the personages in the cartoon "The Departure of the Stork," with which this section started, was none other than this intricate but readily recognizable and widely understood coding.

RECASTING RELIGION IN SOCIAL LIFE

Religion was a constitutive element of Ottoman social life that the republic sought to overtake and modernize. Its influence interlaced many areas of everyday life, social and spiritual. Faith brought people together and marked their rites of passage, structured the flow of time, regulated the cycles of life, defined a focus for their collective allegiances and provided places to reaffirm them, making it a tangible, practical, and pervasive presence in the collective imagination. It connected them to past traditions and conferred on them a sense of identity as well as ways to express that identity. Turkey's leaders were concerned that nationalism would not take root and that the new state and its institutions would not be able to gain legitimacy if religion continued to operate through the same channels and engage people's social allegiances and spatial imagination in so many ways. Religion's intensely powerful social presence, was, in other words, a target for the republican leadership to simultaneously achieve and destroy.

Republican leaders' own conflicted relationship with Islam further complicated the situation. On the one hand, their education in the empire's newer European-style schools and military academies had exposed them to secular thinking and post-Enlightenment ideas about politics and society. They did not turn to religion for ontological questions, favoring instead reason and science for explanations. On the other hand, though they themselves did not embrace Islam, Turkey's leaders understood that they were moving in a world where faith mattered. This was not just because of values with which they were brought up and which many of their contemporaries continued to espouse, but also because religion played an important role in the conduct of international politics and the constitution of national polities. Having grown up in commercial cities of the empire most integrated with the expanding networks of global trade, they enjoyed the modern spaces, sociabilities, and patterns of consumption available in such locales frequented primarily by local non-Muslim mercantile classes and their European counterparts, but they were keenly aware of their exclusion from this new world and its prospects. They resented how Islam had become the basis of their Orientalization and subsequent marginalization in global politics. Nonetheless, forgoing Islam and the bonds it offered was not a realistic possibility. Emergent nineteenth-century nationalisms, which had profoundly transformed the region's demographic makeup, had drawn together new collectivities on the basis of inconsistent mixes of linguistic ethnicities and religions. As a result of decades of migrations, massacres, and population exchanges that culminated in the Treaty of Lausanne, the area corresponding to modern-day Turkey comprised, for the first time in its history, an overwhelmingly Muslim population, a substantial number of whom had no historical or familial ties to the land. From them a nation had to be built, and religion, however flawed, appeared to be the most promising thread to tie them together.

Turkey's leaders had to tread strategically. They selectively co-opted Orthodox Islam's social and cultural infrastructure and tried to subordinate it to the workings of the state, while eliminating the multiple local cores of potential resistance posed by vernacular religion. These processes took place simultaneously and were inextricably intertwined. Orthodox Islam and its leaders, the ulema, had long been associated with the bureaucratic structure of the state, the hierarchical makeup of their ranks was akin to that of a centralized administration, and unlike the leaders of vernacular Islam, they had historically operated under the auspices of the state and in conformity with its policies.[103] With some adjustments, it was conceivable to position and regulate them under the Directorate of Religious Affairs. Moreover, in terms of its formulation and practical mechanisms the *umma*, the Muslim community of believers, was as "imagined" a community as the modern nation itself. Turkey's leaders were quick to seize upon these similarities and deploy them for the constitution of a homogeneous national polity. Because it promoted the unity of all believers as part of a supranational polity, Orthodox Islam conflicted with the premises of the nation-state, but at the time Turkey's leaders did not see this as an actual political danger. In contrast, communities that formed around the myriad Sufi orders were inherently at odds with the policies of centralization and national integration imposed by the state. Whether they espoused beliefs and rituals closer to Sunni Islam or they were closer to Shia, *tarikat*s were perceived as a threat. Hence a closer reading of the laws, with the nature of their practices and their ownership patterns in mind, reveals that the lodges (tekkes) and mosques that belonged to vernacular Islam were more likely to be closed down. Their lands and assets were more prone to appropriation. Their urban real estate and agricultural lands were swiftly handed over to new owners for more "acceptable" use or fell into disrepair as if to bespeak their extinction. But while followers of Sunni *tarikat*s could find a place—however uncomfortable—within the framework of the now state-run Orthodox Sunni Islam, Alevis found themselves in a legal gray zone, with what was effectively a criminalization of the practice of their faith.

The result was a compromised secularism that sought to undercut Islam's grip on political, social, and cultural affairs and confine its sphere of influence to matters of belief and worship, so as to generate a modern and nationalized version of religion. Importantly, it was an effort to redefine religion's role, which stipulated that faith in a modern state was no longer a collective practice one was born into. It was a private choice, self-consciously made by individual citizens and not meant to intersect with the public sphere. The interventions were two-pronged. In addition to legal maneuvers that transformed the distribution of executive powers, the republican administration actively appropriated and dismantled the material bases for the production and expression of that power and attempted to regularize the most quotidian aspects of religious practices. The two strategies combined worked toward the erasure of a cultural landscape shaped by and around religion. The former took place on a rather abstract plane, but the latter brought it home and made it most painfully visible by cutting into the fabric of everyday life, through the elimination or the radical modification of some social and spatial practices. Individually taken, these were small in scale, but they were broad in scope, they happened everywhere and affected the cycles of life in the most immediate environment, in short, they touched the lives of everyone.

In this chapter I have focused on the appropriation of vakıfs, closing down of tekkes and zaviyes, and prohibition of wearing religious clothing and accessories in public as representative sites of a broader process of disestablishing Islam and dismantling the sites and services that brought it to life. But between 1923 and Turkey's transition to multiparty rule in 1946, which eased the restrictions on religious expression, several other policies and laws were designed to loosen religion's grip on society. These included, for example, the requirement that the five daily *ezan*s (calls to prayer) be sung in Turkish rather than the original Arabic, which had a profound effect on the soundscape of villages and towns, and the change of the alphabet from Arabic to Latin, which ostensibly was intended to take advantage of the suitability of the latter to Turkish and to improve literacy rates, but it transformed the signscape of cities and severely limited access to even the most recent years of Ottoman history. For the population at large, official statements and policies were rather unintelligible, if not confusing. The nationalist leaders never accounted in explicit terms for the shifts and contradictions of their approach to vernacular religion. They were interested in expediency and avoided opening such explosive subjects to debate under any circumstances. As the broader cultural and political agenda of the state remained unclear to the polity, so did the relationship between the closure of their local shrines and larger national interests, thus planting the seeds of popular resentment and alienation for decades to come.

CHAPTER 4

OF FORGOTTEN PEOPLE AND FORGOTTEN PLACES

Between the last Ottoman census and the first republican census, the population of the territory that today corresponds to Turkey changed dramatically: whereas in 1914 one in every five people who lived in Turkey was non-Muslim, in 1927, only one in forty was.[1] This remarkable drop in just over a decade was the culmination of more than half a century of population movements in the region surrounding the core Ottoman territories. Emerging nationalisms, competing political and economic interests of various European powers, Russian expansionism, and Ottoman efforts to shore up a disintegrating empire frequently triggered armed conflict accompanied by massacres, deportations, and population exchanges. In 1915, using the First World War and the activities of Armenian nationalists as a pretext, the Young Turk government ordered the mass deportation of all Armenians. With the exception of those residing in Istanbul, Armenians were sent on an arduous trek to what is modern-day Syria, Lebanon, and Iraq. In the process, untold thousands died at the hands of Young Turk officials and marauding bandits, as well as from exposure, disease, and starvation, thus decimating Anatolia's Armenian population. The violence also touched other non-Muslim communities, such as Syriac Christians in the southeast, which suffered severe losses. Later, during the brief period of political disarray following the War of Independence, local Greek Orthodox populations, especially in western Anatolia, became the target of violent attacks, and the majority of them sought refuge in neighboring countries, including Greece, Iraq, Syria, and Lebanon.[2] Then, under the auspices of the Treaty of Lausanne, Turkey's remaining Orthodox Christians—except for those residing in Istanbul—were exchanged with the

Muslim population of Greece, excluding those living in western Thrace. As a means for achieving national homogeneity, population exchange had previously been implemented in the aftermath of the Balkan wars by Bulgaria, Greece, and the Ottoman Empire.[3] But unlike before, this was a compulsory exchange. Although the leaders of both states welcomed it for the much-needed stability they imagined it would bring, the experience was traumatic for the displaced.[4] Executed in a rush, with little logistical preparation and attention to the uneasy overlaps between religion and ethnicity, the process resulted in the departure of almost two million Orthodox Christians, many of whom spoke no Greek, and the arrival of about half a million Muslims, who were a mix of Turkish, Greek, Albanian, and Macedonian speakers. As a result of such large-scale death and displacement, the demographic makeup and distribution of Early Republican Turkey bore little resemblance to what had been there before. Not only had the country become more overwhelmingly (98 percent) Muslim than ever before, but because non-Muslims had tended to concentrate in cities, the percentage of its urban population had dropped from 25 percent to 18 percent, a change that would have long-term economic consequences.

In addition to setting the terms of the Turco-Greek population exchange, the Treaty of Lausanne extended certain protections to ensure the civil rights of the now largely reduced non-Muslim communities living in Turkey. The treaty recognized their cultural and religious rights, which required the Turkish government to grant financial and institutional support for religious and educational facilities and to make provisions for them to continue offering social services through their respective pious foundations. It also extended personal protections for non-Muslims as they conducted their religious rites and used their mother tongues in public. The negotiations also revealed the reservations and calculations of the different parties involved. The Turkish representatives at the conference grudgingly agreed to abide by these ground rules and not to pass a law that would supersede the stipulations of the treaty—a provision that was also underwritten by the Council of the League of Nations.[5] Their staunch refusal to recognize non–Turkish speaking Muslims (such as Kurds, Circassians, and Bosnians) as minorities revealed the deep pervasiveness of Ottoman social categories in their imagination. Ironically, their reluctance to integrate non-Muslims into the polity of the nation-state they were building dovetailed rather conveniently with European designs to use the separate set of rights and protections for minorities as a point of leverage in future negotiations with Turkey. The convergence of these vastly divergent agendas produced a settlement that reproduced some of the strict social demarcations of the Ottoman social structure in ways that contradicted Turkish leaders' professed desires to homogenize the country's polity and denied them the ability to implement homogenizing measures that had long been used by their powerful European counterparts to achieve internal pacification. By facilitating the further homogenization of Turkey according to religion and establishing non-Muslims as a separate category of citizens with equal civil and political rights but special protections, the Treaty of Lausanne both reaffirmed Islam as the basis of membership in the Turkish nation and excluded non-Muslims as an unassimilable category from the outset. In so doing, the treaty made non-Muslims vulnerable to the fluctuations in Turkey's international relations as well as to the vagaries of national politics, wherein their status as "Turks-in-law" would be frequently exploited to mark them as suspect citizens.

The rights and protections outlined in the Treaty of Lausanne interfered in significant ways with Turkey's prospects for exercising sovereignty and attaining national integration. A case in point was the provision that guaranteed minorities the use of their mother tongues not only in private and public conversations but also in business transactions, potentially rendering their books unintelligible to revenue inspectors. Consequently, the Turkish government moved to rescind minority rights and protections in violation of the Treaty of Lausanne. Insofar as they constrained non-Muslim citizens' freedom of movement, undercut their access to and presence in the public sphere, threatened their rightful ownership of businesses and property, and sought to erase the traces of their existence—historical and contemporary—from the national geography, these breaches were remarkably spatial in nature. In this chapter, I examine this process of dismantling Turkey's non-Muslim landscapes on three levels. Concentrating on the scale of the individual self, the first section on minoritization, examines the production of a new subjectivity through official or semiofficial channels in top-down policies as well as opportunistic transgressions by fellow citizens who tactically, within a "permissive" legal climate, performed the recalibration of Turkey's new social hierarchy. Turning to the transformation of local geographies, the second section traces how local cognitive maps were gradually reconfigured as a result of the waves of non-Muslim departures by looking at changes in urban morphology and the state of local landmarks. The last section focuses on the process of "reconquering Turkey" through toponymic erasure and repossession of property and wealth that belonged to non-Muslim citizens.

MINORITIZATION: THE CHANGING EXPERIENCE OF THE SELF IN THE PUBLIC SPHERE

On August 17, 1927, Elsa Niego, a twenty-two-year-old Jewish woman, was murdered in the street by Osman Ratip.[6] An older married man, Osman Ratip, had pursued Elsa for months, despite her repeated rejections, and upon learning she was engaged, stabbed her to death. This was a crime of passion—there were no religious motives behind it. But Osman came from a prominent Istanbul family, and Elsa from a modest Jewish background. Concerned that Osman might get away with a light sentence thanks to his connections, Istanbul's usually reserved Jewish community turned out en masse at her funeral to express their desire for a fair trial.[7] Initially, newspapers also sympathized with Elsa and her family, but the outpouring of support from the Jewish community triggered a sudden negative reaction in the press, which summarily proceeded to accusing Jewish mourners of disturbing order, disrupting traffic, confronting the police, and most important, of turning the funeral into an anti-Turkish rally.[8] Driven by similar suspicions, the police arrested nine prominent members of Istanbul's Jewish community at the funeral on various trumped-up charges. They also raided the local branch of B'nai Brith, the Jewish charitable organization that had helped Niego's family with the funeral expenses, though the search turned up no incriminating evidence.[9] The event sparked further anti-Semitic protests in Izmir, where demonstrators demanded the expulsion from Turkey of Jews who had not done their military service and the closure of Jewish schools, newspapers, and religious institutions. Angry mobs marched to the Izmir Jewish Hospital and then to the rabbinate, trashing signs written in Hebrew in both places. Provoked by the press, which laced its narratives of the events with slurs and insults against Turkey's Jewry as a whole, they called on Muslim Turks to boycott Jewish stores and break off any business relations they had with Jews.[10] With the eruption of violence in several places, within a few days what had started out as a local incident with no political bearing had escalated into a controversy with international repercussions.[11]

Although the events surrounding Niego's funeral had disturbingly anti-Semitic overtones, the incident was symptomatic of broader deliberations over the profound changes in the status of non-Muslims in Turkey. The newly formed nation-state wherein membership was more narrowly defined, lacked the elasticity of Ottoman social categories, which, despite inherent structural inequalities, had historically accommodated the coexistence of diverse ethnic religious and linguistic communities as parallel

FIGURE 4.1. ELSA NIEGO'S FUNERAL PROCESSION MOVING ALONG BANKALAR (BANKS) STREET IN PERA, AUGUST 27, 1927. ISTANBUL'S JEWISH COMMUNITY POURED INTO THE STREETS WITH THE HOPE THAT THEIR SUPPORT WOULD LEAD TO A FAIR TRIAL AND AN APPROPRIATE CONVICTION FOR HER MURDERER. BUT EVENTS TURNED VIOLENT WITH POLICE INTERVENTION. *JOURNAL DE L'ORIENT.*

and equivalent entities. To preserve the cultural and religious freedoms of these groups and protect them against discrimination in the newly forming nation-state, the Treaty of Lausanne stipulated the recognition of Turkey's non-Muslim populations as minorities. But "minority" was a new and unfamiliar social and legal category—one that had yet to be fleshed out. The reconstitution of Turkey's non-Muslims as minority citizens entailed mutual adjustments both between the state and its citizens and among the citizens themselves. Despite signing the Treaty of Lausanne, the republican leadership resented the protections as a compromise over national sovereignty and engaged in various maneuvers to suspend or undercut them and, at various times, pressured non-Muslim communities to renounce them.[12] Non-Muslims continued to be broadly regarded as local extensions of foreign interests and their loyalty to the nation was widely seen to be suspect. That they received protections to guarantee their civil rights further reinforced this perception both among officials and the general public. The transition and its fluctuations affected the different non-Muslim constituencies in unequal ways, generating realignments among them as well.

The conspicuous performance of difference was integral to the process of minoritization, which gradually produced a lesser category of citizenship with diminished participation in Turkey's public, economic, and cultural life.[13] The translation of the Treaty of Lausanne from legal abstraction to lived reality was articulated through manifold encounters, confrontations, and negotiations that took place in streets, schools, workplaces, places of worship, and military camps. As I illustrate below, when imposed from the top through official or semiofficial channels, minoritization took the form of constraints on non-Muslim citizens' ability to move around in the country—including extralegal detentions and internments, limitations on their speech, and restrictions on their presence and activities in public places. At other times, perpetrated by fellow citizens, minoritization was akin to bullying, where relatively minor individual transgressions cumulatively eroded non-Muslims' sense of belonging.

Minoritization was an inherently untidy, uneven, nonlinear, and contentiously negotiated process of differentiation in which various actors vied to extract compromises from one another or to opportunistically insinuate themselves into gaps that opened up along the way. Furthermore, as the sudden shift of the press in the Niego case from sympathy for the victim to an indiscriminate condemnation of Jews suggests, the boundaries between the nation and its others were unstable. On the whole, whereas government policies drove this process to a large extent, its manifestations in different localities varied greatly depending on the attitudes of individual civil servants and the web of relations between Muslim and non-Muslim populations.

Turkish officials used the row at the Niego funeral as an excuse to impose travel restrictions on Jews and to require that they obtain a special permit, as was already required of Christians.[14] Such permits, no matter how necessary, were hard to obtain. They required copious amounts of paperwork, took a long time to process, and were rarely granted.[15] Even short trips between neighboring localities had to be completed under the supervision of the police or gendarmes.[16] Frequent inspections on roads and railroads often thwarted furtive attempts to get around them.[17] Experienced on a daily basis, obstacles to free circulation alienated non-Muslims, thus compelling them to emigrate in droves.[18] Ironically, in stark contrast to the difficulty of getting permits to travel within Turkey, passports were issued promptly on demand. Travel restrictions were very disruptive to the lives of those affected. They kept extended families apart for long periods and weakened social networks that depended on frequent and regular contact. Unable to move without special documentation within their own country, non-Muslims were effectively treated as if they were foreigners and their emigration was encouraged.[19] By confining non-Muslims' movements to very small geographies, the restrictions acted as extralegal instruments of detention, curtailing their basic freedoms as citizens.

Considering how substantial a percentage of Turkey's non-Muslim workforce consisted of merchants and middlemen whose livelihood inherently depended on travel, beyond being an inconvenience, these restrictions served as a tool for limiting their participation in the national economy. Initially, this situation had benefited Jewish merchants, who quickly rose to fill the gap left by Greeks and Armenians, whose numbers had been drastically reduced during the First World War and its aftermath and whose movements had been constrained since the early 1920s.[20] Better disposed than their Muslim Turkish counterparts to facilitate trade due to their broader business experience and, in the case of exports, ability to speak foreign languages, Jewish businessmen dispersed throughout the Turkish countryside and national and international markets. Consequently, in the early years of the republic their businesses expanded significantly.[21] The abrupt restrictions following the Niego incident brought this rise to a halt. Those who, like Lia and Ester Adato of Kırklareli, happened to be traveling at the time found themselves stranded.[22] Unable to go back home and out of funds as their own business in Kırklareli languished unattended, the Adatos were forced to take refuge with relatives in Istanbul. The hastily imposed restriction was driven more by ideology than by any real concern for preserving order. Soon enough, its unforeseen negative side effects on Turkey's economy also revealed its shortsightedness. As suppliers in the countryside began to complain when their ability to send goods to the market was disrupted, the government was compelled to rescind travel restrictions on Jews three months later.[23]

Although the Niego incident and the subsequent travel ban represented a well-publicized moment of crisis, constant myriad transgressions and injustices that shaped non-Muslim experiences went unreported. Official attitudes affected everyday life, forming the broader backdrop for new asymmetries in social and economic exchanges between Turkey's Muslim and non-Muslim citizens. Visibly discriminatory policies such as the travel restrictions, combined with the unwillingness of local authorities to protect non-Muslims when they came under attack, generated a hostile environment in which bullies found license to act on their worst instincts. Religious rites, the performance of which inherently affirmed one's membership in the Jewish or Christian communities, drew much unwanted attention. As a young boy growing up in Tokat, a small town in North Central Turkey, Agop Arslanyan painfully recalled his apprehension of rowdy youths chanting threats as they walked through his neighborhood, and his ordeals in being accosted and harassed by strangers every time he visited local sites with his mother.[24] There were similar stories in other parts of the country. The British Consul in Mersin reported that Orthodox Christians in southern and southeastern Turkey were hounded from "pillow [*sic*] to post."[25] Attending church was akin to an obstacle course, and priests complained about not being able to ring bells to summon believers to service or to mark important occasions. Local authorities took liberties, disrupting their services sporadically and questioning them as to whether there was a justifiable cause for concern or not. When they left church grounds, non-Muslim clergy came under verbal and physical harassment that sometimes endangered their lives.[26] The Armenian Catholic priest of Diyarbakır had been murdered and there were rumors that an Orthodox Christian priest in Mardin had suffered the same fate.[27] In response, many Christians sought to reduce their visibility and resorted to holding church services, baptisms, and weddings in private homes.[28] But funerals were extremely difficult because the deceased had to be taken in a procession, through public paths, to be buried in a cemetery. If Elsa Niego's funeral was an example of what could happen at the heart of Istanbul in full view of the police and foreign observers, in the remote countryside, where the state had a relatively patchy presence, it was not uncommon for unruly locals to follow the mourners, banging tin pans, spitting, and hurling insults and often stones.[29]

What further silenced non-Muslims was a 1926 law that made "insulting or weakening the Grand National Assembly, the government, the army, the navy, or Turkishness" or the "laws of the Turkish Republic" punishable by imprisonment.[30] The wording of the law was vague and open to interpretation and a disproportionate number of the people who were tried under it were non-Muslims. The pretext of "insulting Turkishness" could be used to break up gatherings, justify arrests, withhold justice, even condone violence, and ultimately to intimidate non-Muslims to remain outside the public sphere. As the arrests of Istanbul's prominent Jews at the Niego funeral and their subsequent lengthy trials demonstrated, almost anything someone said or did could, depending on the discretion of the prosecutor, be considered a violation of the law. Moreover, those who attacked or harassed non-Muslims also began to use it as a cover, claiming that their non-Muslim victims had used anti-Turkish slurs, spoken out against Turkey, or engaged in anti-Turkish propaganda, thereby provoking the attack. By 1933, frivolous accusations based on this law had proliferated to the point where *Akşam* newspaper columnist Vala Nurettin argued that the law had become a catchall for the complaints of "any cruel thug who wants his personal enemies, rivals, debtors, creditors, teachers or students, in short anybody whom he fears, loathes, or with whom he has unsettled scores to languish in jail."[31]

Further exacerbating the unease of non-Muslims in public places was the "Citizen Speak Turkish" campaign, launched in January 1928 by Istanbul University law students.[32] Previously, similar sporadic efforts to purge the use of languages other than Turkish in public were often driven by overeager officials, but the "Citizen Speak Turkish" campaign was the most high-profile and concerted effort in this direction.[33] Although it was never officially endorsed, the campaign's advocates counted on implicit support from government agencies and personal commitments from prominent members of the republican administration. To publicize their cause, campaigners placed banners and posters calling for the use of Turkish in social and economic exchanges as a national duty in high-visibility locations such as public transit vehicles, theaters, cinemas, streets, and squares.[34] The campaign gained traction in Ankara as well as commercial cities in the West, such as Istanbul, Izmir, Bursa, and Edirne, which still had sizable non-Muslim populations whose primary language was not Turkish. In many localities, higher education students, backed by the National Turkish Student Union, volunteered their time to run the campaign. In Izmir, students at the Teachers' College took it upon themselves to inspect whether signs and advertisements displayed in local shops were in languages other than Turkish.[35] The campaign also enjoyed frequent and favorable press coverage, which, considering the strict controls over the media, could not have happened without official consent. Editorials stipulated that non-Muslims were "passport Turks" if they did not learn Turkish and suggested various tactics to pressure them to do so.[36] Non-Muslims who were heard speaking other languages among themselves or seen carrying foreign-language publications were harassed in public and reminded to revere the language of the country.[37] In a further encroachment from the public to the private, some campaigners even demanded that phone operators cut the line if they heard anyone speak Ladino or Greek.[38]

To defuse the mounting tensions, Jewish community leaders tried to adopt a conciliatory tone. They visited with the prime minister in Ankara and gave a press release pledging their loyalty to the Turkish state and pleading with the authorities and with the public that Jews be given some time to adjust to the changes under the republic. Some tried to persuade their coreligionists to learn Turkish and assimilate into the national polity as quickly as possible to avoid further trouble. Most notably, Moiz Kohen, who changed his own name to Tekin Alp and wholeheartedly subscribed to the nationalist cause, published *Türkleştirme*, in which he issued "Ten Commandments" for Turkish Jews, recommending that they Turkicize their names, use Turkish to speak among themselves, send their children to Turkish schools, and pray in Turkish.[39]

Despite some misgivings over what some regarded to be the excessive complacency of their community leaders, as fear of intimidation and possible violence flooded the public and private lives of non-Muslims, many chose to withdraw and reduce their visibility in order to avoid harassment.[40] Parents warned their offspring not to use other languages in the street and children stopped their grandparents who inadvertently slipped back to speaking their mother tongues in public.[41] Many non-Muslims changed their names to blend in more easily, as Beki Behar, a Jewish woman who grew up in the 1930s in Ankara, recalled:

> My mother had begun to teach my sister who, at the time, was three or four, how to speak Turkish, and changed her name from Ester to Emel. And I . . . took the name Bedia. We could not not learn the language of the country we lived in and called home, though perhaps one ought to cut older people some slack, allow them some more time to adapt. . . . But those were the "Citizen Speak Turkish" years. The derogatory stereotypes that appeared in cartoons and newspaper articles, the growing presence of German fascist influences: they went beyond making us nervous, they scared us.[42]

The outbreak of the Second World War and the ascent of hardliners within the republican administration marked a sea change in the administration's handling of non-Muslims. Whereas previously non-Muslims were compelled through formal and informal means to reduce their visibility and assimilate, the new policies forced them to put their difference on public display as an expression of a presumed essential and unbridgeable chasm between the nation and its others. Kazım Karabekir, the chairman of the Joint Chiefs of Staff, was adamant that minorities—whom he considered to be "dangerous elements"—living in strategic locations on both sides of the Straits would jeopardize military operations and therefore had to be moved inland to Anatolia.[43] Shortly thereafter, in April 1941, as the scope of the war in Europe broadened, the government conscripted all non-Muslim males between ages twenty and forty.[44] Widely known as the "Twenty Classes conscription" (*Yirmi Kur'a Askerlik*), the decision was presented as a "preemptive measure" to nip in the bud any "fifth column" activities that non-Muslims were suspected of being prone to get involved in.[45]

The mass conscription of 1941 was an incarceration without trial that implicitly criminalized religious difference. The Republican People's Party (RPP) government had been known to impose extended military duty on those who opposed its regime, hence there was already an established precedent for the public to interpret it as a conviction. The arrangement quite conveniently played into widely circulating stereotypes about non-Muslims as overly privileged, disloyal, and dishonest individuals driven solely by personal gain rather than the interests or needs of the nation, and this was their punishment. Non-Muslims were generally imagined to be wealthy, and indeed many of the conscripts—especially those who had been brought from larger commercial cities—were skilled professionals and businessmen who made a good living. That there were thousands who lived hand to mouth and whose modest circumstances were far from this overriding categorization did nothing to mitigate the stereotype or alter perceptions.

From the outset, the gathering of conscripts was a grim spectacle that publicly signaled their membership in a separate and lesser category of citizenship. Regardless of whether they had already completed their compulsory service and with no consideration for the hardships that such an abrupt demand would place on them and their families, non-Muslim men were required to report to their nearest military branch office within forty-eight, hours with strict penalties imposed for evasion.[46] In small towns, the draft was announced by town criers or a prominently located loudspeaker for everyone to hear.[47] As Agop Arslanyan, whose father, two uncles, and older brother were taken, recalled, two days after the notice, on a wintry cold morning, a large and visibly agitated crowd gathered in front of the Tokat City Hall to see loved ones off.[48] In large cities such as Istanbul or Izmir, police or military officials approached men "suspected of being non-Muslim" in the street, at home, or at their business, and detained them if an identity check revealed them to be so. In Istanbul, several men were penned inside a chain-link fence in Sultanahmet, the city's largest square.[49] Although this makeshift solution was implemented because local authorities were just as unprepared as the conscripts for this program, it also had the effect of turning the square into an outdoor jail. Ohannes Garavaryan, who was about five years old at the time, remembered the trauma of seeking his father at Sultanahmet Square shortly after his father was taken into custody by police officers who had come to the family's home: "On the third day when we went to see my dad, there was nobody left inside the pen. Those who had come to look for their fathers, husbands and sons were anxiously looking around and asking each other 'Where have they taken them? What will they do to them?' Nobody knew what was next. I was left without a father. Those were the darkest days of my childhood."[50]

The anxiety experienced by the men and their families, coming in the wake of the First World War deportations, was understandable. Just over two decades earlier, Congress of Union and Progress (CUP) agents had branched out into Anatolia, divided families, rounded the men up to execute them, and sent the rest—the women, children, and elderly—off on what for many became a death march, and thereby decimated Anatolia's Armenian population. Consequently, there was widespread apprehension as to what would happen next, whether the men would ever come back, and whether the women, children, and elderly who had remained behind would be deported.[51] Whereas for the Armenians the conscription program was eerily reminiscent of the tragic events of 1915, for the Jews, overt sympathies toward Nazi Germany and its anti-Semitic policies expressed by some powerful members of the RPP government were extremely unsettling. Some claimed that the detentions of non-Muslims had been carried out at the request of the German government and rumors of impending mass extermination spread like wildfire.[52]

The men were quick to realize that, although it was publicly presented as military service, their conscription was internment by another name. Their recruitment had no military purpose at all. They received no weapons or training. Unlike the regular armed forces, which were overseen by the Ministry of Defense, the non-Muslim regiments were under the direction of the Ministry of Public Works. Their assignments consisted of various construction projects such as roads, railroads, bridges, ports, and urban improvements across the country—tasks for which they had little preparation or training.[53] As they lived and worked under harsh and often unsanitary conditions, they were under the constant surveillance of

FIGURE 4.2. SOLDIERS SERVING AS PART OF THE 20 KURA ASKERLİK (TWENTY CLASSES CONSCRIPTION). COURTESY OF SAİT ÇETİNOĞLU.

military guards, who pulled rank by taunting and tormenting them about the uncertainties of their predicament.[54] Coercing them to perform hard labor and menial tasks was seen as a payback for their perceived command of resources and access to cultural and economic capital that their incarcerators lacked.

The public referred to the conscripts as "infidel soldiers."[55] They were easily identifiable because their uniforms were conspicuously different from those worn by the regular forces. Sloppily stitched together out of blue or brown fabric, not associated with any branch of the military, the "beş düğmeli" (five-buttoned) as they became commonly known, also lacked the detailing of standard-issue uniforms.[56] Similarly, despite their engagement in heavy labor under inhospitable conditions, the conscripts lacked appropriate footwear. Sarkis Çerkezyan, an Armenian conscript from Kayseri, recalled that when they were finally issued boots, an unsettling suggestion that they had been taken from the feet of German soldiers who had died at the Eastern front had begun to circulate.[57] Thus their uniforms associated the conscripts with a stereotypically stigmatized occupation in Turkey and their boots with loot from the fallen. Whether these stories had any truth to them is beside the point, for the widespread belief that they were, both among the conscripts and the general public, was sufficient to mark the wearers of these items as different and inferior.

In contrast to a widely established consensus in nation-building processes, which recognizes military service as a vital instrument for constituting a horizontal comradeship, the mass conscription of non-Muslim men was a practice of segregation—and a very public one at that.[58] Ordinarily, military service is intended to instill a sense of common purpose among conscripts, who are drawn from diverse backgrounds and geographies, through shared, standardized, and repetitive patterns of hard work, exercise, and routines of daily personal maintenance including diet, lodging, and hygiene.[59] For the duration of service, the uniform overrides differences among the conscripts—the wealthy and the privileged serve with the poor and the deprived. But the mass conscription of 1941 was the enactment of the absolute conviction that non-Muslims could never partake in the horizontal comradeship comprising the nation. Every aspect of the process—the high-profile detentions, the penning of men in Istanbul's largest public square, the group send-offs from small towns, to the easily identifiable uniforms—was a public performance of irreconcilable differences between the Turkish nation and non-Muslim Turkish citizens, who shared the same constitutional rights on paper but were denied them in practice.

The process of minoritization, as outlined above, irrevocably transformed Turkey's remaining non-Muslim citizens' experience of the public sphere and of being individuals in the public sphere. Official policies, together with persistent casual harassment that often went unpunished in a lenient legal environment, constrained their ability to freely navigate public spaces, and more critically, eroded their trust in their entitlement to basic protections from the state as citizens. Incidents (such as compulsory conscription) that turned their alleged unassimilability into brazen spectacles, which ironically took place at the same time as demands that they suppress their identities (as Jews, Greeks, Armenians, Assyrians, etc.), altered the way that Turkey's non-Muslims presented themselves in public and the way that they conceptualized the local and regional geographies they inhabited.

OVERLAYS AND ERASURES: A PIECEMEAL PROCESS

The departure of Turkey's non-Muslims and the cautious withdrawal from public life of those who stayed behind had lasting consequences for the way that everyone understood and experienced their everyday environments. Non-Muslim neighborhoods, businesses, civic and religious institutions had historically been integral to the variegated mosaic of the Ottoman cultural landscape and their dismantling could not be seen in isolation from it. Especially in urban areas, which had been home to large concentrations of non-Muslims engaged in urban trades as merchants, businessmen, and trained professionals, the changes were profound. The civilian violence that accompanied the First World War and the War of Independence had destroyed large swaths of the fabric of many Anatolian towns. Entire neighborhoods had been emptied of their inhabitants with the First World War deportation of Armenians and the subsequent departure of Orthodox populations. Bereft of their patrons, the social and religious landmarks that once had anchored these communities also faced attrition. Gradually non-Muslim landscapes were reinscribed with new uses and meanings. This was a piecemeal process that unfolded at different rates and was, to a large extent, inflected by local conditions. In Ankara, which, in its new role, was experiencing unprecedented growth, both the form and the fabric of the city were changing beyond recognition. Meanwhile, wartime scars in formerly thriving mercantile centers such as Izmir lingered on for years as reminders of recent traumas. Depending on demand, in several places, abandoned homes, businesses, or sites of worship were gradually appropriated and repurposed—they housed new families, became warehouses or office buildings, or were converted into mosques. In other places, they were quite literally taken apart to provide materials for the construction of new buildings, which revealed only to the discerning eye the secrets of their provenance. Ultimately, the dismantling of non-Muslim landscapes reconfigured people's mental maps of their cities, redefining the relationships between the whole and its constituent parts, the paths that connected them, and the state and status of local landmarks. Even where individual buildings remained intact, over time, the absence of people and the ebb of activities reduced their visibility. As the representative sampling examined in this section reveals, this process of gradual erasure was central to constructing and maintaining a nationalist narrative of demographic homogeneity in Turkey.

Arguably, in its new role as capital, Ankara underwent the fastest and most complete erasure and reinscription of all cities in Turkey. While the city's extraordinary building boom and population influx are well documented, the massive changes spawned by the loss of almost all of its Greek and Armenian population have been entirely overlooked. Already by the late 1920s the city's linear development along a north–south axis from Ulus toward Çankaya was well established. The daily commutes of the city's new elite and the more ceremonial movements of Mustafa Kemal and his entourage reinforced this pattern, which acquired its visual representation in maps that variously appeared in books, textbooks, city guides, and other promotional materials. In contrast to this distinctive linear form, however, descriptions and maps of Ankara up to the turn of the twentieth century presented it as having a concentric urban form, with a dense core anchored by the Citadel surrounded by an agricultural green belt of vineyards dotting the outlying hills at a distance of about 4–6 kilometers from the center. The plains spreading out toward the west, whence eventually the railroad arrived, were the only exception to this configuration.

Especially for wealthier households, the imperatives of economy and the cycles of ritual and harvest bound together this belt of vineyard estates surrounding the city, integrating them into the geography of Ankara as a whole.[60] Greeks and Armenians, who prospered as modern professionals or from their partnerships with European companies conducting business in the empire had a predilection for settling in Hisarönü, a district of stylish townhouses on the western foothills of the Citadel not far from the new business district expanding toward the train station. Many of them also owned a vineyard estate or enjoyed access to one in the summers to escape Ankara's dry heat and tight quarters in favor of its breezy hills. While Armenians, who by all accounts were the wealthier lot, preferred Çankaya-Kavaklıdere to the southeast of town and the Keçiören-Etlik district in the north; the Greeks concentrated in the south, in vineyards dotting the Dikmen hills. Far from being relaxing vacation homes, though, the vineyard estates were places of production. In addition to growing the more than twenty grape varietals for which Ankara was known, a typical property comprised vegetable gardens and a variety of fruit and nut trees. People enjoyed their produce at the height of the season and celebrated their harvest in annual festivities shared by Muslims and non-Muslims alike, and importantly, they spent the summer months preparing their pantry for Ankara's bitter winters.[61] The vineyard season started as soon as schools were out in early summer and families moved out to their estates accompanied by their relatives and servants. Family patriarchs commuted more regularly to the city in pursuit of business, while the rest of the family—grandparents, wives, and children—stayed at the estate until the end of September, returning after the harvest of the early fall fruits.

FIGURE 4.3. THE TEVONIAN FAMILY AT THEIR VINEYARD HOUSE CIRCA 1910. A TYPICAL VINEYARD HOUSE WAS A TWO-STORY STONE OR BRICK MASONRY BUILDING, OFFERING RELATIVELY MODEST COMFORTS. MANY HAD THEIR OWN ARTESIAN WELLS, AND BY THE EARLY 1900S, IT HAD BECOME QUITE FASHIONABLE TO BUILD A MARBLE POOL AND A FORMAL GARDEN FOR OUTDOOR LIVING. COURTESY OF PROJECT SAVE.

Ankara's concentric urban form was rapidly lost once the interdependencies that had historically linked the center and its agricultural periphery were violently severed with the deportation orders of 1915. The exact chronology of events varies, but prior to the departure of the Armenian community, the contents of the homes, businesses, and religious buildings that belonged to them were moved to the warehouses near the train station under the supervision of specially designated officials and gendarmes, in a process that lasted months.[62] Then, even as these removals were in progress, a fire erupted in Hisarönü and environs. All-consuming fires in Ottoman cities were not uncommon because most residential buildings were made of wood; but the ferocity with which this one spread and devoured Ankara's most elegant neighborhoods was breathtaking—within a few hours it had spread in multiple directions.[63] A young Ottoman bureaucrat (later turned author), Refik Halid Karay, who witnessed the conflagration noted that words fell short of describing the full scale of this disaster, which lasted two nights and two days and finally stopped when there was nothing left to burn. Almost a third of downtown Ankara, including its "most elegant neighborhood, its largest shopping district, its wealth and prosperity had all turned into ashes."[64] The fire and deportations ruptured Ankara's social, economic, and physical fabric and had lasting consequences for Ankara's physical growth and the discourses that surrounded it (see fig. 1.6).

Once Ankara became the capital in 1923, republican leaders' choices regarding institutional and residential development superimposed new spatial hierarchies and patterns of movement onto Ankara's landscape. As examined in previous chapters, Mustafa Kemal's selection of an abandoned vineyard estate in Çankaya that was previously owned by an Armenian family signaled a southbound pull. Although initially abandoned estates in other vineyard districts had appeared to be just as appealing alternatives for housing, as Mustafa Kemal consolidated his grip on power, Çankaya eclipsed them and became a powerful magnet for future development. Many members of the incoming republican elite chose to settle in abandoned properties they acquired from the National Real Estate Office on very convenient terms. Similarly, much of the free land that embassies took from the Turkish government in exchange for their relocation from Istanbul was allocated to them out of abandoned vineyards, further establishing Çankaya-Kavaklıdere as Ankara's prime neighborhood for members of the regime and also the diplomatic corps.[65] Finally, the concentration of new buildings to house the administrative apparatus of the republic along this axis also generated new landmarks that overrode older ones. The government quarter, educational institutions, and bank headquarters became the new references for physical orientation within this rapidly changing cityscape.

These developments reconfigured the formal and functional relationships between what had once been the city center and its agricultural periphery, redefined the sociospatial hierarchies they sustained, and the patterns of land use and economics associated with each. The new settlements in Çankaya were fundamentally different from the vineyards they replaced. In the first place, they were suburban residences, which, despite accessibility problems during winter storms, were meant to be inhabited all year round. Built in the latest fashionable style, these homes also had the symbolic function of showcasing the modern way of life that the republican leadership sought to instill in Turkish society. Furthermore, unlike the departed owners of the former vineyards, none of the new resi-

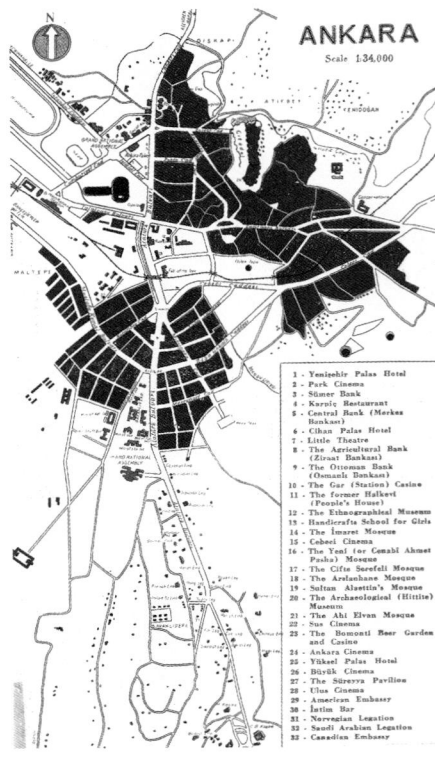

FIGURE 4.4. (LEFT) THE TRANSFORMATION OF ANKARA'S MACROFORM. THIS MAP IS REPRESENTATIVE OF HOW ANKARA APPEARED IN COMMON CITY GUIDES AND TOURIST MAPS. THE NORTH–SOUTH SPINE BETWEEN ULUS AND ÇANKAYA IS DOMINANT, AND THE CITY HAS A LINEAR MACROFORM. AUTHOR'S COLLECTION. (BELOW) THIS IMAGE IS BASED ON A LARGE OFFICIAL MAP THAT SHOWS ANKARA'S BROADER SURROUNDINGS AND POCKETS OF DEVELOPMENT UNDER THE REPUBLIC. THE WHITE RECTANGULAR FRAME OVERLAYING THIS MAP CORRESPONDS TO THE AREA COVERED BY THE MAP ON THE LEFT. THE DARKER CORE OF THE OLD CITY AND THE DOTS REPRESENTING THE VINEYARDS ON THE HILLS AROUND THE CITY REVEAL A CONCENTRIC FORM THAT, BY THE MID-1950S, HAD ALL BUT DISAPPEARED FROM HOW THE CITY WAS IMAGINED. REDRAWN FROM A 1959 MAP; PLEASE NOTE THE UNUSUAL ORIENTATION OF THE NORTH.

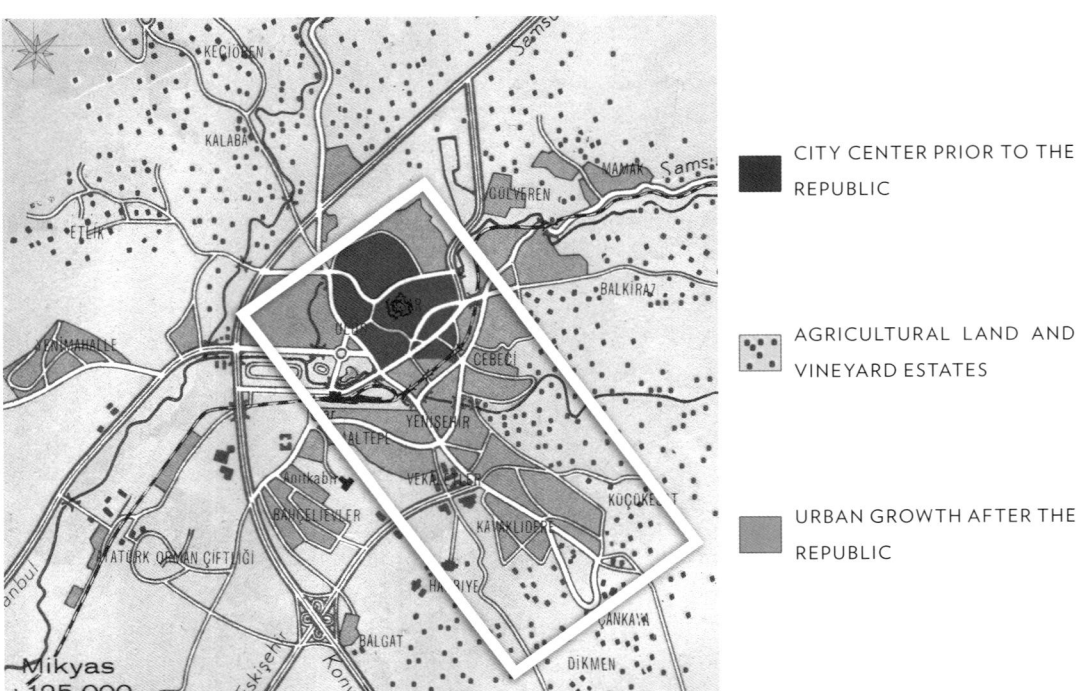

CITY CENTER PRIOR TO THE REPUBLIC

AGRICULTURAL LAND AND VINEYARD ESTATES

URBAN GROWTH AFTER THE REPUBLIC

dents engaged in agricultural production in any way. This made the speculative subdivision of large vineyards for residential development a distinct and very lucrative possibility, leading to the gradual transformation of the size and pattern of property plots and an incipient suburbanization of upper-class residences in the city. Çankaya residents' ability to expedite the provision of utilities—such as water, electricity, and telephone lines—cemented the district's ascendancy over once comparable vineyard districts around town. Meanwhile, the situation in the burned-out district of Hisarönü, which remained in a state of disrepair for several years, was very different. Although some new institutional and commercial structures were built, partially filling the gaps in this area, attention and investment had already shifted away from the Citadel and its immediate vicinity. The property left behind by non-Muslims in downtown Ankara remained on the auction block for extended periods. Over the next few decades, as with most of the city's older neighborhoods, the townhouses that the fire had spared became shoddily subdivided slums that housed Ankara's newest unskilled migrants.

The many Anatolian towns, which, like Ankara had suffered catastrophic fires during the local ethnic clashes that accompanied the two wars, experienced an uneven and unwieldy reconstruction process that transformed the formal, functional, and symbolic significance of the burned districts. To expedite redevelopment in these areas, in 1925 the government amended the Building Development Code to allow the reclassification of urban districts comprising more than 150 burned buildings as fields open for reparcellation.[66] Considering that the owners of many burned out districts had perished or left the country without the possibility of return, let alone of reclaiming their property, the amendment provided local and central government authorities extraordinary opportunities to open up urban land for redevelopment as if they were starting from scratch. Nevertheless, Turkey's constant political and economic instabilities, the lack of expertise and human and material resources combined with corruption that facilitated opportunistic land grabs, all affected the pace and scope of change in different ways in every locality. The process of rebuilding towns and revitalizing their economies was further complicated because the departed populations had also constituted a significant portion of the skilled and specialized workforce in most places. Finally, the reconfiguration of Turkey's borders triggered realignments within the internal geography. Prosperous and populated towns—such as Antep or Edirne—formerly situated at the crossroads of busy trade routes in and out of the empire found themselves redesignated as border towns, largely militarized sites whose diminished economic significance halted their prewar expansion trends.

A case in point was Izmir, which lost its bustling center, most of the people who created and animated it, and, consequently, its key position in the geography of the Eastern Mediterranean. Often derisively called Gavur (Infidel) Izmir, the city was unusual among its Anatolian counterparts for having a plurality non-Muslim majority population.[67] Given its advantageous location, Izmir drew colonies of prospecting Europeans who settled there and, together with entrepreneurial locals drawn primarily from non-Muslim Ottoman communities, turned it into a dynamic business hub that was well integrated into global commercial networks. The second city of the empire had also benefited from Ottoman reforms and local initiatives that modernized its institutions and infrastructure, further reinforcing its rank as a major port. All of this changed at the end of the War of Independence. Shortly after the nationalists retook the city, a devastating fire (the origin of which has been much disputed) burned down almost three-quarters of the living and working quarters of Izmir's non-Muslim population.[68] In addition to the thousands of homes, a substantial portion of the infrastructure that had made Izmir competitive in its region was destroyed, including commercial structures, warehousing facilities, financial institutions, and social and recreational facilities. Physical destruction was paralleled by profound demographic transformation: due to wartime deaths, departures, and the 1924 population exchange, Izmir lost half of its population and an overwhelming majority of its non-Muslim inhabitants, and in the process became 88 percent Muslim.[69] Without its non-Muslim inhabitants, Izmir was drained not only of its historically diverse character but also of a significant portion of the much needed expertise in international finance and commerce, entrepreneurialism, and experience in urban affairs that they possessed.

The reconstruction process fully transformed the urban form, function, and symbolic significance of the fire zone, and by implication the way that people used and understood it and its relationship to Izmir as a whole. Due to fiscal constraints and lack of political will, the gaping hole that opened up in the heart of Izmir remained for almost fifteen years.[70] In the interim, this roughly triangular area hemmed in by the quay to the west, the tight-knit surviving neighborhoods and Turgutlu/Cassaba rail line to the south, and the Aydın line to its east evolved into a discrete mappable entity in the popular depictions of the city. Long-term neglect gradually turned the fire zone into a health and safety hazard, which made it easier for people to conflate the district's image with negative connotations about its former inhabitants circulating through both official and informal channels. Eventually, when Izmir's new mayor Behçet Uz mustered the momentum to revitalize the area, he used the provisions of the

FIGURE 4.5. IZMIR'S STREET MAP BEFORE THE FIRE (TOP) AND PROPOSED DEVELOPMENT (BOTTOM). COURTESY OF CÂNÂ BILSEL.

amended Building Development Code to reconfigure the entire district. The centerpiece of this massive intervention was Kültür Park, a 435,000 square meter urban park, comprising outdoor recreational amenities and the grounds of the annual Izmir International Exhibition, which consolidated the once dense and fine-grained fabric into a single oversize lot. The

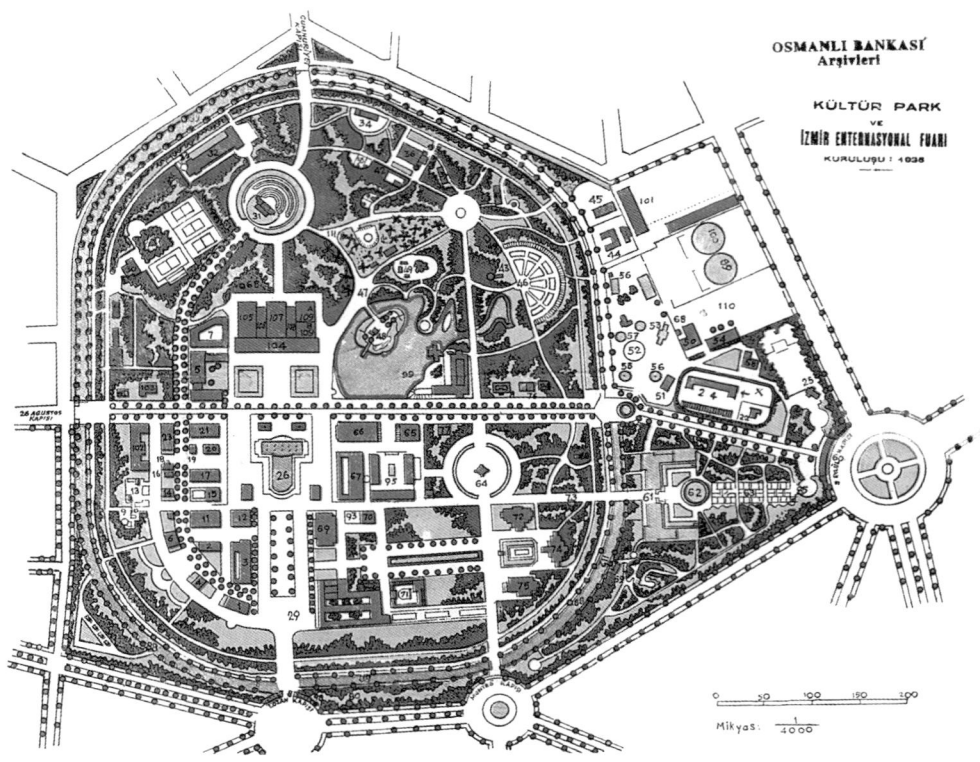

FIGURE 4.6A. IZMIR'S POST-FIRE DEVELOPMENT. KÜLTÜR PARK SITE PLAN. COURTESY OF SALT RESEARCH, MISCELLANEOUS (İZMİR FUARI).

exhibition was intended to raise Izmir's sinking commercial profile, which had been further diminished by the Great Depression. Notably, as the site of an annual government-supported international trade fair, Kültür Park embodied Turkey's adoption of a state-driven model of planned economy, physically replacing the local outposts of imperial capitalism, which had once been based in the fire zone and were intensely abhorred by the republican leadership. Finally, the intervention reconfigured Izmir's symbolic geography. Inaugurated in 1936, four years after the western tip of the fire zone was turned into the Republic Square with an equestrian statue of Mustafa Kemal at its center, and its gateways named after key events leading to the city's reconquest, Kültür Park was part of a deliberate attempt to reorient the city with new nationalist landmarks.

Historically, the religious and institutional buildings pertaining to the various millets constituted most of the landmarks of the Ottoman city. Their relative numbers and prominence varied by region, but churches and synagogues were as familiar as mosques as components of the Otto-

FIGURE 4.6B. KÜLTÜR PARK ENTRANCE AS SEEN FROM THE REPUBLIC SQUARE AND THE ATATÜRK MONU-
MENT. COURTESY OF APİKAM, AHMET PİRİŞTİNA İZMİR CITY MUSEUM AND ARCHIVE.

man townscapes. As landmarks they were as much sites of convergence
for their respective congregations as shared local reference points for everyone regardless of faith. Not only did they punctuate people's mental
maps of their hometowns, but mosques, churches, and synagogues also
structured their understanding of time and space. They mapped the cycles and passage of time onto space with the ebb and flow of footfall they
generated at prayer times and the commotions around religious holidays.
Taken together, they were the embodiments of the pluralistic makeup of
the Ottoman urban society. Churches and synagogues were, in effect, part
of a much larger web of sociospatial relationships that sustained their respective communities both locally and beyond. In much the same way
as their Muslim counterparts, non-Muslim communities also ran pious
foundations that, in addition to catering to religious needs, provided
myriad community support services in orphanages, schools, and hospitals, maintained shrines and cemeteries, and funded these through revenues generated from rental properties, fields, and farms. Furthermore
churches formed part of a hierarchical constellation of institutions scattered throughout the empire in which certain cities stood as major sites

FIGURE 4.7. SAINT THEODOROS GREEK ORTHODOX CHURCH IN DERİNKUYU NEVŞEHİR IN THE EARLY NINE-TEENTH CENTURY WITH ITS CONGREGATION (ABOVE) AND TODAY (OPPOSITE), LEFT IN DISUSE. COURTESY OF OSMAN AYTEKİN.

of ecclesiastic administration and education. These institutions defined and kept alive regional connections beyond the confines of the immediate locality.

As non-Muslim landmarks in various towns lost most of their primary users, government officials and local residents reincorporated them into the routines of everyday life in ways that altered their use and, often, their stature and significance. For instance, Ayvalık, a prosperous coastal town on the Aegean, specializing in olive oil production and export, saw almost its entire population of Orthodox Greek speakers exchanged in 1924 for a smaller number of Muslims from the Aegean Islands.[71] The incoming exchangees supplemented Ayvalık's only mosque by converting several churches into mosques to serve their needs. They used other churches as storehouses or workshops, while still others fell into disuse and gradually crumbled into ruins.[72] The fate of institutional structures such as hospitals, monasteries, or schools was similar. In the absence of imminent pressure to expand and with the availability of surplus building stock, Ayvalık's

new inhabitants—notwithstanding the hardships due to their disloca-
tion—eased gradually into an existing townscape, incrementally remaking
it into their own. In other places, such as the Capadocia-Karaman region
in Central Anatolia, more people were forced to leave than arrived through
the exchange, leaving once vibrant community enclaves to atrophy. The situation was more contentious when incoming exchangees were assigned or
appropriated property over which non-Muslims continued to have claims.
Such was the case in Tokat, where Muslim immigrants from the Balkans
converted local Armenian cemeteries into orchards and used gravestones
and construction materials taken from nearby Armenian churches to
build homes, thus generating tensions between the two communities.[73]

Although vastly reduced in numbers, in the first decades of the republic, there still were small pockets of Armenians who had survived the
deportation in central and eastern towns (e.g., in Kayseri, Elazığ, Antep,
Van, or Sivas) as well as small denominations of Syriacs and Nestorians in
the Southeast (Diyarbakır, Urfa, Mardin). Theirs was a difficult existence
with multiple obstacles to reproducing and transmitting their culture and
sustaining their communities. Constant harassment hindered church attendance, population scarcity made it hard to maintain a parish and offer
relevant religious and charitable services, and foundation revenues that
underwrote operational costs kept falling. Many congregations did not
even have a pastor and relied on itinerant clergy infrequently dispatched

FIGURE 4.8. GAZİANTEP, SURP ASDVADZADZIN CATHEDRAL (ABOVE), CURRENTLY USED AS KURTULUŞ MOSQUE (OPPOSITE). PRIOR TO BEING CONVERTED INTO A MOSQUE, THE CATHEDRAL WAS USED AS A MILITARY WAREHOUSE AND LATER AS A PRISON. COURTESY, RESPECTIVELY, OF HYETERT AND ŞAHİNBEY MÜFTÜLÜĞÜ, GAZİANTEP.

from Istanbul to administer basic rites (performing baptisms and officiating marriages); they also lacked enough students to run schools and resources to retain teachers. This was a downward spiral, which compelled many non-Muslims in the provinces to emigrate or move to Istanbul, which, under nominal international oversight, was turning into the primary city that continued to offer the necessary services in a comprehensive way. Their departure exacerbated the situation for those who remained behind, in turn obliging the latter to leave or stay and face further difficulties and to become more vulnerable to outside pressure—most notably to surrender their assets. Hence, for instance, the main Armenian churches in Diyarbakır (Surp Geragos), Kayseri (Loussavorchakan), and Sivas (Surp Asdvadzadzin Cathedral),[74] as well as smaller parish churches, were seized and converted into government storehouses, military depots, or stables. The services for Surp Geragos's diminished congregation were displaced to the church's nursery school next door.[75] In 1952, the local government demolished the Surp Asdvadzadzin Cathedral in Sivas, claiming that its walls had cracked. The move made room for lucrative new development downtown, thus leaving many local Armenians suspicious as to whether their church was really structurally unsound.[76] In Antep the city's lavish cathedral (also called Surp Asdvadzadzin), completed in 1892, was turned into a prison and then a military warehouse before its eventual conversion into Kurtulus (Liberation Mosque) in the 1980s.

Conversions, almost as a matter of course, included the removal of building components that identified the significance and origins of these landmarks. Hence crosses were removed from doors and domes, walls washed of their iconographic imagery, and bells taken out of belfries—and the building was often treated as if it were no more than a utilitarian structure, with four walls and a roof. Given their distinctive forms, churches, monasteries, and cathedrals remained just as recognizable but looked out of place, disconnected from previous webs of spatial relations that positioned them at the heart of their communities. Such acts of repurposing were not done simply out of necessity—since in towns with large numbers of "abandoned properties" less significant structures would have been available. Rather, they were deliberate demotions in status that replaced a sacred use with a mundane and, at times, sacrilegious one. In so doing, they were meant to marginalize these landmarks both physically and symbolically, as if to purge the non-Muslim communities that had built and kept them alive out of local geographies and histories. Meanwhile the thousands of abandoned structures that were not put to new uses faded into oblivion: exposed to the elements without regular maintenance or looted for building parts, they disappeared completely but nobody could remember just how or when.[77] In the end, the seizure, repurposing, or demolition of non-Muslim sacred sites—churches, cemeteries, schools, orphanages, and miscellaneous other foundation property—was tantamount to the simultaneous dismantling of multiple ethnoreligious cultural landscapes that coexisted within the same geography.

RECONQUESTS, SYMBOLIC AND MATERIAL

Toponyms are potent vessels of local history. They encapsulate broader narratives, imbued with references to historical events, personages, social associations, linguistic clues, and sacred cosmologies. The republic inherited a landscape with a multilingual mix of toponyms that often invoked the heterogeneous heritage of the Ottoman Empire. Names like Tekfurdağı, a compound word, meaning "governor mountain," wherein *tekfur* was a Turkicized Armenian term for a Byzantine governor or feudal lord, revealed more than a thousand years of intermingled histories over the same terrain.[78] Such references undermined the republican elite's desire to constitute in Turkey a homogeneous nation with a common history and shared future.[79] As early as December 1920, even before the outcome of the War of Independence was known, deputies gathered in the first Grand National Assembly expressed their disapproval of the "unnational" character of certain place names despite "our dominance over this land, for more than six hundred years." They argued, notably, that failure to nationalize these names was used by "our enemies" to contest "our rights" over them.[80]

Consequently, republican officials set out to change "foreign" toponyms just as soon as they assumed power. Their interventions were felt at every level—from individual streets to neighborhoods, villages, and provinces. Several historically non-Muslim neighborhoods received explicitly nationalistic new names. Thus Ankara's Jewish Quarter (Yahudi Mahallesi) became İstiklal (Liberation). Tatavla, a heavily Greek neighborhood in Istanbul, was renamed Kurtulus (also meaning Liberation), as was the new avenue that cut across it shortly after a devastating fire that wiped out a large swath of it in 1929. Just north of Tatavla, the Catholic district of Pangaltı's newly laid out orthogonal streets acquired names like Bozkurt (Gray Wolf) or Ergenekon, derived from the ascendant pan-Turanic mythology that celebrated a broader vision of Turkic unity across the wider Central Asian geography and was in vogue among the ultranationalist members of the republican elite.[81] Implicit in such name choices were blanket assumptions about the loyalties of the local residents especially during the recent wars, a desire to put them in their place, and a resolve to unequivocally inscribe the new dominant narrative on the landscape. Other changes vaguely approximated the sound of the previous toponym but hollowed out the historical or cultural bearings underlying the name. Hence, the Thracian border province of Kırkkilise (based on the Greek original Saranta Eklesia, meaning Forty Churches) was renamed Kırklareli, Land of the Forty.[82] Similarly, when the neighboring town of Tekfurdağı was promoted to the status of a province in 1927, it was renamed Tekirdağ, meaning tabby-striped mountain.[83] As the effort intensified, more names, which neither bore resemblance to the sounds of their predecessors nor had any grounding in the locality were also introduced. There were even grassroots demands for name changes, which—as in the decision by the Kirmasti (Kremastre) municipality to rename their town Mustafakemalpaşa—were often likely to be initiated by officious bureaucrats or enterprising notables to score points with the powers that be.[84]

Toponymical engineering was not a republican pursuit alone. Especially from the mid-nineteenth century onward, Ottoman bureaucrats named the numerous new settlements for nomadic tribes compelled to settle by the modernizing state and incoming Muslim refugees fleeing conflict in the Balkans and southern Russia after the sultan, members of his family, or the leaders of these communities.[85] When the CUP came to power, its leaders embraced toponymic interventions with a new zeal. In 1915, they issued a decree to replace existing place names in Armenian, Greek, Bulgarian, or other ancient Anatolian languages with new Turkish ones. Sometimes, in a self-aggrandizing move, they derived toponyms from their own names.[86] Republican officials expanded the scope of the efforts to Turkicize the geographical nomenclature. Although the majority of the changes they made in the first decades of the republic were to Armenian and Greek toponyms, they also targeted Arabic and Kurdish names and anything else that did not sound Turkish enough. A settlements directory published by the Ministry of Interior in 1928 revealed that, at least at the district center (*kaza*) level, many of the Greek names in the west and northeast and Armenian, Arabic, or Kurdish names in the east had already been changed.[87] Republican interventions also conveyed the new leaders' ambivalent relationship to their Young Turk predecessors and their Ottoman heritage, and toponyms that invoked them too overtly also disappeared.[88] Centrally appointed bureaucrats and cartographers, who had little knowledge or interest in local histories or had taken on the task of rendering them illegible, chose rather generic toponyms—such as Şirinköy (Pretty Village), Yeşilköy (Green Village), Çamlıca (Pine Grove)—that they also repeated in other locations, denying them specificity, in much the same way a developer names streets in a new subdivision. In sum, within less than sixty years, what had started as a series of localized and sporadic interventions turned into a systematic project in which the names of twelve thousand out of the nearly forty thousand village names and almost two thousand landforms in Turkey were changed. Republican officials went over the map of Turkey with a fine-tooth comb, over time, zooming in to increasing levels of detail, to cleanse its nomenclature of non-Turkish sounding words. In cities and towns, name changes unequivocally conveyed to the remaining non-Muslim residents their diminished place in the new social order. In the countryside, where Muslim immigrants from the Balkans replaced departed non-Muslims, new toponyms were a means to rhetorically clear up space, as if a new beginning uncompromised by past narratives could be marked.

The administration's efforts to wrest national geography from claims by those it excluded from the definition of "Turkishness" also had an unequivocally material dimension that included their eviction from lands they had inhabited for generations as well as opportunistic seizures of their assets. While the suppression of non-Muslims' participation in the public sphere, obstacles to their economic activities, and the attrition of their religious cultural institutions ensured a steady trickle of outmigrations, draining Anatolia and Thrace of their non-Muslim inhabitants, occasional outbursts of violence triggered sudden mass departures. Arguably, the most notorious among these was the 1934 pogrom in Thrace (Trakya Olayları), when, in late June, anti-Semitic attacks that started with written threats, in Çanakkale, escalated with the physical beatings of Jewish citizens and the boycotting of their businesses. Within a few days the violence had turned into a pogrom, spreading like wildfire in the Thracian cities of Kırklareli and Edirne, which had large Jewish populations.[89] Previous sporadic attacks had intimidated the region's Jews, but nothing had prepared them for the scale of violence that ensued.[90] Emboldened by the passivity of local law enforcement, the rioting mobs brutally assaulted Jews, vandalizing and looting their homes and their businesses. Although many offered shelter to their neighbors under attack, seeing several friends and business partners partaking in the pillage was especially traumatizing for the victims.[91] As distraught families made their way to the train station to flee to Istanbul, townsfolk in Edirne and Kırklareli lined up along the main street to watch their departure.[92] Despite the rapid deterioration of the situation, it took almost a week for the government to intervene and send the gendarmes to restore order. By then, almost a quarter of Thrace's thirteen thousand Jews had arrived in Istanbul (landing in Istanbul's heavily Jewish districts of Balat and Hasköy).[93] In subsequent weeks Sir Percy Lorraine, the British ambassador, estimated that the numbers had reached seven thousand to eight thousand.[94] Very few, if any, returned. They sold what they could, but most had to abandon their homes, businesses, and sites of communal heritage, thus leaving Thrace bereft of its Jewish population.

In 1942, with the passage of the Wealth Tax law, the government formally embraced what was a pattern of sporadic circumstances compelling non-Muslims to urgently liquidate their assets, sell their businesses at a significant loss, and leave their hometowns. Introduced at the height of the Second World War as a one-time levy on professionals, merchants, manufacturers, and owners of large agricultural estates, the implementation of the tax turned into an exercise in the public ostracism of non-Muslims. Public and private statements by government officials as well as editorials and cartoons fomented a discourse that held war profiteers and extortionists, whom they almost invariably implied to be non-Muslim, responsible for Turkey's economic dire straits, which deflected attention from the string of bad economic decisions and defense spending necessitated by the war raging just outside national boundaries.[95] The tax was consequently justified to the broader public as payback for years of unethical practices and ill-gotten gains. Debtors' names and the amounts they owed were posted publicly at local tax offices for everyone to see. More important, these lists, cataloged according to whether the debtor was Muslim, non-Muslim, convert, or foreign, confirmed beyond doubt that while in theory the tax applied to all citizens equally, in practice it targeted non-Muslims.[96] In a throwback to the Ottoman millet system, which the republic putatively rejected, the assessors clearly differentiated between Muslims and non-Muslims, charging the latter exorbitantly higher amounts. The assessments were incontestable and at the end of the fortnight by which payments had to be made in full, the commissions in charge of implementing the law seized the assets of those who failed to comply. Where the funds recouped from seizure were deemed insufficient, police rounded the debtors up to be sent to selected labor camps in Aşkale and Sivrihisar to perform hard labor. Like their

HALKIN SIRTINDAN GEÇİNENLER:
Vurguncu — Haydi, uzun etme, ikimiz de yükümüzü tuttuk!..

FIGURE 4.9. FREQUENTLY NON-MUSLIMS AND, IN THE AFTERMATH OF ARMENIAN AND GREEK DEPARTURES, JEWS, WERE PORTRAYED AS OPPORTUNISTIC PROFITEERS, WHO ENRICHED THEMSELVES AT THE EXPENSE OF THE REST OF THE HARDWORKING TURKISH POPULATION. THE WEIGHT, THE SUIT AND BOWLER HAT, AND THE BIG NOSE WERE STEREOTYPICAL DEPICTIONS THAT IDENTIFIED THE SUBJECT AS BEING JEWISH. VARIATIONS OF THE IMAGE OF NON-MUSLIM PROFITEERS APPEARED FREQUENTLY IN BOTH HUMOR MAGAZINES AND DAILY NEWSPAPERS. COURTESY OF AYHAN AKTAR.

debts, auctions of the debtors' seized property and personal belongings were highly publicized events, reported in newspapers as object lessons. Some auction events took place at repossessed homes and drew massive crowds with an appetite for a good bargain and a curiosity about the now exposed private lives of others. Also, as with the earlier Twenty Classes conscription event, the detention and eventual transfer of wealth of tax debtors was performed as a public spectacle with extensive press coverage offering the details of their miserable journey. In the winter of 1943, crowds braving the freezing cold gathered at train stations along the way to watch the slow transit of "those who profited at our expense but refused to pay their part" in cargo trains to Aşkale.[97] Similarly, the employment of mostly urban professionals—merchants and businessmen as well as doctors, dentists, and lawyers, who ironically were the farthest from mercantile occupations—to work in quarries and road construction under primitive conditions was not the most effective use of their skills (which, as a matter of fact, were much needed in the country). But hard labor was humbling, and that was exactly the point.

The Wealth Tax was a most effective instrument for the transfer of nonmovable assets from non-Muslims to budding Muslim capitalists mediated by the state, albeit using extralegal means.[98] The sums demanded for the tax far exceeded the liquid assets of many of the debtors who were thus compelled to sell the real estate they owned within a very short period of time to come up with the cash. Within the first six months of 1943, in the six central administrative districts of Istanbul, close to nine hundred properties were sold in order to pay for the tax. These property sales constituted only 16 percent of all transactions that year, but since they involved the most expensive real estate in the city, they accounted for almost half of the total monetary value.[99] It is important to note that the sudden availability of a large number of a range of properties including houses, apartments, and multiunit residential buildings as well as commercial structures such as office buildings, shops, arcades, warehouses, and factories drove prices down by up to 40 percent.[100] For those who had enough liquidity, despite the severe cash shortage, this was a buyers' market. The major bulk buyers for the properties were state-owned enterprises, which acquired 30 percent (by value) of the property put on sale, whereas individual Muslim-Turkish buyers bought more than two-thirds. A very modest 2.3 percent of the purchases was made by non-Muslims, who downsized with what was left to them after selling more valuable properties.[101] When all was said and done, some of the most desirable residential and commercial real estate in Istanbul had changed hands within less than a year, thus providing the starter capital and assets for Turkey's emerging entrepreneurial class.

FIGURE 4.10. FRONT-PAGE COVERAGE OF THE WEALTH TAX IN THE ISTANBUL DAILY *TAN*. AT THE TOP LEFT IS AN ARTICLE ANNOUNCING THAT TAX HAD BEEN COLLECTED FROM THREE HUNDRED TAXPAYERS; THE THREE IMAGES BELOW THE HEADLINE SHOW THE VERY PUBLIC COLLECTION OF PERSONAL ITEMS FROM THEIR HOMES TO PAY FOR THEIR TAX DEBTS. JUST BELOW, ANOTHER NEWS ITEM ANNOUNCING THE AUCTION OF HOUSEHOLD ITEMS AND COMMERCIAL STOCK BELONGING TO DEBTORS, ACCOMPANIED BELOW BY AN IMAGE OF ARRESTED DEBTORS BEING TRANSFERRED TO A HOLDING STATION PRIOR TO BEING SENT OFF TO WORK CAMPS IN AŞKALE, ERZURUM.

Government officials and—with notably few exceptions—journalists and other members of the intelligentsia promoted the Wealth Tax as a necessary measure to complete the unfinished business of reconquering Turkey. Explicitly linking it to earlier reforms under Mustafa Kemal,

Prime Minister Saraçoğlu, argued that the Wealth Tax legislation was "the economic reform" that would finally grant "us the opportunity to earn our economic independence . . . and get rid of the *foreigners* who dominate our markets and hand Turkish markets over to Turkish entrepreneurs" (emphasis added).[102] Similarly, the contemporary press defined the tax as a "patriotic duty" (*vatan borcu*) and compared it to the sacrifices made by the soldiers in the battlefield, thereby invoking the nationalistic sensibilities, which were sharpened during the War of Independence and were already heightened due to the Second World War. According to Saraçoğlu, considering how "many apartment and office buildings, commercial structures, and various other means of income" non-Muslims owned, the demand was entirely reasonable.[103] Newspapers noted that the streets of Beyoğlu, which looked like "the streets of a foreign country . . . bedecked in foreign flags and frequently observing holidays and religious festivities that differed from ours" had once been a place where "the most prestigious of Turkish establishments" could not find themselves so much as a store front.[104] With the onslaught of the auctions, however, the most prominent landmarks of Istanbul's commercial heart acquired new Turkish owners. Mere weeks after the tax was imposed, the daily *Cumhuriyet* announced the conversion of His Master's Voice Building into the Sümerbank Domestic Products Beyoğlu Branch, stating that "another beautiful building has been nationalized." The significance of using the language of "reconquest" and "nationalization" to describe this change of ownership (and others like it) was hardly lost on anyone.[105] Founded in 1935, Sümerbank was the quintessential textiles enterprise that embodied the state's forceful involvement in industrial production to put an end to Turkey's dependency on imports and stamp out the prevalence of non-Muslim merchants in this sector of the economy. But beyond the strictly economic, the name Sümerbank (Sumerian Bank) itself was rooted in the Turkish History Thesis, which situated Turks in Anatolia at the outset of history and fabricated ties with ancient tribes of the region, while repudiating the immediate past despite the ubiquity of its traces everywhere. Thus Sümerbank's flagship store in Beyoğlu not only displaced an economic model commonly (and negatively) associated with non-Muslims but also, as with other toponymic engineering projects, sought to Turkicize the landmarks of Istanbul's diverse makeup.

The Wealth Tax temporarily reined in inflationary tendencies by absorbing excess money in circulation, but at the cost of profound long-term effects on Turkey's economy and social fabric. Although at the time, non-Muslims constituted only 1.5 percent of Turkey's population, they paid 53 percent of the Wealth Tax, with Istanbul at the epicenter accounting for

70 percent of the total amount collected nationally.[106] Non-Muslims' heavy involvement in import-export trade, manufacturing, and well-paid professions, made them more likely candidates for Wealth Tax. But the discrepancies between the amounts allotted to them and to Muslims of comparable substance engaged in similar occupations revealed the targeted nature of the appraisals the tax commissions had made.[107] Many non-Muslims who were slated to pay the tax worked in blue-collar or service sector jobs, and their meager incomes would hardly have qualified them for a Wealth Tax had it not been for their religion. The tax spelled the end of many successful businesses and sometimes unintentionally produced ironic consequences such as inducing the collapse of the Yarmayan family's production plant, despite the fact that it produced much needed military defense equipment and could not be readily replaced.[108] The demands for large sums bankrupted many families; for example, Margarios Ohanyan, a wealthy merchant who owned several office and apartment buildings in Istanbul, was reduced to tenancy in the basement apartment of one of his former properties as he and his family tried to rebuild their lives from what little was left.[109] Imposed just two months after their discharge, the tax was especially hard on those returning from the Twenty Classes conscription and, as a result of not having been able to work for sixteen months, were already financially weakened. Long after successive governments admitted the error and repudiated the policy, for those affected the Wealth Tax turned into an experience they did not want to talk about.[110] In the aftermath of the tax, non-Muslims felt skittish about undertaking new enterprises—a gap that was eventually filled by Turkish entrepreneurs like Vehbi Koç or Hacı Ömer Sabancı, whose corporations grew to become Turkey's largest. When they did engage in commerce or industry, they almost always sought a Muslim-Turkish partner, who regardless of skills or experience, they hoped, would provide a shield should they become targets of policies similar to the Wealth Tax.[111] Most noticeably, within two years of the foundation of the new state of Israel, thirty-three thousand Turkish Jews emigrated.[112] Although the Wealth Tax affected a relatively small number of people, it was a profound violation of a fundamental sense of fairness, and in the words of Faik Ökte, who oversaw its implementation in Istanbul, it forever "poisoned the sense of trust between the state and citizens that is indispensable for a thriving . . . economic life."[113]

CONCLUSION

The dismantling of non-Muslim landscapes was remarkably similar to the dismantling of heterodox Islamic landscapes outlined in the previous

chapter. Both were spatial strategies for constituting a homogeneous society, wherein collective allegiances coalesced around the idea of nationhood, overriding all other competing loyalties.

But there were also important differences. In the first place, unlike
the followers of heterodox Islam, whose faith was being co-opted to be
brought under the auspices of the central state, the pressures on non-Muslims were never imposed with an eye toward their eventual assimilation.
They were, instead, geared toward compelling them to leave the country or
forcing them to repress their distinctive identities with the implicit understanding that they would never be able to assimilate. Second, while in the
early years of the republic heterodox Islam came under severe constraints,
Islam's place in Turkey's history was not denied. In contrast, whether
effected directly or perpetrated by individuals and implicitly sanctioned
by the government, the transformation or deterioration of non-Muslim
structures beyond recognition—coupled with their conscious omission
from most historical accounts, as evidenced by their absence on maps
and in local histories and textbooks—was part of an effort to edit non-
Muslims out of Turkey's heritage as well.

Changes in the physical world had long-lasting consequences insofar
as they undercut long-standing notions of land tenure and ownership, reconfigured cognitive maps, and disrupted established cycles of life. From
the catastrophic deportation of Armenians to the petty harassment of
non-Muslims on the streets of small towns, each incident large or small
contributed to the remaking of Turkey's social, economic, and spatial
structure with the range of openings they created for wealth and asset
transfer. These events shook the lives of those who, as targets of such discriminatory policies, lost their homes, livelihoods, and their communal
institutions, while propelling the fortunes of those who, with the implicit
approval of the powers that be, stood to gain from that loss. Beholden to
the regime and with vested interests in its preservation, this emergent
"national bourgeoisie" of local notables and neophyte industrialists was
in turn an indispensable political asset for a state that continued to face
substantial challenges to its solvency and sovereignty. But more broadly,
even for those who had little to lose or gain materially, these changes re-
drew the maps of neighborhoods and towns and generated new economic
and social hierarchies. It is noteworthy that such changes operated in less
discernible, more diffuse ways, thus making their impact harder to grasp
because, for the most part, the physical environment continued to project
an appearance of permanence that masked the disruptions in practice,
transfers of ownership, and concomitant shifts in meaning. And, when
actual physical changes—in the form of demolitions or new construc-

tion—were made to built environments once occupied by non-Muslims, they were gradual and uncoordinated, making them blend easily into other changes in the land.

The exclusionary practices and discriminatory policies outlined in this chapter cumulatively defined the boundaries of what constituted membership in the modern Turkish nation. But the process—as exemplified by the travel restrictions that almost paralyzed national commerce or the chaos during the Twenty Classes conscription with the confinement of the conscripts at the Sultanahmet Square prior to their shipment—was untidy, often shortsighted, and riddled with logistical problems that displayed a pattern of ill-advised clampdowns often followed by hasty pullbacks. Furthermore, republican leaders generally shared a desire to homogenize the polity, but not all of them approached the issue with the same zeal. As in other areas of policy making, the coexistence of both moderates and CUP militants among the RPP's top brass further contributed to this tense and fluctuating state of affairs. Which of the competing factions at different levels of the military and political chains of command prevailed affected both the handling of sudden developments that spiraled out of control (such as the violence after the Niego funeral and the 1934 pogroms in Thrace) and policy reversals (such as the repeal of the Twenty Classes conscription and the Wealth Tax programs within almost a year of their enforcement). Finally, international political alignments also informed domestic policies regarding non-Muslims. Turkish Jews were especially alarmed by the cozy relationship between the ultranationalist members of the RPP establishment and the Nazi regime in Germany. Turkey's minorities were not alone in their anxious existence. Neighboring young nation-states such as Bulgaria, Greece, and Romania, which, like Turkey, were still reeling from the collapse of the Ottoman Empire and the reconfiguration of the region's human and political geography, faced similar challenges to national integration and implemented comparable strategies including minoritization, appropriation and repurposing of the built environment, and toponymic erasure. It is important to note that as kin states to population pockets in each other's territories, they constantly and mutually modulated their policies regarding minorities. Hence, for instance, the fortunes of Istanbul's Greeks and their Turkish-Muslim counterparts in western Thrace were both closely linked to the temperature of Turco-Greek relations. For the people on the ground, however, the unpredictability of living a life so closely indexed to the vagaries of domestic and international politics became an incentive to leave lands inhabited by generations of their ancestors, further homogenizing the nation-states of the region. The resulting regime was inherently lacking in plurality and democracy. It offered a centrally defined, hegemonic cultural identity as the only legitimate public identity and removed all other identity claims, such as language, culture, and belief from the public sphere.[114] In the final part of this book, "An Imaginable Community," I will turn to the spatial construction of this new top-down identity, focusing on the material culture, institutions, and practices of the new state that fomented its reproduction.

PART III

AN

IMAGINABLE

COMMUNITY

CHAPTER 5

NATIONALIZING SPACE

In her renowned memoirs of the Turkish War of Independence (1919–1922), Halide Edip (Adıvar) wrote extensively about the difficulty of mustering support to fight the war even in Ankara, where the nationalists had based themselves. In a conversation during the buildup to the war, local women told her: "Look, of course, we want the good of our country too, but why should [Ankara] struggle and sacrifice herself for a hopeless cause because Istanbul happens to be in the hands of the British? . . . Is it not enough that half of [Ankara] died in [Çanakkale]? And for what? Let each town struggle for itself, for heaven's sake!"[1]

Halide Edip was not alone in voicing apprehension about the profound apathy following the post–First World War occupation of the country, especially in rural Anatolia.[2] The endemic lack of concern among the people for what lay beyond their immediate vicinity appalled the nationalists: How could people not feel compelled to rush to the aid of their compatriots in neighboring towns that came under occupation?

After decades of military conflict, war fatigue was a significant hurdle to mobilization, but people's reluctance to fight for lands and folks they did not necessarily see as their own was an equally important factor. This insular frame of reference persisted after the war, jeopardizing the viability of the neophyte state. The longevity of the Turkish Republic as a political unit depended on national integration. This meant expanding the horizons of people's communal imagination to include a geography that was coterminous with the national borders and establishing enduring affective ties among its inhabitants. In short, it meant ensuring that Istanbul's fate would matter to the inhabitants of Ankara and beyond during emergencies and otherwise.

Complicating the process of integration were the vast regional differences in population profile, geographic conditions, and economic prosperity across the country. Generally speaking, eastern Turkey had a more rugged terrain and a harsher climate than the west; its sparsely populated settlements became all the more isolated during the long and cold winter months. Tribal affiliations were strong, with much of the land and other assets in the possession of a relatively few powerful families. The west, especially the northwest, had more favorable geographic conditions and better accessibility and also benefited from its proximity to the historic seat of power. Its economy was more integrated regionally as well as with international trade, it was more densely populated, and its inhabitants were relatively more prosperous than their eastern counterparts. During the build up to the War of Independence the nationalists had managed to broker makeshift alliances between various groups from different regions. However, struck under extraordinary duress, these were circumstantial in nature and could not hold together constituencies whose living standards, self-definition, and interests were so divergent. Moreover, as discussed in chapter 4, whereas Turkey had lost the bulk of its non-Muslim inhabitants to wartime atrocities and later population exchanges, the remaining predominantly Muslim majority was far from being homogeneous. Existing cleavages between the different religious groups were exacerbated by the administration's policies. Although professing to separate state affairs from religion, the process of secularization had, in practice, co-opted the institutional infrastructure of Orthodox Sunni Islam, thereby favoring its followers over practitioners of indigenous, heterodox forms of Islam, who constituted about a quarter of the population. Finally, a larger conflict loomed ineastern Turkey: The region's large Kurdish population had, for the most part, sided with the nationalists during the War of Independence. They were, however, a distinct ethnic group—even though they were not unified among themselves. Insofar as it called for the Kurds to give up their cultural and linguistic heritage and subordinate themselves to the rule of a central government by relinquishing their tribal social structures, national integration was tantamount to assimilation, which inevitably led to years of violent confrontations that continue today.

National integration may not immediately come across as a spatial problem, but some of the most consequential strategies implemented in Turkey were. Republican leaders understood that in the long run they could not sustain the legitimacy of the new order by imposing the state's authority solely through violent means. Rather, they had to devise and implement policies to instill in the population a sense of unity and continuity as a people with a common history and a united destiny living on a shared piece of land. A central component of this state-driven transformation strategy was the creation of a uniform web of infrastructural services, which would be centrally administered from Ankara.[3] Consequently, despite the severe shortage of resources, Turkey's leaders decided to embark on a large number of public works projects to modernize the country and bring it "to the level of contemporary civilization."[4] Their ambitious endeavor included opening new schools, community centers, and hospitals; remaking the downtown areas of several cities; and building new roads, railroads, and bridges to previously inaccessible parts of the country. Mostly utilitarian structures, the individual components of this undertaking were modest in scale and appearance. Taken together, however, they presented a recognizably uniform physical character as the material culture of the new Turkish state.

Modern states are indisputably territorial.[5] They assert their power not only through their monopoly over the means of violence but also through their ability to transform the physical landscape.[6] The two strategies are inextricably linked and mutually reinforcing. Large-scale infrastructural projects are concrete expressions of power. They require the mobilization of massive human and material resources, which depends on the state's imminent ability to resort to violence if necessary. In turn, as in the Turkish case, the existence of a comprehensive infrastructure is indispensable for the state to deploy its military and police forces effectively. The assertion of authority does not always take the form of open aggression. State power is at its most efficacious when it operates without any visible confrontation, monitoring and channeling people's activities, mediating the transactions between the members of its polity, and controlling the use and distribution of collective resources.[7] The modern state's building stock provides the physical scaffolding in and around which these transactions take place. The barriers, passages, compartments, thresholds, and adjacencies that the built environment engenders shape the rhythms and routines of everyday life and, therefore, are instrumental to disseminating officially sanctioned notions of identity, order, hierarchy, and authority.

The built and written evidence that Turkey's leaders left behind reveals just how central the control of space through the construction of public works was to their national integration strategies. In this chapter, using this rich preserve of records, I examine their zealous attempts to define the form, function, and meaning of a standard, extensive, and centralized web of infrastructural projects, which they envisioned would eventually span the entire country and bind the national territory together. These large-scale projects were not only important for bringing the material comforts of modernity to the population at large but also were central to the functioning of the state and its exertion of power. The roads, railroads, train stations, administrative and military structures, and redesigned town centers surveyed here formed the indispensable physical components of an expanding state apparatus. They facilitated the state's operations, enabling it to enforce laws uniformly, extract taxes in the form of cash or labor, demand compulsory military service, and tighten its control over the newly forged and fragile geopolitical unit. In addition to performing utilitarian functions, this broad infrastructural network carried symbolic meanings to be inscribed in the popular imagination. As the sites of intensified state-citizen transactions, they reminded people of their participation in a national community that stretched beyond the immediately visible. The materialization of these projects was meant to appeal to people's sense of ownership and pride as the fruits of their collective labor as a nation. Most dramatically, Turkey's leaders deliberately deployed the components of this infrastructure for promoting national unity by incorporating them into heavily orchestrated commemorative pageants, in which the traumatic events of the recent past were symbolically reenacted and the shared goals of the nation were collectively reenacted. In short, this chapter foregrounds the material culture of the neophyte Turkish Republic by examining the utilitarian and symbolic functions of state-run sites and services.

WEAVING AN IRON WEB ACROSS THE LAND

A cartoon published shortly after the inauguration of service to Amasya in November 1927 proudly celebrated the Republican People's Party (RPP) government's rail transit policy—albeit with a certain degree of wishful hyperbole.[8] It featured an aged Prime Minister İsmet (İnönü) seated at his official chair, studying a railroad map of Turkey, with a caption that read, "'Fifty Years Later' İsmet Pasha: There is no more room to build new rail lines, we will have to open new lines underground." İnönü was arguably the keenest advocate of "weaving an iron web" across the country and during his long tenure he provided unstinting support for expanding the web's coverage.[9] By the late 1930s, Turkish State Railways (TCDD) officials boasted that in contrast to the 4,100 kilometers of lines built under the Ottoman Empire between 1856 and 1912, 3,100 kilometers of lines were built in the first fifteen years of the republic, tripling the pace of expansion.[10] Remarkably, Ankara, which at the beginning of the War of Independence was the terminus of a secondary service route on the Baghdad–Basra line, emerged as the national hub at the intersection of multiple lines in all directions that reached or were expected to reach Turkey's borders on

FIGURE 5.1. A CARTOON DE-PICTING THE EXPANSION OF TURKISH RAILROADS "'FIFTY YEARS LATER' İSMET PAŞA: THERE IS NO MORE ROOM TO BUILD NEW RAIL LINES, WE WILL HAVE TO OPEN NEW LINES UNDERGROUND."

land and sea. All trains traversing the country had to go through Ankara, reifying the new capital's central position within the country. This new configuration presented a striking contrast to the layout of railroads built during the Ottoman years, signaling a profound shift in Turkey's transportation policy.

The Ottoman government did not make comprehensive long-term rail transit plans nor did it decide the itinerary of routes. Instead, various foreign consortia, often backed by their respective governments, approached Ottoman officials to propose new lines on routes they expected to be lucrative.[11] In exchange for building the lines, they were granted operation rights over a fixed period of time. These concessions also included per-

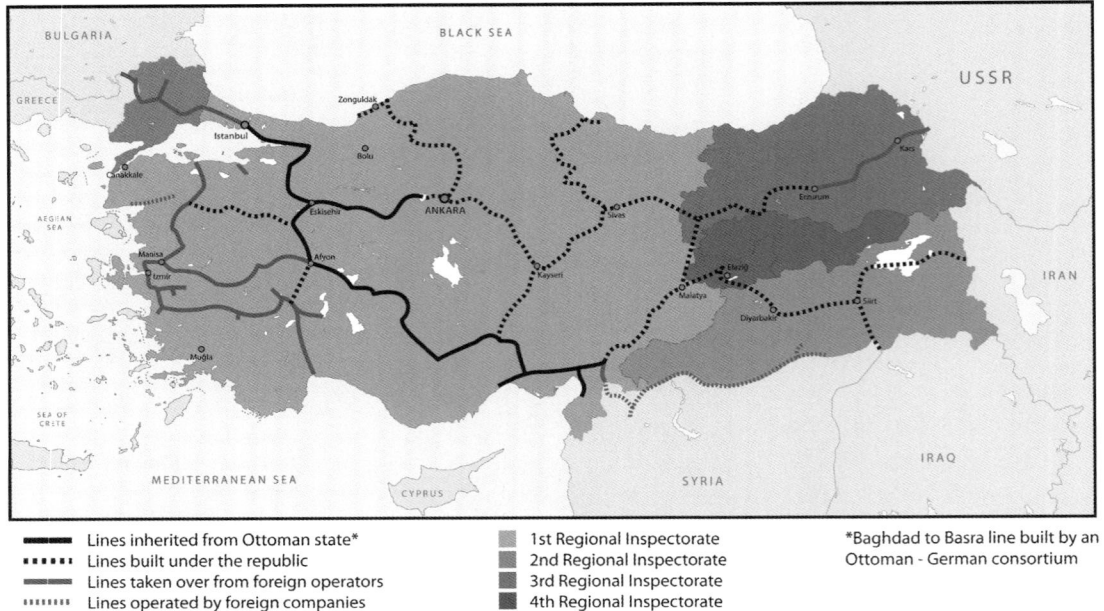

Legend:

- ▬▬▬ Lines inherited from Ottoman state*
- ▪▪▪▪▪▪ Lines built under the republic
- ▬▬▬ Lines taken over from foreign operators
- ▪▪▪▪▪▪▪ Lines operated by foreign companies

- 1st Regional Inspectorate
- 2nd Regional Inspectorate
- 3rd Regional Inspectorate
- 4th Regional Inspectorate

*Baghdad to Basra line built by an Ottoman - German consortium

FIGURE 5.2. THE EXPANSION OF THE RAILROAD NETWORK IN TURKEY. ALSO SHOWN ARE THE AREAS UNDER THE CONTROL OF THE GENERAL INSPECTORATES. MAP DRAWN BY JENNIE WEBB.

quisites such as commercial privileges over agricultural products within the service area and exclusive rights to operate mines found in the close vicinity of the tracks.[12] The Ottoman state, for its part, benefited from the accessibility—albeit piecemeal—provided by the railroads as they facilitated more effective policing and tax collection.[13] Since the Ottoman government agreed at the outset to provide the collateral, cover potential losses, and receive a share of the profits only if these rose above a certain margin, railroad business in the empire was considered to be lucrative and relatively risk-free for foreign investors.[14] Setting up even the most bare-bones line entitled the railroad entrepreneurs to tap into the natural and agricultural resources over a broader region. Given such advantages, obtaining concessions to build new lines was competitive. Although the capitulations gave them little room to maneuver, Ottoman officials were savvy enough to maximize their leverage by pitting the various investors (and the governments behind them) against one another, never allowing one company to completely dominate the sector.

Shaped by the divergent political and economic calculations of the parties involved, Ottoman railroads served narrow and specialized geographic areas.[15] The lines were concentrated mainly in Rumelia and western Anatolia, where the soil was fertile, the climate and topography were agreeable, and the prospects for promoting commercial agriculture were relatively better than the rest of the empire.[16] Their short and segmented itineraries functioned as discrete legal entities controlling fragments of a discontinuous maze.[17] Moreover, routes were selected mainly to capitalize on existing local resources, but once in place, they further widened disparities between regions. As a result, unlike in other countries where railroads opened up previously closed local markets to national and international trade, consolidated labor, and merchandise markets, thereby reinforcing social cohesion, in Ottoman Turkey, railroads did not have a unifying effect.[18]

Republican leaders wanted to reverse all that. They set out to consolidate all lines under the exclusive authority of a single state-owned company because they considered establishing an effective rail transit system indispensable to progress and national integration. To accomplish this, in addition to building new lines to remote and impoverished destinations, which would have been of little interest to private investors, they had to buy out the contracts inherited from the Ottoman Empire or wait until they ran out.[19] Republican leaders resented the continued foreign operation of some lines, which they regarded as the bitter legacy of the empire's subservience to European interests. Taking possession of the country by rail was essentially an act of reclaiming sovereignty and it was as much about conquering uncharted territories with new lines as reconquering those under foreign ownership. During this period of intense reorganization, Turkey's leaders framed their railroad policy in terms of three recurring themes: economy, national integration, and security.

Highlighting the economic dimensions of the task at hand, Hidayet Sertel, director general of TCDD, asserted that "the gains generated by the railroads during the pre-Republican period were unilateral, profiting exclusively foreign investors whose main goal was effortless exploitation." While the lines concentrated in certain profitable regions, other regions, which were often impoverished and had little commercial interest to the investors, were neglected, becoming even less appealing to entrepreneurial appetites.[20] The economic goals of TCDD were different. The company was not an independent moneymaking enterprise but an investment toward spurring economic growth across the country. TCDD charged below cost for shipping agricultural products, metals, industrial goods, and other strategic goods because the long-term benefits of integrating the national market and supporting local industries outweighed short-term profits.[21] Sertel repeated that, unlike commercial carriers, TCDD's mission was not to recoup the initial investment and that its operating expenses should instead be understood

FIGURE 5.3. THE INAUGURATION OF TRAIN LINES WAS A MUCH CELEBRATED EVENT IN THE LOCALITIES ON THE ITINERARY. INAUGURAL TRAINS, ADORNED WITH FLOWERS AND LEAVES, TRAVELED THROUGH OR-NATE MILESTONES AS CHEERING CROWDS LINED UP BESIDE THE TRACKS. THIS IS A PHOTO OF THE FIRST TRAIN SERVICE FROM MERSIN ON THE MEDITERRANEAN COAST TO SAMSUN ON THE BLACK SEA COAST OF TURKEY. THE BANNER IN FRONT OF THE LOCOMOTIVE, DECORATED WITH FLOWERS AND FLAGS, READS "GREETINGS FROM THE MEDITERRANEAN TO THE BLACK SEA."

as an integral part of the overhead costs of operating a nation-state as a whole.[22] Linking the centers of production and consumption was fundamental to Turkey's economic self-sufficiency. He added that railroads were necessary as much for "carrying the coal of Zonguldak to the steel mills of Karabük" as for "bringing bread to our people on the [Black Sea] coast, who not so long ago, were compelled to consume imported wheat."[23]

Railroads were equally vital for their role in facilitating national integration. As they fanned out into the country, they transformed the face of Turkey. Although they were not completely independent of geographic and climatic obstacles, trains broke into the terrain in an unprecedented way. They shortened traveling times considerably and opened new corridors of transit, which in turn reworked established spatial relations of proximity and accessibility between Turkish towns. In eastern Anatolia, where the winters are harsh and the mountains are rugged, remote towns that were part of the itinerary became accessible almost year-round for the first time.[24] Between 1933 and 1938 the total number of passengers quadrupled and the total mileage traveled almost tripled.[25] The increased number of passengers and mileage indicated that railroads were gradually becoming a common means of transportation, enabling more people to reach farther corners of the country. As small enclaves, which in the past had been relatively isolated, gradually became ports of call on a long route, republican leaders hoped their integration to the national unit would be improved as well.

In addition to people and goods, railroads also moved ideas. Turkey's leaders regarded them as crucial agents of social and cultural change. "Without railroads," claimed President Kemal Atatürk, "it would be very difficult even to disseminate ideas about civilization let alone to propagate civilization itself. Railroads chart the path to progress and prosperity."[26] Similarly, in an article titled "Railroads and Turkish Unity," İsmail Hakkı Baltacıoğlu, a professor of education and prolific author, argued:

> Railroads are much more than [an economic investment]. . . . To become a family, a nation, people need to have ties that pull them together. These include a common language, collective duties, spiritual bonds, and last but not least, shared goals and convictions. Such sharing can only happen if certain collective sensibilities are sharpened. What makes a nation is not propinquity but the liveliness of these ties and sensibilities. Yet mountains, seas, deserts, in short, distances, material obstacles stand in the way of establishing and maintaining such ties. What should we do? We should eliminate those natural obstacles, right? How? By getting rid of the mountains, seas, deserts! . . . The only way to do this is to improve railroad and maritime transportation. If this is realized, the constituents of a nation who are of the same ancestry will be drawn closer together and bound together more easily. This will impact collective projects positively, accelerate industrial growth, promote agricultural production, and increase commercial transactions. Out of this revitalization a new generation, which we call the new man, will be born. Nothing can bring the kind of mental transformation that the railroads can.[27]

Finally, and most important, republican leaders stressed the role of railroads in bolstering national security. Republican leaders argued that a decision as important as deciding the routes could not be left to foreign companies and the political powers behind them, as had previously been the case. Owning and operating its own comprehensive network of lines was integral to preserving Turkey's political integrity. The prime minister, İsmet İnönü, firmly believed that to protect and exert its authority in all corners of the country, the central government had to be able to reach those corners in the first place. As he put it, "The safety and prosperity of Izmir can only be assured if we can transport people from Erzurum and Sivas to run to the rescue of Izmir within forty-eight hours."[28] At the time, however, it was just as important—if not more so—to quickly deploy soldiers from Izmir to Elazığ and Tunceli (Dersim), where Kurdish insurrections threatened the authority of the government in Ankara. In Turkey the process of national consolidation had not yet been completed, and the threats were both external and internal. Although the heavily censored press refrained from reporting the details, between 1924 and 1938, various Kurdish tribes, which refused to recognize the authority of the central government, staged seventeen major uprisings in eastern and southeastern Turkey.[29] Almost every spring, after the snow melted, the army made incursions into the rugged territories in an effort to suppress rebellious tribes in guerrilla-style battles. Internal correspondences between civilian and military officials reveal how crucial they regarded making the previously impregnable geography of eastern Turkey accessible to military troops by building roads and bridges to facilitate the passage of vehicles and other heavy equipment, placing military outposts to guard them against attacks, and setting up relay stations to expedite communications.[30] Coupled with regular troop movements, intensified surveillance, new technologies of communication, and reconnaissance flights, railroads produced an unprecedented militarized geography in eastern and southeastern Turkey. Seen through the lens of this chronic conflict, especially in the conflict zones, far beyond a mere metaphorical gesture, taking possession of the land was a very material assertion of state power.

THE REPUBLICAN TOWN

In November 1937, as part of a larger tour of eastern Anatolia, Mustafa Kemal paid a two-day visit to the southeastern city of Diyarbakır, during which he also attended the groundbreaking ceremony for the new rail lines that would connect Turkey to neighboring Iran and Iraq. When his famous white train finally rolled into the train station in the early evening, the crowd of locals who had already been waiting for hours in anxious anticipation cheered with excitement. In preparation for Mustafa Kemal's visit, the entire city of Diyarbakır had been decked out in flags and banners, and temporary archways with welcoming slogans had been erected at prominent locations on the city's main routes along which he was ex-

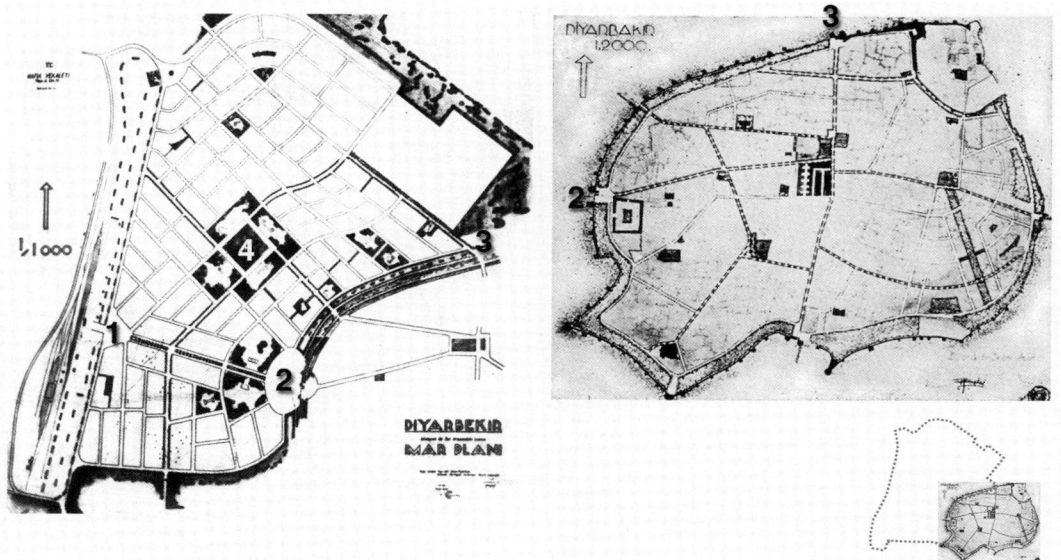

FIGURE 5.4. (LEFT) DİYARBAKIR MASTER PLAN FOR THE WESTERN EXPANSION OF THE CITY OUTSIDE ITS CITADEL, AND (RIGHT) HISTORIC DIYARBAKIR INSIDE ITS WALLS. THE SMALL IMAGE ON THE RIGHT- HAND SIDE INDICATES THE RELATIVE SCALE OF THE EXPANSION TO THE EXISTING CITY. (1) THE SQUARE IN FRONT OF THE TRAIN STATION; (2) URFA GATE, AT THE OTHER END OF STATION BOULEVARD; (3) HARPUT GATE; AND (4) MONUMENT SQUARE, WITH PARK AND NEW INSTITUTIONAL BUILDINGS ON SURROUNDING BLOCKS.

pected to travel. Important buildings such as the Government House and the Governor's Mansion were illuminated with festively strung lightbulbs running off generators because Diyarbakır did not yet have functioning electricity.

The train station served as the staging point for Mustafa Kemal's visit. Between outings, he retreated to his personal car parked at the station, where he met local officials. He used the second-floor terrace of the station to address the crowds—a move that for a brief period turned the building into an outsized podium. The terrace offered an unobstructed view of the new Diyarbakır in the making. Completed in 1935, the building stood at about a kilometer (0.6 meters) to the west of the city wall. Station Boulevard, a newly opened wide road between the train station and Urfa Gate, was conceived as the spine for Diyarbakır's future growth. Most new construction, funded mainly by the government, was located to the north of the avenue, outside the city wall, in the sector between Dağ Kapısı (Mountain Gate) to the north and Urfa Gate to the west. Immediately outside the train station, to the north of Station Boulevard, a large field had been allocated for sporting and ceremonial events. The institutional core of the city, including the Government House, the Courthouse, the Army and Gendarme headquarters, the Offices of the First Regional Inspectorate General were sited around a large park, just three blocks to the north of Station Boulevard. Kapısı Avenue, which eventually turned into the Elazığ Road, demarcated the northern edge of new development, beyond which lay extensive military installations.

During his short but high-profile visit to Diyarbakır, Mustafa Kemal attended a classical music concert at Halkevi (the RPP-run community center), visited the Officers' Club and the Government House (see fig. 6.11). He met with local and regional officials, inquired about the progress of various projects, and examined the long-term plans for the development of old Diyarbakır, inside the city walls, and new Diyarbakır, immediately outside them. He complimented local officials for the latter and ordered some changes in the former, including the widening of Diyarbakır's still discernible cardo-decomanus and the opening of two parallel ring roads on both sides of the city walls.[31] He insisted that historical structures with cultural or artistic significance be preserved during this process so as to retain old Diyarbakır's original character. Yet with the exception of two mansions on the outskirts of the old town, which he had used as residences during his brief deployments to the city as a young Ottoman general, Mustafa Kemal's tour of Diyarbakır was limited exclusively to its newer developments.[32] Much to the disappointment of the local business owners, members of the city's stock and grain exchange and the chamber of commerce, who had contributed to the decoration of the streets of the inner market district, Mustafa Kemal only stopped outside the Urfa Gate to examine the details of its stone carvings and carpentry. Mustafa Kemal's quick and scripted movements about town suggest that he probably had a preconceived notion about the layout of republican Diyarbakır and its landmarks independent of actual conditions on the ground.

Indeed, during the second decade of the republic, the patterns of development outlined above for Diyarbakır were consistent with an urban design template that was becoming increasingly common throughout Turkey. The use of a recurring repertoire of urban design components to endow Turkish cities with a uniform character was as central to the RPP's spatial strategy for national integration as its policy of "weaving an iron web." By providing travelers with similar views to behold at their points of arrival in each city and a townscape that was familiar enough to navigate fluently, republican planners sought to convey a pervasive sense of unity concretized in the physical arrangement of buildings and urban spaces. In this process, Ankara was, par excellence, the model to emulate. As Falih Rıfkı Atay enthusiastically asserted in an editorial he penned for the tenth anniversary of the republic, after succeeding in Ankara, "we could remake the rest of Anatolia . . . which would be like shaping dough using the same mold."[33] In other words, beyond an administrative center, the republican leadership regarded Ankara as the test site for developing the prototypical elements of a modern urban environment and performing the sociospatial practices of a new way of life, which would then be implemented elsewhere. The clustering of institutional buildings, their interior layouts, and their prescribed utilitarian and ceremonial functions in cities across the country would be modeled after those of Turkey's new capital. As the flagship of all republican endeavors, Ankara absorbed a disproportionate amount of Turkey's meager resources and its population grew at a rate incomparable with the rest of Turkish cities.[34] These unique characteristics notwithstanding, practices and ideas first introduced in the new capital were gradually adopted in other Turkish towns. The shortage of funds and labor—especially skilled labor—was even more acute in the provinces, thus projects had to be selected carefully to achieve maximum impact. Consequently, the most prominently representative/ceremonial (and often photographed) urban spaces, such as city entrances, downtowns, and the major thoroughfares between them were given priority, and, in many cases, the projects had to be scaled down or their implementation stretched out over a long period of time. Nevertheless, by the late 1940s, Turkish towns—especially in the arrangement of their main arteries and their institutional cores—began to exhibit remarkably similar characteristics, which are still somewhat recognizable today.

One common gesture, implemented in Diyarbakır and elsewhere, was to use the train station as a generator of urban form. To this end, existing train stations were upgraded and enlarged, and new ones were built as railroad service expanded to new destinations. The new stations along TCDD routes shared common features insofar as they were built according to similar specifications featuring uniform plans, color schemes, and furnishings. There were two standard prototypes. The larger ones built at major provincial destinations such as Diyarbakır, Sivas, Manisa, or Malatya bore the distinctive traits of the style known as "Ankara cubic," characterized by their pronounced horizontal masses accentuated by thick flat bands punctuated by deep windows on the second floor, their apparently flat roofs, and overstretched eaves.[35] Their massing and plan had a distinctly tripartite symmetrical arrangement with a lobby at the center flanked by service spaces and offices on the sides. This simple and pragmatic layout was used across the board, even if the scale or the architectural expression of the building changed. Thus, the small train stations

FIGURE 5.5. IDENTICAL TRAIN STATIONS IN THREE DIFFERENT CITIES, MANISA (ABOVE), SIVAS (TOP, OPPOSITE), AND MALATYA (BOTTOM, OPPOSITE), ON THE DAY OF ITS INAUGURATION. ALTHOUGH NOT FEAURED HERE, THE DIYARBAKIR TRAIN STATION WAS ALSO BUILT TO THE SAME SPECIFICATIONS. COURTESY OF THE TURKISH HISTORICAL SOCIETY LIBRARY.

at minor towns along the route were far less elaborate than their counterparts at the large provincial centers but still had a similar tripartite layout.

In addition, because practical considerations almost always kept the actual railroad at a tangent to existing settlements, the stretch between the settlement and the train station presented itself as a useful development opportunity, and republican planners capitalized on it. In order to frame the approach to town and leave a positive impression on travelers, they designed new squares in front of the train stations and built paved and tree-lined avenues leading into town. They also upgraded existing roads and, where possible, had unsightly objects and buildings around them removed. In localities that remained outside the reach of the iron web, similar improvements were made along the main thoroughfares leading into town. Depending on the availability of land and other local conditions, one of the intersections of these refurbished arteries was enlarged and converted into a square. These new squares were almost invariably named after the republic (Cumhuriyet Meydanı) and were anchored by a mon-

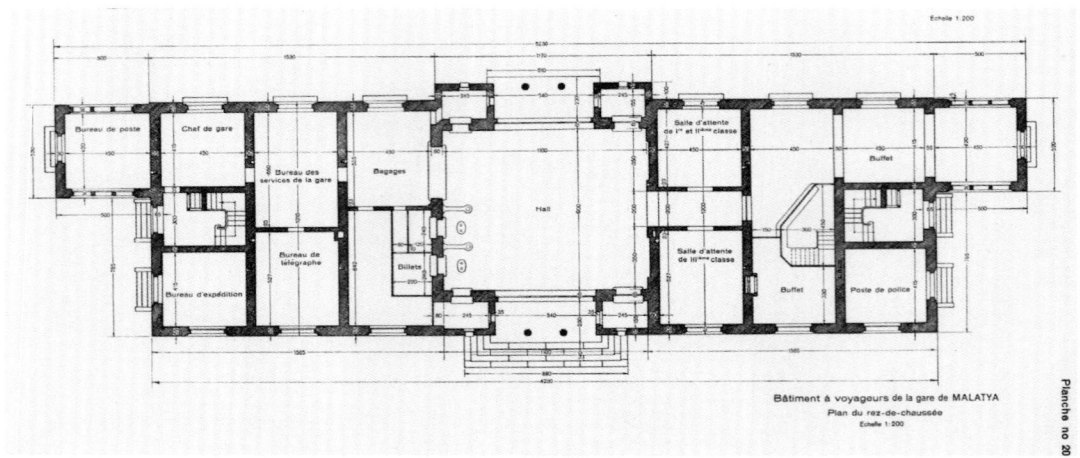

FIGURE 5.6. PROTYPICAL TRAIN STATION PLAN, MALATYA VERSION. COURTESY OF JEAN-PATRICK CHARREY.

FIGURE 5.7. BURSA REPUBLIC SQUARE, PARK, AND ATATÜRK MONUMENT. THE SMALL MODERN BUILD-ING ACROSS FROM THE MONUMENT IS THE BURSA ZIRAAT (AGRICULTURE) BANK MAIN BRANCH OF-FICE. ZIRAAT BANK WAS AND IS THE LARGEST STATE BANK IN TURKEY, AND IT ALSO SERVES AS A LIAISON FOR THE CENTRAL BANK IN THE PROVINCES. LIBRARY OF THE CHAMBER OF ARCHITECTS OF TURKEY.

ument honoring Atatürk and the memory of the War of Independence. Often, a patch of green framed the Atatürk monument, and where land was available, the monument was placed in a park. Although they varied in size and degree of elaboration, these areas were landscaped in a very similar fashion, with geometric parterres bordered by shrubs. Over time, the recurring use of certain plants throughout Turkey—such as salvias, pansies, gladioli, and rosebushes—further reinforced the overall effect of uniformity, as if to complement the standard building stock of republican urbanism with an official flora. The Republic Square, with its monument and landscaping constituted a focal point for new urban development. Buildings that housed the state's administrative apparatus, such as provincial government houses, courts, military command centers, and police departments, were built around it and along the new avenues leading to it. Institutions that served the public directly, including new schools, healthcare centers, and playgrounds, were also located in the same general area. In later years, the local facilities of the ruling Republican People's Party and eventually Halkevleri, the party-run community centers, would follow suit, bringing home the presence of the state and serving as a concrete reminder of the close relationship between the state and the single ruling party.

In the southeastern province of Muğla, for instance, the monument, the square, and the park were not only the conceptual nucleus of the new plan but also its first components to materialize.[36] The new Government House, the Halkevi, and the City Club, also operated by the Halkevi, were completed within the next decade.[37] The new civic core displaced Muğla's city center from the foothills to the plains and brought it closer to the Aydın-Marmaris road, which was also paved, widened, and landscaped. To realize the new town center project, Muğla's old *vakıf*-owned cemetery had to be relocated outside the new development area.[38] The move shifted Muğla's focus away from the city's established core anchored by a handful of mosques, *tekke*s, and commercial buildings owned by miscellaneous vakıfs. It also introduced new venues of casual sociability to replace the old ones. As with so many western Anatolian towns, Muğla had lost its Greek population during the 1923 Turkish–Greek Population Exchange. The local Greeks had owned and operated Muğla's taverns, which despite nominal Islamic proscriptions against alcohol consumption, were well-loved establishments patronized by the town's Muslims and Christians alike.[39] Moreover, the closure of *tekke*s and *zaviye*s in 1924 brought an abrupt end to the social life that flourished around them, leaving early republican Muğla with few venues of socialization outside private homes.[40] By operating the City Club and promoting other social outreach activities

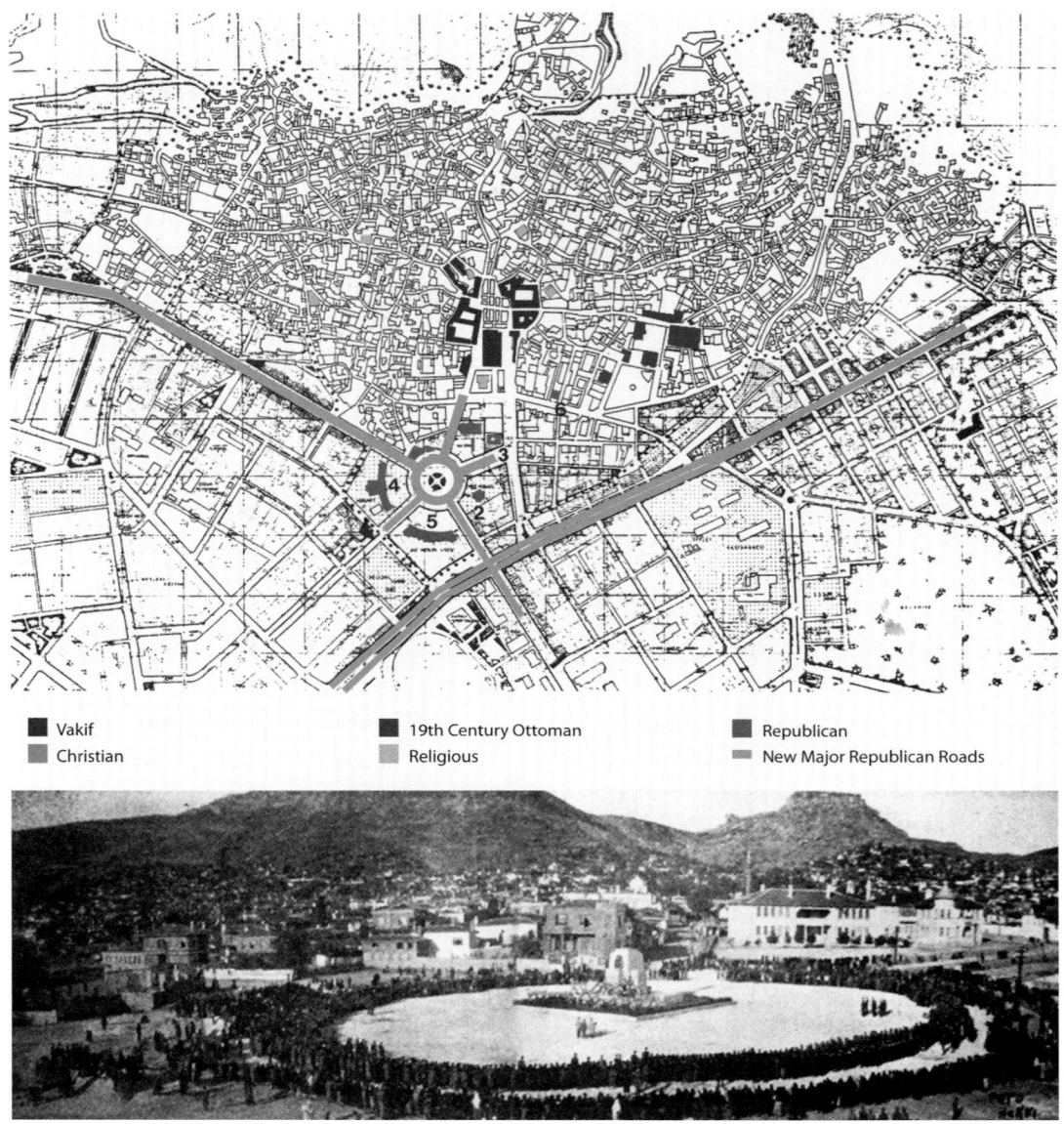

Vakif
Christian
19th Century Ottoman
Religious
Republican
New Major Republican Roads

FIGURE 5.8. (TOP) DOWNTOWN MUĞLA ORGANIZED AROUND A CIRCULAR REPUBLIC SQUARE ANCHORED BY AN ATATÜRK MONUMENT. NOTE THE CONTRAST BETWEEN THE TIGHT FABRIC OF OLDER PARTS OF TOWN NESTLED IN THE FOOTHILLS VERSUS THE NEW DOWNTOWN LOCATED IN THE PLAINS WITH ITS REGULAR GEOMETRICAL LAYOUT. (BOTTOM) A COMMEMORATIVE CEREMONY WITH THE PUBLIC GATHERED AROUND MUĞLA'S REPUBLIC SQUARE. PARADE ROUTES CONCENTRATED ON NEW REPUBLICAN AVENUES AND OMITTED OLDER MORE ESTABLISHED LANDMARKS. MAP REDRAWN BY JENNIE WEBB.

FIGURE 5.9. A TEAGARDEN PARK IN ISPARTA, CENTRAL-WESTERN TURKEY, FLANKED BY THE MUNICIPAL BUILDING AND THE OFFICERS' CLUB. OUTDOOR RECREATIONAL SPACES PROVIDED BY CENTRAL STATE AGENCIES AND SITUATED AMID GOVERNMENT INSTITUTIONS HAD A FORMAL AMBIENCE. THE CONFIGURATION PROLIFERATED IN MANY TOWNS. COURTESY OF THE TURKISH HISTORICAL SOCIETY LIBRARY.

through Halkevleri, RPP was responding to a need that its policies had created in the first place. Not least of RPP operatives' concerns was the political climate in western and southern Turkey. In its short-lived existence, the RPP's rival the Free Republican Party (FRP) had its strongest showing in towns like Antalya, Izmir, Manisa, and Muğla. After Atatürk cornered the FRP leadership to close the party down in 1930 and clamped down on opposition, monitoring civic life in this region continued to be an important preoccupation for the RPP regime. In light of such developments, beyond the generous social services of a welfare state, RPP-run parks, playgrounds, teahouses, and movie theaters, opened mostly in the 1930s, may be seen as attempts by the single-party regime to control and reshape the citizenry's leisure activities in model urban public settings.

As the examples of Muğla, Diyarbakır, and Ankara imply, the development of republican downtowns took place outside established historic town centers. Moving away from historic centers gave republican planners the possibility of avoiding the constraints of working with the tight fabric of historic downtowns and the complex property relations that governed them. By erecting the new buildings as a cluster, within a relatively short period of time, they also hoped to make a more effective statement about the projected image of modern Turkish towns. Most remarkably, the republican downtowns, which comprised strictly secular functions, stood in sharp contrast to their historical counterparts anchored by the social and religious institutions of the Ottoman Empire. The continued centrality of the Ottoman building stock as a physical reminder of a way of life and variegated mosaic of social relations was unacceptable to Turkey's leaders who were committed to instilling secular, modernist, and nationalist values in the polity. Their efforts to shift the focus and traffic away from historic city centers must be seen as part of their strategies to deliberately reconfigure the polity's collective allegiances. In that respect, Istanbul, as the former Ottoman capital, presented the most serious challenge. As Alev Çınar notes, republican planners sought hard to find a site from which the overwhelming presence of Istanbul's myriad Ottoman landmarks could not be felt (or at least could be played down) and that could serve as a new secular urban core. They finally chose Taksim, in the mostly non-Muslim Beyoğlu district, where the only token of official Ottoman presence was the city's water distribution plant, a utilitarian structure that did not have any religious or communitarian associations.[41]

The principles of republican urbanism summarized above constituted a reproducible template, which, despite the odds, gradually cast a recognizable appearance of uniformity over Turkish towns across the board. In that respect, as much as they sought to differentiate themselves from their predecessors, republican efforts were reminiscent of nineteenth-century Ottoman municipal reforms and infrastructural improvement projects, which introduced new public spaces, amenities, and official and institutional buildings in many cities.[42] But whereas Ottoman urban transformations were complemented by a range of civil and private initiatives for the provision of infrastructures (gas, water, lighting, dock and pier construction, etc.), republican projects—even when subcontracted—were under exclusive state supervision.

Although the recurrence of certain formal components made the material culture of republican urbanism recognizable across the country, there were also very substantial differences in the ways that these new urban spaces, the institutions they housed, and the practices they engendered served the process of national integration. Whether rooted in long-standing social and cultural differences, informed by differences in the terrain, variations in accessibility, or the uneven effects of the recent wars on each

FIGURE 5.10. TAKSİM SQUARE, ISTANBUL. THE CIRCULAR TRAFFIC ISLAND AROUND THE ATATÜRK MONU-
MENT. COURTESY OF SALⴀ RESEARCH, PHOTOGRAPH ARCHIVE İSTANBUL FOTOĞRAFLARI.

locality, the national geography exhibited significant regional differences.
The government's response, in return, was similarly varied.

Western Anatolian towns, which had been leveled during the War of
Independence, were among the first to start construction and adopt republican town planning principles. Manisa, located roughly in the middle
of the Izmir–Aydın route, for instance, had suffered severe damage during
the war, and most of its buildings were leveled or burned down. The Government House was the first building to be completed. It stood at the intersection of the east–west avenue, connecting the Manisa to Izmir and the
north–south avenue stretching toward the new train station, which was
built to replace its burned predecessor.[43] The building, which was identical
to the Diyarbakır train station, was completed in 1933. In 1935, Manisa city
government acquired the property in front of the Government House, converted it into a park, and named it after the prime minister, İsmet İnönü.
The İnönü Park contained a paved court facing the balcony of the Government House that was large enough to accommodate crowds during commemorative ceremonies or public speeches.[44] On the southern edge of the
park was the City Hall. In 1938, the Halkevi, the RPP Manisa Office, and
the library would complete the city's official core. That same year, *Manisa*

FIGURE 5.11. A GOVERNMENT OFFICIAL AND MILITARY OFFICERS INSPECTING BRIDGE CONSTRUCTION IN 1938 IN PERTEK (NEAR DERSİM ON THE MURAT RIVER, A TRIBUTARY OF THE EUPHRATES). COURTESY OF THE TURKISH HISTORICAL SOCIETY LIBRARY.

on the Fifteenth Anniversary of the Republic, an official commemorative almanac, enthusiastically noted that the "Republican Government . . . which brought light and life to everything in Turkey" had turned its attention to the "wounded, impoverished, humble, and ailing town of Manisa to heal it."[45] According to the almanac, in the aftermath of the trauma, Manisans had looked to Ankara for more than support and funds—they had also looked for ideas to shape their city:[46] "Under the protective and creative tutelage of the republican administration [Manisa] has attained a degree of perfection unprecedented in its history. . . . Yesterday's charred remains have been replaced with today's stadium, City Club, playgrounds, Halkevi, schools, institutes, RPP offices, movie theaters, libraries, apartment buildings, factories, and hospitals . . . lavish buildings that can be compared to the old palaces of Istanbul. . . . This dedicated passionate work in Manisa has converted a town, once desolate and barren, into the most important and beautiful [train] stop between Izmir and Ankara."[47]

In eastern Anatolia, the expansion of state infrastructure had different meanings and functions. Whereas the challenge in the west was to rebuild, in eastern Anatolia it was to build, often for the first time. Historically, given its distance from the seat of power in Istanbul and the severity of its geographic conditions, state presence had been relatively light in this region, which was also the country's most impoverished. The nineteenth-century bureaucratic reforms, designed to shore up the central authority of the Ottoman state, only had a limited effect in changing regional conditions. The RPP government had a far more ambitious agenda. Unlike their Ottoman predecessors, who tolerated a certain degree of local autonomy, RPP leaders sought complete state penetration in all aspects of social life and cultural practices. RPP policies aimed at infiltrating and dissolving long-standing tribal structures, imposing secularism, and Turkicizing the local Kurdish population met with fierce resistance in eastern and southeastern Anatolia.

Tensions turned into full-blown violent confrontation with the Şeyh Sait Uprising, which threw several provinces in eastern and southeastern provinces into weeks of turmoil. As discussed in earlier chapters, in the aftermath of the uprising, the central government became far more authoritarian, by restricting the public sphere, silencing opposition, and clamping down on heterodox Islam. It also introduced a new military-bureaucratic regime of Inspectorates General in the region, the first of which would be headquartered in Diyarbakır. As inspector general, İbrahim Tali Öngören believed that establishing the state's authority in the region depended first and foremost on expanding its physical infrastructure. In a letter to Prime Minister İnönü, on April 24 1930, he wrote:

> In light of Diyarbekir's [sic] strategic location and its current social and political conditions, erecting a hotel with modern amenities will mean far more than an ordinary construction project. The hotel will play a prominent part in conveying to the people the aims of the infrastructural and social modernization we are in the process of implementing. . . . We understand that difficulties in finding local suppliers for the necessary construction materials and furnishing the building might present challenges and that trying to resolve those might cause delays. However, given the population, the location, and their current importance, the lack of purveyors cannot be an excuse and we cannot afford to even consider getting by with mediocre furnishings.[48]

The hotel as well as the other governmental and institutional buildings were intended to respond to symbolic and utilitarian needs. They were both unmistakable expressions of state power and the sites that facilitated the exercise of that power. The ability to assess and extract taxes, impose the law, arbitrate over conflicts among citizens and between the citizens and the state was contingent on bringing the relevant bureaucrats and technocrats to these locations. While government workers needed buildings in which to perform their various official tasks, they also needed places to live. Hotels served as temporary homes for traveling bureaucrats, tax auditors, and inspectors of various government agencies. In many cases they were permanent homes to officials who, for lack of adequate housing, were unable to bring their families to towns in the more remote parts of the country. Öngören and his successors argued that the shortage of qualified personnel in the region seriously undermined the state's ability to function, noting difficulties in a range of areas including education, tax collection, and construction projects. Building hotels and family housing to attract personnel figured prominently among their proposed solutions to improve the situation.[49] Moreover, they argued that modern housing for government workers would also serve a didactic function, thus providing examples of modern living for local populations to emulate.[50] It is against this background of relentless efforts to impose hegemony and homogeneity that Diyarbakır's simultaneous similarity to and profound difference from Turkish towns in other regions comes into focus. Within this context, it is hardly surprising that during his 1937 visit Mustafa Kemal focused almost exclusively on the new developments, which brought the state to Diyarbakır in a tangible manner.

As the unrest continued unabated in later years, and the scale of Turkey's Eastern Problem (Şark Meselesi) became evident, the First Regional Inspectorate General would be subdivided into three smaller jurisdictions to make the task more manageable. As holders of extraordinary powers, regional inspectors general were capable of mobilizing both military and bureaucratic resources. That a significant bulk of their correspondence with the central government was about providing physical infrastructure and that it took place directly between regional inspectors general and the Prime Minister's Office, bypassing the officials at the Ministry of Settlements and Public Works, reveal that these projects were integral to internal pacification and that they were deliberately designed to secure state penetration through the manipulation of the physical environment. Writing in 1939 as a semiofficial chronicler of the state's expansion in the east in the aftermath of the Dersim rebellion, Naşit Hakkı Uluğ declared that "to bring Dersim in line, it was necessary to build the [rail]line."[51] Uluğ asserted that the Ottoman Empire's failure to pacify Eastern Turkey had been due, in large part, to its inability to establish a permanent network of transport and communications in the region.[52] This time, however, unlike in previous pacification efforts, which "washed away like tides," the state was determined to settle in the region.[53] In Turkey's turbulent East, which, even as of this writing continues to be in a constant state of emergency, the development of city centers, the construction of roads, railroads, and bridges that spanned the distances between them, and the building of military outposts that would monitor and protect them were mutually interdependent parts of a larger strategy to bring the entire region under state authority once and for all.

A LEGAL AND INSTITUTIONAL BASIS FOR UNIFORMITY

In a report he sent directly to İsmet İnönü on May 18, 1931, İbrahim Tali Özgören stated, "I have . . . for the past three years been trying to make plans for the towns in my jurisdiction, but I have succeeded in not even one of the nine provinces."[54] Özgören noted that the scarcity of trained professionals who could prepare urban designs was a nationwide problem and he suggested the creation of a central government agency to provide this service. Should setting up such an agency prove too challenging in the short term, he insisted that some office had to be created to prepare physical plans for the towns lying within the nine provinces of the First Region.[55]

We do not know how influential Özgören's repeated requests were in expediting the process of centralized planning. However, we do know that his reports were forwarded by the Office of the Prime Minister to the Ministry of Public Works, which was already experimenting with the idea because it would streamline the design process, reduce costs, and make the most of the limited number of trained professionals at its disposal.[56] The ministry had begun assigning its in-house architects the development of prototypical projects to be implemented throughout the country—albeit on a modest scale. As illustrated in the *Provinces Album*, published by the Ministry of Interior in 1929, the construction of standard school buildings, which eventually came to be known as the Gazi Schools in popular parlance, was well under way in several towns.[57]

Given the urgent need to start building, between 1930 and 1939, Turkey's leaders enacted a series of laws and created a number of new government agencies, which effectively centralized the production of urban space and the provisions that governed its use and maintenance. The Municipalities Law (1930), the General Public Health Act (1930), and the Roads and Buildings Code were comprehensive pieces of legislation, which together served as a universal set of city ordinances for all Turkish cities.[58] Their provisions outlined a common organizational structure for municipalities, defined the terms of their relationship with the national government,

FIGURE 5.12. A COLLAGE FROM THE FIRST REGIONAL INSPECTORATE'S PROMOTIONAL VOLUME, SHOWCAS-ING SOME OF THE MODERN INSTITUTIONAL BUILDINGS AND INFRASTRUCTURAL PROJECTS COMPLETED IN THE REGION.

and prescribed their responsibilities and jurisdictions. As a result, a range of public concerns, including the construction and maintenance of urban infrastructure, provision of public utilities and various social services, inspection of urban trades, the preparation of maps, and decisions about land use and zoning were brought under a common legal framework. Municipalities were also charged with overseeing a range of services related to public health, including the prevention and treatment of epidemic diseases, control of pests and stray animals, the sale and preparation of food, the checking, prevention, and cleanup of contamination, and the provision of healthy and sanitized funerals and burial sites.[59] At the same time, new government agencies including the Municipalities Bank, the Municipalities Master Plan Commission (1935), and City Engineering Commission were created to oversee the proper design and operation of Turkish cities.[60] These central planning agencies in Ankara served as technical expertise banks, loaning out their teams of planning professionals nationwide, thus making the most of a limited and valuable resource. At the same time, the assignment of several projects to a relatively small number of people, the enforcement of a uniform national building code, and the use of Ankara as the basic reference gradually imparted a certain recognizably uniform physical character to Turkish towns during the early years of the republic. These new laws and state agencies profoundly transformed the production of urban environments in Turkey.[61] Only 14 urban master plans were prepared between 1923 and 1934, but between 1934 and 1945, 238 urban plans were produced by the central planning agencies.[62]

The modernization of Turkish cities was amply advertised in government publications. Perhaps the most striking of these was a series of albums produced by the provinces on the occasion of the republic's fifteenth anniversary. Although their appearances varied somewhat, the books were produced according to a template, which dictated their title "[Name of the Province] on the Fifteenth Anniversary of the Republic" and contents. The heavily illustrated (if poorly produced) volumes documented the "improvements" made under the RPP administration in a range of areas, including construction and urban planning, education, public health, agriculture, industry, community activism, and so on. Rather than the lay public, the audience for this production seems to have been the republican bureaucracy, insofar as, in what appears to have been a mandatory gesture, the books were exchanged between the high-level government officials of the provinces.[63] For officials in the provinces, the books were a venue for proudly displaying the fruits of their labor. The government, in turn, used the series to remind its personnel of their participation in a larger project, the uniformity of which was evident in the illustrations. The possibility of

FIGURE 5.13. REPUBLICAN ELEMENTARY SCHOOLS, A SHARED DESIGN TEMPLATE WITH SLIGHT REGIONAL VARIATIONS IN DIFFERENT LOCALITIES. THE TYPE WAS MODULAR, ALLOWING VARIATIONS DEPENDING ON THE NUMBER OF STUDENTS AND CLASSROOMS. THIS RECOGNIZABLE BUILDING TYPE APPEARED IN MANY PARTS OF THE COUNTRY. ÇORUM CUMHURIYET (REPUBLIC) ELEMENTARY SCHOOL IN CENTRAL TURKEY (TOP), DİYARBAKİR ERGANİ REPUBLIC COMPREHENSIVE ELEMENTARY SCHOOL IN SOUTHEASTERN TURKEY (SECOND FROM TOP), AYDIN UMURLU ELEMENTARY SCHOOL IN WESTERN TURKEY (THIRD FROM TOP), AND MUĞLA ALİKÖY ELEMENTARY SCHOOL IN SOUTHWESTERN TURKEY (BOTTOM). COURTESY OF THE TURKISH HISTORICAL SOCIETY LIBRARY.

FIGURE 5.14. COVERS OF THE *MUĞLA* AND *BOLU* ON THE FIFTEENTH ANNIVERSARY BOOKS. COURTESY OF THE TURKISH HISTORICAL SOCIETY LIBRARY.

getting swift promotions was an incentive for enterprising and ambitious officials who were eager to contribute to this state building project. Hence, for instance, provincial administrators who negotiated for larger government funding, managed their resources judiciously, rallied their subordinates, and squeezed more work out of them, thereby accomplishing more on the ground, quickly rose through the ranks, eventually serving in larger cities, offices of higher responsibility, and sometimes even as members of parliament.[64]

Nevertheless, reality tempered ambitions. Whereas on paper the numbers were encouraging, irate exchanges between government officials in Ankara and the provinces and articles in trade publications, such as *Arkitekt* and *Belediyeler Mecmuası,* reveal the modernization of Turkish cities as a piecemeal process that was riddled with difficulties and blunders. In the first place, building new infrastructural projects and modernizing towns nationwide was very expensive and the government was chronically cash-strapped. Second, the physical challenge of setting up efficient communications between the center and the periphery, the lack of established procedures for relegating duties, the difficulty of coordinating the implementation of so many projects with so few people frequently led to costly mistakes and delays.[65] In one such instance, exasperated by the problems that plagued several municipalities, Halid Ziya, the chief engineering inspector at the State Office of Deeds and Cadastre, chiding the work of overeager government officials, warned:

> Mayors should refrain from getting involved in bigger projects than they can deal with.[66] That is, they should not jump into projects for which they lack funds or trained personnel. . . . We have seen some municipalities that have started to produce detailed building-by-building maps of their city without thinking about the length or the cost of such an enterprise and when what they really need is an accurate topographic survey that shows the roads and city blocks. . . . Maps [on different scales] should be produced gradually and prioritized according to need. How can you make a master plan for a city without producing its map first? This is why the Ministry of Interior mandated that general survey maps be completed as soon as possible. No municipality should engage in any projects before making detailed surveys of existing conditions.[67]

All these obstacles constantly delayed planning and implementation, much to the frustration of those involved. For instance, Tahsin Uzer, inspector general for the Third Region, reporting on the status of the eight provinces under his jurisdiction, ranted in a letter he wrote directly to Prime Minister İnönü:

> The question of government buildings is of utmost importance. [Yet, today, our offices] in many provinces are in [structures] that are even more dilapidated than the homes of the locals. In most county seats there are no government buildings to speak of and where there are, the buildings are in a terrible state of disrepair. Peasants and all other classes of people first look to government buildings to gauge the authority of our government. Yet their homes look much better than government buildings. It is imperative that we solve this problem methodically and soon.[68]

Written in July 1937, Uzer's letter stands in sharp contrast to the celebratory tone of Falih Rıfkı Atay's 1933 claims that the republican administration had radically transformed both the image of Turkish cities and how people lived in them.[69] The tone and contents of numerous letters and reports similar to the one penned by Uzer also reveal that the accomplishments advertised in the provinces on the fifteenth anniversary series were only skin-deep. The uniform applicability of ideas conceived in Ankara to the rest of the country as if "shaping dough using the same mold" was highly questionable.[70] As Turkey's leaders well understood but rarely admitted, both the physical and social landscapes of the country were far too variegated to standardize in a quick and painless manner.

PERFORMING THE NATION'S SPACE

The quest for national integration included strategies that went beyond modifying the physical environment. Taking possession of the national territory also meant controlling the symbolic meanings of that landscape. Turkey's leaders were as adamant about building a standard scaffolding as they were about prescribing how it would be used and understood by the polity. The material culture of the republic obviously had to facilitate routine utilitarian transactions. But it was also meant to serve as tangible proof of Turkey's inexorable journey toward becoming a modern unified nation-state. The individual components of this emerging symbolic landscape were reminders of that larger official narrative of unity and progress. Together they conjured up an imagined web that resided in people's minds and came to life through their bodies as they moved through the structure provided by the roads, railroads, and urban spaces.

To disseminate these notions, Turkey's leaders deployed a variety of means, including print and broadcast media, formal education, and myriad events that called for public participation. Among these, ceremonies that commemorated the anniversaries of the significant events of the nationalist movement constituted prime opportunities to reach out to a broad spectrum of the public and remind them of their achievements and goals as a nation. On these occasions roads, railroads, streets, and ultimately, bodies became the sites of nationwide pageantry in which the repeating patterns of movement, synchronized rhythms, and shared silences were intended to confer a sense of unity on the landscape and its inhabitants. In contrast to the tangibility of the infrastructural webs, these events produced ephemeral webs in space by interweaving the concrete and the abstract, the experiential and the imagined through shared activities. They also complemented the material strategies of nation building, by filling the gaps where the physical structures fell short and presenting those as yet out-of-reach goals of unity, prosperity, and modernity as already having been accomplished. Hence, despite their short life span, these participatory performances were indispensable to the RPP's integration strategies because they generated shared experiences and invested the built environment with lasting meanings that transcended its everyday uses.

Among commemorative celebrations, those performed on the tenth anniversary of the foundation of the republic were, by all accounts, the most ambitious. After a turbulent decade, during which the legitimacy of their rule and the validity of the reforms they introduced were continually challenged, Turkey's leaders were determined to make full use of this meaningful occasion to proclaim their success and publicly reaffirm their resolve to continue pursuing their agenda against all odds. Accordingly, they set up an official preparation committee to ensure that "the celebrations in the largest cities as well as the smallest hamlets would be equally lively, exuberant, bright, meaningful, and thought-provoking."[71] The committee strove to create a recognizably uniform experience of festivities across the country. Their approach closely resembled the standardization that informed the state-provided sites and services. The committee issued detailed guidelines about the schedule, format, and content of the events; specified how to decorate the streets and buildings; designed the flags and banners to be carried by the scout troops, military units, and schools; and went so far as to standardize the clothing and the accessories to be worn in the pageant.[72] In mid-July 1933, more than three months before the festivities, the committee announced that they expected to involve one and a half million people in the ceremonies. This was no small feat, for it meant that one in every ten citizens would partake in the events. To achieve this goal, the committee enlisted the support of high-ranking officials such as provincial governors and regional military commanders and the services of rank-and-file government personnel (teachers, nurses and midwives, military personnel, postal workers, technicians, and civil servants), many of whom were idealistic in their commitment to the goals outlined by the RPP leadership and thus volunteered their time.

For its part, the RPP deployed its national network to help with the preparations and dissemination of information. The party also provided free flags and banners for poor and remote parts of the country.[73] In addition to their festive quality, these posters and banners had an obvious didactic purpose. They were designed to convey to a largely illiterate audience, in visually accessible ways, their achievements as a nation under the republican regime. Most of these posters and banners were crude by any graphic design standards. However, their message of progress—concretized in side-by-side comparisons between the republic and the empire, or charts that graphically depicted constant growth—was hard to miss. Also, the party's undercover public speakers (Halk Hatipleri) were handed their talking points and instructions about how to seize the opportunity to give "spontaneous" speeches extolling the virtues of the republican administration.[74]

As a general rule, the tenth anniversary processions were to start from entrances to towns, and, if possible, at train stations. They were to continue down the newly opened avenues, incorporating the new institutional and administrative buildings into their itinerary, culminating in the Republic Square. In places that did not yet have a Republic Square, the tenth anniversary would be the occasion to make one—even if makeshift. In small villages as well, peasants were ordered to clear up the largest square, place a block of stone as a focal point in its middle, and if possible, crown it with a bust of Atatürk. The date of the tenth anniversary was to be etched on this stone and the square was to be named after the republic. Thus at 8:30 p.m. on October 29, at exactly the time when the republic was proclaimed in Ankara a decade earlier, peasants and urbanites, young and old—in short, the entire nation—could gather around a Republic Square to commemorate the dawn of a new era. If the climactic moment of all commemorative ceremonies in Ankara was paying homage to Atatürk in person, in the provinces, small towns, and villages the Atatürk monument played substitute. Students, scouts, and soldiers laid wreaths at the pedestal in the presence of the highest civil and military officials who brought the ceremony to a meaningful closure with their speeches about the historical significance of the day.

Not only was the entire program for the three-day festivity completely scripted months ahead of time but also the government made sure that everybody knew about it. Newspapers and radio broadcast information about the schedule of the processions so that everyone knew that everywhere in Turkey their compatriots were also engaged in the same activity. Since there were so few radios, loudspeakers were placed in the newly minted Republic Squares so that whoever was downtown within earshot could hear the broadcast and take part in the event. Moreover, people were encouraged to travel and visit other cities and commune with their compatriots to experience this grand festivity. The state railroad company lowered its fares to facilitate transportation, inviting people to explore the "iron web." One such poster urged:

> Compatriots!
> Take advantage of the low fares in effect for the tenth anniversary of our
>   republic
> Visit the four corners of our country.
> Visit friends and family living in other cities,
> Come to see the seat of your government, Ankara.
> Because loving our Republic means loving our country.[75]

In the Turkey of the 1930s few would have had the means to travel long distances just to observe the festivities, although memoirs and contemporary newspapers provide some anecdotal evidence that, taking advantage of the discounts and the extended holiday, some indeed scheduled their visits with family and friends in large towns to coincide with the tenth anniversary celebrations.[76] The most prominent journey was the one scout troops from around the country took yearly to Ankara to perform at the anniversary of the republic, which Cüneyt Arcayürek—though a frequent critic of the regime—wistfully recalls as having enlivened the city:

> Scout troops came to Ankara from every province. Instruction was interrupted for this occasion each year, and every high school building in town was vacated, the desks were moved out of the classrooms. Outdoor kitchens were set up in schoolyards and food was prepared in large pots. And thousands of scouts coming from all parts of the country camped out at the schools, eating, drinking, and sleeping together for an entire week. . . . Cheering crowds watched the daily rehearsals of the troops marching through the streets of the capital toward the Hippodrome, with their bands, horns, and trumpets. Also . . . the schoolyards were used for practice at all hours . . . because [the representatives of] every province wanted to impress İnönü and Atatürk with their discipline during the actual performance.[77]

Clearly, the tenth anniversary celebrations required more effort and funds than had festivities of previous years in order to produce such a comprehensive program supported by ancillary activities such as publications, film screenings, and exhibitions. Such fanfare could only be repeated on important anniversaries like the fifteenth or the twenty-fifth, but the program itself forged a template that could be replicated, albeit more modestly, in all commemorative ceremonies. Over the years, the provisional sites along the parade routes—such as monuments, buildings, and bridges—were replaced with permanent ones. Their inaugurations were often scheduled to coincide with a commemorative event, reinforcing the notion that such ceremonies were part of the narrative of progress, and artifacts were both actual and symbolic milestones.[78]

By synchronizing the course of events and standardizing the material culture of the pageantry, the RPP administration tried to instill a sense of unity in the people. The isomorphic layouts for the new parts of towns, devised by the planners, were to bolster this perception through experience. When woven into the paths of commemorative processions and integrated into the scenario of reenactments, streets, monuments, and other sites that were visited during these events took on new meanings. The sequence of

FIGURE 5.15. CELEBRATIONS OF THE FIFTEENTH ANNIVERSARY OF THE TURKISH REPUBLIC IN SEVERAL CITIES ACROSS THE COUNTRY (WITH IMAGES FROM SİVAS, BALIKESIR, ZONGULDAK, ESKİŞEHİR, MARAŞ, ORDU), AS REPORTED IN THE DAILY SEMIOFFICIAL NEWSPAPER ULUS, 1938.

rituals created new adjacencies and spatial relations among the different elements of the urban landscape based on movement and perception in time rather than evident physical locations. In other words, as part of a fixed series of destinations to be visited, landmarks could be imagined as being arranged linearly over time even though they were not situated as such on the map. This peculiar ability to imagine a web of spatial relationships between physically remote places that were not immediately visible or accessible was an important sensibility that the republican administration intended to cultivate in the citizenry.

The Early Republican townscape had a didactic purpose: it was a reservoir of historical narratives that unfolded as one moved through the city. Lest one missed the point during the processions, the streets and structures that composed this new landscape were named after nationalist heroes, key events from the War of Independence, or the foundational ideas of Turkey's new order, such as nation, liberation, independence, and freedom.[79] The choice of names for specific sites was important, but so were the meanings and associations invoked by their physical juxtaposition. As with interior minister Şükrü Kaya at the inauguration of İnönü Avenue in Izmir, they also took every opportunity to explicate these meanings:

> To honor the name of İsmet Paşa, one of the greatest sons of the Turkish Revolution and foremost heroes of Gazi's reforms, is a privilege for the city that witnessed his birth. To name the road leading to the Gazi Monument after İsmet Paşa is meaningful and ingenious. I sincerely congratulate those who thought of it. The beginning of the road that leads us to the goals defined by Gazi is behind us now. Our journey on this path has been difficult and full of sacrifices. I would like to pay tribute today to those who shed their blood and gave their lives fighting to open our path.[80]

The narrative emanating from these acts of naming and highly stylized reenactments reframed history to lend exclusive legitimacy to the current regime. Republican officials carefully edited the Ottoman heritage out of the official history they disseminated, or they portrayed it in a manner that favored the accomplishments of the republic. Similarly, the landmarks that made the Ottoman city, the spaces, and artifacts associated with the Ottoman past were excluded from the paths of commemorative pageants, even though they were better known and likely to be more meaningful to the people. Official history was selective about its heroes and villains, its miracles and catastrophes. Although internal uprisings during and after the War of Independence were just as threatening as the advances of the Allies-backed Greek armies, they were never acknowledged and their suppression was not venerated in quite the same way. Official history rendered those voices of internal dissent silent, both in ceremonies and in textbooks.[81] Political authority generated the historiographic license necessary to produce narratives that were socially and politically expedient if not true to the facts.[82] The nationalist movement, the War of Independence, and finally the republic were portrayed as Turkey's manifest destiny, which took the collaborative efforts of the entire nation, united under one flag against a common enemy. References to the composite makeup of the citizenry, its divergent experiences and loyalties, were deliberately excluded from this account, as were the effects of these over the course of events.

Whereas official history depicted the rise of a unified nation as a seamless narrative, internal cohesion continued to be a contentious issue for many years after the War of Independence.[83] Forbidden narratives coexisted and often crossed paths with the official one, and when their unfolding threatened the performance of the latter, officials did not hesitate to unleash the state's superior means of coercion at their disposal to preempt their inscription in the same spaces. In the fall of 1937, for instance, having heard that Mustafa Kemal would visit Elazığ as part of his Eastern Turkey tour, the one that had also included Diyarbakır, "six thousand tribesmen from the mountains in their [traditional] white pants" descended on the city in hopes of meeting with him and petitioning him to spare Seyit Rıza's life.[84] Rıza had been caught and placed on trial just weeks before as the lead conspirator in the 1937 Dersim rebellion. Such an unscripted encounter would, at best, be embarrassing for the officials in charge of maintaining order in the region—and at worst, it was dangerous. To prevent it from ever taking place, with the implicit permission of the regional inspector general (Abdullah Doğan) and under the supervision of the National Police Chief (Şükrü Sökmensüer), government officials expedited the process and executed Seyit Rıza and his front men at dawn on November 17, 1937, hours before Mustafa Kemal's arrival. This was in violation even of the laws that already gave them extraordinary powers, but, as Sökmensüer argued, by the time Mustafa Kemal came, "it would have been too late."

In retrospect, this defused confrontation casts Mustafa Kemal's 1937 tour of Eastern Turkey in a different light. It not only exposes the visit for the staged production it was by undermining the laudatory tone of its coverage at the time but also reveals how deep the fractures in the constitution of the new state were, and how close to the surface. When recontextualized in relation to the explosive circumstances within which it actually took place, Mustafa Kemal's visit may be interpreted as a necessary performance to reaffirm state authority against a population that continued to fight it. A visit from Ankara was also important for local officials, who had to deal with the everyday challenges on the ground, since it was public confirmation that they had the central government's support. Similarly, the selection of Mustafa Kemal's itinerary and the largely military composition of his entourage were rhetorical tools to remind the audience of the state's military might. Particularly remarkable within this ensemble was the visibility of Sabiha Gökçen, Mustafa Kemal's adopted daughter, who was also Turkey's first female fighter pilot. Gökçen had just returned from a widely publicized tour of duty having served in the Elazığ-Dersim area, where airpower had given a distinct advantage to the government forces. In this punitive performance, Gökçen stood for the state's superior firepower. Moreover, the fact that her status as a young female warrior impugned the masculinity of the state's opponents could not have been lost on anyone.

An equally important consideration for those who decided to prevent the encounter between Mustafa Kemal and the petitioners was a concern for preserving and disseminating the official narrative. Mustafa Kemal traveled with several journalists and a film crew who would chronicle his tour of the East for the rest of Turkey. In the early years of the republic, the press was strictly censored—those proposing alternative narratives or critiquing the current order paid a heavy price for their actions. As a result, few outside eastern and southeastern Turkey were aware of the scale of the military engagement. It was largely unknown to the rest of the population that fifty thousand troops had been deployed to Dersim, that this was the state's costliest operation, and that thousands of civilians had been killed and additional thousands displaced. The ability to frame the events, editing out inconvenient truths past and present, were integral to the state's self-preservation. Without acknowledging that context, however, our understanding of the meaning and functions of state-sponsored performances—celebratory or punitive—would remain incomplete.

CONCLUSION

In the summer of 1921, in the thick of the Sakarya Battle, during which Greek troops advanced so dangerously close to Central Anatolia that the thunder of gunfire could be heard from the outskirts of Ankara, Mustafa Kemal declared, "There is no *line* of defense; there is a *surface* of defense. And that surface is the entire country."[85] The meaning of this assertion gets lost on us these days, not because so many of Mustafa Kemal's statements are indiscriminately excerpted and circulated for such a variety of ideological purposes that they effectively blend into the background as gray noise but because we are no longer able to imagine why the difference between a "line of defense" and "a surface of defense" mattered. In the early 1920s when Mustafa Kemal issued his call to arms, battleground was a localized concept in the popular imagination: it was confined to the immediate vicinity of the conflagration and dissipated as one moved away. As illustrated in the anecdote from Halide Edip's memoir at the beginning of this chapter, what tied individual communities to the battleground were the men they sent to the front and not the terrain that lay between them and the line of fire. By calling for a "surface of defense" comprising "the entire country," Mustafa Kemal was proposing to bring every inch of that land into the social imagination as part of a collective responsibility. Hence, beyond a statement designed to boost morale at a time when the war looked all but lost, Mustafa Kemal's words must be interpreted as a call for a fundamentally different way of thinking about what constituted community and the object of its allegiances. The idea of nationhood, as Mustafa Kemal pictured it, invoked both a people and the well-bounded territory they inhabited.

In this chapter, by exploring the intimate links between state, space, and ideology, I have sought to demonstrate that Turkey's leaders understood nation building as a spatial challenge and implemented strategies intended to transform the physical shape and prescribe the symbolic meanings of the landscape. National integration called for the maximum mobilization of the human and material resources of the fledgling Turkish state. As amply evidenced in the correspondence of high-ranking officials, asserting the state's presence and prowess by creating new paths of accessibility—thereby breaking open previously isolated communities and linking them to the national unit—and reconfiguring the layout of cities with new buildings, avenues, and monuments were of paramount importance. Republican leaders expected spatial integration to effectively allow the state to permeate the furthest reaches of the national geography to extract resources, provide services, and, importantly, keep the activities and allegiances of the citizenry in check. The performative strategies they devised—ranging from commemorative ceremonies to state visits, designed to convey both the founding myths and the operational tenets of the new state to the public at large—were similarly spatial in nature.

As continued attempts to suppress internal dissent—ranging from censorship to military intervention—indicate, the question of national integration remained a raw nerve for long years after the war. Resistance was rife given Turkey's heterogeneous demography, vast geographic differences, and disparate economic opportunities. Not everybody willingly yielded their critical judgments to the RPP's transparently ideological—

and often self-serving—actions. Yet, over time, the efforts of RPP leaders to carve and sustain a broader jurisdiction for the state and their relentless emphasis on producing the infrastructural scaffolding this required generated a recognizable material culture of the modern state in Turkey. Crucially, the RPP administration instituted the defaults for the procedures of governance and cultivated a growing body of civil servants who had both personal and ideological stakes in the state's functionality. Eventually, the maintenance and expansion of the state's material apparatus became the responsibility of anyone who assumed power regardless of their political persuasions. Though, in later years, local governments gained some degree of autonomy, central government agencies have continued to commission wholesale prototypical schools, offices, and housing for civil servants, and especially the military. Consequently, a certain sense of uniformity remains pervasive in the Turkish landscape.

CHAPTER 6

MANUFACTURING TURKISH CITIZENS

Modern nationality is a spatial concept, much in the way that the nation-state is territorial. The spatiality of national affiliation goes beyond the "willingness to die for a specific piece of land" or claim to self-rule over that land—although it includes those sentiments. In fact, developing such profound affective ties depends on possessing a comparably deep knowledge of a people and their cultural landscape. The concept of modern nationality comprises an amalgam of spatial imagination and spatial practices that are internalized through explicit and implicit lifelong experiences acquired both by immersion and in formal settings—such as schools. Learning to construct a quick map of France, shaped like a hexagon, or grasping the logic by which the Jeffersonian grid confers order on the entirety of the vast American landscape are examples of the skills one acquires as a result of this kind of socialization. More generally, the ideas and practices that constitute the spatial dimension of nationality include familiarity with a particular geography and its organizational logic and internal hierarchies. They comprise the skills to navigate that geography, to recognize the shared and mutually accepted ways of using and organizing space at different scales ranging from that of the near environment to that of the country as a whole, and to orient oneself within them. These ideas and practices operate as interdependent and cumulative webs of skills and information. Their ubiquity and simplicity of use mask the complex developments that brought them into being and the cognitive processes that need to be mobilized by individuals to effectively make use of them. Unspoken and often taken for granted, they become recognizable as cultural constructs only when one is exposed to an unfamiliar context and compelled to cope with equally complex patterns for using and organizing the physical world.

This chapter examines Kemalist leaders' attempts to "produce" a Turkish nation that was unified in its social and territorial allegiances and modern in its outlook. Central to their efforts was the use of spatial strategies designed to inculcate the masses with a sense of territorial attachment, a shared notion of spatial order, and the habits of body and mind to sustain these ideas and transmit them to future generations. Also, the model citizen outlined in the republican rhetoric was urban—yet the majority of Turkey's population was rural, the state had a limited reach into the countryside, and its implicit alliances with rural elites, whose support was vital for internal stability, precluded introducing social reforms that could challenge their long-established authority.[1] The republican drive to incorporate a uniform notion of spatiality into the definition of community was a radical departure from the Ottoman system of millets, which coexisted within overlapping localities and did not necessarily regard exclusive custody of a territory as one of their defining characteristics. To realign the polity's collective allegiances around the idea of a space-bound and homogeneous national community, Turkey's leaders sought to bring all channels of cultural dissemination under strict state control. This strategy was inextricably linked to the decommissioning of the institutions and undermining of the practices through which each millet had historically preserved and transmitted its cultural heritage, covered in part II, "Erasures in the Land."

Republican ambitions for change were all encompassing, consequently they tried to permeate the reaches of social life that had never been part of the state's jurisdiction—or, for that matter, its interests. An exhaustive account of all the sites and services they attempted to take over is beyond the scope of this chapter. Instead, I focus on three of the most representative republican institutions, namely, elementary schools, Girls' Institutes, and Halkevleri, the RPP-controlled community centers, all of which provided formal instructional settings designed to transform individuals into citizens. Specifically, I examine how the spatial practices they engendered contributed to republican efforts to forge a unified, patriotic, and progressive national culture. Despite variations in their respective audiences and the techniques they employed, these institutions displayed striking similarities in their messages and activities. Some of their offerings were practical, such as providing the visual and spatial literacy necessary to orient oneself within Turkey and a working knowledge of republican infrastructure. Others were designed to condition people's ideas about spatial and temporal organization—teaching students by example and through numerous drills to gain an appreciation for the Western-inspired rationalization of tasks, schedules, and spatial layouts. In many places, these institutions also served as the settings for the introduction of European tastes and patterns of socialization into the Turkish repertoire. Finally, ideological concerns were never too far below the surface as participants were expected to internalize values and meanings associated with space, its uses, and its abstractions. In other words, these institutions mediated the propagation of officially sanctioned ideas about selfhood, community, civilization, history, and authority to the public through choreographed collective performances.

This chapter focuses on the role of educational institutions in producing a shared sense of national space and facilitating the social and cultural reproduction of the nation to ensure the longevity of the neophyte state. Modern institutions, especially those facilitating cultural transmission, have long been of interest to scholars for their role in eradicating historical cleavages between regions and communities and expediting the creation of incorporated and rationalized societies.[2] Nevertheless, even in the most insightful analyses, spaces and spatial practices appear at best as backdrops to legal, political, or economic actions. How institutions sort, link, or confine actors and activities through their physical configuration, thereby stitching people to place and nation to land, often eludes scrutiny. A spatial analysis of institutions is necessary not only because they are prominent presences in the landscape and require a substantial investment of resources to build and maintain but also because they are instrumental in reconditioning people's understanding of and relationship to the social and physical world around them.

IMAGINING TURKEY

Republican leaders made nationalizing education a centerpiece of their pursuit of unity and homogeneity even before the end of the War of Independence. Education in the Ottoman Empire had historically been under the jurisdiction of the millets.[3] Although secular institutions of higher learning were introduced with the nineteenth-century reforms, millets retained control over the education of younger pupils. Secular primary and secondary schools were not established until the reign of Abdülhamid II in the late nineteenth century. As with other Ottoman reforms, these new schools did not eliminate existing ones but were added on to an existing and complex panoply of choices. Consequently, multiple types of schools and educational systems that were redundant or even mutually incompatible coexisted in the empire. The Unification of Education Act

(Tevhid-i Tedrisat Kanunu), signed into law with the first wave of republican reforms in 1924, marked a radical departure from this state of affairs by bringing the contents and the delivery of all formal education in Turkey under the exclusive control of the Ministry of Education. The law closed down all schools affiliated with Islamic religious institutions and imposed strict controls over schools operated by minorities, foreign missionary organizations, and other private entities—even at the expense of flouting the provisions of the Treaty of Lausanne.[4] In 1926, a constitutional amendment made elementary education compulsory for all children in Turkey.

In short order, Turkey's leaders established the agencies in charge of articulating comprehensive pedagogical goals and ensuring the uniform implementation of a standard system of education.[5] Among them, the Instruction and Pedagogy Committee (IPC) had—and still has—a strong influence on shaping pedagogical choices and educational policies as the sole authority formulating the curricula, overseeing the content, design, and production of textbooks, suggesting teaching methods, and providing continuing education courses for teachers. In this section, I examine the spatial and material dimension of the pedagogical techniques endorsed by the IPC for elementary and middle school students—a critical period during which children develop lasting ideas about selfhood in relation to a community of peers, individual and cooperative work habits, and the fundamental skills that are valued in their society.[6] The sampling of exercises below illustrates just how central the students' closely monitored participation in the material culture of the republic was to their passage from childhood to citizenship.

In "The Use of Pictures in Geography Education" that he wrote for *İlköğretim Haftası* (Elementary Education Week), Hakkı İzet, a professor at the Gazi Teachers' College, underlined the importance of images in conveying ideas and information. Izet recommended the use of pictures, graphics, and photographs in textbooks and also called for further "exploitation of the magical powers of this means of expression."[7] He argued that students' appreciation of images should be cultivated in order to supplement applied or text-based learning. İzet placed particular emphasis on improving students' cartographic skills. His essay contained several illustrated examples and tips for teaching elementary school students how to construct a quick freehand map of Turkey, how to situate Turkey within its region, and how to estimate the relative proportions of the country's dimensions and those of its neighbors. He outlined various geometric techniques to render the task simple and addressed the potential problems that might be encountered in the classroom. İzet's instructions also included pointers for drawing the map on the blackboard, which, he warned

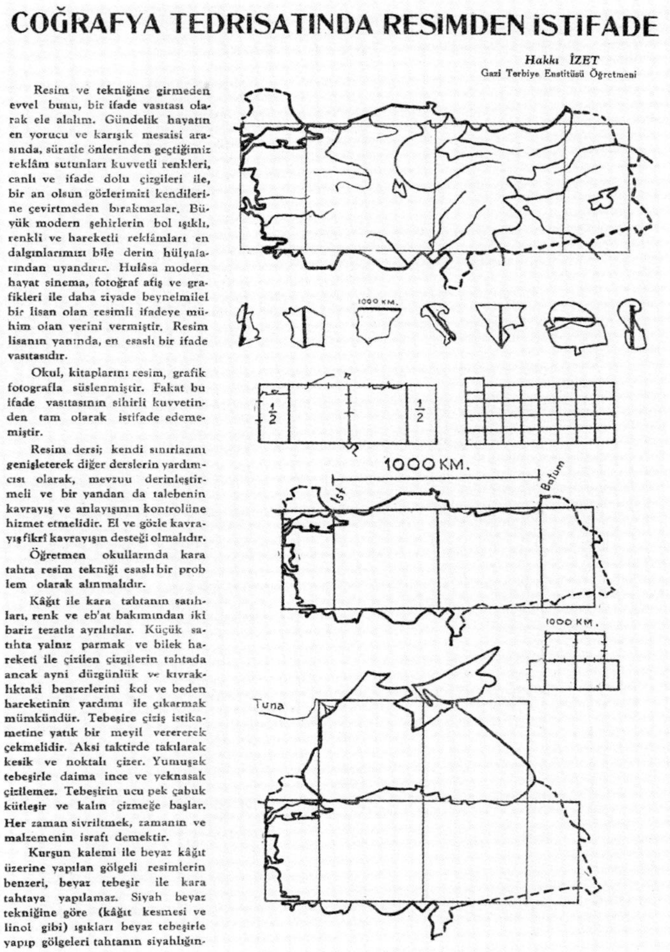

COĞRAFYA TEDRİSATINDA RESİMDEN İSTİFADE

Hakkı İZET
Gazi Terbiye Enstitüsü Öğretmeni

Resim ve tekniğine girmeden evvel bunu, bir ifade vasıtası olarak ele alalım. Gündelik hayatın en yorucu ve karışık mesaisi arasında, süratle önlerinden geçtiğimiz reklâm sutunları kuvvetli renkleri, canlı ve ifade dolu çizgileri ile, bir an olsun gözlerimizi kendilerine çevirtmeden bırakmazlar. Büyük modern şehirlerin bol ışıklı, renkli ve hareketli reklâmları en dalgınlarımızı bile derin hülyalarından uyandırır. Hulâsa modern hayat sinema, fotoğraf afiş ve grafikleri ile daha ziyade beynelmilel bir lisan olan resimli ifadeye mühim olan yerini vermiştir. Resim lisanın yanında, en esaslı bir ifade vasıtasıdır.

Okul, kitaplarını resim, grafik fotografla süslenmiştir. Fakat bu ifade vasıtasının sihirli kuvvetinden tam olarak istifade edememiştir.

Resim dersi; kendi sınırlarını genişleterek diğer derslerin yardımcısı olarak, mevzuu derinleştirmeli ve bir yandan da talebenin kavrayış ve anlayışının kontrolüne hizmet etmelidir. El ve gözle kavrayış fikrî kavrayışın desteği olmalıdır.

Öğretmen okullarında kara tahta resim tekniği esaslı bir problem olarak alınmalıdır.

Kâğıt ile kara tahtanın satıhları, renk ve eb'at bakımından iki bariz tezatla ayrılırlar. Küçük satıhta yalnız parmak ve bilek hareketi ile çizilen çizgilerin tahtada ancak ayni düzgünlük ve kıvraklıktaki benzerlerini kol ve beden hareketinin yardımı ile çıkarmak mümkündür. Tebeşire çiziş istikametine yatık bir meyil vererek çekmelidir. Aksi taktirde takılarak kesik ve noktalı çizer. Yumuşak tebeşirle daima ince ve yeknasak çizilemez. Tebeşirin ucu pek çabuk kütleşir ve kalın çizmeğe başlar. Her zaman sivriltmek, zamanın ve malzemenin israfı demektir.

Kurşun kalemi ile beyaz kâğıt üzerine yapılan gölgeli resimlerin benzeri, beyaz tebeşir ile kara tahtaya yapılamaz. Siyah beyaz tekniğine göre (kâğıt kesmesi ve linol gibi) ışıkları beyaz tebeşirle yapıp gölgeleri tahtanın siyahlığın-

FIGURE 6.1. İZET'S EXERCISES FOR LEARNING TO DRAW AND HOW TO TEACH ELEMENTARY SCHOOL STUDENTS TO DRAW A FREEHAND MAP OF TURKEY. COURTESY OF VEKAM, VEHBİ KOÇ AND ANKARA RESEARCH CENTER.

teachers, presented its own challenges due to the larger scale of the board and the peculiarities of drawing with a light-colored chalk on a dark background. His main concern was not so much to draw perfectly precise maps, such as one would find in an atlas, as it was to acquire a clear mental image of the country through repeated practice. Thus he recommended drawing quick sketches of Turkey, which were identifiable "through the articulation of its most recognizable features."[8]

The progeny of this exercise can be traced to the mutually interdependent development of modern map production technologies and the expansion of the modern state apparatus. Maps presented a particularly useful medium for modern (and mostly western European) states, which were interested in anchoring the loyalty of their polity in a common territory they inhabited, by providing identifiable visual representations of that territory. Hence as several historians of cartography have pointed out, especially during the second half of the nineteenth century, states took a particular interest in the design and dissemination of maps to bolster their territorial claims.[9] Notably, during the same period, exercises designed to teach children how to read and navigate a map or locate themselves on it became increasingly more common in mass public education curricula—in Europe and later the Ottoman Empire—as basic cartographic literacy was among the key sets of skills with which modern states sought to equip their citizens.[10] In addition, improved printing technology—thus the availability of cheaper prints—gradually brought maps out of the exclusive preserve of the privileged elite and increasingly into ordinary/common people's sphere of awareness.

Nineteenth-century Ottoman reformers were similarly interested in forging and disseminating an easily identifiable cartographic image of the empire. This concern was particularly evident in their decision to introduce a new type of map for classroom use. Until the last decade of the century, Ottoman classroom maps were organized by continent, following European practices.[11] These maps, by definition, could not coherently show the empire's landholdings straddling three continents in their entirety, hindering, thereby, the possibility of visualizing it as a single entity. To remedy this problem, Ottoman officials introduced a map that centered on the empire and displayed for the first time the imperial landholdings in Europe, Asia, and Africa on one single sheet.[12] This new map resembled what later scholars have termed a "logo map," which may be described as a readily recognizable, two-dimensional abstraction of the state as a discrete and internally coherent geopolitical unit. This important shift in Ottoman cartography, which took place during the reign of Sultan Abdülhamit II, coincided with increased state investment in expanding basic Western-style public education. Given the number of schools at the time, the new map had limited reach, but its influence as a concept was enduring because the majority of the republic's founding cadre consisted of men who had first acquired their sense of the state and its territoriality from these maps in Hamidian schools.

The republican geography curriculum inherited this incipient conceptualization of the logo map and expanded on it. İzet's proposed pedagogy elicited a more intense cognitive engagement with the shape of the map as it required the ability to reproduce it from memory. His technique had a wide circulation, appearing both in *İlköğretim Haftası*, an influential trade publication for elementary school teachers and administrators, and in textbooks for teachers' colleges, securing its place within the desirable skill set for an elementary school teacher. A ceramicist by training, Hakkı İzet taught mold construction at Gazi Teachers' College—a specialization that had certain parallels to the map exercise in that both required translation between abstract visions and tangible forms.[13] İzet's technique consisted of using simple geometric forms, such as rectangles and triangles, as building blocks to compose more complex geographic forms. Constructing a map of Turkey was not any different from constructing other objects or drawing formal sketches in preparation for building a ceramics mold. Unlike those objects, however, the map of Turkey as a discrete entity—with clearly demarcated boundaries separating it from everything around it—did not exist outside the imagination. İzet's technique associated drawing a map with life drawing but, while the latter was an abstraction of actual objects that were within everyone's reach, the former was the representation of an abstraction that nobody ever actually saw or held. İzet's recruitment to develop this exercise reveals much about the way republican educational policy makers wanted students to imagine Turkey. The common technique used to draw maps and objects tacitly implied the interchangeability between physical reality and its representation, and most important, that Turkey should be thought of as a freestanding object.

The significance of establishing this shape as the default and unalterable image of Turkey through repeated exercises becomes evident especially when viewed in relation to the political climate at the time and the ideological disposition of Turkey's leadership. One of the foundational premises of the new Turkish state was "the country, within its national boundaries, is an indivisible whole." Originally introduced in the wording of the National Oath in 1919 the statement has, over the years, been included in letter or spirit in various subsequent incarnations of the Turkish Constitution. İzet's maps were a visual expression of precisely this premise. However, although the logo map projected a reassuring image of immutable spatial specificity, things were far from stable on the ground. In the first place, Turkey's boundaries remained in flux for years after the Treaty of Lausanne. The disputes between Turkey and Great Britain over the exact location of the southeastern border with modern-day Iraq were not resolved until 1926. Also, until the 1936 signing of the Montreux Convention, Turkey's sovereignty over the Straits was compromised by their demilitarization and oversight by an international Straits Commission. Lastly, after contentious negotiations involving Turkey, France, Syria, and the League of Nations, the southern province of Hatay was annexed in 1939—incidentally, İzet's exercise first appeared in pedagogical publications that same year.[14] Second, internal cohesion remained an elusive goal even after the recognition of Turkey's international borders. As discussed earlier, the country was reeling from the devastation of wars and forced

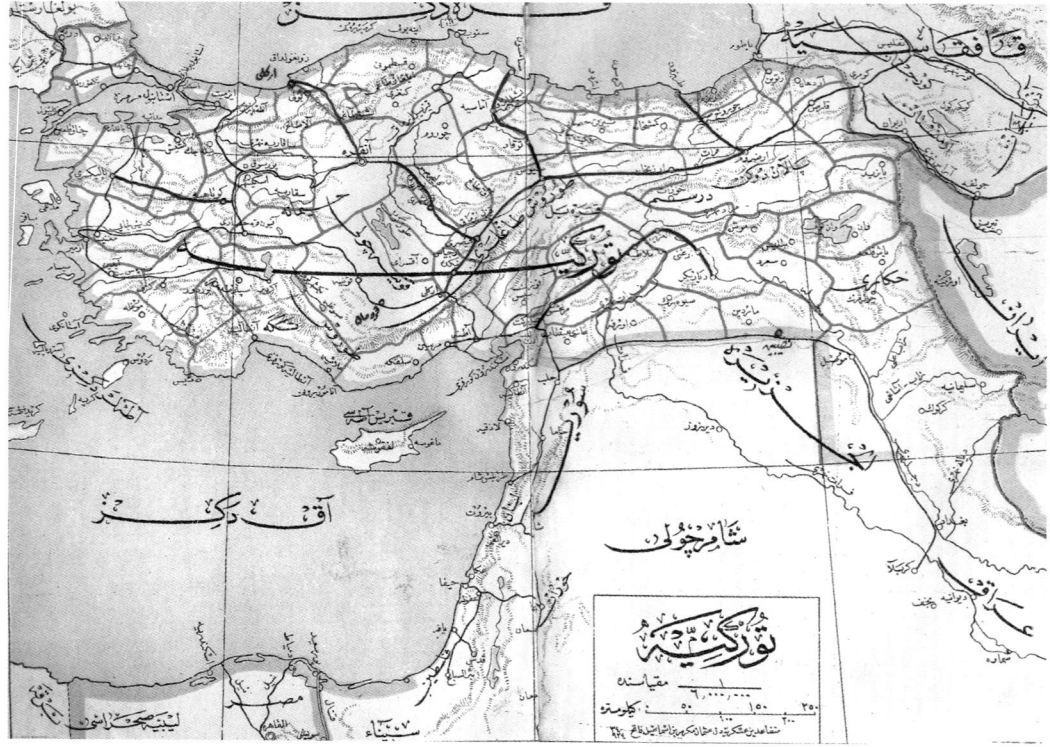

FIGURE 6.2. A GEOGRAPHY TEXTBOOK FROM 1926. NOTE THE UNRESOLVED SOUTHEASTERN BORDER WITH IRAQ. AT THE TIME THE PROVINCE OF HATAY WAS NOT YET PART OF TURKEY AND WAS STILL A FRENCH PROTECTORATE. HATAY BECAME PART OF TURKEY IN 1939. COURTESY OF VEKAM, VEHBİ KOÇ, AND ANKARA RESEARCH CENTER.

migrations and population exchanges, which had substantially transformed its demographic makeup. Sharp geographical differences and the uneven history of economic development and state penetration further impeded achieving stability. The refusal of the predominantly Kurdish population in eastern and southeastern Turkey to submit to the republic's centralizing policies kept the army in a constant state of mobilization in this region. Against this background of external and internal contentions, the logo map of Turkey was a discursive tool that downplayed the discrepancies between ideological desires and reality, depicting the country not as it was but as its leaders would like it to be.[15] Notably, monopoly over education, among other things, gave the state the upper hand in visually framing Turkey's indivisible integrity. Having internalized this image of Turkey as the default once and at a very early stage in their lives, republican generations would find it more difficult to accept alternatives or amendments to the land that they would have grown to know as theirs in its entirety.

In addition to burning the shape of the country into children's minds, map exercises familiarized them with the contents of that form. Students were expected to become knowledgeable enough to draw the course of rivers, locate mountain ranges, pinpoint mining fields and industrial centers, and identify crops grown in different regions on the map. They were frequently prompted to put this image to use in other classes as well. The IPC required that all subjects be infused with patriotic themes and urged teachers to "take every opportunity to foster and reinforce children's national consciousness." Reading assignments thus included a wealth of essays and poems about Turkey's geography, its natural resources, history, and traditions. Mathematics assignments featured road problems about traveling times and distances between different provinces, which were designed to invoke the national map, albeit indirectly.[16] The objective, quite clearly, was not merely to sharpen children's reading or computational skills but, more important, to reinforce by reiteration their awareness of a larger shared national geography.[17]

The IPC recommended complementing the cartography exercises, which were usually completed indoors, with practical projects and field trips. These were to help students acquire the mental agility to move nimbly between physical reality and its representations and understand the relationship between their everyday settings and their cartographic abstraction. The committee noted that what was learned experientially had "more staying power in children's minds" and added, "it is essential that children learn through observation and praxis and that they witness phenomena in situ: this will refine their perspicacity. . . . Providing concrete examples makes the contents of the curriculum—especially elusive concepts—easier to grasp."[18] Accordingly, the IPC oversaw the development of exercises that weaved together the textual and the experiential. These included short excursions, which made use of the immediate vicinity of schools as teaching tools. Kemal Kaya, who authored *İlkokulda Coğrafya Öğretimi* (Teaching Geography in Elementary Schools), the standard manual for elementary education teachers, argued that the vicinity of the school building was an indispensable component of the new learning process and that all subjects—from mathematics to science, history, art, and even Turkish language—in the elementary school curriculum stood to benefit from field trips.[19]

Contemporary trade publications suggested using the republican public works projects as teaching tools and provided sample exercises for teachers across the country to emulate. A rather striking example of good practice, which appeared on the back cover of the November 16, 1939, issue of *İlköğretim Haftası*, featured third-grade students at the Izmir Bayraklı Elementary School, being supervised by their teacher during a mathematics class field trip. In the photograph a group of children appears kneeling on the ground with measuring sticks in their hands, determining the width and length of railroad tracks. According to the caption, the field trip constituted an excellent example of how units of length could be taught through practical exercises. This image is remarkable because, if the goal were merely to teach the units of length by actually measuring the sizes of everyday objects, that certainly could have been accomplished in places less dangerous than railroad tracks. However, given the IPC's emphasis on instilling a sense of belonging to a larger geographic unit extending beyond what was readily visible or accessible, it is possible to think of other motives. Railroad construction was, by all accounts, one of the largest and most important infrastructural undertakings of the republic and was considered vital to national integration. Bringing schoolchildren to see the railroad and watch its tracks disappear into the horizon allowed them to see for themselves that this iron thread did indeed stretch out and connect them to their compatriots in distant parts of the country, constituting, in effect, a vast iron web. By physically touching the rails, the students were also touching a part of the abstract railroad maps that appeared in their textbooks and, by implication, connecting the real with the representational.

Still other exercises turned to the republican landscape directly as the primary object of study. This was where town planning and education crossed paths. *İlkokulda Coğrafya Öğretimi* reminded teachers that only by example and observation could children begin to understand the interdependencies between people and things around them and gain an appreciation for their order.[20] Equipping children with the practical skills to recognize and navigate the deliberate and repetitive spatial configurations of the new republican townscapes, explaining the processes that generated these spaces and the institutions they engendered, and inculcating the official symbolic narratives embedded in that landscape were the province of republican schooling. In addition to these skills, which children growing up in a modernizing world needed to become functional adults, the republican curriculum introduced value judgments, deliberately prompting children to think of their environment in polarized terms. In Kaya's book, a sample exercise for third-grade students addressed both concerns. Developed by a school teacher in Balıkesir, the exercise started with a walk children took around town with their teacher, making notes and sketching diagrams of their itiner-

FIGURE 6.3. ELEMENTARY SCHOOL STUDENTS IN IZMIR LEARNING LONGITUDINAL MEASUREMENTS ON THE TRAIN TRACKS. THIS EXERCISE WAS USED AS A SAMPLE BEST PRACTICE IN THE WEEKLY TRADE MAGAZINE FOR ELEMENTARY SCHOOL TEACHERS PUBLISHED BY THE MINISTRY OF EDUCATION. COURTESY OF VEKAM, VEHBİ KOÇ, AND ANKARA RESEARCH CENTER.

ary.[21] At the end of their walk, they reached a hilltop with a commanding view of Balıkesir and compared what they saw with their maps and diagrams, verifying the locations of important sites. The lesson concluded with sample discussion topics and short essay questions that could be assigned to get students to reflect on their experience. Remarkably, with the exception of two mosques and three government offices inherited from the empire, the only structures deemed worthy of mention in this exercise were the new main street, the new park and public squares, and government buildings, all of which were built under the auspices of the republic. Meanwhile, the public spaces that made up the Ottoman city— the *han*s, bazaars, mosques, churches, synagogues, dervish lodges, and other sites where the civic, the religious, and the commercial mingled seamlessly—were conspicuously absent.[22] Aspects of the old city that exposed the multiethnic, multireligious makeup of the Ottoman society were similarly omitted from this survey. Furthermore, the list of questions suggested for the written portion of the assignment left little doubt about its ideological agenda:

> –Observe the settlement patterns from the hill. Which neighborhoods are more orderly? Which ones are more cramped?
> –Can you tell which streets are more important?
> –Where are our town's new and most impressive buildings? Why are they clustered together? When were they built?[23]

These questions were designed to elicit a very specific type of response: one that pitted the regular low-density layout of republican downtowns, with their wide and straight streets, their large—if somewhat empty—squares and parks, against the densely packed fabric of the Ottoman town, with its irregular streets that conformed to the local topography; a response that, based on this formal observation, associated the former with reason, order, and progress, while framing the latter as irrational, disorganized, and backward. This was yet another reiteration of the official discourse that cast the "successes" of the Turkish Republic against the "failures" of the Ottoman Empire to reaffirm the superiority of the former. What gave this incarnation staying power was that it was taught by praxis. It infused children's process of urban cognitive mapping with ideological meaning, further reinforcing the physical separation between the republican downtown and its Ottoman counterpart introduced by republican planners.

Cartographic exercises and explorations of republican environments advanced the RPP government's agenda by setting the morphological defaults about what constituted Turkey's inviolable territorial integrity and by undercutting the younger generation's ability to detect the ethnic and religious diversity of the Ottoman urban landscape. As exercises that incorporated the experience and abstractions of space into the curriculum, they were unprecedented in the cognitive faculties they targeted. Spaces and artifacts oscillated between serving as mnemonic devices and actual subjects of study in the myriad exercises that called for exploring the built environment, but they always helped anchor the imagined in the real, provided tangible examples of abstract ideological polarities, and made the remote relevant as though it were local.

MOTHERS OF THE NATION

Turkey's founding fathers linked Turkey's progress unequivocally to women's emancipation.[24] Expanding women's participation in public life by conferring on them new rights and responsibilities was key to realiz-

FIGURE 6.4. COVER OF THE AL-PHABET READING BOOK FEATUR-ING ATATÜRK TEACHING HIS AD-OPTED DAUGHTER ÜLKÜ HOW TO READ.

ing Turkey's modernization. Consequently, republican leaders supported broader educational opportunities for women to ensure that they could meet the demands of their new social roles. Mustafa Kemal argued passionately that, in order to catch up with contemporary civilization, it was as necessary to educate women as to educate men because society could not progress as a whole if half of its constituents were left behind. As Nilüfer Göle notes, unlike other contemporary nationalist movements that outlined an "ideal male" as the role model, the Kemalists celebrated the "ideal woman" as the archetypical citizen who embodied the country's transformation. To underline the importance he placed on this matter—in what has since become one of the most memorable images of the period—Mustafa Kemal chose to be depicted on the cover of the new alphabet textbooks as he personally tutors his adopted daughter Ülkü. Similarly,

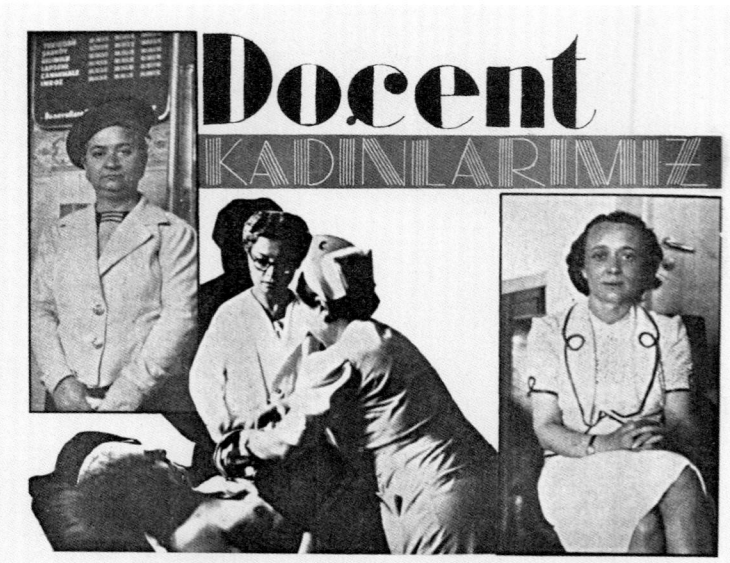

FIGURE 6.5. AN ARTICLE FROM *YENI MECMUA*, FEATURING A STORY ABOUT FEMALE PILOTS WORKING AND FLYING SIDE BY SIDE WITH THEIR MALE COUNTERPARTS AT THE CIVILIAN AVIATION ORGANIZATION, TÜRKKUŞU (TURKISH BIRD). COURTESY OF VEKAM, VEHBİ KOÇ, AND ANKARA RESEARCH CENTER.

his older adopted daughters, who were both educated professionals, frequently accompanied him in public in their capacity as role models for Turkish women. Afet İnan, who completed her doctorate in Geneva, co-authored several history and homeland studies textbooks with Mustafa Kemal, taking on the role of the republic's official historian in the process. More strikingly, Sabiha Gökçen was trained as a female fighter pilot and served a much publicized tour of duty in Eastern Turkey. In addition, early republican publications were replete with images of successful well-educated women who worked as pilots, judges, doctors, academics, mayors, and members of parliament. These publications made a point of depicting women at their respective places of employment and as equals in the company of their male colleagues.

Yet even as he encouraged girls to attend school, assume professional responsibilities, and contribute to the nation's material prosperity, Mustafa Kemal retained the deep conviction that the overriding duty, aspiration, and virtue for all women was motherhood. Although Turkish leaders were not outright opposed to women working outside the home, they regarded child rearing and homemaking as a woman's primary contribution to society.[25] Hence, the ideal Kemalist woman was in a double bind: she was encouraged to obtain an education and pursue a career, but she was also expected to be a perfect homemaker and an enlightened parent. In fact, so important was the latter, that, according to the new Civil Code, a woman's inadequacy in parenting or housekeeping constituted grounds for divorce.[26] Mustafa Kemal maintained that women in their role as mothers were, par excellence, children's first teachers and, consequently, wielded indisputable influence on the formation of future generations. Therefore, he stipulated, if women wanted to become the "mothers of the nation" and support Turkey's bid to modernize, they had to obtain a solid education, which, in turn, would improve their ability to raise their children as productive members of society.[27] In other words, as Zehra Arat notes in her blistering critique, women's education was not an end in itself or a means for their self-realization as individuals but, rather, a selfless investment they were expected to make so as to be better parents to the next generation of men.[28]

The Girls' Institutes were among the most revealing institutional sites that brought into focus the profound ambivalence of Kemalist rhetoric and policy regarding women and their roles in the social life of the nation. Spurred by a desire to educate the enlightened "mothers of the nation," the institutes were vocational schools that admitted female students between the ages of thirteen and seventeen and provided them with a modern education in a formal setting, under the supervision of an overwhelmingly female faculty, only to return them home as "the hundred percent housewife."[29] Originally created in the 1860s to train orphan girls to manufacture military uniforms, over the last decades of the empire the institutes had expanded their offerings to include a wider range of crafts—such as rug and fabric weaving, clothing design, and embroidery—as well as some basic instruction in reading, religion, history, mathematics, and health care. The republic had inherited three Girls' Institutes, all of which were in

Istanbul. Between 1923 and 1938, seven new institutes were opened in Adana, Ankara, Bursa, Elazığ, Izmir, Manisa, and Trabzon, bringing the total to ten.[30] In addition, sixteen two-year evening institutes were established in order to serve a broader range of women between the ages of eighteen and forty-five, who could not attend regular classes but wanted to earn a living through seamstressing or child care.[31] Ten of the evening institutes were operated on the premises of existing daytime programs, another six were opened in Afyon, Diyarbakır, Edirne, Elazığ, Erzurum, and Konya.

İsmet Pasa Girls' Institute in Ankara was the flagship of this educational enterprise. Established in 1928 in a makeshift space borrowed from the Children's Protection Society, the school moved to its very modern-looking, purpose-built facility designed by the Austrian-Swiss architect Ernst Egli on Atatürk Boulevard in 1930. The four-story structure, still considered to be one of the most distinctive buildings from this period, comprised several classrooms, thirty-five ateliers for uses ranging from cooking to handcrafts, and a three-hundred-seat auditorium for performances and movies. In addition, a fifteen-bed infirmary, a sizable dining hall, and bathing and laundry facilities had been made available to accommodate the institute's boarding students.[32] As the standard bearer of Kemalist education in "domestic science," the institute was frequently featured in official and lay publications and received much publicized visits from leading government officials, including Mustafa Kemal and Prime Minister İnönü. In sum, its architectural pedigree, its prominent location along Ankara's prestige corridor, and the high profile guests it hosted reinforced the impression that the mission of Girls' Institutes was comparable in importance to those of its neighbors, which included the most representative financial, educational, and cultural institutions of the Kemalist modernization project.

The republican administration also overhauled the institutes' offerings. According to the Ministry of Education, unlike before, the institutes approached homemaking as an integrated course of study.[33] They provided a composite curriculum, which blended the academic with the vocational, and their graduates were considered to have the equivalent of a high school education. With the reorganization, religious studies were eliminated from the institutes' curriculum, while offerings in Turkish language, history, and homeland studies were expanded. Foundational instruction in subjects such as nutrition science, public health, budgeting, and child development complemented practical courses in cooking, child rearing, and housekeeping. As students acquired advanced standing, they could specialize in a number of fields such as dairy science, domestic agriculture, couture, millinery, home economics, fashion design, and decorative

FIGURE 6.6. ANKARA İNÖNÜ GIRLS' INSTITUTE BUILDING BY SWISS ARCHITECT ERNST EGLI. COURTESY OF THE TURKISH HISTORICAL SOCIETY LIBRARY.

painting—most of which clearly were intended to teach girls how to become both producers and consumers of European-style goods and tastes. In promoting this new comprehensive curriculum, the ministry noted that the institutes provided "the necessary specialized and methodical education" for girls to grow into "knowledgeable and skillful women," who, in addition to having full control over domestic matters, could think for themselves on matters of national concern, earn a living if necessary, and feel as strong, confident, and comfortable working inside their home as they would outside.[34]

In practice, however, the institutes were the only type of vocational school that did not lead to professional employment outside the home.[35] Rather, they offered specializations that reinforced traditional feminine roles; they did not encourage students' intellectual or creative development and did not provide the kind of skills needed to join the workforce.[36] As the principal of the Istanbul Çapa Selçuk Girls' Institute admitted in a magazine interview, an overwhelming majority of its students married soon after graduation. Lack of capital and experience inhibited graduates from opening a business of their own, and the few who did often failed. Consequently, many took the first offer that came their way, which was often marriage. A small number sought employment, but these were often labor-intensive, low-paying jobs such as seamstressing.[37]

The Girls' Institutes were prone to criticism for other reasons as well, including their relatively poor economic returns for the investment and their unrealistic approach to the task at hand. In the first place, women did not really need institute credentials to become homemakers or mothers. Moreover, once folded into family finances, despite being a sizable contribution, their work at home could not be factored into the formal economy of the nation as quantifiable produced value. Such considerations made the original investment hard to justify in fiscal terms.[38] Second, especially in the early years of the republic, few Turkish homes had the amenities or equipment that the students used in their training, and they therefore could not put to use the skills they had mastered at school. In Europe and the United States, whence most of the domestic science techniques were imported, homes already had reliable running water, electricity, and even rudimentary appliances that freed up women's time, thus allowing them to join the workforce. In contrast, at the institutes, as Sibel Bozdoğan notes, rationalizing housework was promoted for its own sake and also because it embodied the idea of modernity and progress.[39] In other words, the institutes took students through the motions of rational and scientific practices without much of the substance, giving them the mental predisposition to accept the superiority of these practices but not the agency to take such an approach to its logical conclusion. These factors, combined with Turkey's meager means, suggest that there were more complex reasons for expansion of the institutes and the government support they received.[40]

From the republican perspective, what must have made Girls' Institutes attractive as instruments of cultural transformation, then, was not that they promised economic productivity or were able to yield quick results, but that they provided a middle ground in which resistance to reform could be mitigated with relatively less friction. The existence of this negotiating terrain suited the founding fathers, who rhetorically framed their reforms as being radical but, in practice, treaded carefully to ensure that they did not upset the fine balance of powers that lent them support. Hence, in potentially controversial matters, they chose to make change attractive rather than compulsory and gradual rather than abrupt. Such, for instance, was the case of veiling: whereas the republican law banned the use of distinctive clothes and accessories that invoked religious allegiances in men, contrary to popular belief it did not require women to take off their veils. Instead republican policies tried to appeal to women's sense of fashion and played up the (upwardly mobile) class associations that came with a Westernized appearance.

Similarly, the institutes did not threaten existing gender divisions or the traditional makeup of the family but introduced rational and scientific work habits into the household, promising to improve women's performance of their customary duties at home. The type of vocational education that the institutes offered put severe limitations on many young women's prospects for self-realization, but, considering that in Turkey girls have historically had low school attendance rates, for many this was the only available schooling beyond elementary education. Notably, an overwhelming three-quarters of the families that did send their daughters to school opted for vocational schools with Girls' Institutes taking the lion's share.[41] That such a sizable percentage of families enrolled their daughters in the institutes suggests that parents who might otherwise have had an objection to sending their daughters to academic schools were less likely to oppose sending them to a single-sex school at which girls would be honing their homemaking skills.

What is noteworthy here is that girls' continued enrollment in the institutes prolonged the duration of their formal education by six years at a crucial period in their lives during which, as adolescents, they would be picking up habits that would last a lifetime. This created an invaluable opportunity for the state to intercept the transmission of domestic culture, determining what, how, and where the students learned and who they learned from. As a result, rather than an individual experience that happened informally in the company of mothers or other older relatives and at home, the acquisition of homemaking and child-rearing skills now took place in a group, under the supervision of an instructor and in the formal setting of a classroom. This reconceptualization of the learning experience was very much in line with the typical pedagogical objectives of a modern state and the mechanisms it uses to implement them.

Institute training was markedly different from the established conventions of housekeeping and child rearing in Turkey. The curriculum emphasized this by choosing to use the Turkicized version of the English word *home* instead of the Turkish word *ev*, asserting that the students would be learning "hom teknigi" (home technique), thus implying that this was a kind of knowledge for which no words existed in Turkish yet.[42] An examination of their settings and the contents of their instructional program reveals that much of the training at the institutes involved coaxing the students to reimagine the relationships between space, time, and their own bodies through their labor in a manner that was remarkably different from what they would have observed in their parents' home. In turn, the expectation was for them to re-create this new order in their own homes. The institutes, in the rational spirit of modern domestic sci-

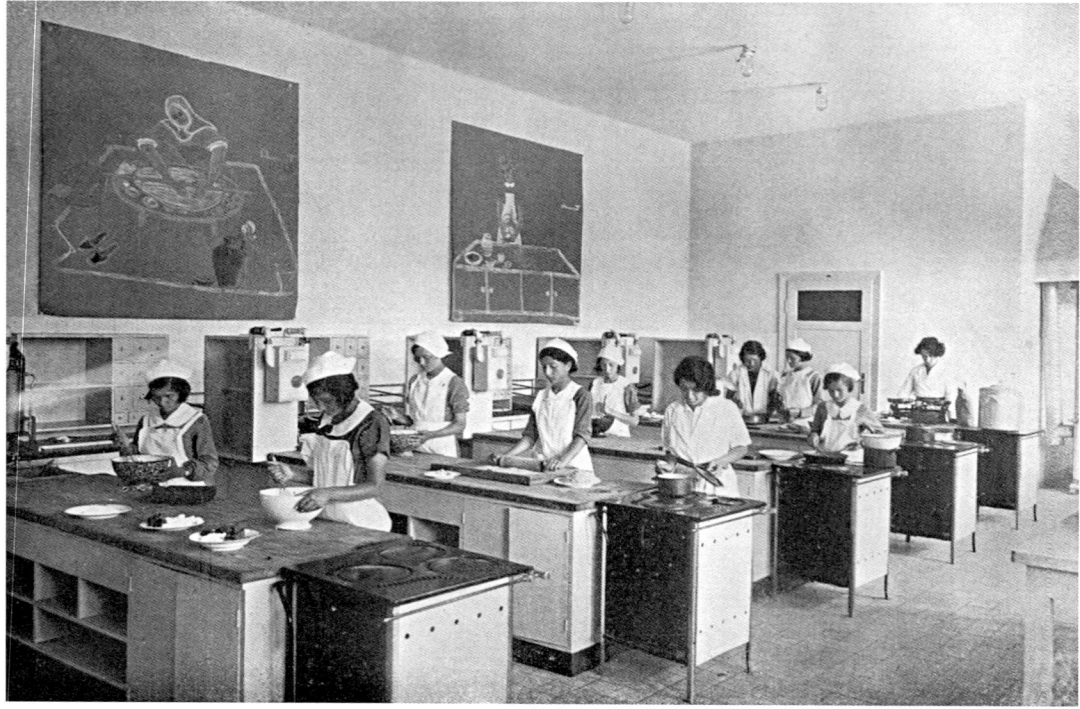

FIGURE 6.7. STUDENTS AT A COOKERY CLASS. DISTINCT FROM LEARNING HOUSEHOLD TASKS AT HOME, THE INSTITUTE OFFERED A RATIONALIZED SPATIAL LAYOUT WHEREIN THE TASKS WERE DIVIDED INTO SMALLER SUBROUTINES. EXPLANATIONS OF THE SUBROUTINES CAN BE SEEN ON THE WALLS OF THE INSTRUCTIONAL KITCHEN. COURTESY OF THE TURKISH HISTORICAL SOCIETY LIBRARY.

ence, brought a certain reflectiveness to housekeeping practices. Students learned to work from written lists of instructions, use recipes, and make precise measurements. New tools and techniques, which would previously have been considered extraneous to household tasks, were introduced to the process of training. Notably, these included the use of visual aids (such as posters, charts, and diagrams) for communicating ideas, measurement tables and various scales for calculations, and, especially in the couture and millinery classes, sketches and mock-ups prior to the final version of a given project. Students were taught that abiding by these principles would yield successful results as in a science experiment and eliminate waste—which during the postwar years of frugality was itself a desirable virtue. In a particularly favorable page-long article, the semiofficial daily *Ulus* provided a detailed description of the revolutionary scientific approach institutes brought to homemaking, emphasizing the laboratory-like quality of the teaching environment:

> Inside a glass cabinet, there are Robenal [*sic*] system scales, funnels, various scales and measuring cups, zinc containers. . . . But this is a chemistry lab, did we come to the wrong place? No, this is not a mistake. This really is where they prepare the food. You measure the gravel and the sand you mix when you are building a house, why not measure the ingredients that we expect to supply us with energy and that we put into our far more delicate stomachs? Can't you accept that these raw ingredients also have to be measured? . . . Why would you put more or fewer ingredients than you need and spoil the taste?[43]

Students also learned to manage their time efficiently. They were prompted to chart timetables to organize housework and to use new industry-inspired techniques for carrying out common chores more efficiently.[44] Everyday tasks such as dishwashing, laundry, or dressmaking were broken down into discrete subroutines. Most remarkably, the sequential nature of these subroutines were then mapped out onto space during class: students were assigned to rotating groups working on a specific part of a given project, as though they were factory workers along a conveyor belt.

It is important to note that the institutes also served ideological functions. First, conditioned through their own experiences to believe in the superiority of methods they learned at school, the students were quick to criticize the shortcomings of the households whence they came. Thus, for instance, a student essay titled "Taylorism in Our Homes," cited by Yael Navaro, drew sharp contrasts between the neat and rational kitchens she was taught to organize and the old Ottoman kitchens, which were "disorganized and dirty."[45] This comparison's terms are reminiscent of the ubiquitous binary comparisons used in official rhetoric of the republic. Written by a student at the Izmir Girls' Institute, however, it is a powerful reminder of how this binary logic permeated the minds of the new generation, and a testament to the effectiveness of corporal and spatial techniques in teaching. Trained as modern homemakers, the girls were (and came to see themselves as) agents in charge of creating and maintaining that neat and rational order in the modern Turkish household, and they were therefore hardly disinterested judges of the differences in question.

Second, the institutes introduced a whole new notion of frugality as a virtue by linking it directly to protectionism, Turkey's national economic policy after the Great Depression. In Turkey, where traditionally watchful in-laws were known to keep an eye on how thinly a bride-to-be could peel potato skins, people already had an appreciation for thrift. But the institutes pushed students to move beyond family finances to consider their contribution to supporting the national economy, teaching them not only to cut costs but also to pay attention to using domestically produced ingredients. As the *Ulus* article noted, "What is most impressive about a typical institute girl is that should she find herself having to use an ingredient that is not grown or produced in our own country, she is pained as if her hands were burning even from just touching it."[46]

As patriotic homemakers of the future, the students were taught to think of themselves as "defenders of the Revolution" and to "express their love of country even in their choice of ingredients."[47] By encouraging the consumption of domestic agricultural products, home economics courses at the institutes brought national economic concerns to the family dinner table. Also, as suggested by the praise received by students for a cake recipe featuring "Izmir raisins and Central Anatolian rye," the institutes ushered an awareness of national geography based on a knowledge of Turkey's regions through their respective crops that was akin to the applied geography exercises suggested for elementary schools.

Finally, the institutes served as a middle ground for negotiating the characteristics of the material culture of modern Turkey. By virtue of their offerings, which included food preparation and a range of handcrafts such as needle- and lacework, couture, and millinery, the institutes brought the state into terrains of cultural production (and tastemaking) over which it previously had little or no influence. Students were trained in both *alaturka* (Turkish) and *alafranga* (Western) skills and were encouraged to experiment with "updating" the former using techniques derived from the latter.[48] They were taught how to make soufflés, cakes, sauces, and pastries, all of which were new and unusual to the Turkish palate, but they also learned how to cook traditional Turkish dishes "using modern preparation techniques" to make them "lighter and more practical."[49] The *Ulus* reporter praised the students at İsmet Paşa Girls' Institute for reforming alaturka cuisine, while assuring his more skeptical readers that they "need not worry, this does not mean that familiar foods we like are replaced with concoctions made of strange ingredients that we do not even have a name for. No, what has happened at the institute is that *oriental* foods have been *Westernized*" (emphases added).[50] Similarly, the students learned to design and sew anything from lingerie to coats, and the school took commercial orders for bed and table linen, bridal gowns, and evening dresses. Many of these items were entirely new additions to Turkish women's wardrobes or wedding chests. Here, "Westernization of the oriental" often implied the application of formal elements drawn from the vocabulary of traditional crafts onto modern objects of new kinds of domestic products/ artifacts or clothing. Such, for instance, was an evening gown prepared at the institute for Mevhibe İnönü, Prime Minister İnönü's wife.[51] The shape of the ensemble reflected contemporary European fashions, but the em-

FIGURE 6.8. MEVHIBE İNÖNÜ'S DRESS DESIGNED AND MADE BY STUDENTS AT THE INSTITUTE. COURTESY OF VEKAM, VEHBİ KOÇ, AND ANKARA RESEARCH CENTER.

broidered patterns on the velvet jacket made recognizable references to *Bindallı*, the traditional bridal dress from Erzurum in Eastern Anatolia. The schools' dual offerings in alaturka and alafranga techniques could be read as signs of a long-running conflict between a feverish determination to adopt modern but (disturbingly) foreign cultural practices and a deep reluctance to forgo the familiar. But their simultaneous inclusion in the institutes' curriculum undeniably broadened students' repertoire and opened to them the decision of just "how modern to be," giving young women a new—if unsung—agency for reconciling established local patterns of everyday life and imported ones in their own homes. Relegated to the domestic sphere, their work has received significantly less credit and academic attention even from feminist historians, although women's deliberations over reconciling the inherited and the imported were quite comparable to those in other areas of cultural production, such as music and architecture, and as everyday productions they were far more ubiquitous.

Women's informal and private networks are only beginning to receive attention within the context of nation-building processes, although they were indispensable for the transmission and diffusion of the republican culture. Girls' Institutes drew a mixture of students from families of civil servants and local elites in the towns in which they were located. An institute degree diversified young women's prospects for marriage, as matches between graduates and locally stationed government workers, military officials, or engineers were common. For the men in question, marrying an institute graduate (*enstitü mezunu*) was a savvy move that publicly bolstered his credentials as a progressive in his social circle, and especially in the eyes of his superiors. Such couplings were desirable because they helped the diffusion of the new cultural practices through informal means. The stay-at-home wives of these republican middle-class professional men created their own circles of socialization, which had hierarchies parallel to those of their husbands but had more fluid boundaries and expanded to include neighborhood ties.[52] Women came together on reception days (*kabul günleri*), semiformal gatherings that happened regularly and on a rotating basis, during which they exchanged news and views about manners, fashion, child-rearing practices, family relations, and, depending on the context, even politics.[53] Such informal channels were indispensable for amplifying the reach of officially endorsed cultural tastes, practices, and ideologies.

The institutes' role in recruiting and training young women to generate reform-friendly households is easy to miss—especially in places like Ankara, the republican stronghold, or Istanbul, the households of which already displayed many modern traits. Their centrality to the nation-building project, however, snaps into focus in a place like Elazığ, where the initiative to establish an institute came not from the Ministry of Education but from the regional inspector general, Abdullah Alpdoğan, who took office shortly after the violent suppression of Kurdish tribes in Dersim in 1937. Unlike its counterparts elsewhere, the first priority of the Elazığ Institute, exceeding modern homemaking skills in importance, was to train "mothers who spoke Turkish with their children." In addition to the typical cohort recruited from families of civil servants and local elites, the institute's enrollment included a sizable number of boarding students all of whom were Kurdish. The latter was a mixed crowd, ranging from the daughters of government-friendly tribal chiefs, who cemented their association with the RPP administration by sending their offspring to the institute, to orphans whose parents had died in clashes with government

FIGURE 6.9. ELAZIĞ GIRLS' INSTITUTE BUILDING.

forces.[54] The Inspectorate General closely monitored the institute's activities and the students' progress, leaving no doubt as to what the institute's real function was. As one member of parliament, grabbing the hand of a student who had just been examined by visiting officials, put it, "This hand will not hold a gun, this hand will not hold a sword, this hand is now the hand of a friend . . . now it holds a pen, now it holds a needle."[55]

Schooling Kurdish girls was a strategy for achieving internal pacification by cultural assimilation. The Elazığ Girls' Institute was, in the words of one government official, similar to the ultramodern American factory in the proverbial Turkish joke, which took cows from one end and churned out sausages from the other.[56] The institute in Elazığ was a factory that "churned out civilized human beings." It took "pigheaded and disobedient" girls with no language skills from "the poorest and the most primitive backgrounds imaginable" and turned them into well-mannered young women who "make conversation in Turkish" and "graciously serve you coffee." The disturbingly graphic factory analogy was not far from the destruction and reconstruction of identity that the Kurdish girls experienced, a process that school officials meticulously documented in albums filled with before and after photographs. Especially in the early years of the institute, girls were brought to school with the "assistance" of the gendarmes. Forcefully severed from their families and the only homes they

BİR İNSAN YARATMA
HİKÂ

Yanyana gördüğü
resim, mükemmel b
ratmanın kısa hikâ
gün bir masal ismi
köylerine yayılmış,
pette mütevazı, a
Türk kadınının nel
ceğini bu üç mini
raftan daha iyi gö
bir vesika olamaz. S
yıllardan beri yaptı
tal yuvası halindeki
rinden gene aldığı k
atının terkisinde ş
yor. Elâziğ'daki mek
riyor. Onlara en sıc
katini gösteriyor.
sadece yemekte ça
kullanmaktan ibare
öğretiyor. Okutuyo
yor ve sonra da bu
nelerini birer ışık l
linde köylerine gön

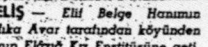

ELİŞ — *Elif Belge Hanımın*
ilka Avar tarafından köyünden
ulıp Elâziğ Kız Enstitüsüne geti.

MEKTEPTE — *Bir sene sonra*
Elif mektepte. Beyaz yakalı, siyah
öğrenci elbisesi içinde Elif iyi ta.

VE NİHAYET — *Mektep bitmiş-*
tir. Tertemiz Türkçe konuşan, tah-
sili yerinde bir Türk kızının kar-

FIGURE 6.10. NEWSPAPER CLIPPING BASED ON THE COLLECTIONS OF BEFORE AND AFTER PHOTOGRAPHS BY ONE OF THE TEACHERS AT THE ELAZIĞ INSTITUTE. THE PRACTICE OF COLLECTING BEFORE AND AFTER PHOTOS AS PROOF OF THE GIRLS' TRANSFORMATION WAS ROUTINE AT THE INSTITUTE. THE NEWSPAPER STORY IS TITLED, "THE STORY OF PRODUCING A PERSON." THE STUDENT IS BROUGHT IN BAREFOOT AND LONGHAIRED WITH RATHER WORN-OUT CLOTHES. THE MIDDLE PICTURE SHOWS THE SAME STUDENT, ELIF BELGE, NOW BEARING A TURKISH NAME, WITH A UNIFORM AND HER HAIR TIED AT THE BACK. THE PHOTO TO THE RIGHT SHOWS HER TRAINED AS A NURSE, SPEAKING "THE PUREST TURKISH."

knew, the girls were further traumatized upon arrival as their clothes were taken and burned, their hair was shaved to get rid of head lice, and they were quarantined in separate quarters for days before they could join other students. Even when implemented in the name of health and hygiene, these measures scarred them for life. Decades later they still recalled how they felt branded as otherness was inscribed on them with their government-issued uniforms and their bald heads.[57] Almost none of them spoke Turkish when they arrived, and hence their coursework, which consisted of several hours of language drills a week, differed from that of their Turkish schoolmates.[58] They were not allowed to speak Kurdish among themselves and were afraid to do so even when they were alone.[59] Language and ethnicity coupled with the visible signs of the abject poverty whence they came became painful markers of a disparity felt by those on either side of the divide at the institute.[60]

Unlike their Turkish counterparts, whose education was designed and presented as a carefully considered updating of Turkish traditions with Western scientific techniques, Kurdish girls were forced to shed their cultural identity altogether to become modern and civilized, revealing, not so subtly, the official prejudices about the inferiority of Kurdish heritage. When top-level officials pronounced Kurdish students to be untrustworthy, their derision gave everybody down the command chain, who identified themselves as ethnically Turkish, the license to treat Kurdish girls with contempt. The positional superiority projected by government workers also informed the relations between students, who self-segregated by ethnicity in the common areas of the school, reifying perceived hierarchies in space. In places such as the dining hall, it was understood that the daughters of civil servants would serve as role models, demonstrating civilized manners, by example, and that Kurdish girls would emulate—without the slightest consideration that the latter could have anything to bring to this exchange. As an unintentional consequence of forced recruitment, many Kurdish families, suspicious of the government's intentions, refrained from sending their daughters to school; instead they hid them, and, in some cases married them off en masse at an even earlier age than was already traditional in this region, just to disqualify them from enrollment.[61]

Education at the institute entailed complete immersion in the official culture. The journey from the remote mountain villages whence Kurdish girls came was often long and sometimes dangerous. The students traveled to school only once at the beginning of the academic year and returned home at the end, in early summer. As boarding students, consequently, their entire stay, not just their hours of formal instruction, was structured with activities that were integral to their formation as modern, urban, loyal Turkish citizens. Despite the hardships and humiliation they had to face, life at the institute expanded the boarders' outlook. In their vocational courses, much like those of their counterparts in other parts of the country, they began to acquire an understanding of Turkey's geography as they learned about regional culinary ingredients and craft traditions. The difference in this isolated corner of Eastern Anatolia in the years before the integration of the national market, however, was that many had never seen lemons or olive oil before, let alone knowing their provenance or how to cook with them. The students' sense of what lay yonder expanded further as some of them found the opportunity to travel to other cities, including Ankara, and saw for themselves the expanse of national territory that stretched beyond the narrow confines of their self-contained world.

Schooling introduced new daily, weekly, and annual cycles defined not by the familiar rhythms of local seasons and rites of religion but by the requisites of the official calendar. Located in the new expansion to the west of town, the Elazığ Girls' Institute was part of a model urban landscape, comprising the most prominent cultural-didactic institutions of the republic, including the Halkevi and the stadium. This rather compact—and rudimentary—urban stage facilitated the expansion of the girls' education outside the institute's own premises into the city and its institutions. Through their regular and compulsory participation in functions held at these quintessential enclaves of official culture, the daughters of tribal Kurdish families, along with their Turkish cohorts, became fluent in the kind of modern citizenship roles they would assume as mothers of the next generation.

The institute mediated some of the most complex interactions between the state and its Kurdish citizens. Despite the schisms and the asymmetry of means and power, the Elazığ Institute, like its counterparts in different parts of the country, was a site of negotiation, which refracted the state's single-minded mandate into a spectrum of diverse experiences. For the Kurdish students, initially, the experience was one of forcible cultural assimilation, one that mixed profound trauma with the uncertain promise of material rewards and social mobility in exchange for conforming to the exigencies of the dominant culture. As they took to their education, however, the girls gained new agency as emissaries who inhabited both cultures. They shared their newly acquired skills with their fellow villagers when they went back for the summer or after completing their studies and, as living models of conversion, participated in the recruitment of new students.[62] A few even made their stay at Elazığ a stepping-stone toward further education and became village teachers or nurses. As with all cultural go-betweens, the girls found themselves in the difficult position of adjusting the terms of their existence within the expectations of their original communities.[63] If they married within their village, when they tried to put their training to use they found themselves alone against established ideas about child rearing, hygiene, and nutrition that were held by other more powerful women in their immediate spheres of existence.[64] But many of them married outside, spoke Turkish at home, and acquired roles that were quite similar to those of the modern middle-class women they were taught to emulate. Ironically, many parents who initially had to be convinced to permit their daughters' education did not want them to marry below their newly acquired station in life.[65]

The Elazığ Girls' Institute deserves attention not because it became an influential prototype that was widely replicated, but because it reveals the extent to which women's education was linked to some of the core tensions within the official ideology. The republic's leaders were torn between investing in cultural and economic institutions to modernize the region, on the one hand, and fears that such efforts would increase Kurdish ethnic consciousness and fuel separatist movements, on the other. If the building of new schools, community centers, and urban amenities was representative of the first approach, the militarization of the landscape and implementation of new techniques for surveillance and communication were representative of the latter. Ultimately, as with all other cases of cultural divergence or political opposition in Turkey, those who saw the "Eastern Problem" (Şark Meselesi) primarily through a security lens prevailed. More broadly speaking, the tensions between the civic and the military embodied by Turkey's twin landscapes are among the most enduring legacies of early republican corporatism. The profound ambivalence between integrating dissent into the political process and suppressing it by force continues to be a defining characteristic of statecraft in Turkey today.

PERMEATING THE PUBLIC SPHERE

Academic and vocational schools targeted the next generation in its formative years, but the RPP administration was equally concerned about winning over the current generation of adults—or at least forming alliances with a critical mass. In a revealing front-page editorial he wrote for *Hakimiyet-i Milliye* on October 8, 1929, Zeki Mesut Alsan argued that building a society that shared the same principles and goals as a nation was an even more pressing need than achieving literacy. "To frame people's outlook, shape their morality and ethics, and prescribe their national and military duties," he suggested, "it [is] necessary to regulate not just school activities, but also to exercise control over [people's] leisure time," like Italy's Fascist government was doing "so creatively."[66] Zeki Mesut's wistful portrayal of the Fascists' success at consolidating the Italian nation came at a time when the RPP's own repeated efforts to compel the Turkish Hearths Association (THA) to serve in a similar capacity were failing. Not only was the THA unwilling to relinquish its autonomy or perform functions outside its charter, but it had gone so far as to provide a forum for dissent.[67] In early 1931, as part of his larger efforts to reinforce the RPP's hold on power, Mustafa Kemal forced the THA to disband and replaced it with Halkevleri, which were inaugurated in January 1932.

A nominally autonomous network of multipurpose community centers modeled after contemporary state-supported communitarian organizations in Italy, Germany, Hungary, and Czechoslovakia, Halkevleri effectively functioned as the RPP's public outreach division. Unburdened by the fiscal and political problems that the THA faced, Halkevleri expanded its national network rather quickly, from 14 provincial branches to 55 within a year and to 478 by 1945.[68] The RPP tried to prioritize the launching of Halkevleri in areas that presented particular challenges to national integration. These included Thrace and parts of Northern Turkey, which served as intake regions for the diverse Balkan immigrants, and east of the Euphrates, a region frequently rocked by violent uprisings.[69] Furthermore, in 1940, the RPP created an affiliated network of Halkodaları (singular, Halkodası), which allowed party expansion into smaller more remote settlements, albeit with more limited functions—by 1945, 4,322 of them existed across the country.[70]

The creation of Halkevleri was an attempt by the state to permeate areas of social life that had previously remained outside its purview for the ultimate goal of achieving national integration. While the specifics varied depending on the availability of local personnel and resources, Halkevleri provided a broad range of educational and charitable activities. They offered instruction in arts and crafts and in practical areas such as literacy, numeracy, typewriting, and bookkeeping, so as to increase employability in mostly urban office jobs. Halkevleri also organized lectures, performances, and commemorative events. In addition, they tried to provide assistance in cash and kind to the needy and scholarships to poor students, and they offered free medical consultations and advice on issues from agriculture to bureaucratic procedures. The RPP regarded these as long-term investments in stabilizing a society hard hit by long years of war and large-scale population movements. No less important was the legitimacy party leaders expected this kind of benevolent paternalism to lend to their rule—not unlike their Ottoman and Seljuk predecessors who founded *vakıf*s and used them to foment urban development.[71]

The RPP intended for Halkevleri to anchor city life, serving as both physical landmarks and nodes of activity in their respective towns. Because it was a pressing concern to get as many branches as possible up and running in many places, Halkevleri started out in makeshift facilities often inherited from the defunct THA, moving gradually into custom-built premises as these became available. However, when building a new facility, RPP officials emphasized site selection, stipulating that the location be prominent and close to the new downtown, with other governmental and institutional buildings nearby. According to the organization's manual, Halkevi buildings had to "go beyond the simply utilitarian" and "lead the advancement of modern architectural culture in Turkey by example," gaining recognition as symbols of "the state's civilizing mission."[72] In this respect, the Diyarbakır Halkevi is a good example. With its compact cubic mass and protruding glass corners that gave it a lighter appearance and revealed what to the locals was its unusual structural system, the building stood in sharp contrast to the massive stone architecture for which this region was renowned. As Mustafa Kemal himself articulated in his 1937

FIGURE 6.11. DIYARBAKIR HALKEVI UNDER CONSTRUCTION (TOP) AND FINISHED (BOTTOM) WITH OTHER IN-STITUTIONAL STRUCTURES OF THE NEW STATE—INCLUDING THE TEACHERS' AND OFFICERS' CLUBS, GOV-ERNOR'S MANSION, AND A GIRLS' INSTITUTE—THAT WERE BEING SITED IN THE SAME AREA. SOME OF THESE APPEAR IN THE BACKGROUND. COURTESY OF THE TURKISH HISTORICAL SOCIETY LIBRARY.

trip to Diyarbakır, during which he attended a classical music recital at the Halkevi shortly after the building's completion, modernity of form and modernity of function went hand in hand as indicators of progress: "I am visiting Diyarbakir for the first time in twenty years. [I am] in one of the world's most beautiful and modern buildings, listening to exquisite modern music . . . with one of the world's most civilized peoples. You can surely appreciate how pleased and proud I am to visit this Halkevi, and I am happy to publicly make a note of this."[73]

Official events, such as commemorative ceremonies or Mustafa Kemal's visit, were the only type of activity that animated republican downtowns insofar as the buildings around them generally provided bureaucratic services that had little interaction with the street. The commercial and religious institutions that generated constant foot traffic continued to operate in the historic cores of towns. Republican urbanism was a work in progress; construction projects—dogged by chronic shortages of money, materials, and labor—took years to complete, and as a result, outside of special events, the new urban spaces looked rather desolate. To animate these spaces, the RPP encouraged Halkevleri and municipal authorities to hold functions in the newly minted public outdoor spaces to draw a range of audiences throughout the day.

One such occasion was the RPP's call for public gatherings at local squares throughout the country on the occasion of the July 20, 1936, signing of the Montreux Convention, which restored Turkey's sovereignty over the Straits. The signing ceremony, expected to take place around midnight local time, would be broadcast by the Ankara radio for all to hear. To amass the necessary crowds and keep them in the square that late, local Halkevi branches were urged to put on a show to entertain the public. In Merzifon, a small town in central northern Turkey, local officials dispatched the gendarmes to small hamlets and nearby towns to bring people out from their homes. That night, the Merzifon Halkevi organized an impromptu program to teach people the geographic location and importance of the Straits and the significance of the treaty, followed by the recitation of patriotic poetry, and performances by the Halkevi band and local singers. With the "help" of the gendarme forces, people were "entertained" at the Republic Square until 3:00 a.m.[74] The event not only turned public space into a didactic place but also put a twist on the act of listening to the radio, typically a private indoor activity, and made it a collective ritual.

Attempts to permeate or tweak collective events and bring them under surveillance were telltale signs of a single-party regime that was seeking to consolidate its control over the public sphere. Having clamped down on long-standing sociospatial practices that characterized Ottoman cities, the RPP and its local operatives also tried to monopolize collective activities such as team sports, leisure, and recreation. For instance, in Western Anatolian towns, the forced exchange of local Orthodox Greek populations had also led to the closure of the taverns they ran, well-loved establishments that provided occasions for leisurely sociability for Muslims as well.[75] Moreover, the closure of *tekke*s and *zaviye*s in 1924 had brought an abrupt end to the social life that flourished around them, leaving these towns with few venues for sociability outside private homes.[76] By operating establishments such as the city clubs, municipal tea gardens, and movie theaters and by promoting other outreach activities, the RPP was responding to a need that its policies had created in the first place. Anxieties about popular movements that could threaten the party's grip on power drove the RPP's desire to intercept social exchange.[77] The party discouraged the formation even of organizations that had no political agenda—such as sports clubs—outside the purview of the local Halkevi, and encouraged existing organizations to come under its patronage.[78] In light of such developments, rather than the generous social services of a welfare state, the RPP-run parks, playgrounds, teahouses, movie theaters, and sports grounds that opened mostly in the 1930s may be seen as attempts by the single-party regime to control and reshape the citizenry's leisure activities in model public settings.

These new venues of casual sociability also had the not-so-subtle purpose of teaching provincial populations, by example, how to be "modern urban citizens." Frequented mainly by civil servants and their families, they were mixed-gender establishments where men and women, dressed in European style (*alafranga*) clothes engaged in Western patterns of recreation and consumption. As such, depending on the region and its previous exposure to European cultural forms, they were likely to be perceived as extraneous by the locals. As noted by Muhlis Koner, an official of the Konya chapter, Halkevleri were in danger of becoming a gathering place almost exclusively for the republican middle classes, especially civil servants.[79]

The RPP's heavy-handed and crudely ideological attempts to monitor urban social interaction met with the resistance of their intended audience and also came under scholarly criticism in later years.[80] Provincial populations were generally reticent to embrace cultural forms and spatial practices they considered to be alien. Rather than overt protestations though, bearing in mind the state's coercive power, people opted for passive forms of resistance by refusing to participate in organized events when given the choice.[81] As Sefa Şimşek documents, in the Black Sea town of Giresun,

Küçük tip Halkevi

Küçük Halkevleri TiP projeleri

Y. Mimar Sabri Oran

C. H. Partisi Müşavir Mimarı

Cumhuriyet Halk Partisi Genel Sekreterliği tarafından, yurdun muhtelif kaza ve nahiye merkezle-
rinde yapılması düşünülen, halkevleri için tip pro-
je hazırlattırılmıştır. Halk Partisi, bilhassa kaza ve
köylerde, halkevleri faaliyetine çok ehemmiyet ver-
diğinden bunlara lüzumlu binaların sür'atle ve bir
program dahilinde meydana getirilmesine çalışmak-
tadır. Bu maksatla, Genel Sekreterlikte bir müşavir
mimarlık ihdas edilmiş ve yüksek mimar Ahmet
Sabri Oran tayin olunmuştur.

Müşavir mimarlık; memleketimizde yapılan
halkevleri projelerini tetkik etmekle beraber bazı
halkevlerinin projelerini de tanzim etmektedir. Bu
meyanda Konya vilâyeti halkevi projesini müşavir mimarlık yapmıştır. Bundan başka bu sayımız-
da neşrettiği müzproeler kaza merkezleri için, küçük
ve büyük iki tip olarak hazırlanmış bulunmaktadır.

Küçük A tipi Halkevi projesini tetkik edersek:
Bu bina takriben 275 metrelik bir sahaya mâ-
liktir. İdare kısmı altında küçük bir bodrum katı va-
dır. Büyük salonun ve diğer kısımların altı doludur.
Binanın mühim bir kısmını merasim salonu işgal etmektedir. İdare kısmı bu salonun irtifaı içinde iki kat
olarak tanzim edilmiştir. Zemin katta bir
okuma odası vardır. Binanın plânı iktisadî düşünce-
lerin tahtı tesirinde çok küçük olarak tanzim edilmiştir. Küçük A tipi plân bir kaza merkezi
için değil belki bir nahiye merkezine kifayet edebilir.
Küçük bir antre ile zemin kat holüne giriliyor, sa-

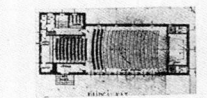

Birinci kat plânı

lonun grişi bu hol üzerindedir. Karşıya vestiyer ve bir
küçük kat merdiveni geliyor. Vestiyerin yanında bulunan helâların kapıları bu hole karşıdır. Bu helâların hol üzerinde olması bilhassa, tazikli suyu ol-
mıyan bazı kasabalarımızda hiç de doğru değildir.
Helâlar kasaba evlerinde olduğu gibi acaba binadan
biraz daha uzakta tesis edilemez mi? Hiç olmazsa
kapıları hol üzerinde olmayarak plânın biraz sapa
ve uzak bir köşesine götürülürse daha iyi olacaktır.

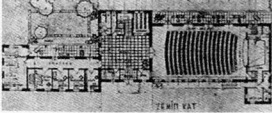

Zemin kat plânı

FIGURE 6.12. SMALL-TYPE HALKEVI BUILDING TEMPLATE PROPOSED BY THE ARCHITECTURE OFFICE OF THE REPUB-LICAN PEOPLE'S PARTY. NOTE THAT THE PLAN FEATURES AN AUDITORI-UM THAT IS LARGER IN COMPARISON WITH SPACES FOR OTHER FUNCTIONS OFFERED BY THE FACILITY, THUS EMPHA-SIZING ITS DIDACTIC FUNCTION. COUR-TESY OF THE LIBRARY OF THE CHAMBER OF ARCHITECTS OF TURKEY.

parents who refused to enroll their children in free music classes at the Halkevi were publicly chastised by the local Halkevi journal, *Aksu*, for hiring the same teacher to privately tutor their children. Because both the subject and the instructor were the same, concludes Şimsek, parents were not necessarily opposed to their children studying music, but they were wary of the extra dose of propaganda that was infused into every Halkevi activity.[82]

Didactic objectives also seeped into ostensibly recreational events, which had strong moral messages or were intended to introduce im-ported cultural forms. Although the official RPP literature claimed that Halkevleri were sites for the exchange of expertise and ideas in both di-rections, the centerpiece of the standard architectural brief for a Halkevi building was a two-hundred-person auditorium for lectures and ideolog-ical plays, which suggested otherwise, and the public took notice of their assigned role as passive recipients in this spatially implied hierarchy.[83] Halkevleri's failure to resonate with the public's sensibilities was already evident to party officials, as exemplified in a bleak report filed from Mar-din Halkevi:

> Before our committee started work . . . recreation in Mardin amounted to
> no more than going to coffeehouses, listening to inferior and vulgar mu-
> sicians, and watching absurd plays. . . . Our drama committee has gone to
> great lengths to change this. The city did not have a place for people to gather
> or a stage for plays. Halkevi hall and auditorium are gifts to the people of
> Mardin. . . . However, after providing them with an experience they had
> been awaiting for many years, we expected people would rush to see our play
> willingly. . . . This expectation did not materialize, and despite all our ef-
> forts, we did not see even one local person come to our play. The attendance
> did not number more than sixty, and consisted totally of out-of-town civil
> servants.[84]

The inability of Halkevleri to fulfill their stated mission should not,
however, detract from attending to the organization's indispensable service as an instrument of state building. Halkevleri provided venues for reifying the state as a concrete entity, offered much-needed logistical support
for the expansion of its operations, and helped generate the human capital
needed to secure its longevity. Excavating the workings of Halkevleri lays
bare the negotiated process by which a new culture of state was constituted in Turkey.

The urban location and interior configuration of Halkevleri set the
stage for the performance of state authority in a tangible way for all to
both take part and witness. The buildings overlooking Republic Squares,
including the Halkevi, were often designed with a second-floor balcony
or a roof terrace that could be used as a podium from which to address
crowds at public gatherings. During these ceremonies, the abstract hierarchy of government offices, ordinarily known to few outside the bureaucracy, came to life in the calculated acts of deference and projections
of authority performed by the actual officials in attendance.[85] Even as
both the RPP and Halkevleri publicly claimed that nobody had special
privileges in a "classless and horizontally integrated society," the organization's manual distributed nationwide already established seating protocols that closely replicated the local line of succession. Official gatherings rendered publicly visible not only the distance between the guests of
honor at the top and the ordinary folks at the bottom but also the entire
circuitry of power between them, which was essential to the continued
maintenance of local order. The repeated and public acknowledgment of
power in both official and extracurricular capacities by the entire body of
civil servants in these events contributed to shaping a performance-based
institutional culture of deference that continues to characterize the Turkish state today.

FIGURE 6.13. REPUBLIC DAY CELEBRATIONS IN FRONT OF BANDIRMA HALKEVI, FACING MÜTAREKE SQUARE. THE ORDERLY ARRANGEMENT MAKES VISIBLE THE LOCAL HIERARCHY OF GOVERNMENT OFFICIALS AND MILITARY OFFICERS. THE SQUARE'S NAME COMMEMORATES THE END OF THE WAR OF INDEPENDENCE: *MÜTAREKE* MEANS "ARMISTICE." COURTESY OF THE TURKISH HISTORICAL SOCIETY LIBRARY.

Halkevleri were the primary conduit through which the RPP leadership tried to secure the cooperation of rank-and-file government workers and provincial notables in propping up a new order. As a cursory look at the organizational charts of local chapters reveals, teachers constituted an overwhelming majority of the officers, whereas the presence or contribution of blue-collar workers, farmers, or local business owners was virtually undetectable.[86] Civil servants were particularly vulnerable to this kind of pressure to commit their "free time" because they were at the mercy of their superiors for promotions and geographic rotations. The pressure to contribute and produce was applied all the way down the chain of command, each level keeping tabs on the contribution of the next. Meticulous reporting and the scrutiny of peers and superiors were the major operational instruments for extracting the necessary involvement. Each chapter was compelled to produce participation logs for inspection by Halkevi and party brass in Ankara, who in turn issued reviews that commended the productivity of a given chapter or publicly shamed its officers into action through party publications.[87] False reports and fudged numbers were not uncommon insofar as greater numbers of events and participants got the praise.[88] The demand to increase participation blurred the distinction between the private and official identities

FIGURE 6.14. HALKEVLER PROVIDED A SOCIALLY ACCEPTABLE INSTITUTIONAL SETTING SANCTIONED BY THE STATE FOR MIXED-GENDER ACTIVITIES. BUT TO FUNCTION, THEY ALSO DEMANDED THAT CIVIL SERVANTS CONTRIBUTE THEIR FREE TIME. THE PHOTO FEATURES CIVIL SERVANTS FROM TOKAT WHO PARTICIPATED IN THE PERFORMANCE (*GÖSTERIT*) COMMITTEE OF THE LOCAL HALKEVI. COURTESY OF THE TURKISH HISTORICAL SOCIETY LIBRARY.

of civil servants, who, even as they engaged in purportedly voluntary activities, were expected to abide by existing workplace hierarchies because the organizational chart of a Halkevi closely resembled the hierarchy of government offices.

Although the relationship between the state and its workforce presented an asymmetric balance of powers, it was also undeniably symbiotic. Halkevi branches were safe harbors for civil servants traveling into remote corners of the country. In her trips to recruit students for the Elazığ Girls' Institute, for instance, Sıdıka Avar reported spending several nights with her students at the Bingöl Halkevi.[89] Also, especially in isolated and conservative localities, Halkevleri provided an invaluable social outlet for civil servants who felt lonely.[90] Whereas it would have been impossible for a man and a woman to be seen together even in a public place such as a teahouse, it was acceptable for them to work in groups under the chaperonage of the state on Halkevi projects such as staging a play, organizing a concert, or even going on extended field trips to nearby villages. As a consequence, marriages between civil servants who met during their postings at provincial towns were not uncommon.

While civil servants were, par excellence, Halkevleri's natural base, the organization sought to recruit and retain new members by rewarding their participation. For those with a genuine interest in literature or the arts, Halkevleri provided the initial, and sometimes only, opportunities to cultivate their talent. As an aspiring author in Diyarbakir, İhsan Bey-sanoğlu was grateful for the opportunity to publish at the local Halkevi's monthly for what was a generous remuneration at the time.[91] Similarly, Halkevleri served as the launching pads for the careers of some of Turkey's nationally renowned authors, poets, and musicians.[92] Similarly, for those with political ambitions, Halkevleri offered opportunities for mobility up the party ranks—even if this came at the expense of their peers. Hardworking staffers who were successful in recruiting more members and organizing events received promotions, were summoned to higher positions in the bureaucracy, and were even invited to serve as members of parliament.

The need to pull people in eventually compelled party leaders to become more flexible about their mission and rethink the location, contents, and format of Halkevi activities.[93] In fact, using loudspeakers to broadcast Halkevi lectures, thereby turning urban public spaces into didactic environments, was part of such an attempt to broaden the party's reach. So was scheduling major events to coincide with local market days when peasants came to town to trade goods. Officials also began to move away from strictly Western types of activities, for, as one dissatisfied audience member noted after a piano and violin recital at the Merzifon Halkevi, people "do not want to listen to this strange *alafranga* music, which is so foreign to [their] ears."[94] Following the dismal performance of its classical music division, however, Merzifon Halkevi went on to establish a Turkish music division, which did attain popularity.[95] Although Halkevleri failed to popularize the imported contents of their cultural offerings, the format they introduced for the government-funded scientific study and performance of music, dance, and dramatic arts, which was equally foreign, proved acceptable.

The give-and-take between the party and the polity transformed existing spaces and spatial practices, thus generating new crossovers that neither conformed to RPP's initial vision nor were strictly conventional. Acknowledging the contingent nature of this process reveals that the cadre that ran Halkevleri was not a monolithic body, and that the rejection of their efforts by the public at large was far from categorical. It opens up the possibility of imagining Halkevleri not as exclusive playgrounds for the republican elite but as sites of encounter, at which party officials, rank-and-file civil servants, and locals met and adjusted their expectations of themselves and each other, despite the inherent asymmetry of their relative positions and access to resources and power.

CONCLUSION

Official historiography and development theories have variously represented the early republican ideology prescribed by Mustafa Kemal and implemented by the single-party regime as a secular, enlightened, rational, and pragmatist ideology. It condoned the use of militant measures only temporarily to expedite Turkey's progression into a modern society. However, as recent scholarship has made amply clear, authoritarianism was integral to the Kemalist ideological framework from its inception. Kemalists regarded the public sphere and its institutions not as platforms for true political negotiation and exchange of ideas but as sites that had to be dominated.[96] They tried relentlessly to monopolize the public sphere and eliminate alternative ideologies, potential political opposition, and competing sources of loyalty.[97] This resulted in the suppression of religious activities, purges of political rivals, and the demise of ethnic and religious minorities.

A new order cannot be forged by proscriptive actions alone, however. Rather it is contingent on seizing control over the popular imagination and making the artificial appear natural, almost inevitable. Access to the state's resources gave Kemalists the upper hand in this process, but the dearth of a serviceable infrastructure, a consolidated market, and a sizable competent workforce in a war-torn country severely limited their actual transformative prowess. Nevertheless, even as they continually rescaled their ambitions to fit the constraints imposed by Turkey's realities, RPP leaders sought to put in place strategic mechanisms that would facilitate the continued reproduction and expansion of a core constituency comprising the state's military-judiciary-bureaucratic establishment and private entrepreneurs who depended on the state for their success. This constituency would be loyal to the state and take on itself the responsibility to uphold the foundational tenets of the Kemalist republic. As institutions of cultural production and transmission with the potential to shape collective and individual actions and outlook for generations to come, the schools, Girls' Institutes, and Halkevleri examined in this chapter were indispensable tools for this process of establishing ideological hegemony. They mediated some of the most intense encounters between the citizenry and the Kemalist state and they familiarized a broad spectrum of the population with the constitutive practices of that state. Most important, they translated Kemalism from rhetoric into action, by engaging both minds and bodies in carefully structured and closely monitored activities that played out in real time and space.

EPILOGUE

There is a certain poignancy about finalizing a book on the making of the modern Turkish nation-state just as the very premises of that state, its fundamental symbols, and the ties that bind its polity together have become subjects of intense contention. What triggered this latest wave of unrest was the violent police intervention, in late May 2013, against a handful of environmentalists who had camped out at Gezi Park, near Istanbul's Taksim Square, to stop the construction of yet another shopping mall in the city—this one supposedly a replica of an Ottoman army barracks that had once been in the same location. Overnight, Gezi became an unexpected catalyst for previously unconnected constituencies to publicly express their long-brewing resentments about the country's direction and to find—albeit temporary and unstructured—solidarity in each other's company as they took to the streets across Turkey.[1] Many shared a generalized unease about then prime minister (now president) Erdoğan's increasingly authoritarian policies and were disappointed that what had started out as a promise to democratize Turkey, wresting it from decades-long military tutelage, had turned into a brutal witch hunt, similar to what was previously seen after coups.[2] Others were troubled by the government's intensifying intrusions into private life, with tactics ranging from nudging to legal restrictions, in areas such as family planning, alcohol consumption, Internet use, and even personal attire.[3] People were also concerned about hawkish and deeply flawed attempts to reposition Turkey as a regional leader, with thinly veiled neo-Ottomanist ambitions, most visibly in Egypt and Syria.[4] In short, what started out as a debate over rights to the city spiraled into an unprecedented and spectacular collective interrogation of the relationship between the state and its citizens, the modes, channels, and sites of their encounters.

Erdoğan, who, for more than a decade, has ruled with minimum friction thanks to his party's comfortable majority in the parliament and the opposition's considerable incompetence, was unwilling to negotiate or hear grievances and was harsh in his response to these developments. As protests spread to almost all the provinces, he endorsed the continued use of excessive police force even as the demonstrators deliberately chose to avoid confrontation. By the time violence subsided, 8 people had died and more than 7,500 people had been wounded.[5] Erdoğan also silenced the already largely subservient media and, in subsequent months, constrained the activities of various professional bodies and civic organizations that could serve as platforms for the dissemination of critical opinions.[6] To galvanize broader public support, especially among his base, he argued that these events had been incited by malicious foreign governments and organizations that could not stand Turkey's booming economy and rising international stature. He also cannily tapped into his electorate's religious (read Sunni) sensitivities by personally circulating what were eventually proved to be false stories of sacrilegious acts perpetrated by the protesters, further deepening extant religious cleavages.[7]

Erdoğan's Justice and Development Party (AKP) drew its strength from a population that had long been marginalized in Turkish politics and elite cultural life. From the outset, members of a powerful military-judiciary-bureaucratic triad (i.e., primary wielders of power, as shown in in this book) had run the country according to what they considered to be strict Kemalist principles, prioritizing the state's interests in matters political, economic, and cultural.[8] Together with a distinctive class of entrepreneurs and industrialists, who were beholden to them for imposing discriminatory policies that reduced non-Muslims' dominance in the private sector and for implementing protectionist measures that shielded them from foreign competition, they had acted as gatekeepers. Upward mobility had been available to those who espoused the same principles— if extremely unevenly. But those who embraced more conservative ways of life, who resented republican restrictions on religious expression, who were alienated by the growing influence of imported cultural forms and values or the disruptions in social order brought on by modernization were, for the most part, shut out of decision-making processes. Moreover, even if they found financial success, they lacked the cultural capital to join the ranks of the country's elite. The AKP only came to power after several of its previous incarnations were outlawed for threatening to undermine the secular principles of the state.[9] To accomplish this, the party adopted a carefully calibrated strategy, brought into the fold a coalition of liberal intellectuals and business elite, who also felt stifled by the unending tutelage and ideological rigidity, and obtained the financial backing of a rising conservative entrepreneurial class (Anatolian tigers) that had successfully taken advantage of expanding global economic opportunities. The AKP also benefited from a changed international climate that no longer overlooked military or judicial interventions against popularly elected governments. Despite some setbacks and disagreements, the experiment seemed successful and the party expanded its lead in the 2007 and 2011 elections.[10] But thereafter an air of invincibility set in as a confident Erdoğan set out to establish one-man rule. In response, popular discontent surged and the coalition of intellectuals, business people, and religious leaders dissolved, culminating in the extraordinary flare-up at Gezi, which has since become the reference point for a new grassroots more inclusive and liberal movement in Turkish politics.[11]

The actions and rhetoric of the government and the protesters not only resonated with the now familiar formative themes of the Turkish nation-state, but, notably from this book's perspective, they revolved around the meanings and use of public space, eliciting direct comparisons between the Early Republican and AKP governments. In the first place, Gezi Park and Taksim Square have long been considered Istanbul's most quintessentially modern sites. Selected as Istanbul's Republic Square because it had almost no physical trace of official Ottoman building stock, with the erection of one of the earliest Atatürk monuments in the country, Taksim became the focal point for commemorative ceremonies, public exhibitions, and collective reenactments of Turkey's foundation narratives. Just nearby, the courtyard of the abandoned nineteenth-century Ottoman Army barracks was used for sports, variously as a makeshift football stadium—including Turkey's inaugural national game against Romania—and a wrestling arena. In 1942, the barracks were demolished to make room for Istanbul's first modern park, which became a popular destination for urban outings.[12] Redesigning the square and reconstructing the barracks would be tantamount to erasing Taksim's republican heritage, and as such, it was a move that resonated with the AKP's sustained efforts across the country to raze modernist landmarks closely identified with the Early Republic and downgrade—if not altogether eliminate—the commemorations and celebrations that have become Republican traditions in the past eight decades.[13]

As the most Europeanized part of Istanbul, Taksim had been selected as the ideal location for showcasing the modern sociospatial practices promoted by the republican leadership, corroborating its aspirations for accession to the ranks of modern civilized nations. It was not just the official or recreational uses of the square or the park itself, but the myriad venues of urban sociability around it that made Taksim worthy of such an assertion. Istanbul's theaters, best restaurants, hotels, stores, and social clubs had long been located in this district, and for the first few decades of the Turkish Republic, Taksim continued to be the city's prime business district, as the head offices of national and branches of international companies concentrated around it. Despite the ups and downs in its fortunes and its changing place within Istanbul's macroform, as the city firmly establishes itself within the geography of twenty-first-century globalization and other larger purpose-built business districts rise, Taksim has remained a lively urban hub, a cultural center, and a window to the world.

Nonetheless, in the run-up to the Gezi events, activities once proudly touted as evidence of modern lifestyles were caught in the crosshairs of the AKP's social discourse for being alien, decadent, and immoral. Restrictions on sidewalk cafés, bans on the public consumption of alcohol, which was also heavily taxed, increasingly loud criticism of mixed gender socialization, disparaging remarks on the appropriate attire for women—all in all seemingly minor interferences in public life—were instrumental in driving a large number of youths to the protests at Gezi. The protesters saw these as visible manifestations of more sinister and invasive policies that stunted the public sphere and imposed a certain kind of orthodox religiosity on social and personal life choices. These interventions constituted a deliberate reversal of the norms that governed public life under the republic. Whereas Early Republican leaders had promoted a Western-style sociability and relegated religious expression to the private sphere, the AKP rewarded the public display of piety and faith, while marginalizing sociospatial practices that unmistakably invoked Early Republican aspirations to modern urbanity. Such interventions also revealed that the AKP leaders, much like their predecessors, whom they ruthlessly maligned, did not envision a truly public sphere in which individuals make choices, express themselves, or assemble to demand their rights. Despite their profound ideological differences, ultimately they both preferred a heavily monitored public sphere with little room for dissent or deviation from prescribed modes of association.

Taksim also encapsulated the republic's complicated relationship with religion and its incoherent history with secularism. Together with the Galata district, of which it formed part, Taksim was a ready-made site of Westernized urban imagery because for centuries it had been the historic business and residential enclave for European merchants and their

Ottoman counterparts, who were reviled by the republican leadership as a comprador bourgeoisie compromising the empire's economy. Stamping the district with the republic's distinctive cache was, therefore, the realization of a thinly veiled desire to symbolically reconquer this last bastion of foreign interests in the bosom of Istanbul.[14] Despite exclusionary practices against non-Muslims, however, the republican takeover of the square was deliberately secular in terms of the symbols and activities chosen. Later governments continued with this mission, framing the eastern end of the square with the Atatürk Cultural Center (1946–1969), a state-of-the art venue for the performing arts and arguably one of the most elegant interpretations of international modernism in Turkey.[15] Used as a way of purging the district's non-Muslim history, while selectively co-opting its cultural legacy, this heightened sense of secularism became firmly embedded in republican Taksim's image and remained in effect for decades. In the late 1980s, however, rumors of a proposed grand mosque in Taksim began to circulate as the first signs of a sea change indicating the rise of Islamist politics, which over the next couple of decades would pave the way to the AKP's election victories.[16]

Coming out of decades of not just political but also cultural marginalization, the AKP's leaders also sought to rebuild Taksim in their own image, showcasing a peculiar reinterpretation of Ottoman heritage as if it were purely a Turco-Islamic invention, writing out the plurality that had been germane to the empire's power and longevity, and presenting their projects as if almost nine decades of Western-oriented republican rule had had no influence on cultural production in the country. The reconstruction of a faux Ottoman barracks, supposedly restoring the district to its former glory, was in line with AKP's other attempts to build *truer than original* Ottoman landmarks throughout Istanbul—and the rest of the country.[17] Building an ultramodern mosque with vaguely Ottomanesque references on the opposite end of the square, meanwhile, was meant as a direct counterstatement against the modernism of the Atatürk Cultural Center and the uses it engendered. Remarkably, there were two inherent ironies in this posturing, both expressed through architecture: first, by embracing and building on this imagined Ottoman legacy, Erdoğan defined himself in full opposition to the republican leadership who had so categorically sought to repudiate it. But the spectacular performance of religiosity notwithstanding, his rewriting of history replicated the republican desire to edit the empire's non-Muslim subjects out of its history. That the barracks and, later, Gezi Park stood on a former Armenian cemetery and that the park's marble stairs were made of gravestones from surrounding Armenian cemeteries displaced by republican urban renewal were not lost on the protestors, who had allied themselves with some of the city's key non-Muslim communities.[18] Second, by 2013, the AKP's urban moves, largely portrayed as heritage preservation, were failing to mask the neoliberal crony capitalism underlying various transactions that transferred public land to political supporters in direct contravention of Ottoman state tradition, which the party claimed to faithfully uphold and emulate. Indeed, the increasing rejection of these narratives by a growing critical mass was what ultimately sparked the protests of 2013.

Contentions over modernization and how to regulate its scope, the place of civil society vis-à-vis the state, the boundaries of the public and the private, and the recognition of ethnoreligious diversity that violently surfaced in Taksim, have been the pervasive themes of republican history, the formative years of which I have examined in this book. Although power has changed hands and the military-judiciary-bureaucratic triad that long underpinned it has been all but dismantled, the strategies for silencing critical dissent have not. Neither has the discourse that equates modernization exclusively with material improvements, presented often in the form of celebrated infrastructural projects—roads, railroads, urban improvement projects—without attending to the myriad concomitant transformations that individuals and society experience and demand. Meanwhile, over the past decades, deliberations about what belongs in the public sphere and what should be relegated to the private sphere have continued unabated. Although it is not the only issue of this kind, the expression of faith has been the most polarizing of these issues, discussed primarily, though not exclusively, in term's of women's bodies—specifically regarding the use of the headscarf in public institutions.[19] Similarly, tapping into the nation's latent anxieties about malicious foreign interference in domestic affairs and about marginalization for being Muslim—by the West or by its local agents—remains a well-worn recourse for shoring up public support whenever questions about the country's direction emerge and a difficult public debate looms. Last, but not least, historiography continues to be a strategic arena of intervention for whoever takes the reins, and this project always involves reshaping the built environment to fit the desired narrative, demolishing buildings, rewiring functional and symbolic relationships between spaces and their uses, and thus erasing certain unwanted meanings from the landscape and reinscribing new ones onto it. The Gezi events represent yet another layer woven out of these very themes, but one that cannot be fully deciphered without examining the underlying layers.

Methodologically speaking, establishing a relational framework within which actors positioned themselves and sites and practices acquired meaning is just as important as identifying the enduring themes pertaining to the making of modern Turkey and the latest milestone of this story at Gezi. Building a nation-state is an inherently spatial process that unfolds simultaneously and on different yet interdependent scales. In that regard, a principal goal of this book, from the outset, has been to demonstrate the concurrence between the creative and destructive processes that have transformed Turkey's landscape. Hence, the deliberate dismantling of ethnoreligious enclaves—Muslim and non-Muslim alike—and the use of their land and assets to realize ambitious modernization projects have played crucial roles in structuring my narrative. But the anxieties that shaped the official culture and decision making would be hard to recognize without attending to the intersections of the intentionally calculated and the relatively unpredictable parallel processes evolving independently of state control. Suffice it to say that the self-confident pronouncements of unmitigated sovereignty over Anatolia—at the expense of other cultures that had long coinhabited it—at the 1937 History Exhibition were made against the background of one of the most violent Kurdish uprisings in republican history, which were brutally suppressed just in time for Atatürk's visit to the region mere weeks after the exhibition's conclusion.[20] An equally important aim of this book has been to recognize the multiple spatial scales at which an event might register and to locate the threads running across those different scales. As I have illustrated, within the idiosyncratic context of diplomacy in Turkey, a seeming formality like the spectacular arrival of Russian dignitaries with a flotilla down the Bosphorus to celebrate the tenth anniversary of the Turkish Republic (1933) was also the enactment of much larger cartographic calculations about the balance of geopolitical powers in the eastern Mediterranean, at once sending signals to Italy and Great Britain, both of which had designs on the region. Making the nation imaginable through tangible means and imaginational practices was a similarly multipronged process that operated on several scales. Hence, for instance, elementary school drills that trained students to visualize Turkey through maps and site visits in which they could actually see segments of the large infrastructure projects that crisscrossed the country, consolidating it operationally, were just as important for developing the mental dexterity to move nimbly between the national space and its abstractions.

All told, expanding on the widely accepted notion that building the nation-state is a spatial enterprise, this book has zoomed into the texture of the nation's demarcated territory to explore how the state and its citizens activate it and bestow it with meaning. It has posited that neither the paths and nodes of activity that structure the national space nor the practices that animate it can be viewed in isolation, but much like texts or images, they are contingent on and derive meaning from one another. Beyond the specifics of this monograph, I would argue, using a relational framework that foregrounds *interspatiality* provides an indispensable tool for studying nation-state building processes in general. This approach reveals the resonances between spaces and practices at different scales, uncovers the interdependences between concurrent events, and exposes the lineages of meaning between cumulative chronological layers. It is, after all, at the confluence of these multifarious and, at times, seemingly disparate spaces that the nation-state finds its full expression.

NOTES

Introduction: Ambivalences and Anxieties

1. "Turkey: Matbuat Umum Müdürlüğü, 'L'Exposition d'Histoire,'" *La Turquie Kemaliste* (Número Spécial Consacré à La IIe Congrés d'Histoire Turque et a l'Exposition d'Histoire 20–26 septembre 1937), nos. 21–22 (1937): 13–22.

2. In Turkish: "Tarih yazmak, tarih yapmak kadar mühimdir. Yazan yapana sadık kalmazsa değişmeyen hakikat, insanlığı şaşırtacak bir mahiyet alır."

3. For the creative mobilization of the notions of history, heritage, and archaeology in nation building, see, among others Benedict Anderson, *Imagined Communities: Reflections on the Origin and the Spread of Nationalism* (New York: Verso, 1983); E. J. Hobsbawm, *Nations and Nationalism since 1780: Programme, Myth, Reality*, 2nd ed. (Cambridge: Cambridge University Press, 2012); Eric Hobsbawm and Terence Ranger, *The Invention of Tradition*, Past and Present Publications (Cambridge: Cambridge University Press, 1984). See also comparisons and case studies by Eugen Weber, *My France: Politics, Culture, Myth* (Cambridge, MA: Belknap Press of Harvard University Press, 1991); Rogers Brubaker, *Citizenship and Nationhood in France and Germany* (Cambridge, MA: Harvard University Press, 1992); Nadia Abu El-Haj, *Facts on the Ground: Archaeological Practice and Territorial Self-Fashioning in Israeli Society* (Chicago: University of Chicago Press, 2008); Afshin Marashi, *Nationalizing Iran: Culture, Power, and the State, 1870–1940* (Seattle: University of Washington Press, 2008); D. Medina Lasansky, *The Renaissance Perfected: Architecture, Spectacle, and Tourism in Fascist Italy* (University Park: Pennsylvania State University Press, 2004). For a general overview of the political uses of cartography, including for corroborating nationalists' claims, see John Brian Harley, "The Map and the Development of the History of Cartography," in *The History of Cartography, Volume 1*, ed. David Woodward and John Brian Harley, accessed June 22, 2012, http://www.press.uchicago.edu/ucp/books/book/chicago/H/bo3620863.html; Jeremy Black, *Maps and Politics* (Chicago: University of Chicago Press, 2004); Mark S. Monmonier, *How to Lie with Maps* (Chicago: University of Chicago Press, 1996).

4. For the ideologically heavy content of curricula as informed by the exhibition

and history congresses in Turkey see Etienne Copeaux, *Tarih Ders Kitaplarında (1931–1993): Türk Tarih Tezinden Türk İslam Sentezine* (Istanbul: Tarih Vakfı Yurt Yayınları, 1998); Büşra Ersanlı Behar, *İktidar ve Tarih: Türkiye'de 'Resmi Tarih' Tezinin Oluşumu (1929–1937)* (Istanbul: AFA Yayınları, 1992); Faith Childress, "Republican Lessons: Education and the Making of Modern Turkey" (PhD diss., University of Utah, 2001).

5. There is an expansive body of literature on the empire's integration into the global networks of nineteenth-century capitalism and how these networks transformed social structures and life in general. For a few representative general overviews of the process see Behar, *İktidar ve Tarih*; Copeaux, *Tarih Ders Kitaplarında*; Childress, "Republican Lessons." For studies focusing on the transformation of Ottoman cities, see Sevgi Aktüre, *19. Yüzyıl Sonunda Anadolu Kenti Mekansal Yapı Çözümlemesi* (Ankara: Orta Dogu Teknik Üniversitesi Yayınları, 1978); Reşat Kasaba, Çağlar Keyder, and Faruk Tabak, "Eastern Mediterranean Port Cities and Their Bourgeoisies: Merchants, Political Projects, and Nation-States," *Fernand Braudel Center Review* 10, no. 1986 (n.d.): 121–35; Zeynep Çelik, *Empire, Architecture, and the City: French-Ottoman Encounters, 1830–1914* (Seattle: University of Washington Press, 2008).

6. For a concise summary of the millets, the empire's ethnoreligious communities, and their structural transformation, see Fatma Müge Göçek, "Ethnic Segmentation, Western Education, and Political Outcomes: Nineteenth-Century Ottoman Society," *Poetics Today* 14, no. 3 (1993): 507–38. A very valuable overview of the accommodative pluralistic constitution of the Ottoman Empire and the gradual emergence of rigid divisions between the constituent communities is offered by Karen Barkey, *Empire of Difference: The Ottomans in Comparative Perspective* (Cambridge: Cambridge University Press, 2008).

7. For a comparative study of these changes within the empire, see Anna Phrankoudakē and Çağlar Keyder, *Ways to Modernity in Greece and Turkey: Encounters with Europe, 1850–1950* (London: I. B. Tauris, 2007). For the way that these transformations informed the urban public sphere, see Gilles Veinstein, ed., *Selânik 1850–1918: "Yahudilerin Kenti" ve Balkanlar'ın Uyanışı* (İstanbul: İletişim, 1999); Sibel Zandi-Sayek, *Ottoman Izmir: The Rise of a Cosmopolitan Port, 1840–1880* (Minneapolis: University of Minnesota Press, 2012). Insights about how modern European-style education informed these changes can be found in Selçuk Akşin Somel, "Osmanlı Ermenilerinde Kültür Modernleşmesi, Cemaat Okulları ve Abdülhamid Rejimi," *Tarih ve Toplum: Yeni Yaklaşımlar*, no. 5 (2007): 71–92.

8. Çağlar Keyder, *State and Class in Turkey: A Study in Capitalist Development* (London: Verso, 1987); Karen Barkey, "Thinking about the Consequences of Empire," in *After Empire: Multiethnic Societies and Nation-Building*, ed. Mark von Hagen, 94–114 (Boulder, CO: Westview Press, 1997).

9. See Carter Vaughn Findley, *Turkey, Islam, Nationalism, and Modernity: A History, 1789–2007* (New Haven, CT: Yale University Press, 2010), esp. ch. 4; and M. Şükrü Hanioğlu, "The Second Constitutional Period (1908–18)," in *The Cambridge History of Turkey: Volume 4, Turkey in the Modern World*, 1st ed., ed. Reşat Kasaba, 62–111 (Cambridge: Cambridge University Press, 2008).

10. Findley, *Turkey, Islam, Nationalism, and Modernity*, 204.

11. Reşat Kasaba, *A Moveable Empire: Ottoman Nomads, Migrants, and Refugees* (Seattle: University of Washington Press, 2009), 123–26.

12. Hanioğlu, "The Second Constitutional Period (1908–18)," 68–70.

13. For the politics and activities of the CUP, see Feroz Ahmad, *The Young Turks:*

The Committee of Union and Progress in Turkish Politics 1908–14 (London: C. Hurst, 2009); M. Şükrü Hanioğlu, *A Brief History of the Late Ottoman Empire* (Princeton, NJ: Princeton University Press, 2008); Hanioğlu, "The Second Constitutional Period (1908–18)"; Erik J. Zürcher, *The Young Turk Legacy and Nation Building: From the Ottoman Empire to Atatürk's Turkey* (London: I. B. Tauris, 2010).

14. Major fronts were opened in Eastern Anatolia (Kafkasya), Gallipoli, and the Arabian Peninsula, Sinai-Palestine, and Iraq (including Sinai-Palestine, Iraq, and the Hejaz-Arabian Peninsula against the British. There were also relatively minor battles in Iran, Macedonia, and Galicia.

15. Ayhan Aktar, *Varlık Vergisi ve "Türkleştirme" Politikaları* (Istanbul: İletişim Yayınları, 2000); Taner Akçam, *Ermeni Meselesi Hallolmuştur: Osmanlı Belgelerine Göre Savaş Yıllarında Ermenilere Yönelik Politikalar* (Istanbul: İletişim Yayınları, 2008).

16. The literature on the deportations and massacres to which Anatolian Armenians were subjected is broad. Recent scholarship that takes advantage of both Ottoman and foreign sources includes Akçam, *Ermeni Meselesi Hallolmuştur*; Uğur Ümit Üngör, *The Making of Modern Turkey: Nation and State in Eastern Anatolia, 1913–1950* (Oxford: Oxford University Press, 2011); Ronald Grigor Suny, Fatma Müge Göçek, and Norman M. Naimark, *A Question of Genocide: Armenians and Turks at the End of the Ottoman Empire* (New York: Oxford University Press, 2013); Hans-Lukas Kieser, *Iskalanmış Barış: Doğu Vilayetlerinde Misyonerlik, Etnik Kimlik ve Devlet 1839–1938*, trans. Atilla Dirim (Istanbul: İletişim, 2005); Taner Akçam, *The Young Turks' Crime against Humanity: The Armenian Genocide and Ethnic Cleansing in the Ottoman Empire* (Princeton, NJ: Princeton University Press, 2012).

17. Zürcher, *The Young Turk Legacy and Nation Building*, 139. Although sources differ on the total death toll from 800,000 to 2.5 million, in recent years most estimates agree on 1.5 million dead. For a comparison of different calculations, see Taner Akçam, *The Young Turks' Crime against Humanity: The Armenian Genocide and Ethnic Cleansing in the Ottoman Empire* (Princeton, NJ: Princeton University Press, 2012), 253–64.

18. For detailed studies of demographic transformation in Turkey from empire to republic, see Kemal Karpat, *Osmanlı Nüfusu 1830–1914 (Demografik ve Sosyal Özellikleri)* (Istanbul: Tarih Vakfi Yurt Yayınları, 2003); Justin McCarthy, *Muslims and Minorities: The Population of Ottoman Anatolia at the End of the Empire* (New York: New York University Press, 1983).

19. For a systematic study of the alliances with and continuities between the CUP and the nationalists, see Zürcher, *The Young Turk Legacy and Nation Building*.

20. The economist Joseph Schumpeter's conceptualization of capitalist expansion processes have found resonance among scholars interested in modernization and nation-state formation processes as well. Critical works with significant spatial implications that have been instrumental to my interpretation of the Turkish experience include Marshall Berman, *All That Is Solid Melts into Air: The Experience of Modernity* (London: Verso, 1983); David Harvey, *The Condition of Postmodernity: An Enquiry into the Origins of Cultural Change* (Oxford: Blackwell, 1989). An influential book detailing the intertwinement for creative and destructive forces in the making of a modern nation-state is Eugen Weber, *Peasants into Frenchmen: The Modernization of Rural France 1870–1914* (Stanford, CA: Stanford University Press, 1977). For the layering (and occasionally displacement) of competing practices, see also Alice Garner,

A Shifting Shore: Locals, Outsiders, and the Transformation of a French Fishing Town, 1823–2000 (Ithaca, NY: Cornell University Press, 2005).

21. For references on forced homogenization processes central to nation-state building, see, among others, Ernest Gellner, *Nations and Nationalism* (Ithaca, NY: Cornell University Press, 1983); Heather Rae, *State Identities and the Homogenisation of Peoples* (Cambridge: Cambridge University Press, 2002). More specific to the Turkish experience with reference to the suppression or elimination of ethnic and religious identities are, among others, Martin van Bruinessen, *Agha, Shaikh, and State: The Social and Political Structures of Kurdistan* (London: Zed Books, 1992); Resat Kasaba, "Izmir 1922: A Port City Unravels," in *Modernity and Culture: From the Mediterranean to the Indian Ocean*, ed. Leila Fawaz, C. A. Bayly, and Robert Ilbert, 204–30 (New York: Columbia University Press, 2002); Nilüfer Göle, *The Forbidden Modern: Civilization and Veiling*, Critical Perspectives on Women and Gender (Ann Arbor: University of Michigan Press, 1996); Kasaba, *A Moveable Empire*; Mesut Yeğen, *Devlet Söyleminde Kürt Sorunu*, 1. baskı. (Istanbul: İletişim Yayınları, 1999); Taner Akçam, *Türk Ulusal Kimliği ve Ermeni Sorunu* (Istanbul: İletişim Yayınları, 1992); Akçam, *The Young Turks' Crime against Humanity*; Serif Mardin, *Religion and Social Change in Modern Turkey* (Albany: State University of New York Press, 1989); Karen Barkey and Mark Von Hagen, *After Empire: Multiethnic Societies and Nation-Building: The Soviet Union and the Russian, Ottoman, and Habsburg Empires* (Boulder, CO: Westview Press, 1997).

22. See Theda Skocpol's seminal discussion of the balance between internal pacification and international recognition for the constitution of a modern state, and, more recently, Heather Rae's summary of internal-external considerations in state formation. Theda Skocpol, *States and Social Revolutions: A Comparative Analysis of France, Russia, and China* (Cambridge: Cambridge University Press, 1979); Heather Rae, "Theories of State Formation," in *International Relations Theory for the Twenty-First Century*, ed. Martin Griffiths (London: Routledge, 2007), 123–34.

23. For critical views on the tools and practices of the kind of social engineering that modern states have deployed to produce loyal citizens with a shared repertoire of knowledge and skills, see Michel Foucault, *Discipline and Punish: The Birth of the Prison* (New York: Penguin, 1988); Michel Foucault, "Governmentality," in *The Anthropology of the State: A Reader* (London: Blackwell, 2006), 131–43; Etienne Balibar and Immanuel Maurice Wallerstein, *Race, Nation, Class: Ambiguous Identities* (New York: Verso, 1991); James C. Scott, *Seeing like a State: How Certain Schemes to Improve the Human Condition Have Failed* (New Haven, CT: Yale University Press, 1998).

24. There is a broad literature about the use of museums for public edification, often with the underlying design to instill the dominant ideology. On museums, see, for instance, Tony Bennet, *The Birth of the Museum: History, Theory, Politics* (London: Routledge, 1995); Eilean Hooper-Greenhill, *Museums and the Shaping of Knowledge*, ed. Andrew Wheatcroft, The Heritage Care and Preservation Management (London: Routledge, 1992); Susan Pearce, *Museums, Objects and Collections* (Washington, DC: Smithsonian Institution Press, 1992). Agendas that justified the industrial capitalism and colonial enterprise also drove world fairs (Burton Benedict, *The Anthropology of World's Fairs: San Francisco's Panama Pacific International Exposition of 1915* [London: Scolar Press, 1983]; Patricia A Morton, *Hybrid Modernities: Architecture and Representation at the 1931 Colonial Exposition, Paris*, illustrated ed. [Cambridge, MA: MIT Press, 2000]). Building or rejuvenating the nation was never far from the

concerns of museum and exhibition organizers. (Becky Conekin, *The Autobiography of a Nation: The 1951 Festival of Britain* [Manchester: Manchester University Press, 2003]; David Boswell and Jessica Evans, *Representing the Nation: A Reader: Histories, Heritage and Museums*, 1st ed. [London: Routledge, 1999]).

25. For trenchant critiques of the tensions and incongruities involved in adopting this binary trope, first identified in Edward Said's influential work (Edward Said, *Orientalism* [New York: Vintage Books, 1978]), by non-Western intellectuals and political leaders to advance their modernizing agendas, see Partha Chatterjee, *Nationalist Thought and the Colonial World: A Derivative Discourse* (Minneapolis: University of Minnesota Press, 1993); Meyda Yeğenoğlu, *Colonial Fantasies: Towards a Feminist Critique of Orientalism* (Cambridge: Cambridge University Press, 1998).

26. The selective appropriation of an idealized classical heritage into European cultural history—informing, among other areas, arts, architecture, philosophy, and historiography—became fairly common in the nineteenth century. *The Invention of Tradition*, with Eric Hobsbawm's seminal introduction, has been particularly influential in opening up a critical debate about such manufactured histories and heritages, often at the service of thinly veiled political agendas (Hobsbawm and Ranger, *The Invention of Tradition*). Despite the controversy it spurred, the publication of *Black Athena* has been similarly important for reexamining the selective appropriations of classical cultures, reconstructed in isolation from their broader historical context. Martin Bernal, *Black Athena: The Afroasiatic Roots of Classical Civilization* (New Brunswick, NJ: Rutgers University Press, 1987). For recent scholarship on the grafting of classical cultures into national narratives, see Lasansky, *The Renaissance Perfected*; Katerina Zacharia, *Hellenisms: Culture, Identity, and Ethnicity from Antiquity to Modernity* (Hampshire: Ashgate Publishing, 2008); Can Bilsel, *Antiquity on Display: Regimes of the Authentic in Berlin's Pergamon Museum* (Oxford: Oxford University Press, 2012).

27. An excerpt from Atatürk's speech at the inauguration of the third term of the assembly (Zabıt Ceridesi, Devre: III, Içtima I, cilt: I, pp. 3–4 [November 1, 1927]).

28. Behar, İktidar ve Tarih, 103–8; Copeaux, *Tarih Ders Kitaplarında*, 45–53.

Chapter 1. Political Capital

1. "Ankara-Istanbul," *La Turquie Kamaliste*, no. 47 (n.d.): 38.

2. Henri Lefebvre, *The Production of Space* (Oxford: Blackwell, 1991), 53–54.

3. Ruşen Keleş, *Eski Ankara'da Bir Sehir Tipolojisi* (Ankara: Ankara Üniversitesi Siyasal Bilgiler Fakültesi Yayınları, 1971), 5.

4. Report from Geoffrey Knox, Charge d'Affairs in Ankara to the Foreign Office, dated May 20, 1927, Doc. 13, Inclosure in Doc. 12, Letter from Sir George Clerk to Sir Austen Chamberlain, dated June 9, 1927 (FO E/2711/257/44).

5. TBMM Ceridesi 2. Devre, 1. Sene Cilt 2 [Session Transcripts of the Turkish Grand National Assembly, 2nd assembly, 1st session, vol. 2], 666–70 (abbreviated as TBMM, 666–70 below).

6. TBMM Zabıt Ceridesi 2. Devre, 1. Sene Cilt 2, 666–70.

7. "Devlet Merkezi," *Hakimiyet-i Milliye*, October 16, 1923.

8. TBMM Zabıt Ceridesi 2. Devre, 1. Sene Cilt 2, 666–70.

9. That there was a direct relationship between the making of a new state and

its capital was frequently stated explicitly and often by those at the forefront of the nationalist movement. Among them, see: Falih Rıfkı Atay, *Çankaya: Atatürk Devri Hatıraları* (Ankara: Dünya Yayınları, 1958); Kemal Atatuğ, *Çocuklara Ankara* (Ankara: Yeni Cezaevi Matbaası, 1949); Mahmut Goloğlu, *Atatürk ve Anadolu Kulübü* (Ankara: Ajans-Türk Matbaacılık Sanayii, 1981); Yakup Kadri Karaosmanoğlu, *Ankara* (Istanbul: İletişim Yayınları, 1991). In his report for final draft of the city plan, Hermann Jansen, who, as I will explain later in this chapter, had been commissioned to prepare the plan, also made similar remarks about the relationship between city building and state building. See Hermann Jansen, *Ankara İli İmar Planı* (Istanbul: Alaaddin Kıral Matbaası, 1937), 7. Similarly, French diplomat and journalist Jacques Bénoist-Mechin wrote that Ankara was the most tangible instance of Turkey's rebirth as a modern nation. See Jacques Bénoist-Méchin, *Mustafa Kemal: Bir İmparatorluğun Ölümü*, trans. Zeki Çelikkol (Ankara: Bilgi Yayinevi, 1995), 295.

10. Zabıt Ceridesi, February 25, 1341/1925 Devre 2 İçtima 2 Cilt 14–15 i 64, c 3, 329.

11. Quoted in Bernard Lewis, *The Emergence of Modern Turkey* (Oxford: Oxford University Press, 1962), 266 (from Kemal Atatürk, *Atatürk'ün Söylev ve Demeçleri*).

12. "Asya'da bir Avrupa sehri" *Yedigün* 8, no. 191, November 4, quoted in Sibel Bozdoğan, *Modernism and Nation-Building: Turkish Architectural Culture in the Early Republic* (Seattle: University of Washington Press, 2001), 68.

13. Meyda Yeğenoğlu, *Colonial Fantasies: Towards a Feminist Critique of Orientalism* (Cambridge: Cambridge University Press, 1998), 123.

14. Johannes Fabian, *Time and the Other: How Anthropology Makes Its Object* (New York: Columbia University Press, 1983), 17, 25, 31.

15. Fabian, *Time and the Other*, 147.

16. Partha Chatterjee, *Nationalist Thought and the Colonial World: A Derivative Discourse* (Minneapolis: University of Minnesota Press, 1993), 38–42. Chatterjee maintains that insofar as it "accepts and adopts the same essentialist conception based on the distinction between the East and the West, the same typology created by the transcendent studying subject, and, hence, the same objectifying procedures of knowledge constructed in the post Enlightenment age of Western science" (38), non-Western nationalist thought is complicit with imperialism and consequently, it perpetuates the legacies of both Orientalism and Eurocentrism.

17. Although Mustafa Kemal and his supporters called for a complete break from the empire, others demanded continuity. Even some of Mustafa Kemal's closest wartime allies had declared themselves to be committed royalists who were "bound by conscience and sentiment to the Sultanate and Caliphate. Among the royalists were some of the most prominent heroes of the War of Independence such as Refet (Bele) Pasha, who had led the nationalist forces to victories in the battleground, and Rauf (Orbay) Bey, who had traveled to Anatolia in Mustafa Kemal's first entourage and had been a prominent member of the first cabinet (see Lewis, *The Emergence of Modern Turkey*, 257.) Meanwhile, in the Grand National Assembly, the contingency of representatives who had led persistent opposition to Mustafa Kemal's leadership throughout the entire war were clearly loath to support his imminent bid for power. This particular group was fiercely opposed to Mustafa Kemal's leadership and on more than one occasion tried to undermine it. During the transitional period (between the war and the dissolution of the Grand National Assembly) they even tried to pass legislation stating that those born outside the national boundaries as deemed by

the Lausanne Treaty could not become president or member of parliament. This was a serious enough threat but was remedied by a symbolic move by Ankara's notables who conferred honorary citizenship of Ankara to Mustafa Kemal so that there would be no risk of his not making it to the congress. See Bilal Şimsir, *Ankara . . . Ankara: Bir Başkentin Doğuşu* (Ankara: Bilgi Yayınevi, 1988) for further detail.

18. Other authors with close loyalties to the official narratives have also favored versions that honor the support given by the people of Ankara or attribute it to the pragmatism of preserving Ankara's status quo as the established headquarters of the nationalists. Among these works, see Atay, *Çankaya: Atatürk Devri Hatıraları*; Gönül Tankut, "Cumhuriyet Döneminin İlk Toplu İmar Deneyimi: Ankara," *Amme İdaresi Dergisi* 14 (December 1981): 113–19; Şimsir, *Ankara . . . Ankara*. However, such justifications remain weak in explaining the choice given what was at stake and the eventual treatment Ankarans received from the republican administration, which I discuss in this chapter.

19. "Ankara Ankara güzel Ankara / Seni görmek ister her bahtı kara / Senden yardim umar her düşen dara / Yetersin onlara güzel Ankara / Burcuna göz diken dik baslar insin / Türk gücü orada her zoru yensin / Yoktan varedilmiş ilk şehir sensing / Varolsun toprağın taşın Ankara."

20. Sevgi Aktüre, *19. Yüzyıl Sonunda Anadolu Kenti Mekansal Yapı Çözümlemesi* (Ankara: Orta Doğu Teknik Üniversitesi Yayınları, 1978), 124–25.

21. Aktüre, *19. Yüzyıl Sonunda Anadolu Kenti*, 127–29.

22. Şimsir, *Ankara . . . Ankara*, 26–44.

23. Karaosmanoğlu, *Ankara*, 27.

24. Karaosmanoğlu, *Ankara*, 27.

25. TBMM Zabıt Ceridesi 2. Devre, 1. Sene Cilt 2 [Session Transcripts of the Turkish Grand National Assembly, 2nd Assembly, 1st session, vol. 2], 666–70 (here 668).

26. Vala Nureddin, quoted in Önder Şenyapılı, "Ankara '70," *Mimarlık* 3 (1970): 30.

27. For a discussion of how large fires transformed the urban fabric and served as occasions for importing new building regulations on large urban districts in Istanbul, Zeynep Çelik, *The Remaking of Istanbul: Portrait of an Ottoman City 1838–1908* (Seattle: University of Washington Press, 1986), ch. 3; and Murat Gül, *The Emergence of Modern Istanbul: Transformation and Modernisation of a City* (London: Tauris, 2009), ch. 1 and 2. For similar postfire reconstructions in nineteenth-century Izmir, see Sibel Zandi-Sayek, *Ottoman Izmir: The Rise of a Cosmopolitan Port, 1840–1880* (Minneapolis: University of Minnesota Press, 2012), ch. 3.

28. A very detailed analysis of the Lörcher plan can be found in Ali Cengizkan, *Ankara'nın İlk Planı /1924–1925 Lörcher Planı* (Ankara: Arkadaş Yayınevi, 2004).

29. Cengizkan, *Ankara'nın İlk Planı*, 21.

30. Cengizkan, *Ankara'nın İlk Planı*, 47–48.

31. For a detailed comparative study of the limited competition with three invited proposals, see Gönül Tankut, *Bir Başkentin İmarı: Ankara (1929–1939)* (Ankara: Orta Doğu Teknik Üniversitesi Yayınları, 1990).

32. Zeynep Kezer, "Contesting Urban Space in Early Republican Ankara," *Journal of Architectural Education* 52, no. 1 (September 1998): 13.

33. Jansen, *Ankara İli İmar Planı*, 6–7.

34. Charles Sherrill, *Gazi Mustafa Kemal Nezdinde Bir Yıl Elçilik* (Istanbul: Muallim Ahmet Halit Kitaphanesi, 1935), 7.

35. Carl Ch. Lörcher, "Das Neue Regierungsviertel Der Stadt Angora," *Städtebau* 20 (1925): 144–45.

36. Zeynep Kezer, "The Making of a National Capital: Ideology and Socio-Spatial Practices in Early Republican Ankara" (PhD diss., University of California, Berkeley, 1999), 59–69.

37. Ackbar Abbas, "Building, Dwelling, Drifting: Migrancy and the Limits of Architecture. Building Hong Kong: From Migrancy to Disappearance," *Postcolonial Studies* 1, no. 2 (1998): 191–94.

38. Cengizkan, *Ankara'nın İlk Planı*, 77–78.

39. Lörcher, "Das neue Regierungsviertel der Stadt Angora."

40. For details of name and form changes, see Cengizkan, *Ankara'nın İlk Planı*.

41. Dipl.-Ing. Walther Bangart, "Stadtgestaltung in Der Türkei," *Deutsche Bauzeitung* 70:1, no. 4 (1936): 68–80.

42. Holzmeister was a leading figure in the right-wing Austrofascist movement when he began to work in Turkey. After the Nazi ouster of the Austrofascists, he would move all his operations to Turkey, taking an even more active role in shaping both the physical form of the new capital and more broadly the architectural culture of modern Turkey.

43. Reading between the lines in Jansen's own final report about the making of Ankara, one finds frequent expressions of tacit resentment over these disruptions, especially with reference to various military office buildings and modifications of the plans for the government quarter. See Jansen, *Ankara İli İmar Planı*.

44. Bernd Nicolai, *Moderne und Exil: Deutschsprachige Architekten in der Türkei, 1925–1955* (Berlin: Verlag fur Bauwesen, 1998), 56–57.

45. Well-known criticisms appear variously in the memoirs of Falih Atay (*Çankaya: Atatürk Devri Hatıraları*) and foreign observers such as Paul Dumont (*Mustafa Kemal invente la Turquie moderne : 1919–1924* [Brussels: Editions Complexe, 1983]) as well as in fictionalized accounts of Early Republican Ankara and its ambitious new elite in the novels of Yakup Kadri Karaosmanoğlu (*Ankara*; and *Panorama* [Istanbul: Remzi Kitabevi, 1953]).

46. For instance, the Ministry of Education was finished in the 1970s and the new Grand National Assembly Complex was not completed until 1962, even though the competition to obtain the project had been held in 1942.

47. "Catching up with modern civilization" in Turkish is "Muasır medeniyet seviyesine ulaşmak" and was a popular turn of phrase. Variations such as "muasırlaşmak" (to become contemporary) also appear commonly in contemporary newspapers, journals, and statements made by various officials.

48. Coronel Reşat Hallı indicates that between 1923 and 1931 seventeen uprisings took place in Turkey, of which, fifteen were staged by Kurdish nationalists in southeastern Anatolia. In 1927 some tribes went so far as to declare independence and proclaim the eastern province of Ağrı their capital. For a detailed discussion of these incidents, see Resat Hallı, *Türkiye Cumhuriyetinde Ayaklanmalar (1924–1938)* (Ankara: Genel Kurmay Harp Tarihi Başkanlığı Yayınları, 1972).

49. For a thorough account of the gradual consolidation of the single-party regime and the sidelining of Atatürk's rivals over the years, see Mete Tunçay, *Türkiye'de Tek Parti Yönetiminin Kurulması (1923–1931)*, 3rd rev. ed. (Istanbul: Tarih Vakfı Yurt Yayınları, 1999).

50. Bülent Gökay, *British Documents on Foreign Affairs: Reports and Papers from the Foreign Office Confidential Print, Series B: Turkey, Iran, and the Middle East 1918–1939. Volume 31: Turkey, March 1927–December 1929* (University Publications of America, 1997), 11–12.

51. Some of the most ostentatious revivals of these performances took place under the military regime that came to power in the military coup of 1980. Kenan Evren, the coup's leader, wanted to buttress his image by imitating Atatürk. To accomplish this he sought to create occasions where he could be depicted in the same poses as Atatürk's best known photographs, often also wearing almost identical clothes.

52. There is a very wide literature of memoirs about Atatürk's life, penned not only by members of his inner circle but also by civil servants, service personnel, journalists, diplomats, and politicians who had been part of these—almost nightly—events. See, for instance, Atay, *Çankaya: Atatürk Devri Hatıraları*; Haldun Derin, *Çankaya Özel Kalemini Anımsarken (1933–1951)* (Istanbul: Tarih Vakfı Yurt Yayınları, 1995); and İsmet Bozdağ, *Atatürk'ün Fikir Sofrası* (Istanbul: Tekin Yayınevi, 1998).

53. Necdet Evliyagil, *Çankaya* (Ankara: Ajans-Türk Matbaacılık Sanayii, 1986), 28.

54. Kevin Hetherington, *The Badlands of Modernity: Heterotopia and Social Ordering* (London: Routledge, 1997), viii.

55. Joseph C. Grew, *The Turbulent Era: A Diplomatic Record of Forty Years 1904–1945*, vol. 2 (Boston: Houghton Mifflin, 1952), 86.

56. The memoirs of Haldun Derin, who served in the office of the chief of staff of both Atatürk and İnönü, contain many episodes of such exchanges (Derin, *Çankaya Özel Kalemini Anımsarken*, 50, 88, 103, 108–10).

57. Grew, *The Turbulent Era*, 784–85.

58. Letter from Mr. Hoare to Sir Austen Chamberlain, dated March 30, 1927. FO E 1575/17/44. Gökay, *British Documents*, vol. 31.

59. Letter from Sir George Clerk to Sir Austen Chamberlain, dated February 1928. Gökay, *British Documents*, vol. 31, 148.

60. Derin, *Çankaya Özel Kalemini Anımsarken*, 60–61.

61. İlhan Tekeli and Selim İlkin, *Bahçeli Evlerin Öyküsü: Bir Batı Kurumunun Yeniden Yorumlanması* (Ankara: Kent Koop Yayınları, 1984).

62. The Ankara train station and the headquarters building for the Turkish Hearth sAssociation each had a room for Atatürk's personal use. Burak Erdim notes that the Faculty of Language, History, and Geography also had a room labeled "Cumhur Reisi Dairesi" (President's Quarters). Their building had a separate driveway and a door leading directly from the exterior into this room reserved for him, which featured a window overlooking the main entrance and another looking into the main auditorium. See Burak Erdim, "Lost in Translation: The Encounter between Bruno Taut and the Turkish Republic from 1936–38" (PhD diss., University of Virginia, 2004), 29–30.

63. Emin Karakuş, *40 Yıllık Bir Gazeteci Gözü İle İşte Ankara* (Istanbul: Hür Yayın ve Ticaret, 1977), 17; Mehmed Kemal, *Türkiye'nin Kalbi Ankara* (Istanbul: Çağdas Yayınları, 1983), 165–71.

64. Selim Deringil, *The Well-Protected Domains: Ideology and the Legitimation of Power in the Ottoman Empire, 1876–1909* (New York: Palgrave Macmillan, 1998), 16–17.

65. Deringil, *The Well-Protected Domains*, 17.

66. Joel Migdal, *State in Society: Studying How States and Societies Transform and Constitute One Another* (Cambridge: Cambridge University Press, 2001), 112.

Chapter 2. Theaters of Diplomacy

1. Austin Chamberlain's dispatch to Lord Crewe (FO 371/10194p; E9848/210/44) quoted in Ömer Kürçüoğlu, "Turco-British Relations since the 1920's," in *Four Centuries of Turco-British Relations: Studies in Diplomatic, Economic and Cultural Affairs*, ed. Ali İhsan Bağış and William Hale, 80–102 (North Humberside: Eothen Press, 1984).

2. Controlling strategic waterways was in accordance with long-term British strategies. In the Mediterranean, in addition to the Gibraltar Strait, over time the British had also taken possession of the islands of Malta and Cyprus, which were crucial to controlling navigation in the eastern Mediterranean. As early as 1919, Lord Curzon, who would later head the British delegation at Lausanne, publicly disclosed this as the most favorable strategy for long-term peace in the Middle East. According to his biographer, Earl of Ronaldshay, already in early 1919, Lord Curzon had suggested "the ejection of the Turk from Europe and the establishment of a much reduced but compact and homogeneous Turkish State in Asia Minor" to be "the essentials of any permanent settlement of this age-old question. Such a policy entailed the amputation of large tracts even of the Asiatic dominions of the former Turkish Empire." Earl of Ronaldshay, *The Life of Lord Curzon, Being the Authorized Biography of George Nathaniel Marquess Curzon of Keddleston, K.G.* (London: Ernest Benn, 1928), 262.

3. Former viceroy of India, Lord Curzon was an influential figure in British politics, especially in international matters. Although a vocal and influential person, Lord Curzon did not dominate the British Foreign Office at the end of the First World War. However, his views are important because they formed the basis of his arguments as the head of the British delegation at the Lausanne Peace Conference and they were pivotal in drafting the final agreement, shaping as a result the borders of modern-day Turkey.

4. James Shotwell and Francis Deák provide a useful summary of the situation in Lausanne and later modifications made in Montreaux in 1936 with references to more detailed legal interpretations. For a concise overview of international disputes over the Bosphorus and Dardanelles Straits. See James Shotwell and Francis Deák, *Turkey at the Straits: A Short History* (New York: MacMillan, 1940), 115–77.

5. The former Ottoman province of Musul and Kirkuk, located in modern-day northern Iraq, were occupied by British troops a few days after the cease-fire at the end of the First World War. The nationalists, who regarded the British occupation to be illegal, intended this region to be a part of the nation-state they were fighting to create and thus included it in the National Pact.

6. The Turkish government claimed that the British occupation was illegal and that the Musul-Kirkuk region had a mainly Turkish-speaking population and should therefore be returned to Turkey. The British delegation argued that the region was inhabited mostly by Arabs and Kurds and therefore British dominion was legitimate and Turkey had no business claiming land in the area. However, although the British argued for the rights of the population in Musul and Kirkuk, they were primarily interested in the region's rich oil fields. In addition, the British government wanted to ensure that the boundaries were positioned strategically to favor British troops stationed in the area, bolstering Britain's military foothold in the Middle East.

7. Kürçüoğlu, "Turco-British Relations since the 1920's," 80–85. For a more de-

tailed study of Turco-British relations in the early years of the republic, see also Ömer Kürkçüoğlu, *Türk Ingiliz İlişkileri (1919–1926)* (Ankara: Ankara Üniversitesi Siyasal Bilgiler Fakültesi Yayınları, 1978), part 3, chs. 1–3.

8. There were other strategies too. As I mention later, British diplomats frequently referred to Turkey's need for credit financing postwar reconstruction as a potential instrument of political leverage. Also, Turkish authorities were suspicious of British involvement in stirring up Kurdish tribes in the southeastern regions of the country, where central state penetration was weak.

9. Bilal Şimşir, *Ankara . . . Ankara: Bir Başkentin Doğuşu* (Ankara: Bilgi Yayınevi, 1988), 219–33, 249–350. For extensive examples of British correspondence on the matter, see also Bülent Gökay, *British Documents on Foreign Affairs: Reports and Papers from the Foreign Office Confidential Print, Series B: Turkey, Iran, and the Middle East 1918–1939. Volume 30: Turkey, August 1923–February 1927* (Frederick, MD: University Publications of America, 1997) (repeat citations are given as Gökay, *British Documents*, vol. 30).

10. A physician by training, Adnan Adıvar was an articulate man of letters. He was also the husband of famed novelist Halide Edip (Adıvar) whom I quote frequently in the introduction to chapter 5. Husband and wife were both very active in the nationalist front during the National Struggle and worked with Mustafa Kemal in Ankara on various strategic decisions.

11. Complaining about the situation to London, the British ambassador Ronald Lindsay wrote: "Bad as it is, the situation is likely to be even worse if and when as is now threatened, Adnan Bey is replaced by an official of even lower standing. There is no real contact between the Government of Turkey and those of the Great Powers of Europe and America, and no efficient means by which the latter can make their views known to the former, or apply any methods of pressure or persuasion. It will be all the more important to remedy this state of affairs when the Treaty of Lausanne comes into force and the application of its stipulations has to be insisted on. Nor can any serious attempt be made to wean Turkey from her violent xenophobia until some more efficient contact has been established." Letter from Mr. Lindsay to Mr. MacDonald, dated March 19, 1924. FO E2586/210/44. Gökay, *British Documents*, vol. 30, 155.

12. Letter from Mr. Lindsay to Mr. MacDonald, dated March 11, 1924. FO E 2344/32/44. Gökay, *British Documents*, vol. 30, 150.

13. Dispatches to the Foreign Office regularly mentioned the difficulty of conducting business at the Istanbul location, this was one of the most revealing of the diplomats' frustration.

14. Letter from Ronald Lindsay to Chamberlain dated February 6, 1925. Quoted in Şimşir, *Ankara . . . Ankara*, 336–37. (Retranslated to English by the author.)

15. Lindsay was Sir George's predecessor, and he served from early 1925 to the end of 1926. In 1927 he was replaced by Sir George Clerk, who was more amicable in his dealings with Turkey. The excerpt quoted above is taken from a letter from Sir R. Lindsay to Mr. Austen Chamberlain, dated May 18, 1925. FO E3015/3015/44. Gökay, *British Documents*, vol. 30, 310–11.

16. Şimşir, *Ankara . . . Ankara*, 289.

17. Şimşir, *Ankara . . . Ankara*, 291–93.

18. Memorandum from the Minister of Foreign Affairs to the Prime Minister dated February 8, 1925. Quoted in Şimşir, *Ankara . . . Ankara*, 292.

19. Rudolf Nadolny, *Mein Beitrag: Erinnerungen eines Botschafters des Deutschen Reiches* (Cologne: DME-Verlag, 1985), 178.

20. Şimşir, *Ankara . . . Ankara*, 292.

21. "Constantinople or Angora?" *Times*, December 22, 1924.

22. Şimşir, *Ankara . . . Ankara*, 340; Alwyn Parker, "Representation at Angora," *Times*, December 18, 1925.

23. Joseph C. Grew, *The Turbulent Era: A Diplomatic Record of Forty Years 1904–1945*, vol. 2 (Boston: Houghton Mifflin, 1952), 845–46.

24. The front forged by the intense British campaign was never a stable one. An examination of British Foreign Office correspondence suggests that the differences of opinion between France, Italy, and Britain were quite strong from the beginning. See, for instance: Annual Report, 1925 from Mr. Hoare to Sir Austen Chamberlain, dated August 12, 1926. FO E/4798/4798/44, in Gökay, *British Documents*, vol. 30, 372. See also Annual Report 1928, from Sir George Clerk to Sir Austen Chamberlain, dated February 6, 1929. FO E 906/906/44, in Bülent Gökay, *British Documents on Foreign Affairs: Reports and Papers from the Foreign Office Confidential Print, Series B: Turkey, Iran, and the Middle East 1918–1939. Volume 31: Turkey, March 1927–December 1929* (Frederick, MD: University Publications of America), 250 (repeat citations are given as Gökay, *British Documents*, vol. 31),

25. Letter from Sir George Clerk to Lord Cushendun, dated October 4, 1928. FO E 4854/708/44, in Gökay, *British Documents*, vol. 31, 211.

26. Dilek Barlas, *Etatism and Diplomacy in Turkey: Economic and Foreign Policy Strategies in an Uncertain World, 1829–1939*, ed., Suraiya Faroqhi and Halil Inalcik. The Ottoman Empire and Its Heritage: Politics, Society and Economy (Leiden: Koninklijke Brill, 1998), 149.

27. Şimşir, *Ankara . . . Ankara*, 340–43.

28. "Constantinople or Angora?" *Times*, December 22, 1924, 11.

29. Annual Report 1929, from Sir George Clerk to Mr. A. Henderson, dated February 3, 1921. FO E 729/729/44, in Gökay, *British Documents*, vol. 31, 367.

30. The Friendship and Fraternity was signed on March 16, 1921, after a brief confrontation between the Red Army and the Turkish forces. With this agreement, the Soviet government became the first to recognize Turkey's claims to sovereignty in the area covered by the National Pact, and capitulations between the two countries were canceled. Another agreement signed on October 13, 1921, defined the Soviet-Turkish border. Turkish forces withdrew from Batum, and the Soviets returned Kars and Ardahan to Turkey. In addition, throughout the National Struggle, the Soviets provided monetary and material aid to Turkey. Barlas, *Etatism and Diplomacy in Turkey*, 120. See also Suat Bilge, *Güç Komsuluk: Türkiye-Sovyetler Birliği İlişkileri 1920–1964* (Ankara: Türkiye İş Bankası Kültür Yayınları, 1992); Stefanos Yerasimos, *Türk Sovyet İlişkileri* (Istanbul: Gözlem Yayınları, 1979).

31. Nonriparian states, meaning states that did not border the Black Sea. In fact, the acceptance by the Turkish representatives of the clause calling for the demilitarization of the Straits and the opening up of the Black Sea to free navigation temporarily soured the Turco-Soviet alliance that had been quite steadfast throughout the National Struggle. Shotwell, *Turkey at the Straits*, 112.

32. Nadolny, *Mein Beitrag*, 170. All translations from German are by Stephan Heilmayr.

33. Nadolny, *Mein Beitrag*, 175–76.

34. Nadolny, *Mein Beitrag*, 170.

35. Nadolny, *Mein Beitrag*, 170

36. Nadolny, *Mein Beitrag*, 175, 178.

37. Annual Report 1927 from Sir G. Clerk to Austen Chamberlain, dated February 27, 1928. FO E/1149/1149/44 in Gökay, *British Documents* vol. 31, 94.

38. Dicle Oğuz and Renan Erdogan, *Ankara Kentinde Ender Bulunan Ağaç Türleri Üzerine Bir Araştırma* (Ankara: Ankara Üniversitesi Araştırma Fon Müdürlüğü, 2002).

39. Nadolny, *Mein Beitrag*, 178.

40. Nadolny, *Mein Beitrag*, 178.

41. Nadolny, *Mein Beitrag*, 178.

42. Nadolny, *Mein Beitrag*, 179, 178.

43. Nadolny, *Mein Beitrag*, 178, 192, 265.

44. Nadolny, *Mein Beitrag*, 171.

45. The most outstanding of these was the annual winter ball featuring performances by reputable German artists, which always caused "much ado at the embassy." Nadolny wrote: "So in different winters I had Mr. Kempff, Baron Munchausen, Opera singer Schlusnus, Graf Keyserlang, Ms. Olaff, Mr. Kulinkampf, and Mr. Bruckmann with his theater company." Nadolny, *Mein Beitrag*, 182.

46. Nadolny, *Mein Beitrag*, 170.

47. Nadolny, *Mein Beitrag*, 194.

48. Enclosure in Doc. 267. General Notes on a Visit to Angora, September 16–17, 1925, in Gökay, *British Documents*, vol. 30, 338.

49. Gönül Tankut, *Bir Başkentin İmarı Ankara (1929–1939)* (Ankara: Orta Doğu Teknik Üniversitesi Yayınları, 1990), 75–78. In addition to documenting the close working relationship between Herman Jansen and Robert Oerley, an Austrian architect-planner who was already working with the government in Ankara and who provided Jansen with crucial insider information about the workings of the decision-making process in Ankara, Tankut emphasizes that Turkish authorities, in general, preferred to work with German and other German-speaking Central European architects and planning professionals in various projects. Tankut also infers from the correspondence of Jansen and Oerley, that Oerley identified himself as being German.

50. Reporting on Ali Haydar's visit to Germany, the *Times* wrote: "though he visited several other towns, such as Bucharest and Budapest, Ali Haidar Tiregöl Bey seems to have been principally impressed by the various towns in Germany that he saw, and its is pretty clear that the new Angora will be largely on the neo-Teutonic style, both of town planning and of architecture." "A Turkish Capital." *Times*, December 22, 1924, 9.

51. Nadolny, *Mein Beitrag*, 175–78, 185–88.

52. Barlas, *Etatism and Diplomacy in Turkey*, 152–53.

53. "Vali" means provincial governor in Turkish. However, during the early years of the republic, the governors of major provinces such as Ankara, Istanbul, or Izmir also served as mayors. Hence the closest counterpart of the *vali* title in Ankara would be "prefect."

54. The observations of the London *Times* reporter ("A Turkish Capital") were echoed in the correspondence of the Foreign Office personnel stationed in Turkey. In a 1925 report he wrote about a two-day visit to Ankara, the British ambassador Sir

Ronald Lindsay remarked that many construction projects in the Turkish capital were under German supervision, and that the crews of workmen at these sites "only spoke German." See enclosure in Doc. 267. General Notes on a Visit to Angora, 338.

55. Leland James Gordon, *American Relations with Turkey 1830–1930: An Economic Interpretation* (Philadelphia: University of Pennsylvania Press, 1932), 69.

56. Gordon, *American Relations with Turkey*, 68–69.

57. Letter from Sir G. Clerk to Sir Austen Chamberlain, dated June 22, 1927. FO E 2832/1672/44, in Gökay, *British Documents*, vol. 31, 21.

58. "Constantinople Embassy," *Times*, December 23, 1925.

59. "Constantinople Embassy."

60. Parker, "Representation at Angora."

61. Nezahat Demirhan, "Türkiye Cumhuriyeti'nin Onuncu Yıl Kutlamaları," *Atatürk Araştırma Merkezi Dergisi*, August 20, 2007, http://www.atam.gov.tr/dergi/sayi-37/turkiye-cumhuriyetinin-onuncu-yil-kutlamalari; "Jew for Nazis," *Time*, June 18, 1934, http://www.time.com/time/printout/0,8816,747494,00.html.

62. "Turkey: Oh, What Happiness," *Time*, November 6, 1933, http://www.time.com/time/printout/0,8816,746241,00.html.

63. "Soviet Cinderellas," *Time*, December 4, 1933, http://content.time.com/time/magazine/article/0,9171,746417,00.html.

64. "Jew for Nazis."

65. Demirhan, "Türkiye Cumhuriyeti'nin Onuncu Yıl Kutlamaları."

66. Robert C. Tucker, "The Emergence of Stalin's Foreign Policy," *Slavic Review* 36, no. 4 (1977): 563–89.

67. "Jew for Nazis"; "Allies v. Soviets," *Time*, April 8, 1940.

68. Mehmet Köçer, "Bolşevik İhtilali Sonrasında Afganistan Üzerinde İngiliz-Rus Mücadelesi," *İlahiyat Fakültesi Dergisi*, August 19, 2007, http://www.firat.edu.tr/ilahiyat/DergiYazilari/09-1_2004/05MehmetKocer.pdf.

69. "Jew for Nazis"; and Letter from Sir R. Lindsay to Sir Austen Chamberlain, dated April 20, 1926. FO E 2768/2768/44, in Gökay, *British Documents*, vol. 30, 398.

70. Grace Ellison wrote the following of the British Embassy: "People in England are curious to know what the British Embassy in Angora is like. 'England, as she always does,' said Boghetti of the Ottoman Bank, 'has chosen for herself the very best site in Angora.' Whether this was just good luck, or deliberately done I cannot say, but the view from the British Embassy overlooking the wide stretch of Tchan-Kaya and Angora is really beautiful." Grace Ellison, *Turkey To-Day* (London: Hutchinson, 1928), 78.

71. Letter from Sir George Clerk to Lord Cushendun, dated October 4, 1928. FO E 4854/708/44, in Gökay, *British Documents*, vol. 31, 211.

72. For instance, the Soviet embassy was granted 3,000–4,000 square meters, because it had become clear that the lot in its possession was insufficient for its needs. (See Başbakanlık Cumhuriyet Arşivi, *Bakanlar Kurulu Kararnamesi* no. 3547, May 6, 1926.) In August 1929 the Italian embassy demanded the 3,000 square meter piece of land that had initially been granted for access to a service road that belonged exclusively to it during construction. The request was granted on September 16, 1929. (See Başbakanlık Cumhuriyet Arşivi, *Bakanlar Kurulu Kararnamesi* no. 8362, September 16, 1929.) The British embassy, claiming that its lot was extremely steep, twice requested additional pieces of land. (See Başbakanlık Cumhuriyet Arşivi, *Bakanlar Kurulu Kararnamesi* no. 2675, October 10, 1925, and no. 3635, May 25, 1926.)

73. Ellison, *Turkey To-Day*, 61. See also Dispatch from Mr. Hoare to Sir Austen Chamberlain, March 30, 1927, in Gökay, *British Documents*, vol. 31, 4–5. Grace Ellison described life atop Ankara's social pyramid, which she had a chance to watch closely, in the following terms: "Society in Angora turns around the Ministers, functionaries of the Government, députés, and the Diplomatic Corps. After two or three parties you have met everyone, for the same people are invited everywhere. . . . In a place where unlike Constantinople, entertaining is the only distraction, society would have been colourless indeed if the only entertainers had been the corps diplomatique as is the custom in all other Muslim countries" (Ellison, *Turkey To-Day*, 62).

74. Ellison, *Turkey To-Day*, 76.

75. Grew, *The Turbulent Era*, 752. For instance, in 1927, the Ministry of Foreign Affairs was housed in an old mansion that was, in the words of the United States ambassador Joseph Grew, "a ramshackle building, dark and dingy and crowded" (752) and the minister's office was a "cubbyhole—one could hardly call it a room" (719).

76. "Thé dansant," which appears in both Turkish and British documents, is a French term that means a tea party that also includes music and dance.

77. Letter from Sir George Clerk to Sir John Simon, dated November 2, 1932. FO E6033/34/44, in Bülent Gökay, *British Documents on Foreign Affairs: Reports and Papers from the Foreign Office Confidential Print, Series B: Turkey, Iran, and the Middle East 1918–1939, Volume 32: Turkey, January 1930–December 1932* (Frederick, MD: University Publications of America), 313.

78. Message from Sir George Clerk to Sir Austen Chamberlain, dated Angora February 21, 1928. FO E 984/ 560/44, in Gökay, *British Documents*, vol. 31, 148.

Chapter 3. Dismantling the Landscapes of Islam

1. *Seğmen* refers to a semimilitary organization composed of local civilians that can be mobilized to fight a war. This practice is closely associated with Central Anatolia, and Ankara in particular.

2. Mazhar Müfit Kansu, *Erzurum'dan Ölümüne Kadar Atatürk'le Beraber*, XVI. Seri-Sa. 6a (Ankara: Türk Tarih Kurumu Yayınları, 1968), 492–97; Alptekin Müderrisoğlu, *Kurtuluş Savaşında Ankara* (Ankara: Ankara Büyükşehir Belediyesi Yayınları, 1993), 66–74; Bilal Şimşir, *Ankara . . . Ankara: Bir Başkentin Doğuşu* (Ankara: Bilgi Yayınevi, 1988), 160–64.

3. Fuat Bayramoğlu, *Hacı Bayram-ı Veli: Yaşamı, Soyu, Vakfı* (Ankara: Türk Tarih Kurumu Yayınları, 1983), 93; Kansu, *Erzurum'dan Ölümüne Kadar Atatürkle Beraber*, 482–84; Müderrisoğlu, *Kurtuluş Savaşında Ankara*, 71.

4. A *müezzin* is a person who makes the call to prayer; the *hafız* is a person who has memorized the Koran and can recite it at religious ceremonies.

5. Müderrisoğlu, *Kurtuluş Savaşında Ankara*, 83–84.

6. See also Kansu, *Erzurum'dan Ölümüne Kadar Atatürk'le Beraber*, 492; Şimşir, *Ankara . . . Ankara*, 165.

7. A *fetwa* is a decree issued by religious scholars sanctioning a particular action.

8. The colonizing dervishes belonged to religious orders that were primarily Islamic in character but also bore the heritage of Central Asian shamanic practices. They settled in towns as well as in the countryside and mixed with the local peoples. Under their guidance, new vernacular versions of Islam, fused with ancient Tur-

kic tribal practices and the beliefs the local peasantry, flourished and several sects with strong Sufi tendencies were formed. For extensive information, see also Ömer Lütfi Barkan, *Kolonizatör Türk Dervişleri* (Istanbul: Hamle Yayın Dağıtım, 1939), 492; Raymond Lifchez, *The Dervish Lodge* (Berkeley: University of California Press, 1992).

9. For a detailed history of these, see Barkan, *Kolonizatör Türk Dervişleri*; John Robert Barnes, *An Introduction to Religious Foundations in the Ottoman Empire* (Leiden: Brill, 1986); Nazif Öztürk, *Menşei ve Tarihi Açısından Vakıflar* (Ankara: Vakıflar Genel Müdürlüğü Yayınları, 1983); Yaşar Nuri Öztürk, *Tasavvufun Ruhu ve Tarikatler* (Istanbul: Sidre Yayıncılık, 1988).

10. Öztürk, *Tasavvufun Ruhu ve Tarikatler*, 78.

11. Öztürk, *Tasavvufun Ruhu ve Tarikatler*, 80–82.

12. Lifchez, *The Dervish Lodge*, 3–5.

13. Kansu, *Erzurum'dan Ölümüne Kadar Atatürk'le Beraber*, 492–94.

14. Bayramoğlu, *Hacı Bayram-ı Veli*, 96.

15. Şimşir, *Ankara . . . Ankara*, 172–84.

16. Bayramoğlu, *Haci Bayram-ı Veli*, 98.

17. Müderrisoğlu, *Kurtuluş Savaşında Ankara*, 87.

18. Bayramoğlu, *Hacı Bayram-ı Veli*, 96; Hıfzı Veldet Velidedeoğlu, *İlk Meclis ve Milli Mücadele'de Anadolu* (Istanbul: Çağdaş Yayınları, 1990), 15. The new, turbaned representatives summoned to the first Grand National Assembly included both Mehmed Tayyib Efendi and Çelebi Cemalettin Efendi.

19. Müderrisoğlu, *Kurtuluş Savaşında Ankara*, 87–88.

20. Halifetin İlgasına ve Hanedan-ı Osmani'nin Türkiye Cumhuriyeti Memalik-i Haricine Çıkarılmasına Dair Kanun Maddesi, *Resmi Gazete*, no. 63, March 6, 1924, article no. 431.

21. *Medrese* means "school" in Arabic, but in the Ottoman context it referred to a higher institution of religious learning.

22. For a concise overview of these umbrella institutions, see Howard Crane, "Ottoman Sultan's Mosques: Icons of Imperial Legitimacy," in *The Ottoman City and Its Parts: Urban Structure and Social Order*, ed. Irene Bierman, R. Abou El-Haj, and Donald Preziosi, 173–243 (New Rochelle, NY: A. D. Caratzas, 1991).

23. *Vakıf* (plural *evkaf* and *vakıflar*) is originally an Arabic term, which means to seize something and bring it to a standstill. In Islamic law, the term is used to describe a general category of institutions most closely translated into English as pious foundations or endowments. Establishing a vakıf entails setting aside a revenue-generating property (buildings or land) as an endowment in order to support some religious or charitable service in perpetuity. According to the law, vakıf assets are immune to changes of ownership that could be detrimental to their survival since according to sharia they are sacrosanct and inalienable. Taken out of the sphere of commercial transactions, they are, in effect, at a legal standstill. John Robert Barnes, "Evkaf-I Humayun : Vakıf Administration under the Ottoman Ministry for Imperial Religious Foundations, 1839 to 1875" (PhD diss., University of California, Los Angeles, 1989), 9. The original plural in Arabic is *evkaf*. In Turkish, *vakıflar* as a grammatical hybrid is also used to denote plural. While both words are grammatically correct in Turkish and still in wide usage, I will refer to the *evkaf* as the broad institutional framework of all vakıfs, and will use *vakıfs* for the plural of *vakıf* when referring to a number of them.

24. Nazif Öztürk, *Türk Yenileşme Çerçevesinde Vakıf Müessesi* (Ankara: Diyanet Vakfı Yayınları, 1995), 76.

25. Cengiz Orhonlu, *Osmanlı İmparatorluğu'nda Aşiretlerin İskanı* (Istanbul: Eren Yayıncılık ve Kitapçılık, 1987), 16.

26. Öztürk, *Türk Yenileşme Çerçevesinde Vakıf Müessesi*, 31; Halim Baki Kunter, "Türk Vakıfları ve Vakfiyeleri," *Vakıflar Dergisi* (1934), 105.

27. Reşit Çelik, "Vakıflar Genel Müdürlüğündeki Kayıtlara Göre II. Meşrutiyet Döneminden Cumhuriyetin İlanına Kadar Tesis Edilen Eğitim ve Kültür Müesseseleri," report submitted to the national archives of Turkey (Ankara: T.C., Başbakanlık Cumhuriyet Devlet Arşivi, 1986), 1–3.

28. Robert Barnes notes that observations about abuse of the system appear as early as the seventeenth-century reports by the Ottoman bureaucrat and imperial adviser Koçi Bey. Barnes, "Evkaf-ı Humayun."

29. MA Ubicini in Letters on Turkey (London: John Murray, 1850), 260, quoted in Barnes, "Evkaf-ı Humayun," 37.

30. Öztürk, *Türk Yenileşme Çerçevesinde Vakıf Müessesi*, 68–86.

31. Karen Barkey, *Empire of Difference: The Ottomans in Comparative Perspective* (Cambridge: Cambridge University Press, 2008), 164–81; Carter Vaughn Findley, *Turkey, Islam, Nationalism, and Modernity: A History, 1789–2007* (New Haven, CT: Yale University Press, 2010), 15–22, 122–23.

32. T.C. Medeni Kanun [The Civil Code of the Turkish Republic], *Resmi Gazete*, April 4, 1926, article no. 743.

33. Öztürk, *Türk Yenileşme Çerçevesinde Vakıf Müessesi*, 92.

34. Çelik, "Vakıflar Genel Müdürlüğündeki Kayıtlara Göre II."

35. "Ankara Şehri İmar Müdüriyeti Teşkilat ve Vazaifine Dair Kanun," *Resmi Gazete*, no 902, May 30, 1928, article no. 1351.

36. This becomes rather obvious when the resolutions made by the Council of Ministers and the sums involved are examined in sequence. The accompanying letter with each request also reveals that vakıfs around the country were frequently tapped for the purposes of making the new city.

37. Öztürk, *Türk Yenileşme Çerçevesinde Vakıf Müessesi*, 75.

38. Umumi Muvazeneye Giren Vekalet ve Daireler ile Vakıflar Umum Müdürlüğü Arasındaki Bütün Alacak ve Vereceklerin Karşılıklı Olarak İbrasına Dair 2879 Sayılı Kanun, *Resmi Gazete*, no. 3197, January 4, 1936, article no. 2879.

39. Öztürk, *Türk Yenileşme Çerçevesinde Vakıf Müessesi*, 421.

40. For a detailed history of this transition, see Osman Ergin, *Türkiye'de Sehirciliğin Tarihi İnkişafi* (Istanbul: Cumhuriyet Gazete ve Matbaası, 1936).

41. Öztürk, *Türk Yenileşme Çerçevesinde Vakıf Müessesi*, 427.

42. "Belediye Mezarlıklar Hakkında Nizamname," *Resmi Gazete*, no. 1868, August 9, 1931.

43. Öztürk, *Türk Yenileşme Çerçevesinde Vakıf Müessesi*, 428–30.

44. Öztürk, *Türk Yenileşme Çerçevesinde Vakıf Müessesi*, 421.

45. "Guraba Hastanesi'nde Üniversite için ayrılacak olan iki binanın devamlı masraflarının vakıflarca karşılanmasına imkan olmadığı" (BCA: 30. . 10.0.0/ 139.997. .4. /13341), May 12, 1934

46. The law granting land to landless farmers is a good example of this practice. Çiftçiyi Topraklandırma Kanunu, *Resmi Gazete*, no. 6032, June 15, 1945, article no. 4753.

47. TBMM Zabıt Ceridesi, Devre VI, Cilt 17, İçtima 45, p. 132 (April 28, 1941).

48. The discussions about the 1941 appropriations for the Pious Foundations Administration is a revealing (yet hardly unique) discussion in which various violations against vakıf properties and assets were brought up by both the administration's director general Faruk Kiper and various representatives sympathetic to the destruction of the national patrimony. The examples in this section are drawn from these discussions. (TBMM Zabıt Ceridesi, Devre VI, Cilt 11, İçtima 60, pp. 482–91 [May 30, 1940].)

49. TBMM Zabıt Ceridesi, Devre VI, Cilt 11, İçtima 60, p. 490 (May 30, 1940).

50. "Vakıflar Mezarlıkları Devretmemektedir," *Cumhuriyet*, March 26, 1931.

51. "Ankara imar planındaki yeni yollar dışında, kapanması gereken yolların, arsa hükmüne girmesinden dolayı İmar Müdürlüğüne terk edilip edilmeyeceği" (BCA: 30. . 10/ 189.296. .2. /22S22), January 14, 1934.

52. "Evkaf İle İstanbul Belediyesi Arasındaki Su Meselesi," *Akşam*, March 19, 1932.

53. Öztürk, *Türk Yenileşme Çerçevesinde Vakıf Müessesi*, 427.

54. Bayram Sakalli, "Tekke, Zaviye ve Türbelerin Türk Toplumundaki Rolleri, Kapatılmaları ve Tepkiler," *Türkiye Günlüğü* (July–August 1994): 205–7; Ergun Aybars, *İstiklal Mahkemeleri 1921–1927* (Izmir: Dokuz Eylül Üniversitesi, Atatürk İlkeleri ve İnkilap Tarihi Enstitüsü, 1988), 328.

55. "Tekke ve Zaviyelerin Seddine ve Türbedarlıklar ile Bir Takım Ünvanların men'i İlgasına Dair Kanun," *Resmi Gazete*, no. 243, December 13, 1925, article no. 677.

56. Baha Tanman, "Settings for the Veneration of the Saints," in Lifchez, *The Dervish Lodge*, 133.

57. Tanman, "Settings for the Veneration of the Saints," 136.

58. Tanman, "Settings for the Veneration of the Saints," 133.

59. Öztürk, *Tasavvufun Ruhu ve Tarikatler*, 78. The *ahi* chambers had tight control on the trades and supervised both the quality of production and the integrity of commercial transactions. The ahis were also active members of the community who engaged in charity work, gave food to the poor and provided shelter for travelers and the homeless, founded savings collectives and offered financial help to those in debt, and contributed to the provision of urban services. They were not only well-organized in towns but had branched out into the countryside through filial organizations such as the *yaran* chambers.

60. Tanman, "Settings for the Veneration of the Saints," 134.

61. "Tekke ve Zaviyelerin Seddine ve Türbedarlıklar ile Bir Takım Ünvanların men'i İlgasına Dair Kanun"; Vakıflar Mecmuası, 9–13. See also Öztürk, *Türk Yenileşme Çerçevesinde Vakıf Müessesi*; Hikmet Tanyu, *Ankara ve Çevresinde Adak Yerleri* (Ankara: Ankara Üniversitesi İlahiyat Fakültesi Yayınları, 1967).

62. Lucy Mary Jane Garnett, *Mysticism and Magic in Turkey: An Account of the Religious Doctrines, Monastic Organisation, and Ecstatic Powers of the Dervish Orders* (London: Pitman, 1912), 8.

63. John Robert Barnes, "A Short Note on the Dissolution of the Dervish Orders in Turkey," *Muslim World* 64, no. 1 (1974): 33. Reporting from Samuel Anderson's "Dervish Orders of Constantinople" (1922), Barnes notes the number at 258 but that, until two catastrophic fires in short succession destroyed 61 of them, the number of *tekke*s in Istanbul was 319.

64. Klaus Kreiser, "Dervish Living," in Lifchez, *The Dervish Lodge*, 49. Kreiser

estimates that between 1820 and 1920, in the provinces of Anatolia and Rumelia, the number of *tekke*s (dervish lodges) was between two thousand and three thousand. He emphasizes the distinction between urban and rural lodges. Urban lodges especially those in Istanbul were heavily dependent on endowment (vakıf) funds and gifts and donations from high-ranking officials. In contrast, for the rural lodges, this constituted only a minor portion of the revenues. Citing from Faroqhi, Kreiser reports that rural lodges, descendants of the initial colonizing process in the countryside, were self-supporting units that "were directly involved with economy as landowners, moneylenders, and urban landlords." The imperial generosity with endowments, donations, and other gifts may also help to explain the high concentration of lodges in the former capital.

65. Ahmet Yüksel, *Ankara Şehri Salnamesi 1325/1907* (Ankara: Ankara Araştırmaları Vakfı, 1995), 87.

66. There are several reports of clandestine activity following the closing down of *tekke*s where believers gathered at the home of the sheikh to perform ritual dances, readings, and chanting. For example, in Rize, on the Black Sea Coast, Derviş Baba, leader of a Kadirî *tarikat,* and Feyzioğlu Hacı Cemal Efendi, leader of the Halvetî *tarikat,* had multiple run-ins with the authorites as they continued to hold chanting sessions (*zikir meclisi*) and readings with their followers at the *tekke* premises and their homes. Underground activities, including musical instruction were also known to take place in Çorum, a central Anatolian town. Ubeydullah Sekizli, "Çorum'da Bir Mûsikîşinas Hâfız Recep Camcı," *İstanbul Üniversitesi İlahiyat Fakültesi Dergisi*, no. 22 (2012): 267–84.

67. Vakıflar Mecmuası (Ankara: Vakıflar Umum Müdürlüğü, 1942), 10. For more examples of clandestine activities and arrests, see also Bünyamin Kocaoğlu, "Atatürk Dönemi Laiklik Uygulamalarına Yönelik Bazi Toplumsal Tepkiler," *Turkish Studies* 2, no. 4 (fall 2007): 1297–307.

68. The Turkish word for the sufi order *tarikat* also means "path," which quite literally refers to the path of one's search for god and spiritual enlightenment. Although the translation into English is somewhat awkward, it is important to keep both meanings of the word in mind as the pun is intentional.

69. Mustafa Selim İmece, *Atatürk'ün Sapka Devriminde Kastamonu ve İnebolu Seyahatleri* (Ankara: Türkiye İş Bankası Kültür Yayınları, 1975), 82.

70. "Tekke ve Zaviyelerin Seddine ve Türbedarlıklar ile Bir Takım Ünvanların men'i İlgasına Dair Kanun"; Vakıflar Mecmuası, 12

71. Vakıflar Mecmuası, 9.

72. Tanyu, *Ankara ve Çevresinde Adak Yerleri*, 82–84.

73. Tanyu, *Ankara ve Çevresinde Adak Yerleri*, 76–77, 81; Nezihe Araz, *Anadolu Evliyaları* (Istanbul: Atlas Kitabevi, 1975), 79.

74. Tanyu, *Ankara ve Çevresinde Adak Yerleri*, 68; Araz, *Anadolu Evliyaları,* 147–48.

75. Ahmed Yüksel Özemre, *Hasretini Çektiğim Üsküdar*, 1. baskı. (İstanbul: Kubbealtı Neşriyâtı, 2007), 21, 26.

76. Özemre, *Hasretini Çektiğim* Üsküdar, 15–26.

77. Barnes, "A Short Note," 35–39.

78. Anat Lapidot, "Islamic Activism in Turkey since the 1980 Military Takeover," *Terrorism and Political Violence* 8, no. 2 (1996): 67, doi:10.1080/09546559608427346.

79. *Ankara Haftasi*, December 6, 1934.

80. Bazı Kisvelerin Giyilemeyeceğine Dair Kanun [Law Regarding the Ban on Certain Outfits], *Resmi Gazete,* no. 2879, December 3, 1934, article no. 2596.

81. İmece, *Atatürk'ün Sapka Devriminde,* 84.

82. İmece, *Atatürk'ün Sapka Devriminde,* 63.

83. İmece, *Atatürk'ün Sapka Devriminde,* 84.

84. TBMM Zabıt Ceridesi Dönem II, Cilt 19, İçtima 14, pp. 221–24 (25.11.1341/1925).

85. Ahmed Nedim, *Ankara İstiklal Mahkemesi Zabıtları 1926,* ed. Belgelerle Kurtulus Savaşı (Istanbul: İşaret Yayınları, 1993), 78.

86. Nedim, *Ankara İstiklal Mahkemesi Zabıtları,* 82.

87. TBMM Zabıt Ceridesi Dönem II, Cilt 19, İçtima 14, pp. 221–22 (25.11.1341/1925).

88. TBMM Zabıt Ceridesi Dönem II, Cilt 19, İçtima 14, p. 224 (25.11.1341/1925).

89. Öztürk, *Tasavvufun Ruhu ve Tarikatler,* 109–10.

90. Nurhan Atasoy, "Dervish Dress and Ritual: The Mevlevi Tradition," in Lifchez, *The Dervish Lodge,* 253–55.

91. Öztürk, *Tasavvufun Ruhu ve Tarikatler,* 140–41.

92. Öztürk, *Tasavvufun Ruhu ve Tarikatler,* 44–47.

93. İmece, *Atatürk'ün Şapka Devriminde,* 84.

94. TBMM Zabıt Ceridesi Dönem II, Cilt 19, İçtima 9 ,, ek p. 1–3 (16.11.1341/1925).

95. Ahmed Nedim the editor of the transcripts states that there were several protests in quick succession and he gives the following dates and locations: November 14, 1925, in Sivas, November 22, 1925, in Kayseri, November 24, 1925, in Erzurum, November 25, 1925, in Rize, November 26, 1925, in Maraş, and December 4, 1925, in Giresun. Nedim, *Ankara İstiklal Mahkemesi Zabıtları,* 349.

96. Gavin D. Brockett, "Collective Action and the Turkish Revolution: Towards a Framework for the Social History of the Atatürk Era, 1923–38," *Middle Eastern Studies* 34, no. 4 (1998): 49.

97. Aybars, *İstiklal Mahkemeleri 1921–1927,* 309–11.

98. Letter from Consul Knight to Sir G. Clerk, dated May 12, 1927, enclosure in FO [E 3234/257/44], Bülent Gökay, *British Documents on Foreign Affairs: Reports and Papers from the Foreign Office Confidential Print, Series B: Turkey, Iran, and the Middle East 1918–1939. Volume 31: Turkey, March 1927–December 1929* (Frederick, MD: University Publications of America, 1997), 40–42. Brockett, "Collective Action and the Turkish Revolution," 53.

99. According to Camilla Nereid, fifty-seven people were executed in Ankara alone. Camilla T. Nereid, "Kemalism on the Catwalk: The Turkish Hat Law of 1925," *Journal of Social History* 44, no. 3 (2011): 707, doi:10.1353/jsh.2011.0003. In Erzurum about a hundred people were tried, but information about how many were executed is conflicted. See Brockett, "Collective Action and the Turkish Revolution," 49. Nedim, *Ankara İstiklal Mahkemesi Zabıtları,* 349–51.

100. Nedim, *Ankara İstiklal Mahkemesi Zabıtları,* 328; Necip Fazıl Kısakürek, *Son Devrin Din Mazlumları* (Istanbul: Toker Yayınları, 1969), 69.

101. Tahir Olgun, *Matbuat Alemindeki Hayatım ve İstiklal Mahkemeleri* (Istanbul: Nehir Yayınları, 1990), 330.

102. Olgun, *Matbuat Alemindeki Hayatım,* 323–24, 352, 358. See also Letter from Consul Knight to Sir G. Clerk.

103. Bernard Lewis, *The Emergence of Modern Turkey* (Oxford: Oxford University Press, 1962), 414.

Chapter 4. Of Forgotten People and Forgotten Places

1. Çağlar Keyder, *State and Class in Turkey: A Study in Capitalist Development* (London: Verso, 1987), 67; Kemal Kirişçi, "Migration and Turkey: The Dynamics of State, Society and Politics," in Reşat Kasaba. *The Cambridge History of Turkey: Volume 4, Turkey in the Modern World*, 1st ed. (Cambridge: Cambridge University Press, 2008), 175–77.

2. There is a growing literature about the experiences of the empire's non-Muslim communities during this difficult period of transition. See, among others, Keyder, *State and Class in Turkey*; Erik Jan Zürcher, *Savaş, Devrim ve Uluslaşma: Türkiye Tarihinde Geçiş Dönemi (1908–1938)* (Istanbul: İstanbul Bilgi Üniversitesi Yayınları, 2005); Uğur Ümit Üngör, *The Making of Modern Turkey* (Oxford: Oxford University Press, 2011); Taner Akçam, *Ermeni Meselesi Hallolmuştur: Osmanlı Belgelerine Göre Savaş Yıllarında Ermenilere Yönelik Politikalar* (Istanbul: İletişim Yayınları, 2008); Kirişçi, "Migration and Turkey"; Aktar, *Varlık Vergisi ve 'Türkleştirme' Politikaları*; Ayhan Aktar, *Türk Milliyetçiliği, Gayrimüslimler ve Ekonomik Dönüşüm* (Istanbul: İletişim Yayınları, 2006).

3. Ayhan Aktar, *Varlık Vergisi ve "Türkleştirme" Politikaları* (Istanbul: İletişim Yayınları, 2000), 26–32.

4. For the exchange process and the difficulties experienced, see Kemal Ari, *Büyük Mübadele: Türkiye'ye Zorunlu Göç* (Istanbul: Tarih Vakfı Yurt Yayınları, 1995); Renee Hirschon, *Crossing the Aegean: An Appraisal of the 1923 Compulsory Population Exchange between Greece and Turkey* (Oxford: Berghahn Books, 2003); Renee Hirschon, *Heirs of the Greek Catastrophe: The Social Life of Asia Minor Refugees in Piraeus* (Oxford: Clarendon Press, 1989); M. Ali Gökaçtı, *Nüfus mübadelesi* (Istanbul: İletişim Yayınları, 2003).

5. Treaty of Lausanne, section III, Protection of Minorities, article 37.

6. "Turkish Jewry Agitated over Murder Case," *Canadian Jewish Review*, 1927; "Funérailles d'Elza Niego" *Le Journal d'Orient*, August 19, 1927; Avner Levi, *Türkiye Cumhuriyeti'nde Yahudiler* (Istanbul: İletişim Yayınları, 1996), 75–84.

7. Osman Ratib, the son of a former governor and himself a former guard of Sultan Abdülhamid II, was indeed found innocent by reason of insanity and sent to a mental institution, where ten years later, he would be killed by another inmate.

8. Levi, *Türkiye Cumhuriyeti'nde Yahudiler*, 75–77.

9. "Turkish Jewry Agitated over Murder Case."

10. "Turkish Jewry Agitated over Murder Case"; Levi, *Türkiye Cumhuriyeti'nde Yahudiler*, 81.

11. "Turkish Jewry Agitated over Murder Case."

12. For an extensive discussion of the legal underpinnings and inconsistencies of the "minority" status in Turkey, see Baskın Oran, *Türkiye'de Azınlıklar: Kavramlar, Teori, Lozan, İç Mevzuat, İçtihat, Uygulama* (Istanbul: İletişim Yayınları, 2004).

13. As part of the growing literature on this matter, see Rıfat Bali, *Bir Türkleştirme Serüveni (1923–1946)* (Istanbul: İletişim Yayınları, 1999); Samim Akgönül, *Türkiye Rumları: Ulus-Devlet Çağından Küreselleşme Çağına* (Istanbul: İletişim Yayınları, 2007); Levi, *Türkiye Cumhuriyeti'nde Yahudiler*; Aktar, *Varlık Vergisi ve "Türkleştirme" Politikaları*; Aktar, *Türk Milliyetçiliği, Gayrimüslimler*; M. Çağatay Okutan, *Tek Parti Döneminde Azınlık Politikaları* (Istanbul: İstanbul Bilgi Üniversitesi Yayınları; Siyaset Bilimi, 2004.

14. "Turkish Jewry Agitated over Murder Case"; Annual Report 1927, from Sir George Clerk to Sir Austen Chamberlain, dated February 1928 (FO E1149/1149/44).

15. "Turkish Treatment of Minorities," FO E6101/225/44.

16. "Tour in Southern Anatolia," FO E223/223/44.

17. Erol Haker, *Bir Zamanlar Kırklareli'de Yahudiler Yaşardı* (Istanbul: İletişim Yayınları, 2002), 185–86.

18. "Alleged Infringements of Minority Rights by the Turkish Civil Code," FO E1682/143/44.

19. The British Consul in Mersina reported that a local official had confided in him that the intention was to get Syrian Christians to "clear out" voluntarily and that if they went to a government office with a request or complaint, they were being told "if you do not like it, get out." Report by BJ Catton, Acting British Consul in Mersina, dated October 28, 1929, FO E 6101/255/44.

20. Akgönül, *Türkiye Rumları*, 81–84; Aktar, *Varlık Vergisi ve "Türkleştirme" Politikaları*, 114–18.

21. Levi, *Türkiye Cumhuriyeti'nde Yahudiler*, 17.

22. Haker, *Bir Zamanlar Kırklareli*, 185–86.

23. "Turkish Jewry Agitated over Murder Case." The effect of this travel ban appears to have been registered as larger than it actually was. According to Erol Haker, who bases his story on narrative provided by his extended family, the travel ban lasted ten months. According to Avner Levi, who bases his estimate on contemporary newspapers, the ban lasted three months.

24. Arslanyan, at his advanced age, still remembers the verses of the taunt: Ge-Ge-Gevur [*sic*] / Boynunu satırla vur / Kazana koy, hindi gibi kavur / Ge-ge-gevur [*sic*]! [In-In-Infidel infidel! / Slash him in the neck with a machete / Put him in a pot and roast him like a turkey / In-In-Infidel infidel!]. During a visit to an outdoor shrine at Hac Dağı (Mountain of the Cross) with his mother, Arslanyan was accosted by a man who first swears at Arslanyan's mother, then urinates in front of them on the shrine they have come to worship. He also relates that there had previously been a church at the site, which was demolished, and those who demolished it took much pride in their act. Agop Arslanyan, *Adım Agop, Memleketim Tokat* (Istanbul: Aras Yayıncılık, 2005), 73–75.

25. Report by BJ Catton, October 28, 1929.

26. Report by BJ Catton, October 28, 1929. Hampartzoum Vasilian, "Two Months in the Interior of Turkey," *Armenian Review* 5, no. 1 (1952): 115.

27. Letter from George Clerk to Secretary of State for Foreign Affairs, Arthur Henderson, FO E 6101/255/44; Report by BJ Catton, October 28, 1929. In his dispatch Catton notes that the murder of the second priest, which he relates in gruesome detail, may be an alternative version of the murder of the priest in Diyarbakır, though he notes receiving confirmations of this second incident from the American Mission in Adana and the Catholic Mission in Mersina.

28. Arslanyan, *Adım Agop*, 75–76; Vasilian, "Two Months in the Interior"; Mığırdiç Margosyan, *Gâvur Mahallesi* (Istanbul: Aras Yayıncılık, 1994). 56.

29. Vasilian, "Two Months in the Interior."

30. For a detailed examination of the impact of this law in action, see Cemil Koçak, "Ayın Karanlık Yüzü: Tek-Parti Döneminde Gayri Müslim Azınlıklar Hakkında Açılan Türklüğü Tahkir Davaları," *Tarih ve Toplum Yeni Yaklaşımlar*, no. 1 (2005): 147–208. Koçak notes that in 1926–1927, out of the 105 lawsuits based on this law, 62

were opened against non-Muslims. The lack of proportion looms especially large considering that in 1927, non-Muslims composed only 2.5 percent of the population. Koçak also notes that within the Muslim population an overwhelming proportion of the accused were either Muslims who were not ethnically Turkish or Muslims who claimed or were known to be converts. Of the more than 600 cases tagged with the term "insult to Turkishness" between 1925 and 1935, in the National Archives database, an overwhelming majority (by about ten to one) lists non-Muslim citizens as the subjects of prosecution.

31. Vala Nureddin, "Vay! . . . Türklügü Tahkir Etti Ha?" *Akşam,* April 20, 1933.

32. Avram Galanti, *Vatandaş Türkçe Konuş (Yahut Türkçe'nin Tamimi Meselesi)* (Istanbul: Hasan Tabiat Matbaası, 1928), 1.

33. "Turkish Jewry Agitated over Murder Case"; Levi, *Türkiye Cumhuriyeti'nde Yahudiler,* 58–59, 85–94; Haker, *Bir Zamanlar Kırklareli,* 191–92.

34. Senem Aslan, "'Citizen, Speak Turkish': A Nation in the Making," *Nationalism and Ethnic Politics* 13, no. 2 (1007): 245–72. Aslan provides a detailed description and insightful analysis of the campaign.

35. Aslan, "'Citizen, Speak Turkish,'" 254.

36. Aslan, "'Citizen, Speak Turkish,'" 256.

37. In an attempt to defuse growing tensions, Yunus Nadi, publisher of the daily *Cumhuriyet,* penned an editorial titled "Citizen Do Not Fight!" discouraging the use of violence in this important campaign. Nadi and Falih Rifki (Atay), who wrote similar essays in *Hakimiyet-i Milliye,* advocated the use of nonviolent methods to persuade non-Turkish speakers to use the language and recommended long-term strategies for the government to realize this goal. Neither Yunus Nadi nor Falih Rifki were particularly known for their sympathies for disenfranchised minorities, but they were influential journalists who were in Mustafa Kemal's inner circle, and considering Mustafa Kemal's own moderate position and concern for the volatility of the situation, it is possible that they were asked to help rein in the violence. (Yunus Nadi, "Vatandaş Kavga Etme," *Cumhuriyet,* April 5, 1928 quoted in Aslan, "'Citizen, Speak Turkish,'" 255.)

38. Aslan, "'Citizen, Speak Turkish,'" 245.

39. Similarly, Avram Galanti authored a book titled *Vatandaş Türkçe Konuş* [Citizen Speak Turkish] in which he provided both a historical and geographic background of Jewish linguistic distribution in Turkey and a long-term proposal with heavy emphasis on educational programs for Turkish Jewry to become Turkicized. In another tome, *Türkler ve Yahudiler* [Turks and Jews], Galanti focused on the history of Turkish–Jewish relations, painting the former as tolerant and the latter as a loyal community, while editing out the less pleasant episodes of their interaction. Both authors were known for their support of Turkish nationalism and their close involvement with the Kemalist cadres. Their advocacy was met with skepticism, and the Jewish community did not necessarily heed their recommendations. As Avner Levi points out, rather than Jews, their intended audience was influential Turks, whose perception of Jews could affect the introduction of campaigns like Citizen Speak Turkish, and the official support they would get. Galanti, *Vatandaş Türkçe Konuş*; Levi, *Türkiye Cumhuriyeti'nde Yahudiler,* 88–89.

40. Beki L. Bahar, *Efsaneden Tarihe Ankara Yahudileri* (Istanbul: Pan Yayıncılık, 2003), 164.

41. Bahar, *Efsaneden Tarihe Ankara Yahudileri,* 164–65.

42. Bahar, *Efsaneden Tarihe Ankara Yahudileri,* 164.

43. Rıdvan Akar, *Aşkale Yolcuları: Varlık Vergisi ve Çalışma Kampları* (Istanbul: Belge Yayınları, 1999), 173–75.

44. Long overlooked in the annals of official history, the program, known as the Incident of the Reserves, left profound scars in the memory of Turkey's non-Muslim communities but has only recently received critical attention. The Turkish name for the program was Yirmi Kur'a Ihtiyatlar or Yirmi Sinif Askerlik. It appears as Las Vente Klasas in the narratives of the Ladino-speakers, as Ikosi Ilikeis among the Greek, and Kisan Tasagark among Armenians.

45. Akar, *Aşkale Yolcuları*, 173–74.

46. As young Vitali Hakko, who had opened a small millinery business in Beyoğlu, recalled: "One day the police came to my shop, asking after me. After confirming that I indeed was Vitali Hakko, they told me to come with them because I was being conscripted. I was shocked, and though I tried to explain to them that there must be a mistake, that I had just been discharged, I could not reason with them. They told me there was no mistake and took me to the Selimiye Barracks to serve out my third deployment" (Vitali Hakko, *Hayatım, Vakko*, 2. baskı [Istanbul: Sedele Matbaacılık, 1997], 88–90).

47. Arslanyan, *Adım Agop*, 39.

48. Arslanyan, *Adım Agop*, 39. Tokat is in eastern Turkey, which has long winters. Thus, although the marching orders were issued in April, it is quite likely that the weather was still quite cold.

49. Ohannes Garavaryan, "6–7 Eylül 1955: Ohannes Garavaryan Anlatıyor," Interview by Kemal Yalçın, April 3, 2004, http://www.kemalyalcin.com/index.php/menu-ogesi-soylesiler/170-6-7-eyluel-1955-ohannes-garavaryan-anlatyor.

50. "Gurbette Kırk Yıl: Ohannes ve Karmen Garavaryan'dan 6-7 Eylül," *Agos*, September 8, 2007.

51. Arslanyan, *Adım Agop*, 40–42; Kemal Yalçın, *You Rejoice My Heart*, translated by Paul Bessemer (Watertown, MA: Garod Books, 2007), 76–80.

52. In Izmir and Istanbul, large-scale construction projects triggered rampant speculations that the buildings might eventually be used as incinerators. Thus, following the death from typhus of a young Jewish conscript, when the commanders ordered the sterilization of the Bursa Mollaköy Military Camp, Jewish soldiers panicked for fear they were going to be gassed. Akar, *Aşkale Yolcuları*, 175–78.

53. Men from different parts of the country were first sent to holding camps in Afyonkarahisar, Sivas, and Yozgat where they awaited their assignments. Sarkis Çerkezyan, *Dünya Hepimize Yeter* (Istanbul: Belge Yayınları, 2003), 113.

54. Jewish soldiers who dug canals in western Turkey were told by their attendants that they were digging their own graves. Sarkis Çerkezyan remembers their fear of their Kurdish attendant—Armenians were scared of Kurds because in the past they were deployed in the massacres. Çerkezyan, *Dünya Hepimize Yeter* 111.

55. Çerkezyan, *Dünya Hepimize Yeter*, 113.

56. Word had it that they were street-sweeper uniforms originally sent to Turkey from Greece as part of an emergency assistance shipment following the 1939 Erzincan earthquake. Çerkezyan, *Dünya Hepimize Yeter*, 114; Akgönül, *Türkiye Rumları*, 101.

57. Çerkezyan, *Dünya Hepimize Yeter*, 114.

58. For a detailed discussion of the place of the military within modern Turkish culture, see Ayşe Gül Altınay, *The Myth of the Military Nation* (New York: Palgrave Macmillan, 2004). However, Altınay does not look at the "Incident of the Reserves" in her work.

59. Eugen Weber, *Peasants into Frenchmen: The Modernization of Rural France 1870–1914* (Stanford, CA: Stanford University Press, 1977), 294–302.

60. Alice Odian Kasparian, *The History of the Armenians of Angora and Stanos (From Prechristian and Galatian Periods up to 1918)* (Beirut: Doniguian Press, 1968), 22–25.

61. Kasparian, *The History of the Armenians of Angora and Stanos*, 24.

62. Refik Halit Karay, *Deli* (Istanbul: Semih Lütfi Kitabevi, 1939), 55. Decrying the lawlessness of the looting that ensued, Alice Odian Kasparian recalled "Many officers expropriated anything they wanted." In addition to the goods stored in shops owned by the deportees, she lamented the confiscation of common household goods, family heirlooms and jewelry—in short, she wrote, "everything that was removable was removed from the city as well as the summer homes." Kasparian, *The History of the Armenians of Angora and Stanos*, 36.

63. Karay, *Deli*, 48.

64. With mothers crying over lost children, distressed pregnant women going into labor, young girls running and screaming with their hair ablaze, and unattended casualties stranded in stretchers in narrow streets. Karay, *Deli*, 49.

65. In some cases (for example, the site for the British embassy), the chosen sites belonged to a member of the republican elite from whom the property would be expropriated at market rate to be given to the embassy making the request. However, the owner prior to the current holder was more than likely to have been a departing Greek or Armenian family.

66. Ebniye Kanununun 20, 21, 22, 23, 24, 25inci Maddelerine Muadil Kanun, *Resmi Gazete*, no. 96, April 29, 1925, article no. 642.

67. The Ottoman census of 1880 indicates that the city's population was 208,000 of which 60 percent were non-Muslims of various descriptions. According to Kasaba, estimates of the city's population on the eve of the First World War vary, but despite absorbing Muslim migrants and refugees as the empire continued to shrink, non-Muslims continued to constitute more than half the population. Reşat Kasaba, "Izmir 1922: A Port City Unravels," in *Modernity and Culture: From the Mediterranean to the Indian Ocean*, ed. Leila Fawaz, C. A. Bayly, and Robert Ilbert (New York: Columbia University Press, 2002), 204–30.

68. Biray Kolluoğlu Kırlı, "From Ottoman Empire to Turkish Nation-State: Reconfiguring Spaces and Geobodies" (PhD diss., State University of New York-Binghamton, 2002), 225. Kolluoğlu also provides a good overview of the discrepant accounts of the start of this catastrophic fire.

69. Kasaba, "Izmir 1922," 207.

70. Kırlı, "From Ottoman Empire to Turkish Nation-State"; Behçet Uz and L. Ece Sakar, *Atatürk'ün İzmir'i: Bir Kentin Yeniden Doğuşu* (Istanbul: Türkiye İş Bankası Kültür Yayınları, 2007). The massive revenue losses Izmir suffered following its demotion within the region as a major international port, coupled with the diminished demand for redevelopment, and a general lack of political will and vision within the city's municipal administration were the principle causes of this delay. The broader nationwide lack of resources further exacerbated things. Biray Kırlı discusses the process extensively in chapter 5 of her dissertation (Kırlı, "From Ottoman Empire to Turkish Nation-State").

71. Mainly from Crete (Hirschon, *Crossing the Aegean*, xii, 218–19). Akar, *Aşkale Yolcuları*; Aktar, *Varlık Vergisi ve "Türkleştirme" Politikaları*.

269

72. For a detailed list of the fate of the religious and social institutions that belonged to Ayvalık's Greek Orthodox community, see Neriman Şahin Güçhan, "Tracing the Memoir of Dr Şerafeddin Magmumi for the Urban Memory of Ayvalık," *METU Journal of the Faculty of Architecture* 25, no. 1 (2008): 67–68.

73. Arslanyan, *Adım Agop*, 34.

74. B. Kushikian, "One Month in Turkey," *Armenian Review* 6, no. 2 (1953): 117, 119.

75. Vasilian, "Two Months in the Interior," 114.

76. Kushikian, "One Month in Turkey," 120.

77. Arzu Öztürkmen, "Remembering through Material Culture: Local Knowledge of Past Communities in a Turkish Black Sea Town," *Middle Eastern Studies* 39, no. 2 (2003): 184–85.

78. *Tekfur* originates from the Armenian term *Takavor*, meaning crown bearer, which in turn appears to have Persian origins in the word *Tac-aver*. Bilge Umar, *Türkiye'deki Tarihsel Adlar* (Istanbul: İnkilap Kitabevi, 1993), 775.

79. Recently, the study of republican "toponymical engineering" has become a rather popular subject. For further and more detailed discussion, see Kerem Öktem, "The Nation's Imprint: Demographic Engineering and the Change of Toponyms in Republican Turkey," *European Journal of Turkish Studies*, Thematic Issue no. 7, Demographic Engineering, part 1 (February 23, 2009), http://www.ejts.org/document2243 .html; Suavi Aydın, "Bir Tilkinin Ettiği: İsimler Milli Birliği Nasıl Bozar?" *Toplumsal Tarih*, November (2005), 90–97; Selim Özcan, "XX Yüzyıl Başlarında, Canik (Samsun) Sancağında İsimleri Değiştirilmek İstenen Kaza, Köy, Mahaleler ve Yeni İsimleri," in *Geçmişten Geleceğe Samsun*, ed. Cevdet Yılmaz, 671–85 (Samsun: Samsun Büyükşehir Belediyesi Kültür ve Eğitim Hizmetleri Daire Başkanlığı, 2006); among others.

80. Aydın, "Bir Tilkinin Ettiği," 95.

81. Didem Danış and Ebru Kayaalp, *Elmadağ: A Neighborhood in Flux* (Istanbul: IFEA, 2004), 4.

82. "Kırk Kilise isminin 'Kırklareli' ne tahviline Tahvili Hakkında Kanun," *Resmi Gazete*, no. 82, January 14, 1925, article no. 537. The name was post-rationalized in various media (local guidebooks, almanacs, etc.) as a reference to the putative forty Turks who died during the Ottoman conquest of the city in the fourteenth century.

83. Umar notes that other place names containing the word *Tekfur* subsequently had it replaced with *Tekir*, suggesting that rather than the colors of the local mountain, the choice was informed by the similarity of sound (Umar, *Türkiye'deki Tarihsel Adlar*, 775).

84. The decision to make the change was made by the local municipality on December 24, 1922; on the same day, the Greek neighborhood in town was also renamed after Captain Sarıbey, who had fought with the nationalist forces (http://www.mus tafakemalpasa.gov.tr/tarihce1.html). A similar decision was made in 1925 by the city council in Artvin, replacing all Georgian toponyms with Turkish ones. See Harun Tunçel, "Türkiye'de İsmi Değiştirilen Köyler," *Fırat Üniversitesi Sosyal Bilimler Dergisi / Fırat University Journal of Social Science* 10, no. 2 (2000): 27.

85. Names like Reşşdiye, Hamidiye, and Mamüret-ül Aziz commemorated Ottoman sultans and princes, whereas Mehmetbey, Arifiye, and Mesudiye honored community leaders. For further discussion, see Aydın, "Bir Tilkinin Ettiği"; Özcan, "XX Yüzyıl Başlarında."

86. Aydın, "Bir Tilkinin Ettiği," 674–75; Özcan, "XX Yüzyıl Başlarında," 656.

87. Öktem, "The Nation's Imprint," §26. Öktem also notes that with the adminis-

trative restructuring of eastern and outheastern Anatolia following the bloody suppression of a series of Kurdish uprisings in the mid-1930s, along with sweeping changes and widespread militarization of the region, further name changes were made.

88. Toponymic changes under the republic came in waves, particularly intensifying at times of trauma. For a critical examination of these successive waves and their consequences, see Kerem Öktem, "The Nation's Imprint: Demographic Engineering and the Change of Toponyms in Republican Turkey," *European Journal of Turkish Studies*, Thematic Issue 7, Demographic Engineering, part 1 (February 23, 2009), http://www.ejts.org/document2243.html.

89. For detailed eyewitness accounts of the pogrom, especially in Kırklareli, see Haker, *Bir Zamanlar Kırklareli*.

90. Haker, *Bir Zamanlar Kırklareli*.

91. Haker, *Bir Zamanlar Kırklareli*, 255–68.

92. Haker, *Bir Zamanlar Kırklareli*, 254.

93. Hatice Bayraktar, "The Anti-Jewish Program in Eastern Thrace in 1934: New Evidence for the Responsibility of the Turkish Government," *Patterns of Prejudice* 40, no. 2 (2006): 95–96.

94. Letter from Sir P. Lorraine to Sir John Simon, dated July 7, 1934. FO4633/4633/44, in Bülent Gökay, *British Documents on Foreign Affairs: Reports and Papers from the Foreign Office Confidential Print, Series B: Turkey, Iran, and the Middle East 1918–1939, Volume 33: Turkey, December 1932–November 1935* (Frederick, MD: University Publications of America), 131–32.

95. For a detailed discussion of Turkey's economic situation during the First World War leading to the imposition of the tax, see Akar, *Aşkale Yolcuları*; Aktar, *Varlık Vergisi ve "Türkleştirme" Politikaları*. A pro-state counterargument that seeks to justify the implementation of this extralegal taxation can be found in Cahit Kayra, *Savaş Türkiye Varlık Vergisi*, 1st ed. (Istanbul: Tarihçi Kitabevi, 2011).

96. Faik Ökte, *Varlık Vergisi Faciası* (Istanbul: Nebioğlu Yayınevi, 1951). Ökte, the top Treasury bureaucrat in Istanbul penned his remorseful observations years later in this memoir, laying out the arbitrary and discriminatory process by which the amounts were decided and the levies were imposed.

97. *Tasvir-i Efkar*, January 28, 1943; Bahar, *Efsaneden Tarihe Ankara Yahudileri*, 168–69. The press, fascinated by the process, provided continued coverage of the shipment of the first two groups. (See, for instance, issues of *Cumhuriyet, Tasvir-i Efkar*, and *Tan* of January 20–28, 1942; February 10–14, 1943.) The Istanbul daily *Tasvir-i Efkar* sent a young journalist, Feridun Kandemir, who traveled with the debtors and reported for a short period on the hardship of their daily lives but was summoned back to Istanbul when details began to look as if they could induce sympathy among the readership, and thus backfire on the government.

98. Both the bureaucrats and politicians involved in formulating and implementing the law appear to have been well aware of its extralegality. See Ökte, *Varlık Vergisi Faciası*, 64; Faik Ahmet Barutçu, *Siyasi Anılar (1939–54)* (Istanbul: Milliyet Yayınları, 1977), 260–65; Süleyman Inan, "Varlık Vergisi Ile İlgili Değerlendirmelere Türk Ekonomisi Açısından Kısa Bir Bakiş," *Türk Yurdu* 22, no. 182 (2001): 33.

99. Edward Clark, "The Turkish Varlık Vergisi Reconsidered," *Middle Eastern Studies* 10 (July 2009): 2008, http://dx.doi.org/10.1080/00263207208700205; Aktar, *Varlık Vergisi ve "Türkleştirme" Politikaları*; Akar, *Aşkale Yolcuları*. In his meticulous study, Aktar has examined the six central districts (*kaza*) Kadıköy, Beyoğlu,

Şişli, Fatih, Eminönü, and Adalar. The last one is not part of the central districts but was a popular residential area for non-Muslims, especially for weekend homes. The majority of the property sold (by value) belonged to Jewish citizens (39 percent), followed by Armenians (29 percent), Greeks (12 percent), minority-owned companies (10 percent), foreign nationals (5 percent), other non-Muslims (i.e., Bulgarian, Russian, 0.3 percent), and Muslim non-Muslim jointly owned businesses (2 percent).. In the same period only 0.8 percent of the property sales to pay for the tax were made by Muslims and 0.1 percent by businesses solely owned by Muslims. Aktar, *Varlık Vergisi ve "Türkleştirme" Politikaları*, 201–3.

100. Ayhan Aktar who has produced the most thorough inquiry into the transformation of real estate ownership triggered by the Wealth Tax in Istanbul has calculated that the average price of the real property auctioned off by the Treasury was 3,053 Turkish lira, whereas the same properties were assessed at an average of 5,101 Turkish lira prior to the tax. Individuals who sold their properties to pay the tax—rather than having them seized and auctioned—did only marginally better and many had to declare bankruptcy (Clark, "The Turkish Varlık Vergisi Reconsidered," 208–9). In general, the prices were significantly depressed, making it a buyers' market for those who had cash. For a detailed discussion of movements in Istanbul's property resulting from the Wealth Tax, see Aktar, *Varlık Vergisi ve "Türkleştirme" Politikaları*, 196–206.

101. Aktar, *Varlık Vergisi ve "Türkleştirme" Politikaları*, 205.

102. Barutçu, *Siyasi Anılar*, 263. This particular statement by Saracoğlu was made behind closed doors in a meeting involving RPP top brass, ministers, and high-level bureaucrats. Although his contemporary public speeches were less explicit about the motivation behind the tax, they clearly outlined a revanchist agenda against Turkey's non-Muslim citizens. The chairman of the Joint Chiefs of Staff, Kazım Karabekir, made no secret of his ultranationalist views at the time of the Twenty Classes conscription incident. Present at the discussions leading to the imposition of the tax, despite the fact that this was notably an economic measure, Karabekir argued that the stronghold minorities had in all areas of commercial activity needed to be reined in (Karabekir, quoted in Bali, *Bir Türkleştirme Serüveni*, 423).

103. Saracoğlu's closing statement at his party's Sixth Convention was remarkable in that it denied allegations that non-Muslims were a target and implicitly admitted that they indeed were. (*Ulus*, June 16, 1943, quoted in Cemil Koçak, *Türkiye'de Milli Şef Dönemi [1938–1945]*, 2 vols. [Istanbul: İletişim Yayınları, 1996], 2:511.)

104. Feridun Kandemir (*Tasvir-i Efkar*, March 8, 1943), quoted in Aktar, *Türk Milliyetçiliği, Gayrimüslimler*, 206.

105. Two neighboring office buildings were acquired by İş Bankası—a bank founded in 1924 by Mustafa Kemal and supported with funds donated by Indian Muslims to support the nationalists during the War of Independence, the Pious Foundations Administration. Another office building abutting His Master's Voice, Generali Han, was purchased by a private individual, and called Bozkurt (Gray Wolf), a name closely associated with ultranationalist Turanic mythology.

106. Akar, *Aşkale Yolcuları*, 160–61; Aktar, *Varlık Vergisi ve "Türkleştirme" Politikaları*, 140.

107. In later years, Faik Ökte, the chief officer of the Treasury in Istanbul (Defterdar), who was deeply involved in the process, penned a memoir in which he detailed, with some degree of remorse, the arbitrary nature of the tax, and how it targeted non-Muslims (Ökte, *Varlık Vergisi Faciası*, 71–87, 173–86). At an individual level, according to

the tables compiled by the British Consulate in Istanbul, whereas a Muslim Turkish wool merchant with an estimated business capital of 60,000 Turkish lira was assessed a levy of 2,000 Turkish lira, a Turkish citizen of Orthodox Greek origin was expected to pay 75,000 Turkish lira on an estimated business capital of 25,000 Turkish lira. A resident British citizen of Jewish origin, with an estimated business capital of 20,900 Turkish lira , meanwhile.was levied a tax of 90,000 Turkish lira. Akar, *Aşkale Yolcuları*, 100–105. See also, Aktar, *Varlık Vergisi ve "Türkleştirme" Politikaları*, 181–200.

108. Gülay Dinçel, "Yarmayanlar: Üç Kuşak Sanayici Bir Ermeni Ailesi," *Toplumsal Tarih* 12, no. 69 (1999): 22–33.

109. Rıfat Bali, "1952 Yılı Hizmet Gazetesinin Varlık Vergisi İle İlgili Yayını," *Toplumsal Tarih*, no. 173 (2008): 28.

110. My personal anonymous interviews with members of the Jewish and Armenian communities resonate with the more widely publicized interviews conducted with more prominent members of these communities by Akar and Bali. See Akar, *Aşkale Yolcuları*, 234–43; Akgönül, *Türkiye Rumları*, 157; Rıfat Bali, *Devlet'in Yahudileri ve "Öteki" Yahudi* (Istanbul: İletişim Yayınları, 2004), 206–7.

111. Vasilian, "Two Months in the Interior"; Clark, "The Turkish Varlık Vergisi Reconsidered."

112. Aktar, *Türk Milliyetçiliği, Gayrimüslimler*, 241–42. For detailed stories of the immigration of Turkish Jews to Israel, see Haker, *Bir Zamanlar Kırklareli*; Rıfat Bali, *Cumhuriyet Yıllarında Türkiye Yahudileri: Aliya: Bir Toplu Göçün Öyküsü, 1946–1949* (Istanbul: İletişim, 2003).

113. Ökte, *Varlık Vergisi Faciası*, 209–10.

114. Ahmet İçduygu and Özlem Kaygusuz, "The Politics of Citizenship by Drawing Borders: Foreign Policy and the Construction of National Citizenship Identity in Turkey," *Middle Eastern Studies* 40, no. 6 (2004): 41.

Chapter 5. Nationalizing Space

1. Çanakkale Wars (1915–1916), better known as the Gallipoli Campaign in the English-speaking world. See Halide Edip Adıvar, *Türkün Ateşle İmtihanı; İstiklâl Savaşı Hâtıraları* (Istanbul: Can Yayınları, 1962). Also published in English as *The Turkish Ordeal* (New York: Century, 1928).

2. Karaosmanoğlu's novel *Yaban* is revealing about the shock and consternation the nationalists experienced as they discovered the lack of national consciousness in Anatolia. In his famous speech, a political oratory delivered over three days embodying his perspective on the foundational narrative of the Turkish state, Mustafa Kemal makes similar observations. Yakup Kadri Karaosmanoğlu, *Yaban* (Istanbul: Remzi Kitabevi, 1932).

3. Monographs of individual buildings and urban designs exist, but critical studies that examine these projects as components of a larger plan are scarce. Most of the research in the latter category can be found in the work of Ilhan Tekeli and his frequent collaborator Selim Ilkin. A comprehensive three-volume collection including their joint research was published recently: İlhan Tekeli and Selim İlkin, *Cumhuriyetin Harcı*, 3 vols. (Istanbul: Bilgi Üniversitesi Yayınları, 2003).

4. The expression "Muasır medeniyet seviyesine ulaşmak" (reaching the level of contemporary civilization) was a common motto during this period.

5. Chandra Mukerji, "The Political Mobilization of Nature in Seventeenth-Century French Formal Gardens," *Theory and Society* 23, no. 5 (1994): 652. Mukerji notes that sociologists after Eugen Weber have focused on state power articulated primarily as access to the means of political violence. Refreshingly, she traces the intimate connections between the expansion of the modern state and transformation of the physical landscape. Her analysis includes the construction of roads, canals, bridges, and drainage systems in addition to the development of weapons and defense systems. Prior to Mukerji, Anthony Giddens, in his seminal book, *The Nation-State and Violence* (Berkeley: University of California Press, 1987) makes similar observations about the physical apparatus of the modern state, referring to the physical components of the state's administrative apparatus as "containers of power." However, Giddens's analysis remains rather abstract as he does not examine how actual sites in specific contexts facilitate the implementation of state power.

6. Giddens, *The Nation-State and Violence*, 84–88. Mukerji, "The Political Mobilization of Nature," 652. See also Nicos Poulantzas, "The Nation," in *State/Space: A Reader*, ed. Neil Brenner, Bob Jessop, Martin Jones, and Gordon Macleod, 65–83 (Oxford: Blackwell, 2003); Michael Mann, "The Autonomous Power of the State: Its Origins, Mechanism and Results," in Brenner et al., *State/Space*, 53–64; Henri Lefebvre, "Space and the State," in Brenner et al., *State/Space*, 84–100; and Peter J. Taylor, "The State as Container: Territoriality in the Modern World System," in Brenner et al., *State/Space*, 101–14.

7. Giddens, "The Nation-State and Violence," 61–120.

8. TCDD was the acronym for Türkiye Cumhuriyeti Devlet Demiryolları (Turkish Republic State Railroads). The agency was founded in 1927.

9. First stanza of the "Tenth Anniversary March" (lyrics by Behçet Kemal Çağlar and Faruk Nafiz Çamlıbel; music by Cemal Reşit Rey).

10. Salahaddin Bilge, a high-ranking official at the Ministry of Public Works, stated that, while in the fifty-six years between 1856 and 1912 approximately 4,100 kilometers of railroads had been built, in just the first fifteen years of the Turkish Republic 3,100 kilometers had been added to the existing lines. (Not all 4,100 kilometers remained within the boundaries of the republic.) The rate of railroad expansion had risen from 73.21 kilometers/year to 206.67 kilometers/year. Salahaddin Bilge, "Cumhuriyet Devrinde Nafia İşleri," in *Cumhuriyetin 16: Yıldönümünde Hitabeler ve Konferanslar* (Ankara: Ulus Basımevi, 1939), 49.

11. These consortia often consisted of some combination of import/export companies, venture capitalists, engineering firms, and so forth. For instance, the first rail line in the empire between the port city of Izmir and the agricultural town of Aydın, located in the fertile plains of the Meander River, was financed by a group of British venture capitalists. In exchange for their investment in the construction, the British group was granted operation rights and profits on this line for seventy years. In the next few decades the Ottoman government granted further concessions with similar conditions for the construction and operation of railroads by foreign companies. Between 1856 and 1912, thirty-five more railroad contracts were signed between Ottoman officials and various European consortia to build and run 6,877 kilometers of railroads. The Ottoman state, for its part, built the 1,564 kilometer Hejaz line between Istanbul and Hejaz on the Arabian peninsula with contributions from private individuals and by deploying conscripted soldiers in the construction process. Of these, 4,100 kilometers remained within the boundaries

of the Turkish Republic. According to Yerasimos the breakdown of the shares of investments by country in the period immediately preceding the First World War was: France 39.92 percent; Belgium, Switzerland, and Austria 1.85 percent; Germany 12.7 percent; Great Britain 7.71 percent; and Ottoman 7.21 percent. Stefanos Yerasimos, *Az Gelişmişlik Sürecinde Türkiye*, 3 vols. Bilim Arastirma Dizisi (Istanbul: Gözlem Yayınları, 1974–1976), 3:965. For more information about the expansion of railroads in Turkey, see Yerasimos, *Az Gelişmişlik Sürecinde Türkiye*, 2:916–26, 966–71.

12. Cumhuriyet Halk Partisi, *On Beşinci Yıl Kitabı* (Ankara: Cumhuriyet Matbaası, 1938), 242.

13. Yerasimos, *Az Gelişmişlik Sürecinde Türkiye*, 3:942.

14. Obtaining these concessions was competitive. Ottoman officials kept the competition up by pitting the different consortia and governments against one another. By engaging them in this competition, they managed to have power.

15. Reşat Kasaba, "Migrant Labor in Western Anatolia 1750–1850," in *Landholding and Commercial Agriculture in the Middle East*, ed. Çağlar Keyder and Faruk Tabak, 113–21 (Albany: State University of New York Press, 1991).

16. Kasaba, "Migrant Labor in Western Anatolia 1750–1850," 113–21.

17. Due to the lengthy and highly contested nature of the bidding, planning, and building processes, the operations of each line and sometimes even of particular segments within a given line were governed by different bilateral agreements signed over a long period of time. For instance, it took eleven years to build the 130-kilometer line between Izmir and Aydın. Yerasimos, *Az Gelişmişlik Sürecinde Türkiye*, 3:937.

18. Examples of the unifying effect have been discussed in detail by Eugen Weber, *Peasants into Frenchmen: The Modernization of Rural France 1870–1914* (Stanford, CA: Stanford University Press, 1977); Wolfgang Schivelbusch, *The Railway Journey: The Industrialization of Time and Space in the 19th Century* (Berkeley: University of California Press, 1986); William Cronon, *Nature's Metropolis: Chicago and the Great West* (New York: Norton, 1991).

19. These contracts were a thorn in the side of the republican administration. They regarded them as the undesirable reminders of the continued operation of European interests in sovereign Turkish territory, a bitter legacy of the empire's subservience to European interests.

20. Cemal Hidayet Sertel, "Türk Demiryolculuğu," in *Cumhuriyetin 16: Yildönümünde Hitabeler ve Konferanslar* (Ankara: Ulus Kitabevi, 1939), 99.

21. Sertel, "Türk Demiryolculuğu," 101; Partisi, *On Beşinci Yıl Kitabı*, 250–52.

22. Sertel, "Türk Demiryolculuğu,: 101. Sertel was not alone in advocating the importance of taking over and expanding railroads under a single national company for economic development and market integration. For example, in an official letter he wrote to Prime Minister İnönü, Abidin Özmen, the inspector general of Thrace, complained bitterly about the Orient Express company, which was still operating the rolling stock in the region. He argued that "this foreign company, which focuses exclusively on maximizing its own profit slaps heavy charges for shipping and handling making it unaffordable for our farmers whose crops, as a result, rot in the fields. Discouraged by this state of affairs, the farmers grow only for their own subsistence or give up on farming all together.... To provide an opportunity for economic development in Thrace ... it is imperative to bring this line under the control of our national

railroad company." Cited in Cemil Koçak, *Umumi Müfettişlikler (1927–1952)* (Istanbul: İletişim Yayınları, 2003), 140.

23. "Erzurum Demiryolu," *Ülkü*, 1939, 165.

24. "Erzurum Demiryolu," *Ülkü*, 1939, 164.

25. Partisi, *On Beşinci Yıl Kitabı*, 251.

26. Quoted on the inner cover of the public works exhibition. *Nafia Sergisi* (Ankara: Devlet Basımevi, 1942).

27. İsmail Hakkı Baltacıoğlu, "Demiryolu ve Türk Bütünlüğü," *Yeni Adam*, 1934, 8.

28. "Erzurum Demiryolu," *Ülkü*, 1939, 165.

29. Baskın Oran, *Atatürk Milliyetçiliği ilResmi İdeoloji Dışı Bir İnceleme* (Ankara: Dost Kitabevi, 1988).

30. Koçak, *Umumi Müfettişlikler*, 91, 236–38.

31. Cardo-decomanus: Cardo (North–South) and Decumanus (East–West) were the cruciform main streets of Roman cities, of which Diyarbakır had been one.

32. During the First World War, Mustafa Kemal was posted twice in Diyarbakır, March 26–June 3, 1916, and March 11–July 9, 1917. See Mehmet Önder, *Atatürk'ün Yurt Gezileri* (Ankara: Türkiye, 1998), 135.

33. Falih Rıfkı Atay, "Ankara," *Hakimiyet-i Milliye*, October 29, 1933.

34. See Tansı Şenyapılı, *Ankara Kentinde Gecekondu Gelişimi* (Ankara: Kent-Koop Yayınları, 1985). The city's population increased from approximately 20,000 in 1923 to 75,000 in 1927 and to 123,000 in 1935. Ruşen Keleş, *Eski Ankara'da Bir Şehir Tipolojisi* (Ankara: Ankara Üniversitesi Siyasal Bilgiler Fakültesi Yayınları, 1971), 5.

35. The style, as Sibel Bozdoğan notes, was inspired by the work of Central European architects who were commissioned to design some of the earliest institutional buildings for the new state. The flat roofs were in demand because of the image of modernity they projected, but Turkish builders did not have the technology and expertise to construct flat roofs that did not leak. Early Republican modern buildings thus had sloped roofs concealed by parapet walls. Sibel Bozdoğan, *Modernism and Nation-Building: Turkish Architectural Culture in the Early Republic* (Seattle: University of Washington Press, 2001), 185.

36. İlhan Tekeli, "1923–1950 Döneminde Muğla'da Olan Gelişmeler," in *Tarih İçinde Muğla*, ed, Tekeli (Ankara: Orta Doğu Teknik Üniversitesi Yayınları, 1993), 169.

37. Meanwhile, the courthouse, the gendarme headquarters, and the municipality remained on the edge of the historic downtown in buildings that had been built during the previous wave of bureaucratic expansion under Ottoman reformers.

38. Tekeli, "1923–1950 Döneminde Muğla," 173.

39. Tekeli, "1923–1950 Döneminde Muğla," 165.

40. Tekeli, "1923–1950 Döneminde Muğla," 165.

41. Alev Çınar, *Modernity, Islam, and Secularism in Turkey: Bodies, Places, and Time* (Minneapolis: University of Minnesota Press, 2005), 110–12. Although Taksim did not have the imprint of the Ottoman state or its pious institutions, of course, it was an important enclave for the city's non-Muslim citizens and their commercial establishments and communal institutions.

42. For a study of Ottoman urban transformations in the nineteenth century, see Zeynep Çelik, *Empire, Architecture, and the City: French-Ottoman Encounters, 1830–1914* (Seattle: University of Washington Press, 2008).

43. Cenap Refik Orkon, *Manisa Coğrafyası* (Istanbul: Resimli Ay Matbaası, 1937), 70. Manisa was on the oldest train route in Turkey, between Aydın and Izmir. During the war its train station was burned along with the rest of the town. The completion of Manisa's train station antedated that of Ankara by three years. However, it would not be anachronistic to argue that Manisa's plan used the same principles for establishing the spatial connection between the downtown and the station, because even though the new large train station in Ankara was not completed until 1936, the spatial patterns were established and the Ankara government had already been working on reinforcing them.

44. *Cumhuriyetin 15. Yılında Manisa* (Istanbul: Kemal Matbaası, 1938), 78. The municipality had acquired the property in 1935, and in 1938, it organized a competition for the design of the Atatürk monument to be built on the site.

45. *Cumhuriyetin 15. Yılında Manisa*, 73.

46. Orkon, *Manisa Cografyası* , 70.

47. *Cumhuriyetin 15. Yılında Manisa*, 73.

48. Öngören and Inönü, interview. Cited in Koçak, *Umumi Müfettişlikler*, 122.

49. For example Abidin Özmen wrote "with the exception of seven to eight of our forty-eight districts, there is no housing available for government personnel that would provide them the possibility of living with their families and working productively and with commitment." Özmen, cited in Koçak, *Umumi Müfettişlikler*, 124. Koçak includes additional similar examples of correspondence, 116–25,

50. In another report that reiterated the pressing need for housing, Özmen demanded funding for two hundred apartments that were slated to be built in the twenty-eight districts within the provinces of Diyarbakır, Urfa, Mardin, Siirt, Bitlis, Mus, Van, and Hakkari. These units, consisting of three bedrooms, a living room, and a bathroom each, would be modest, "but as they would be models for the local population to emulate, they would serve an additional purpose, contributing to national progress and development in every possible way." Özmen, cited in Koçak, *Umumi Müfettişlikler*, 124.

51. Naşit Hakkı Uluğ, *Tunceli Medeniyete Açılıyor* (Istanbul: Cumhuriyet Matbaası, 153.

52. Uluğ, *Tunceli Medeniyete Açılıyor*, 161.

53. Uluğ, *Tunceli Medeniyete Açılıyor*, 161.

54. Öngören and Inönü, interview. Cited in Koçak, *Umumi Müfettişlikler*, 115.

55. Koçak, *Umumi Müfettişlikler*, 115–16.

56. See Sibel Bozdogan's account of criticisms that appeared in *Arkitekt*, the only professional journal of the Early Republican years. Bozdoğan, *Modernism and Nation-Building*, 89–91. In fact, as discussed in the May–June 2004 issue of *Mimarlik*, the main professional journal published by the Turkish Chamber of Architects, despite Turkey's vastly different circumstances, changes in styles, tastes, and the availability of architects and construction workers, the practice of producing school buildings based on a few national prototypes continues to this day.

57. *Vilayetler Albümü* (Ankara: Dahiliye Vekaleti, 1929). For an analysis of the

debates within the architectural profession about government funded centrally designed projects, and especially schools, see Bozdoğan, *Modernism and Nation-Building*, 181–82.

58. Municipalities Law (*Belediyeler Kanunu*), *Resmi Gazete*, April 3, 1930, article no. 1580, and later addendum in *Resmi Gazete*, June 7, 1935, article no. 2763.

59. General Public Health Act (*Umumi Hıfzısıhha Kanunu*), *Resmi Gazete*, May 16, 1930, article no. 1539. Municipality Road and Buildings Code (*Belediye Yapı ve Yollar Kanunu*), *Resmi Gazete*, June 21, 1933, article no. 2290.

60. Modeled after the Ankara Master Planning Bureau, the commission consisted of representatives from the Ministries of Public Works, Finance, and Treasury, Health and Social Security, the head counsel of the Interior Ministry, and the directors general of local governments, the Municipalities Bank, and Ankara Master Planning Bureau. Municipalities Master Plan Commission Charter, *Resmi Gazete*, March 17, 1935, article no. 2799, see also İlhan Tekeli, "Türkiye'de Kent Planlamasının Tarihsel Kökleri," in *Türkiye'de İmar Planlaması Konferansı*, ed. Tamer Gök (Ankara: Orta DoğuTeknik Üniversitesi Şehir ve Planlama Bölümü, 1980), 59. In 1939, with an amendment to the Charter Law of the Ministry of Public Works, the authority of the City Engineering Commission to prepare plans and supervise their realization was formally recognized (64). See also, Partisi, *On Beşinci Yıl Kitabı*, 78–79.

61. Two important developments brought major changes to urban planning practices in Turkey in the aftermath of the First World War. The first one was the country's transition into a multiparty system that dissolved the strictly hierarchical centralizing control exercised by the RPP in all areas of public life. The second was the sudden and rather enormous influx of rural immigrants to cities in search of jobs.

62. For a full listing of all the urban plans produced between 1933 and 1945, see Ilhan Tekeli, "Cumhuriyetin Altmış Yıllık Belediyecilik Deneyiminin Değerlendirilmesi Üzerine," in *Türk Belediyeciliğinde 60. Yıl Uluslararası Sempozyumu*, ed. Tekeli (Ankara: Metropol İmar A.S. Ankara Büyükşehir Belediyesi, 1990), 113–21.

63. On more than one occasion, at the Library of the Turkish Historical Society in Ankara, while browsing books from the provinces in the fifteenth anniversary series, I have found the cover letters addressed to officials from one province to their counterparts in another suggesting that this was a resource to be mutually shared.

64. A good example would be Lütfü Kırdar, who was promoted from the governorship of Manisa to that of Istanbul and eventually became the MP for Istanbul. For similar examples of local officials' rise in Diyarbakır, see Şevket Beysanoğlu, "Anılarımda Diyarbakır Halkevi," *Kebikeç* 2, no. 3 (1996): 161–67. The pattern was repeated in several towns across the country.

65. Halid Ziya, "Belediyeler Nasıl Bir Haritaya Muhtaçtır?" *Belediyeler Dergisi* 1, no. 10 (1934): 29–30.

66. In the early years in many cities, the position of mayor and governor were held by the same person. Thus local government was very tightly controlled from the center, through the Ministry of Interior.

67. Ziya, "Belediyeler Nasıl Bir Haritaya Muhtaçtır?"

68. Uzer and Inönü, interview. Cited in Koçak, *Umumi Müfettişlikler*, 201.

69. Atay, "Ankara."

70. Atay, "Ankara."

71. "Büyük Bayram Nasıl Kutlulanacak," *Hakimiyet-i Milliye*, July 7, 1933.

72. See, for instance, T. C. Kültür Bakanlığı, *Cimnastik Senlikleri Talimatnamesi*

(Istanbul: Devlet Basımevi, 1938); T. C. Kültür Bakanlığı, *Okullarda Kullanılacak Milli Bayrak ve Okul Filaması Hakkında Talimatname* (Istanbul: Devlet Basımevi, 1938).

73. "Büyük Bayram Nasıl Kutlulanacak," *Hakimiyet-i Milliye*, July 7, 1933, BCA 490.01/1150.36.1.

74. Halk Hatipleri was a program designed to enlist local notables to propagate official views on all matters that affected the public. A broader study of the program can be found in Sefa Şimşek, *Bir İdeolojik Seferberlik Deneyimi: Halkevleri, 1932–1951* (Istanbul: Boğaziçi Üniversitesi Yayınevi, 2002).

75. From an advertisement in *Cumhuriyet*, October 15, 1933.

76. Adalet Ağaoğlu, *Ölmeye Yatmak* (Ankara: Yapı ve Kredi Yayınları, 1994), 88–90; "Cumhuriyet Bayramı: En Büyük Bayramı, Ankara Şehri Halkı ve Bütün Memleket 29-10-1936 Perşembe Günü Görülmemiş Bir Heyecan ve Alaka İle Kutladı," *Karınca Kooperatif Postası* (November 1936); "Cumhuriyetimizin 10. Yılı Coşkuyle Kutlulandı," *Ankara Haftası*, no. 55 (1933).

77. Cüneyt Arcayürek, *Cüneyt Arcayürek Açıklıyor: Demokrasinin İlk Yılları* (Ankara: Bilgi Yayınevi, 1983), 146.

78. Official holidays such as the Republic's Anniversary or Armed Forces Day also began to serve as markers of the government's annual calendar as mass appointments of bureaucrats and military promotions were also scheduled to coincide with them.

79. Avenues were named after nationalist heroes such as Mustafa Kemal Atatürk, Ismet Inönü, and Fevzi Çakmak; children went to schools named after battles of the War of Independence, and concepts such as nation, liberation, independence, and freedom were frequently used in the naming of new urban spaces.

80. "Ismet Pasa Bulvarı İzmirlilerin Coşkun Sevinclerile Açıldı," *Ankara Haftası*, April 13, 1933, 5

81. In the process of conducting my field work, I examined several history textbooks written for students ranging from elementary school to the end of high school. None of them mentioned the internal strife that plagued the War of Independence.

82. In addition to history textbooks used in schools, conferences where teachers were trained were also instrumental in the dissemination of these ideas such as the weekly for elementary school teachers İlköğretim Haftası, or university week in Elazığ (*Üçüncü Üniversite Haftası, 23–30 Eylül 1942, Elazığ*, no. 196 [Istanbul: İstanbul Üniversitesi Yayınları, 1943]).

83. Martin van Bruinessen quotes from the observations of Turkish sociologist İsmail Beşikçi concerning the pervasive cultural ethnic divide in Turkey: "It was said that the Kurds were Turks by origin and their language derived from Turkish, that Kurdish was a Turkish dialect. But in Elazığ, I was confronted, in various districts, with different social and cultural realities: a different language, a different culture. . . . [I saw that] realities on the ground and what was claimed by the universities and the press were at variance with one another. This planted in me the seed of fundamental doubts that were later to come to flourish." M. M. van Bruinessen, "Genocide in Kurdistan? The Suppression of the Dersim Rebellion in Turkey (1937–38)," in *Conceptual and Historical Dimensions of Genocide*, ed. George J. Andreopoulos, 141–70 (Philadelphia: University of Pennsylvania Press, 1994).

84. İhsan Sabri Çağlayangil, *Anılarım*, 2. baskı (Istanbul: Yılmaz Yayınları, 1990), 44–55.

85. "Hatt-ı müdafaa yoktur sath-ı müdafaa vardır. O satıh bütün vatandır."

Chapter 6. Manufacturing Turkish Citizens

1. For discussions of the relationship between constituencies with which the republican leadership built alliances to shore up the neophyte state see, among others, Doğan Avcıoğlu, *Türkiye'nin Düzeni* (Ankara: Bilgi Yayınevi, 1968); Çağlar Keyder, *State and Class in Turkey: A Study in Capitalist Development* (London: Verso, 1987).

2. For institutional transformations and changing state-citizen relations in modern nation-state formation processes, see Ernest Gellner, *Nations and Nationalism* (Ithaca, NY: Cornell University Press, 1983); Eugen Weber, *Peasants into Frenchmen: The Modernization of Rural France 1870–1914* (Stanford, CA: Stanford University Press, 1977); Henry Jacoby, *The Bureaucratization of the World* (Berkeley: University of California Press, 1973); Scott, *Seeing like a State: How Certain Schemes to Improve the Human Condition Have Failed* (New Haven, CT: Yale University Press, 1998).

3. Faith Childress, "Republican Lessons: Education and the Making of Modern Turkey" (PhD diss., University of Utah, 2001), 16–20.

4. Nazif Öztürk, *Türk Yenileşme Çerçevesinde Vakıf Müessesi* (Ankara: Diyanet Vakfı Yayınları, 1995), 66–75; Zeynep Kezer, "Contesting Urban Space in Early Republican Ankara, " *Journal of Architectural Education* 52, no. 1 (September 1998): 14–15.

5. Childress, "Republican Lessons," 38. Education inspectors visited schools to examine activity logs, audit classes, and test students. To ensure constant preparedness, their visits were unannounced—if somewhat predictable—and they remain, to this day, among the most intimidating experiences for teachers and students alike.

6. Jacquelynne S. Eccles, "The Development of Children Ages 6 to 14," *Future of Children* 9, no. 1 (1999): 30–44.

7. Hakkı İzet, "Coğrafya Tedrisatında Resimden İstifade," *İlköğretim Haftası* (1939), 252.

8. İzet, "Coğrafya Tedrisatında Resimden İstifade," 254.

9. Jeremy Black, *Maps and Politics* (Chicago: University of Chicago Press, 1997); Eugen Weber, *My France: Politics, Culture, Myth* (Cambridge, MA: Belknap Press of Harvard University Press, 1991), 57–71.

10. Benjamin Carr Fortna, "Change in the School Maps of the Late Ottoman Empire," *Imago Mundi* 57 (2005): 23–34.

11. Fortna, "Change in the School Maps," 25–26.

12. Fortna, "Change in the School Maps," 26.

13. Interestingly, Hakkı İzet's background was not in geography or cartography. Originally trained as an architect and a graphic artist, he then studied fine arts in Germany and went on to become one of Turkey's first ceramicists. Deniz Onur Erman, "Cumhuriyet Sonrası Türk Seramik Sanatının Çağdaşlaşma Süreci," accessed December 19, 2014, http://sanatvetasarim.gazi.edu.tr/web/makaleler/6_deniz.pdf.

14. Hatay was part of the French mandate over Syria in the post–First World War partition of former Ottoman lands. Its annexation to Turkey after long years of negotiations and a contested plebiscite was later challenged by Syria, which included the province in its maps until well into the 1990s.

15. Historians of cartography have convincingly argued that maps disclose more about their makers than about what they depict. See, among others, Black, *Maps and Politics*; John Brian Harley, "The Map and the Development of the History of Cartography," in *The History of Cartography, Volume 1*, ed. David Woodward and John Brian Harley, accessed June 22, 2012, http://www.press.uchicago.edu/ucp/books/book/

chicago/H/bo3620863.html; Mark S. Monmonier, *How to Lie with Maps* (Chicago: University of Chicago Press, 1996).

16. For example, the use of word problems that involved republican infrastructural projects, national products, or national geography was highly recommended.

17. Türkiye Cumuriyeti [*sic*] Kültür Bakanlığı, ed., *İlkokul Programı* (Istanbul: Devlet Basımevi, 1936), 20–21.

18. The same idea is repeated with very similar wording throughout the book, in chapters dealing with various subjects such as history, homeland studies, geography, and so on.

19. Kaya was a professor of education at the Gazi Teachers' College. Kemal Kaya, *İlkokulda Coğrafya Öğretimi* T. C. Maarif Vekilliği İlkokul Öğretmeni Kılavuzları (Istanbul: Maarif Matbaası, 1942), 51.

20. Kaya, *İlkokulda Coğrafya Öğretimi*, 51.

21. Kaya, *İlkokulda Coğrafya Öğretimi*, 57–60.

22. Kaya, *İlkokulda Coğrafya Öğretimi*, 57.

23. Kaya, *İlkokulda Coğrafya Öğretimi*, 58.

24. For trenchant feminist critiques of the Kemalist ideal of the modern Turkish woman, see Yeşim Arat, "The Project of Modernity and Women in Turkey," in *Rethinking the Project of Modernity and National Identity in Turkey*, ed. Reşat Kasaba and Sibel Bozdoğan, 95–112 (Seattle: University of Washington Press, 1997); Zehra F. Arat, "Turkish Women and the Reconstruction of Tradition," in *Reconstructing Gender in the Middle East: Tradition, Identity, and Power*, ed. Fatma Müge Göçek and Shiva Balaghi, 57–89 (New York: Columbia University Press, 1994); Nilüfer Göle, *The Forbidden Modern: Civilization and Veiling*, Critical Perspectives on Women and Gender (Ann Arbor: University of Michgan Press, 1996); Deniz Kandiyoti, *Cariyeler, Bacılar, Yurttaşlar: Kimlikler ve Toplumsal Dönüşümler* (Istanbul: Metis Kadın Yayınları, 1996); Jenny B. White, "State Feminism, Modernization and the Turkish Republican Woman," *NWSA Journal* 15, no. 3 (2003): 145–59.

25. Arat, "Turkish Women and the Reconstruction of Tradition"; Kandiyoti, *Cariyeler, Bacılar, Yurttaşlar*, 65–83.

26. Arat, "Turkish Women and the Reconstruction of Tradition," 64.

27. Arat quotes a number of speeches and writings by Mustafa Kemal, drawn primarily from Atatürk, *Atatürk'ün Söylev ve Demeçleri* (Ankara: Türk İnkılâp Tarihi Enstitüsü, 1946), and his manuscripts from books he cowrote with Afetinan. Arat, "Turkish Women and the Reconstruction of Tradition," 60–62.

28. Arat, "Turkish Women and the Reconstruction of Tradition," 60.

29. "Yüzde Yüz Ev Kadını Yetiştiren Bir Müessese: İsmet İnönü Enstitüsü," *Ulus*, August 8, 1938.

30. *Kız Enstitüleri ve Sağnat Okulları* (Ankara: Devlet Matbaası, 1938), 35.

31. Graduation from the evening institutes took two years. *Kız Enstitüleri ve Sağnat Okulları*, 41.

32. "L'Institut de Jeunes Filles d'Ismet Inönü," *La Turquie Kamaliste*, no. 6 (April 1935): 6–9.

33. For the curriculum and principles of these schools see *Kız Enstitüleri ve Sağnat Okulları*; *Türkiye Cumhuriyeti Maarif Vekaleti Ismet Paşa Kız Enstitüsü* (Ankara: Hakimiyet-i Milliye Matbaası, n.d.).

34. *Kız Enstitüleri ve Sağnat Okulları*, 32.

35. Government publications classified Girls' Institutes as vocational schools, along with commercial high schools, building trades high schools, and boys crafts schools, which included specializations in various areas including, among others, metalworking, carpentry, electrical systems, and so on.

36. In Turkey, girls' school attendance has historically been low. Of the families that did send their daughters to school, a large number chose vocational. Arat notes that a "limited number of career-oriented schools that were open to female students led to mostly labor-intensive and low wage jobs that did not allow women to participate in decision-making processes at work. Consequently, the specialization and recruitment in vocational schools resulted in an educational system that perpetuated traditional gender roles." Even in academic high schools, prior to the integration of male and female schools, male students received longer hours of instruction in the form of field trips or laboratory work, while girls were assigned modern housekeeping tasks. Some differences remained even after integration in the 1930s, especially in the areas of crafts and physical education. Arat, "Turkish Women and the Reconstruction of Tradition," 67–70.

37. Naci Sadullah, *Yeni Mecmua*, no. 5 (1939): 33.

38. *Kız Enstitüleri ve Sağnat Okulları*, 32.

39. Sibel Bozdoğan, *Modernism and Nation-Building: Turkish Architectural Culture in the Early Republic* (Seattle: University of Washington Press, 2001), 200.

40. By 1938, the institutes accounted for 10 of the 49 vocational schools (which included boys' technical vocational schools and mixed-gender commercial-accounting schools) in operation. There were also 16 evening institutes, some of which shared facilities with the day schools, mainly for young working or married women. These schools had a total of 14,749 students (*Kız Enstitüleri ve Sağnat Okulları*, 10, 22). According to Elif Akşit, by the 1937–38 academic year 2,000 girls were in day schools and 8,000 students were in the evening schools. Elif Ekin Akşit, *Kızların Sessizliği: Kız Enstitülerinin Uzun Tarihi* (Istanbul: İletişim Yayınları, 2005), 153.

41. In 1942–1943, the first year for which statistical data are available, only 26 percent of girls were enrolled in academic high schools, while 74 percent were in vocational schools. The Girls' Institutes took the lion share with 47.7 percent of the total enrollment, while vocational schools in the health care area (nursing, midwifery, child care), which also recruited exclusively female students, constituted 4.22 percent of female high school enrollment. (Arat, "Turkish Women and the Reconstruction of Tradition," 69.)

42. *Türkiye Cumhuriyeti Maarif Vekaleti Ismet Paşa Kız Enstitüsü*, 3. Although it is not uncommon for terms from Western languages to be imported into Turkish, "hom" was not one that gained any sort of common circulation.

43. "Yüzde Yüz Ev Kadını Yetiştiren Bir Müessese."

44. Bozdoğan, *Modernism and Nation-Building*, 200.

45. Bozdoğan, *Modernism and Nation-Building*, 203.

46. "Yüzde Yüz Ev Kadını Yetiştiren Bir Müessese."

47. "Yüzde Yüz Ev Kadını Yetiştiren Bir Müessese."

48. *Türkiye Cumhuriyeti Maarif Vekaleti Ismet Paşa Kız Enstitüsü*, 5; *Maarif Sergisi Rehberi* (Ankara: Maarif Vekaleti, 1933), 72. Duplications were common in tasks ranging from food preparation to lingerie production and needlework for bed linen.

The students were expected to master the skills necessary to satisfy a broad range of tastes and needs, old and new. At other times, as in the case of house cleaning, material circumstances dictated the need to learn both "modern" and "old-fashioned" ways of doing things: students learned to clean both with a broom and with a vacuum cleaner.

49. *Türkiye Cumhuriyeti Maarif Vekaleti Ismet Paşa Kız Enstitüsü*, 5.

50. "Yüzde Yüz Ev Kadını Yetiştiren Bir Müessese."

51. Mevhibe İnönü, wife of Ismet İnönü, often served as the de facto first lady. Mustafa Kemal was single, and she was the wife of the second highest ranked officer of the republic.

52. Peter Benedict, "The Kabul Günü: Structured Visiting in an Anatolian Provincial Town," *Anthropological Quarterly* 47, no. 1 (January 1974): 28–47, doi:10.2307/3317025; Kandiyoti, *Cariyeler, Bacılar, Yurttaşlar*; Mahmut Tezcan, *Türk Ailesi Antropolojisi*, 1st ed. (Kızılay, Ankara: İmge Kitabevi, 2000).

53. Ferhunde Özbay, "Gendered Space: A New Look at Turkish Modernisation," *Gender and History* 11, no. 3 (1999): 561; Tezcan, *Türk Ailesi Antropolojisi*.

54. Sevim Yeşil, "Unfolding Republican Patriarchy: The Case of Young Kurdish Women at the Girls' Vocational Boarding School in Elazig" (MA thesis, Middle East Technical University, 2003), 86–87. "Later, when Sıdıka Avar was there, they collected homeless, orphan girls from the rural area and caves of Tunceli with trucks. They were like the African children shown on the TV; they were just skin and bones, with swollen abdomens. They had fed themselves with grass; they were hungry. First, they treated those children. Then they accepted those at the appropriate age. It was the time of Ms Sıdıka. They made all those girls at unfitting age maidservants. All of them had to be maidservants, what else could they do?"

55. Sıdıka Avar, *Dağ Çiçeklerim* (Ankara: Öğretmen Yayınları, 1986), 124.

56. The anecdote appears in both Sıdıka Avar's and Muhtar Körükçü's recollections. Avar, *Dağ Çiçeklerim*, 232–33; Körükçü, *Köyden Haber*, 55.

57. From Sevim's oral history interviews. Yeşil, "Unfolding Republican Patriarchy," 110–13.

58. Yeşil, "Unfolding Republican Patriarchy."

59. Yeşil, "Unfolding Republican Patriarchy," 104, 113.

60. Yeşil, "Unfolding Republican Patriarchy," 117. Sevim's interviewees provide extensive details about how children from different backgrounds were sorted in the shared spaces of the institute. None of the interviewees report particularly bad treatment by other (Turkish) students, but they acknowledge that their relationships were always frosty. One of them notes that she had been verbally bullied. This was not unlike previous United States and contemporary Canadian or Australian attempts to "civilize" indigenous children by severing them from their families and familiar surroundings.

61. Avar, *Dağ Çiçeklerim*, 147.

62. Avar, *Dağ Çiçeklerim*, 273–74.

63. Avar, *Dağ Çiçeklerim*, 337–40.

64. Avar, *Dağ Çiçeklerim*, 357.

65. Yeşil, "Unfolding Republican Patriarchy," 157.

66. Zeki Mesut (Alsan), "Inkilap ve Terbiye," *Hakimiyet-i Milliye*, 1929.

67. Günver Güneş, "Serbest Cumhuriyet Fırkası Döneminde Türk Ocakları ve Siyaset," *Toplumsal Tarih* (May 1999): 11–18.

68. What follows is a table showing Halkevleri expansion:

Year	Number of Halkevi chapters	Number of Halkodası chapters
1932	14	—
1933	55	—
1934	80	—
1935	103	—
1936	136	—
1937	167	—
1938	209	—
1939	376	—
1941	379	141
1945	478	4,322

See Kadri Kaplan, "Halkevleri," in *Atatürk ve Halkevleri: Atatürkçü Düsünce Üzerine Denemeler*, ed. Kaplan (Ankara: Türk Tarih Kurumu Basımevi, 1974), 135–37.

69. The correspondence of the inspector general for the Thrace region suggests that these immigrants were not seen as a security threat but, rather, lacked language skills and familiarity with the region in which they had been settled. According to the inspector general of Thrace, the immigrants in that region did not pose a threat of violence as did the Kurdish tribes in Eastern Turkey. They did, however, need cultural services such as language skills, knowledge about their new homeland, and information about the rules and duties that came with their citizenship, which could be delivered most effectively by Halkevleri. The first group of Halkevleri included that of Çanakkale, which had one of the largest percentages of non-Turkish speakers in the population. Similarly Samsun on the Black Sea coast, Eskişehir in Central Anatolia, and Izmir on the Aegean were among the first provinces that acquired a Halkevi (Koçak, *Umumi Müfettişlikler*, 153–54). In the East, Diyarbakır Halkevi was among the first fourteen inaugurated in February 1932 and was followed by the addition of Van in the summer of that year, and Urfa, Siirt, Muş, Bitlis, and Silvan in 1934. The capital investment for the construction of these facilities was remarkable: Mardin, Bitlis, and Van each had received 50,000 Turkish lira for the construction of Halkevi facilities in their provincial seats; 140,000 Turkish lira had been spent on the construction of the new Halkevi building in the provincial seat of Diyarbakır, which was completed in early 1937. (Koçak, *Umumi Müfettişlikler*, 97–99). For comparison purposes, Koçak notes that 200,000 Turkish lira had been allocated to install water infrastructure for the entire city of Diyarbakır (116) and that in 1934 the annual spending for the entire municipality of Diyarbakır was 281,800 Turkish lira, 49,900 Turkish lira for the municipality of Mardin ("Uray Bütçeleri ve Bayındırlık," *Belediyeler Dergisi*, n.d.).

70. For a detailed assessment of the various activities of the organization see Sefa Şimşek, *Bir İdeolojik Seferberlik Deneyimi: Halkevleri, 1932–1951* (Istanbul: Boğaziçi Üniversitesi Yayınevi, 2002).

71. Benevolent paternalism in the form of social welfare offerings has historically been an integral part of Muslim-Turkish state programs. Both Seldjuk and Ottoman sultans established *vakıf*s—pious foundations—in several towns to foment urban development and reinforce the legitimacy of their rule. What distinguished the republican programs from those of their predecessors was their aggressive secularism and their attempt to bring all such activity under state control.

72. *Halkevleri ve Halkodaları* (Istanbul: Alaeddin Kıral Matbaası, 1942), 19–20.

73. Until that date, Diyarbakır was known as Diyarbekir. It appears that Mustafa Kemal deliberately mispronounced it. (Kadri Kemal Kop, *Atatürk Diyarbakır'da ve 'O'nun Hatıraları* [Istanbul: Cumhuriyet Matbaası, 1938], 35.) According to Beysanoğlu, from that day on the city's name was changed. The law, which changed the name officially was passed on December 10, 1937. (Diyarbekir Beldesi Adının Diyarbakır Olarak Değiştirilmesi Hakkında Kararname, *Resmi Gazete*, no. 3786, December 18, 1937, 2/ 7789.) During the 1937 trip, Mustafa Kemal changed the names of several eastern toponyms that invoked the Kurdish or Arabic heritage of the region. This was quite similar to the toponym changes intended to eliminate traces of Greek, Armenian, and other non-Turkish histories.

74. For a detailed account of the event see Kop, *Atatürk Diyarbakır'da*, 35.

75. İlhan Tekeli, *Tarih İçinde Muğla* (Ankara: Orta Doğu Teknik Üniversitesi Yayınları, 1993), 165.

76. Tekeli, *Tarih İçinde Muğla*, 165.

77. Güneş, "Serbest Cumhuriyet Fırkası Döneminde."

78. Ahmet Yüksel recalls that in Merzifon (Central Turkey), sports in clubs other than those run by the Halkevi were proscribed (Ahmet Yüksel, "Merzifon Halkevi ve Taşan Dergisi," *Kebikeç* 2, no. 3 [1996]: 173). Halkevleri did not permit sports competitions with teams other than those pertaining to Halkevleri (*Halkevleri ve Halkodaları*, 7). Similar proscriptions appeared in various local Halkevi publications in the provinces. But, as with other policies, the crackdown seems not to have been uniform. In Istanbul, which already had several sports clubs, state interventions appear to have been minimal.

79. Koner quoted in Şimşek, *Bir İdeolojik Seferberlik Deneyimi*, 112.

80. A more critical approach is provided, for instance, by Eyal Ari, "The People's Houses and the Theatre in Turkey," *Middle Eastern Studies* 40, no. 4 (2004): 32–58; Şimşek, *Bir İdeolojik Seferberlik Deneyimi*. Others offer a view that is loyal to the party line: Anıl Çeçen, *Atatürk'ün Kültür Kurumu: Halkevleri*, 2nd rev. ed. (Istanbul: Cumhuriyet Kitapları, 2000); Uluğ İğdemir, "Halkevleri ve Halkodaları," *Aylık Ansiklopedi*, March 1945; Kadri Kaplan, *Atatürk ve Halkevleri: Atatürkçü Düsünce Üzerine Denemeler* (Ankara: Türk Tarih Kurumu Basımevi, 1974); Ziya G. Muğulkoç, "Halkevlerinin Gelişme Dönemi: Sosyal Bir İnceleme," in Kaplan, *Atatürk ve Halkevleri*.

81. Zafer Çetin, "Tales of Past, Present and Future," *Journal of Muslim Minority Affairs* 24, no. 2 (2004): 347–65.

82. Şimşek, *Bir İdeolojik Seferberlik Deneyimi*, 111.

83. İğdemir, "Halkevleri ve Halkodaları," 121.

84. *CHF Mardin Broşürü* (Mardin: Ulus Sesi Basımevi, 1935).

85. *CHP Halkevi Öğreneği* (Ankara: Recep Ulusluoğlu Matbaası, 1938).

86. Various Halkevi branches produced magazines on a monthly, bimonthly, or trimonthly basis. A sampling from various regions, including *Altan* (Elazığ), *Başpınar* (Gaziantep), *Anafarta* (Çanakkale), *Çukurova* (Adana), *Uludağ* (Bursa) and some randomly available issues reveals a large degree of overlap between local bureaucrats and teachers and the organizers of activities and authors of the Halkevi publications.

87. Simsek, *Bir İdeolojik Seferberlik Deneyimi*, 102–3. A survey of Ülkü editorials—the publication of the Ankara branch of Halkevleri—reveals the urge felt by the organization's central administration to monitor the activities nationwide. A close reading

of the published reports about various branches suggests that there was pressure from above as evidenced in the former by attempts to hold local administrative officials (governors, prefects, etc.) personally responsible for the local lack of participation and attempts to discipline civil servants whose attendance was seen to be lackluster. Similarly, there is evidence of resistance from below, in the form of stalling tactics that can be gleaned from repeated, frustrated reports of requests for the same pieces of information about local activities and developments by administrators at the center.

88. Ilhan Başgöz, "The Meaning and Dimension of Change of Personal Names in Turkey," *Turcica* 15 (1983), 201–18; Şimşek, *Bir İdeolojik Seferberlik Deneyimi*; Ari, "The People's Houses and the Theatre."

89. Avar, *Dağ Çiçeklerim*, 139–40.

90. Avar, *Dağ Çiçeklerim*, 115, 247, 257.

91. Şevket Beysanoğlu, "Anılarımda Diyarbakır Halkevi," *Kebikeç* 2, no. 3 (1996): 161.

92. Beysanoğlu, "Anılarımda Diyarbakır Halkevi," 162–64; Ari, "The People's Houses and the Theatre," 41–43.

93. Neşe Gürallar Yeşilkaya, *Halkevleri: İdeoloji ve Mimarlık* (Istanbul: İletişim, 1999), 94–98; Ari, "The People's Houses and the Theatre," 48.

94. Gürallar Yeşilkaya, *Halkevleri: İdeoloji ve Mimarlık*, 172–73.

95. Gürallar Yeşilkaya, *Halkevleri: İdeoloji ve Mimarlık*, 173. According to Beysanoğlu, the same pattern was repeated in Diyarbakır, which opened musical branches for both *alafranga* and *alaturka* music. The former atrophied, but the latter flourished, launching the careers of several performers who went on to national success (Beysanoğlu, "Anılarımda Diyarbakır Halkevi," 164). Beysanoğlu makes a reference particularly to the work of Celal Güzelses. Once a week, on Sunday afternoons, he notes, Güzelses who headed the traditional music section of the Diyarbakır Halkevi offered open public concerts in the Halkevi garden. These concerts, which lasted until sundown, were very popular and the garden would always be filled with enthusiastic listeners. He went on to a recording career in Istanbul and at the time of his death in 1959, he had recorded sixty-six albums, which sold well both in Turkey and in neighboring countries.

96. Taha Parla and Andrew Davison, *Corporatarist Ideology in Kemalist Turkey: Progress or Order* (Syracuse, NY: Syracuse University Press, 2004), 51.

97. Parla and Davison, *Corporatarist Ideology in Kemalist Turkey*, 36.

Epilogue

1. An ample web archive of the developments in Gezi is kept by several news organizations as well as nongovernmental organizations, comprising a timeline of events, news items, audiovisual materials, and the like. See, for example, *Radikal* newspaper's archive (http://www.radikal.com.tr/taksim_gezi_parki_olaylari), CNN Turk's dedicated pages (http://www.cnnturk.com/guncel.konular/gezi.parki/1090/). Comprehensive and bilingual archives assembled by independent researchers and activists are also available at http://everywheretaksim.net/tr and http://www.geziparkikitabi.com/. An English-language summary can also be found at http://www.bbc.com/news/world-europe-22780773.

2. Turkey experienced military coups in 1960, 1971, and 1980. A memorandum

issued by the Joint Chiefs of Staff in 1998 forced the coalition government, led by the Islamist Party (Refah Partisi), to resign and the incident has since been dubbed "the postmodern coup."

3. As early as 2009, Prime Minister Erdoğan urged families to have at least three children ("Erdoğan: İş Işten Geçmeden En Az 3 Çocuk," October 10, 2009, http://www.ntvmsnbc.com/id/25008774/). The government has since put in place an incentive package "'En Az 3 Çocuk' a Teşvik Yolda," *TRT Haber*, May 9, 2013, http://www.trthaber.com/haber/ekonomi/en-az-3-cocuk-a-tesvik-yolda-85415.html; "Üç Çocuk Formülü Hazır: Nakit+Prim Teşviki," September 10, 2014, http://siyaset .milliyet.com.tr/uc-cocuk-formulu-hazir-nakit-prim/siyaset/detay/1761411/default .htm. Another bone of contention has been restrictions on the sale and consumption of alcohol in public spaces, which started with local ordinances that made obtaining liquor licenses more difficult as early as the mid-1990s when mayors of the Islamist Party first gained dominance. A rather strict legislation with a range of constraints was enacted in May 2013, at about the same time as the Gezi protests erupted. (Neşe Karanfil, "Yeni Alkol Düzenlemesi Neler Getiriyor? Türkiye Haberleri-Radikal," *Radikal*, June 10, 2013, http://www.radikal.com.tr/turkiye/yeni_alkol_duzenlemesi_ neler_getiriyor-1137075; "Alkol Yasağı Sorularına Yanıt! Ekonomi Haberleri-Radikal," accessed May 12, 2014, http://www.radikal.com.tr/ekonomi/alkol_yasagi_sorularina_ yanit-1143955; "İçki Satış Yasağı Uygulamaya Başlandı," September 10, 2013, http:// www.radikal.com.tr/turkiye/icki_satis_yasagi_uygulamaya_baslandi-1150085.) On a seemingly lighter note, the new uniforms and makeup instructions for female flight attendants of the flagship airline, THY (which, despite being a commercial company, as a legacy of Turkey's statist past, is not entirely independent of the government's authority) introduced weeks before Gezi were widely parodied. These also attracted criticism for harking back to an Ottomanesque appearance and for excessive intru- siveness in the personal choices of female staff, and the move taken to imply a partic- ularly restrictive view of women's self-presentation in the public sphere in the context of broader conversations at the time. ("THY'de Yeni Kıyafet Polemiği," *Ntvmsnbc*, February9, 2013, http://www.ntvmsnbc.com/id/25420810/; "Kabin Ekibi mi Fasıl Ek- ibi mi?" *Hürriyet*, February 10, 2013, http://www.hurriyet.com.tr/gundem/22559401 .asp.)

4. Nerves were especially raw after more than fifty people died just a fortnight before in the southern province of Hatay in a powerful explosion largely seen to be the consequence of meddling in neighboring Syria's intensifying civil war. (Mahmut Hamsici, "Deadly Blasts Hit Turkey Border Town of Reyhanlı," *BBC News*, accessed May 13, 2014, http://www.bbc.co.uk/news/world-middle-east-22494128; Tülin Daloğ- lu, "Reyhanli Worst Terror Attack Turkey Has Witnessed, Al-Monitor: The Pulse of the Middle East," *Al-Monitor*, accessed May 13, 2014, http://www.al-monitor.com/ pulseen/originals/2013/05/reyhanli-bombing-turkey-syria-policy.html.)

5. Between May 28 and June 16, as the protests spread to the country, there were incidents in 79 out of the 81 provinces. About 7,300 civilians and 800 police officers were wounded, and there were 8 deaths. For reports on the events and casualties, see Tolga Şardan, "2.5 Milyon Insan 79 Ilde Sokağa İndi," *Milliyet*, June 23, 2013, http:// www.milliyet.com.tr/2-5-milyon-insan-79-ilde-sokaga/gundem/detay/1726600/ default.htm; "Berkin Elvan: Gezi'de Yitirilen Sekizinci Can," *Radikal*, March 11, 2014, http://www.radikal.com.tr/turkiye/berkin_elvan_gezide_yitirilen_sekizinci_can -1180607; Amnesty International, *Gezi Park Protests: Brutal Denial of the Right to*

Peaceful Assembly in Turkey (London, 2013), http://www.amnesty.org.tr/ai/system/files/GeziParkiEN.pdf.

6. In what became a widely criticized decision, Turkey's mainstream media, already restrained by the government, initially chose not to report on the developments in Gezi. In later weeks the government, and especially Erdoğan personally leaned on the media bosses to limit critical reporting. For an overview of pressures on the media, see Amnesty International, *Gezi Park Protests*, 49–50. In the aftermath, fifty-nine journalists were forced out of their jobs, and *ntv-Tarih*, a monthly popular history journal that was to publish a special issue about the events was closed down by its parent company. Elif Akgül, "Gezi Direnişinde 59 Gazeteci İşten Çıkarıldı, İstifaya Zorlandı," *Bianet, Bağımsız İletişim Ağı*, accessed May 13, 2014, http://www.bianet.org/bianet/medya/148636-gezi-direnisinde-59-gazeteci-isten-cikaril-di-istifaya-zorlandi. In subsequent months, the president of the Turkish Business Association, which had originally lent its support to the AKP, criticized the prime minister for heavily damaging brand Turkey and triggered a very public sparring between the two. ("TÜSİAD'ta Ağır Sözler: Türkiye Markası 4 Noktada Ağır Hasarlı!," *t24.com.tr*, accessed May 13, 2014, http://t24.com.tr/haber/tusiadta-agir-sozler-turkiye-markasi-4-noktada-agir-hasarli/249127.)

7. In a claim that was later proved false, Erdoğan disseminated in his public speeches the story that a young veiled mother had been attacked by about eighty topless hooligans who also urinated on her, supposedly as retribution for her religious and political views overtly expressed through her choice of clothes. "'Hâlâ 'Kabataş'ta Başörtülü Bacımı Sürüklediler' Diyorsun, Boyundan Utan," *t24.com.tr*, accessed May 13, 2014, http://t24.com.tr/haber/hala-basortulu-bacimi-suruklediler-diyorsun-boyundan-utan/251366; "Turkish PM Erdoğan Defiant over Attack Claims on Veiled Women during Gezi Protests," accessed May 13, 2014, http://www.hurriyet dailynews.com/turkish-pm-erdogan-defiant-over-attack-claims-on-veiled-women-during-gezi-protests.aspx?PageID=238&NID=62554&NewsCatID=338/.

8. For a thorough overview see Kerem Öktem, *Angry Nation: Turkey since 1989* (London: Zed Books, 2011).

9. Islamist parties in Turkey have repeatedly faced closure by judicial fiat, and as with the pro-Kurdish parties, they have always regrouped and reentered politics. The AKP's predecessors Virtue (Fazilet) Party and Welfare (Refah) Party have been dissolved for contravening the constitution in 1998 and 2001, respectively. The National Salvation Party was ended with the 1980 military coup, which shut down all political parties. The AKP has been the most successful and long-lived of them so far, but it too faced a serious closure threat in 2008.

10. Under the AKP's rule, in the initial years, negotiations for accession to the European Union were started, and Turkey became one of the twenty largest economies in the world. On the diplomatic front, the party made a promise of zero tensions with Turkey's neighbors as the country began to position itself as a regional powerbroker. After the 2007 election, an attempt to bring down elements in the military plotting to overthrow the democratically elected government grew into a much criticized witch hunt that provided an excuse for specious accusations and subsequent detentions of those the government considered to be a threat. Premature and risky moves in the Arab Spring also soured relations with the neighboring countries.

11. In June 2015, just as I was making the last revisions to this manuscript, a general election brought an end to the AKP's unchallenged twelve-year rule. The election

brought into the Grand National Assembly previously excluded constituencies (mainly Kurds and various left-wing groups), which formed a coalition to overcome the 10 percent electoral threshold that had kept them outside parliament for decades. The Gezi events were seminal in bringing about this new type of alliance. It remains to be seen whether this shift will have lasting and significant consequences and what they may be.

12. Aysegul Baykan and Tali Hatuka, "Politics and Culture in the Making of Public Space: Taksim Square, 1 May 1977, Istanbul," *Planning Perspectives* 25, no. 1 (2010): 49–68; Murat Gül, John Dee, and Cahide Nur Cünük, "Istanbul's Taksim Square and Gezi Park: The Place of Protest and the Ideology of Place," *Journal of Architecture and Urbanism* 38, no. 1 (2014): 63–72; İlay Romain Örs, "Genie in the Bottle: Gezi Park, Taksim Square, and the Realignment of Democracy and Space in Turkey," *Philosophy and Social Criticism* 40, nos. 4–5 (May 1, 2014): 489–98, doi:10.1177/0191453714525390.

13. For a sampling of proscriptions of celebrations on national holidays, see "30 Ağustos Törenlerinde Çelenk Koyma Savaşı," *Taraf.com.tr*, August 31, 2012, http://www.taraf.com.tr/haber-30-agustos-torenlerinde-celenk-koyma-savasi-101359/; "29 Ekim'e Başkent'te Yasak, İstanbul'da Bayrak Gerginliği," *Hürriyet*, October 24, 2012, http://www.hurriyet.com.tr/gundem/21755621.asp; "Erdoğan '29 Ekim Yasağı'na Destek Verdi: Valilik Üzerine Düşeni Yaptı," *t24.com.tr*, October 25, 2012, http://t24.com.tr/haber/erdogan-bdp-konusunda-bakis-acimiz-meclis-baskanindan-farklidir/215981.

14. Arus Yumul, "'A Prostitute Lodging in the Bosom of Turkishness': Istanbul's Pera and Its Representation," *Journal of Intercultural Studies* 30, no. 1 (2009): 57–72, doi:10.1080/07256860802579444.

15. The site has an oddly tortured history. Plans for a performing arts center at this site go back to the early years of the republic. The construction of a project in 1946 with a somewhat austere design, possibly inspired Central-European interwar modernism by architects Rükneddin Günay Feridun Kip, was abandoned. Later, in 1956, the project was commissioned to Hayati Tabanlıoğlu and completed in 1969. In 1970 an electrical fire almost completely burned the building down. It was restored and reopened in 1978 and throughout the 1980s and 1990s became Istanbul's prime performing arts center. The building was closed down for restoration and repairs in 2008 with substantial support from the Sabancı family foundation and it was closed during the Gezi protests. ("AKM'nin Restorasyonuna Sabancı'dan 30 Milyon Lira," *Dünya Gazetesi*, February 15, 2012, http://www.dunya.com/akmnin-restorasyonuna-sabancidan-30-milyon-lira-146025h.htm.) Protesters who snuck into the building to hang banners also discovered that the building had been gutted internally and, much to public consternation, no restoration work was going on.

16. Rumors about the possibility of building a mosque in Taksim have always been rife. (Ahu Antmen, "Bir Biblo Sehpası Olarak Taksim Meydanı . . .," *Radikal*, October 10, 2010, http://www.radikal.com.tr/radikal.aspx?atype=haberyazdir&articleid=1012759.) One memorable uptick was at the time of an international urban design competition for the area, which took place in 1987, though notably neither the winning plan (by the father-son team of Vedat Hakan Dalokay) nor the mosque materialized.

17. Construction and architectural style has occupied a central place in AKP's agenda and its attempts to carve itself a legacy. Erdoğan has repeatedly called for the use of Ottoman or Seljuk architecture in official buildings and has encouraged the

use of a similar stylistic language among developers, especially those who are also ideologically close to his party. (For a small sampling of related news, see "Sulukule'ye 'Osmanlı Mimarisi,'" *Hürriyet*, January 8, 2008; "Yeni Sulukule Böyle Olacak," news, *Ntvmsnbc*, September 23, 2011, http://www.ntvmsnbc.com/id/25282019/; "Osmanlı ve Türk Mimari Özellikleri Birarada," July 20, 2012, http://www.akparti.org.tr/site/haberler/osmanli-ve-turk-mimari-ozellikleri-bir-arada/28886#1; "Kamuda Neo-Osmanlı Modası," *Radikal*, August 13, 2013, http://www.radikal.com.tr/hayat/kamuda_neo_osmanli_modasi-1145889.)

18. Non-Muslims were part of the coalition that voted for AKP. Having been kept out of national politics by the RPP, Turkey's non-Muslims have often voted for center right parties, which, in their push back against the RPP's rigid secularism, have been—at least at election time—more friendly to non-Muslim constituencies, though the policies of these parties, once at the helm have not been all that different.

19. In this regard, Nilüfer Göle's work was groundbreaking. Others have joined in with critical assessments of the politicization of women's bodies, especially with a focus on veiling. Nilüfer Göle, *The Forbidden Modern: Civilization and Veiling* (Ann Arbor: University of Michigan Press, 1997; Yael Navaro-Yashin, *Faces of the State: Secularism and Public Life in Turkey* (Princeton, NJ: Princeton University Press, 2002); Alev Cinar, *Modernity, Islam, and Secularism in Turkey: Bodies, Places, and Time*, 1st ed. (Minneapolis: University of Minnesota Press, 2005); Jenny B. White, *Muslim Nationalism and the New Turks*, with a new afterword (Princeton, NJ: Princeton University Press, 2014).

20. The uprising in Dersim had started in spring 1937. By October many of the leaders of the Kurdish tribes in question had been caught. In November 1937 Atatürk would embark on an Eastern Anatolian trip, as if symbolically to assert the state's dominance in the region. Nonetheless the conflagrations were not over, the violence continued in 1938, and the death toll for the local population was very high.

BIBLIOGRAPHY

Books and Articles

Abbas, Ackbar. "Building, Dwelling, Drifting: Migrancy and the Limits of Architecture. Building Hong Kong: From Migrancy to Disappearance." *Postcolonial Studies* 1, no. 2 (1998): 185–99.

Adana Cumhuriyetten Evvel ve Sonra. Ankara: Ulus Basımevi, n.d.

Adıvar, Halide Edip. *The Turkish Ordeal*. New York: Century, 1928.

Adıvar, Halide Edip. *Türkün Ateşle İmtihanı: İstiklâl Savaşı Hâtıraları*. Istanbul: Can Yayınları, 1962.

Afyon Valilik. *Afyon: Cumhuriyetin 15 Yılı İçinde*. Istanbul: Tan Matbaası, 1938.

Ağaoğlu, Adalet. *Ölmeye Yatmak*. Ankara: Yapı ve Kredi Yayınları, 1994.

Aghatabay, Cahide Zengin. *Mübadelenin Mazlum Misafirleri: Mübadele ve Kamuoyu (1923–1930)*. Istanbul: Bengi Yayınları, 2007.

Ahmad, Feroz. *The Making of Modern Turkey*. London: Routledge, 1993.

Ahmad, Feroz. *The Young Turks: The Committee of Union and Progress in Turkish Politics 1908–14*. London: Hurst, 2009.

Akar, Rıdvan. *Aşkale Yolcuları: Varlık Vergisi ve Çalışma Kampları*. Istanbul: Belge Yayınları, 1999.

Akçam, Taner. *Ermeni Meselesi Hallolmuştur: Osmanlı Belgelerine Göre Savaş Yıllarında Ermenilere Yönelik Politikalar*. Istanbul: İletişim Yayınları, 2008.

Akçam, Taner. *A Shameful Act: The Armenian Genocide and the Question of Turkish Responsibility*. New York: Henry Holt, 2006.

Akçam, Taner. *Türk Ulusal Kimliği ve Ermeni Sorunu*. Istanbul: İletişim Yayınları, 1992.

Akçam, Taner. *The Young Turks' Crime against Humanity: The Armenian Genocide and Ethnic Cleansing in the Ottoman Empire*. Princeton, NJ: Princeton University Press, 2012.

Akçura, Necva. "Muğla'da Geleceğe Yönelik Çabalar, Tarihi Çevre Koruması." In *Tarih Içinde Muğla*, edited by İlhan Tekeli, 240–339. Ankara: Orta Doğu Teknik Üniversitesi Yayınları, 1993.

Akekmekçi, Tuba, Muazzez Pervan, and Necmeddin Sahir Sılan. *Dersim Harekâtı ve Cumhuriyet Bürokrasisi (1936–1950)*. Vol. 4. Istanbul: Tarih Vakfı Yurt Yayınları, 2011.

Akgönül, Samim. *Türkiye Rumları: Ulus-Devlet Çağından Küreselleşme Çağına*. Istanbul: İletişim Yayınları, 2007.

"AKM'nin Restorasyonuna Sabancı'dan 30 Milyon Lira." *Dünya Gazetesi*, February 15, 2012. http://www.dunya.com/akmnin-restorasyonuna-sabancidan-30-milyon-lira-146025h.htm.

Akşit, Elif Ekin. *Kızların Sessizliği: Kız Enstitülerinin Uzun Tarihi*. Istanbul: İletişim Yayınları, 2005.

Aksoy, Yaşar, and Neşe Yurdkoru Özgünel. *70 Yıllık Sevda: İzmir Fuarı*. Izmir: İzmir Büyükşehir Belediyesi, 2001.

Aktar, Ayhan. *Türk Milliyetçiliği, Gayrimüslimler ve Ekonomik Dönüşüm*. Istanbul: İletişim Yayınları, 2006.

Aktar, Ayhan. *Varlık Vergisi ve "Türkleştirme" Politikaları*. Istanbul: İletişim Yayınları, 2000.

Aktüre, Sevgi. "19. Yüzyılda Muğla." In Tekeli, *Tarih İçinde Muğla*, 34–113.

Aktüre, Sevgi. *19. Yüzyıl Sonunda Anadolu Kenti Mekansal Yapı Çözümlemesi*. Ankara: Orta Doğu Teknik Üniversitesi Yayınları, 1978.

Alonso, Ana Maria. "The Politics of Space, Time and Substance: State Formation, Nationalism and Ethnicity." *Annual Review of Anthropology* 23 (1994), 379–405.

Alpkaya, Faruk. *Türkiye Cumhuriyeti'nin Kuruluşu (1923–1924)*. Istanbul: İletişim Yayınları, 1998.

Altınay, Ayşe Gül. *The Myth of the Military Nation*. New York: Palgrave Macmillan, 2004.

Amnesty International. *Gezi Park Protests: Brutal Denial of the Right to Peaceful Assembly in Turkey*. London, 2013. http://www.amnesty.org.tr/ai/system/files/Gezi-ParkiEN.pdf.

Anderson, Benedict. *Imagined Communities: Reflections on the Origin and the Spread of Nationalism*. New York: Verso, 1983.

Anderson, M. S. *The Rise of Modern Diplomacy, 1450–1919*. 1st ed. London: Longman, 1993.

Anderson, Perry. *Lineages of the Absolutist State*. London: Verso, 1979.

Andrews, Peter Alford, and Rüdiger Benninghaus. *Ethnic Groups in the Republic of Turkey*. Wiesbaden: Ludwig Reichert Verlag, 1989.

Ankara Belediye Zabıtası Talimatnamesi. Ankara: T. C. Ankara Belediyesi, 1952.

Ankara Belediyesi Talimatnameleri. Ankara: T. C. Ankara Belediyesi, 1942.

"Ankara-Istanbul." *La Turquie Kamaliste*, no. 47 (1943): 37–49.

Ankara Kalesi Koruma Gelistirme İmar Planı Projesi Yarışma Şartnamesi. Ankara: Altındağ Belediyesi, 1988.

"An Outpost of Modern Architecture.' *London Studio* 7, no. 107 (March 1934): 139–42.

Anzerlioğlu, Yonca. *Karamanlı Ortodoks Türkler*. Ankara: Phoenix Yayıncılık, 2003.

Arat, Yesim. "The Project of Modernity and Women in Turkey." In Bozdoğan and Kasaba, *Rethinking Modernity and National Identity*, 95–112.

Arat, Zehra F. "Turkish Women and the Reconstruction of Tradition." In *Reconstructing Gender in the Middle East: Tradition, Identity, and Power*, edited by Fatma Müge Göçek and Shiva Balaghi, 57–78. New York: Columbia University Press, 1994.

Araz, Nezihe. *Anadolu Evliyaları*. Istanbul: Atlas Kitabevi, 1975.

"Arbeiten von Prof. Ernst Egli, Ankara." *Das Werk* 25, no. 9 (1938): 275–78.

Arcayürek, Cüneyt. *Cüneyt Arcayürek Açıklıyor: Demokrasinin İlk Yılları*. Ankara: Bilgi Yayınevi, 1983.

Arendt, Hannah. *The Origins of Totalitarianism*. New York: Harcourt Brace Jovanovich, 1973.

Ari, Eyal. "The People's Houses and the Theatre in Turkey." *Middle Eastern Studies* 40, no. 4 (2004): 32–58.

Arı, Kemal. *Büyük Mübadele: Türkiye'ye Zorunlu Göç*. Türkiye Araştırmaları. Istanbul: Tarih Vakfı Yurt Yayınları, 1995.

Arıcanlı, Tosun. "Property, Land and Labor in Nineteenth Century Anatolia." In Keyder and Tabak, *Landholding and Commercial Agriculture*, 123–133.

Arslanyan, Agop. *Adım Agop, Memleketim Tokat*. Istanbul: Aras Yayıncılık, 2005.

Aslan, Senem. "'Citizen, Speak Turkish': A Nation in the Making." *Nationalism and Ethnic Politics* 13, no. 2 (2007): 245–72.

Aslan, Senem. "Everyday Forms of State Power and the Kurds in the Early Turkish Republic." *International Journal of Middle East Studies* 43, no. 1 (January 2011): 75–93. doi:10.1017/S0020743810001200.

Aslan, Senem. "Incoherent State: The Controversy over Kurdish Naming in Turkey." In "State-Society Relations in the Southeast," edited by Nicole F Watts. *European Journal of Turkish Studies*, no. 10 (December 29, 2009). http://ejts.revues.org/index4142.html.

Aslanoğlu, İnci. *Erken Cumhuriyet Dönemi Mimarlığı*. Ankara: Orta Doğu Teknik Üniversitesi Yayınları, 1980.

Atasoy, Nurhan. "Dervish Dress and Ritual: The Mevlevi Tradition." In Lifchez, *The Dervish Lodge*, 253–58.

Atatuğ, Kemal. *Ankara*. Ankara: İstiklal Matbaası, 1956.

Atatuğ, Kemal. *Çocuklara Ankara*. Ankara: Yeni Cezaevi Matbaası, 1949.

Atatürk. *Atatürk'ün Söylev ve Demeçleri*. Ankara: Türk İnkılâp Tarihi Enstitüsü (Turkey), 1946.

Atatürk, Kemal. *Nutuk–Söylev: Cumhuriyet Halk Partisi'nin 15–20 Ekim 1927 Tarihleri Arasında Toplanan İkinci Büyük Kongresinde Söylenmiştir*. Yayınlar / Türk Tarih Kurumu. 23 Dizi, sa. 2-2a. Ankara: Türk Tarih Kurumu Basımevi, 1981.

Atay, Falih Rıfkı. *Çankaya: Atatürk Devri Hatıraları*. Ankara: Dünya Yayınları, 1958.

Atay, Falih Rıfkı. *Zeytindağı*. Ankara: Hakimiyet-i Milliye Matbaası, 1932.

Atilhan, Cevat Rifat. *Meşhur Yahudi Casusu Suzi Liberman'in Hatıra Defteri*. Istanbul: Türkiye Matbaası, 1935.

Avagyan, Arsen, and Gaidz F. Minassian. *Ermeniler ve Ittihat ve Terakki: İşbirliğinden Çatışmaya*. Istanbul: Aras Yayıncılık, 2005.

Avar, Sıdıka. *Dağ Çiçeklerim*. Ankara: Öğretmen Yayınları, 1986.

Avcıoğlu, Doğan. *Türkiye'nin Düzeni*. Ankara: Bilgi Yayınevi, 1968.

Aybars, Ergun. *İstiklal Mahkemeleri 1921–1927*. Izmir: Dokuz Eylül Üniversitesi, Atatürk İlkeleri ve İnkilap Tarihi Enstitüsü, 1988.

Aydemir, Sevket Süreyya. *Tek Adam: Mustafa Kemal'in Hayatı*. Istanbul: Remzi Kitabevi, 1963.

Aydın, Suavi. "Bir Tilkinin Ettiği: İsimler Milli Birliği Nasıl Bozar?" *Toplumsal Tarih* (November 2005): 90–97.

Aydın, Suavi. "Türk Tarih Tezi ve Halkevleri." *Kebikeç* 2, no. 3 (1996): 107–30.

Aydın, Suavi, Kudret Emiroğlu, Ömer Türkoğlu, and Ergi D. Özsoy. *Küçük Asya'nın Bin Yüzü: Ankara*. Ankara: Dost Kitabevi, 2005.

Aytaç, Fethi. "Belediye Kanununun Oluşumu, Uygulanması ve Değişiklikler." In *Türk Belediyeciliğinde 60: Yıl Uluslararası Sempozyumu*, edited by İlhan Tekeli. Ankara: Metropol İmar A. S. Ankara Büyükşehir Belediyesi, 1990.

Aytürk, Yaşar, Yaşar Çelik, and Enver Şahinarslan. *Diyanet İşleri Başkanlığı Teşkilat Tarihçesi*. Ankara: Diyanet İşleri Başkanlığı APK Dairesi Başkanlığı, 1987.

Baghdjian, Kevork K. *La confiscation par le gouvernement turc des biens arméniens dits abandonnés*. Montreal: K. K. Baghdjian, 1987.

Bağış, Ali Ihsan. *Osmanlı Ticaretinde Gayri Müslimler: Kapitülasyonlar, Beratlı Tüccarlar, Avrupa ve Hayriye Tüccarları (1730–1839)*. Ekonomik ve Sosyal Araştırmalar. Ankara: Turhan Kitabevi, 1983.

Bahar, Beki L. *Efsaneden Tarihe Ankara Yahudileri*. Istanbul: Pan Yayıncılık, 2003.

Balcıoğlu, Mustafa. *Belgelerle Milli Mücadele Sırasında Anadolu'da Ayaklanmalar ve Merkez Ordusu*. Ankara: YÖK Basımevi, 1991.

Balin, Remzi. *Diyarbakır: Tarihçe, Eski Eserler, Coğrafya, İlçeler, Kültür, Yetiştirdiği Adamlar*. Diyarbakır: Kısmet Kitabevi, 1963.

Bali, Rıfat. *Bir Türkleştirme Serüveni (1923–1946)*. Istanbul: İletişim Yayınları, 1999.

Bali, Rıfat. *Cumhuriyet Yıllarında Türkiye Yahudileri: Aliya: Bir Toplu Göçün Öyküsü, 1946–1949*. Istanbul: İletişim, 2003.

Bali, Rıfat. *Devlet'in Yahudileri ve "Öteki" Yahudi*. Istanbul: İletişim Yayınları, 2004.

Bali, Rıfat. *Musa'nın Evlatları Cumhuriyet'in Yurttaşları*. Istanbul: İletişim Yayınları, 2001.

Bali, Rıfat. "1952 Yılı Hizmet Gazetesinin Varlık Vergisi Ile Ilgili Yayını." *Toplumsal Tarih*, no. 173 (2008): 25–33.

Bali, Rıfat. "20 Sınıf Ihtiyat Olayı." *Cumhuriyet Dergi (Pazar Eki)*, December 19, 1999.

Bali, Rıfat N. *II. Dünya Savaşında Gayrimüslimlerin Askerlik Serüveni: Yirmi Kur'a Nafıa Askerleri*. Istanbul: Kitabevi Yayınları, 2008.

Balibar, Etienne, and Immanuel Maurice Wallerstein. *Race, Nation, Class: Ambiguous Identities*. New York: Verso, 1991.

Baltacıoğlu, İsmail Hakkı. "Demiryolu ve Türk Bütünlüğü." *Yeni Adam*, March 5, 1934.

Bambach, Charles R. *Heidegger's Roots: Nietzsche, National Socialism, and the Greeks*. Ithaca, NY: Cornell University Press, 2005.

Bardakçı, İlhan. *Taşhan'dan Kadifekale'ye*. Milliyet Yayın Ltd. Şti. Yayınları. İstanbul: Milliyet Yayınları, 1975.

Barkan, Ömer Lütfi. *Kolonizatör Türk Dervişleri*. Istanbul: Hamle Yayın Dağıtım, 1939.

Barkan, Ömer Lütfi. *Türk Toprak Hukuku Tarihinde Tanzimat ve 1274 (1858) Tarihli Arazi Kanunnamesi*. Istanbul: Maarif Matbaası, 1940.

Barkey, Karen. *Empire of Difference: The Ottomans in Comparative Perspective*. Cambridge: Cambridge University Press, 2008.

Barkey, Karen. "Thinking about the Consequences of Empire." In Barkey and von Hagen, *After Empire*, 99–114.

Barkey, Karen, and Mark von Hagen. *After Empire: Multiethnic Societies and Nation-Building: The Soviet Union and the Russian, Ottoman, and Habsburg Empires*. Boulder, CO: Westview Press, 1997.

Barlas, Dilek. *Etatism and Diplomacy in Turkey: Economic and Foreign Policy Strategies in an Uncertain World, 1829–1939*. Leiden: Koninklijke Brill, 1998.

Barlas, Dilek. "Friends or Foes." *International Journal of Middle East Studies* 36, no. 2 (2004): 231–52.

Barlas, Uğurol. *Gaziantep Tıp Fakültesi Tarihi ve Azınlık Okulları*. Gaziantep: Gaziantep Kültür Derneği Yayınları, 1971.

Barnes, John Robert. "Evkaf-ı Humayun: Vakıf Administration under the Ottoman Ministry for Imperial Religious Foundations, 1839 to 1875." PhD diss., University of California, Los Angeles, 1989.

Barnes, John Robert. *An Introduction to Religious Foundations in the Ottoman Empire*. Leiden: E. J. Brill, 1986.

Barnes, John Robert. "A Short Note on the Dissolution of the Dervish Orders in Turkey." *Muslim World* 64, no. 1 (1974): 33–39.

Barret, Maurice. "Concours pour le Palais du Parliament de Turquie." *L'Architecture d'Aujourd'hui* (May 1939): 6–10.

Barutçu, Faik Ahmet. *Siyasi Anılar (1939–54)*. Istanbul: Milliyet Yayınları, 1977.

Başar, Haşim. "Bir Ders Vasıtası: Zaman Şeridi-Tarih Şeridi." *İlkögretim Haftası* 1, no. 37 (n.d.): 294–98.

Başgöz, İlhan. "The Meaning and Dimension of Change of Personal Names in Turkey." *Turcica* 15 (1983): 201–18.

Basmacıyan, Krikor Hagop. *Şark'ta Toplumsal ve Dinsel Hayat*. Istanbul: Aras Yayıncılık, 2005.

Baydar, Gülsüm. "Tenuous Boundaries: Women, Domesticity and Nationhood in 1930s Turkey." *Journal of Architecture* 7, no. 3 (2002): 229–44.

Baykal, Kazım, and Süleyman Savcı. *Diyarbakır Şehri*. Diyarbakır: CHP Diyarbakır Halkevi Neşriyatı, 1942.

Baykan, Aysegül, and Tali Hatuka. "Politics and Culture in the Making of Public Space: Taksim Square, 1 May 1977, Istanbul," *Planning Perspectives* 25, no. 1 (2010): 49–68.

Bayman, Mustafa Adli. *Tandoğan: Şahsiyeti-Ölümü-Hatıraları*. Istanbul: Tan Matbaası, 1948.

Bayraktar, Hatice. "The Anti-Jewish Progrom in Eastern Thrace in 1934: New Evidence for the Responsibility of the Turkish Government." *Patterns of Prejudice* 40, no. 2 (2006): 95–111.

Bayramoğlu, Fuat. *Hacı Bayram-ı Veli: Yaşamı, Soyu, Vakfı*. Ankara: Türk Tarih Kurumu Yayınları, 1983.

Behar, Büşra Ersanlı. *İktidar ve Tarih: Türkiye'de 'Resmi Tarih' Tezinin Oluşumu (1929–1937)*. Istanbul: AFA Yayınları, 1992.

Belge, Ceren. "State Building and the Limits of Legibility: Kinship Networks and Kurdish Resistance in Turkey." *International Journal of Middle East Studies* 43, no. 1 (2011): 95–114. doi:10.1017/S0020743810001212.

Belge, Murat, and Aydın Oran, *Ataturk Devrimleri İdeolojisinin Türk Muzik Kültürüne Doğrudan ve Dolaylı Etkileri*. Boğaziçi Üniversitesi Türk Müziği Kulübu Yayınları. Istanbul: Boğaziçi Üniversitesi, 1980.

Bellah, Robert N. "Religious Aspects of Modernization in Turkey and Japan." *American Journal of Sociology* 64, no. 1 (July 1958): 1–5.

Bendix, Reinhard. *Kings or People: Power and the Mandate to Rule*. Berkeley: University of California Press, 1978.

Benedict, Burton. *The Anthropology of World's Fairs: San Francisco's Panama Pacific International Exposition of 1915*. London: Scolar Press, 1983.

Benedict, Peter. "The Kabul Günü: Structured Visiting in an Anatolian Provincial Town." *Anthropological Quarterly* 47, no. 1 (January 1974): 28–47. doi:10.2307/3317025.

Benevolo, Leonardo. *The Origins of Modern Town Planning*. Cambridge, MA: MIT Press, 1971.

Bennet, Tony. *The Birth of the Museum: History, Theory, Politics*. London: Routledge, 1995.

Bénoist-Méchin, Jacques. *Mustafa Kemal: Bir İmparatorluğun Ölümü*. Translated by Zeki Çelikkol. Ankara: Bilgi Yayınevi, 1995.

Berezin, Mabel. *Making the Fascist Self: The Political Culture of Interwar Italy*. Ithaca, NY: Cornell University Press, 1997.

Berman, Marshall. *All That Is Solid Melts into Air: The Experience of Modernity*. New York: Penguin Books, 1988.

Bernal, Martin. *Black Athena: The Afroasiatic Roots of Classical Civilization*. New Brunswick, NJ: Rutgers University Press, 1987.

Beysanoğlu, Şevket. "Anılarımda Diyarbakır Halkevi." *Kebikeç* 2, no. 3 (1996): 161–67.

Beysanoğlu, Şevket. *Diyarbakır Coğrafyası*. Istanbul: Şehir Matbaası, 1961.

Bilal, Melissa. "The Lost Lullaby and Other Stories about Being Armenian in Turkey." *New Perspectives on Turkey* (spring 2006): 67–92.

Bilge, Suat. *Güç Komşuluk: Türkiye-Sovyetler Birligi İlişkileri 1920–1964*. Ankara: Türkiye İş Bankası Kültür Yayınları, 1992.

Bilsel, Can. *Antiquity on Display: Regimes of the Authentic in Berlin's Pergamon Museum*. Oxford: Oxford University Press, 2012.

Bilsel, Cana. "Ideology and Urbanism during the Early Republican Period: Two Master Plans for Izmir and Scenarios for Modernization." *METU Journal of the Faculty of Architecture* 16, nos. 1–2 (1997): 13–30.

Bischoff, Norbert. *Ankara: Türkiye'deki Yeni Oluşun Bir İzahı*. Ankara: Ulus Basımevi, 1936.

Black, Jeremy. *Maps and History: Constructing Images of the Past*. Chicago: University of Chicago Press, 2000.

Black, Jeremy. *Maps and Politics*. Chicago: University of Chicago Press, 2004.

Boli, John, Francisco O. Ramirez, and John W. Meyer. "Explaining the Origins and Expansion of Mass Education." *Comparative Education Review* 29, no. 2 (1985): 145–70.

Bonell, Victoria E. *Iconography of Power: Soviet Political Posters under Lenin and Stalin*. Berkeley: University of California Press, 1997.

Börtücene, Demet. *Once upon a Time Ankara*. Ankara: Belko Limited Sirketi, 1993.

Boswell, David, and Jessica Evans. *Representing the Nation: A Reader: Histories, Heritage and Museums*. 1st ed. London: Routledge, 1999.

Boyacıoğlu, Levent. "Tek Parti Döneminde İnkilap Temsilleri-I." *Tarih ve Toplum*, no. 102 (June 1992): 30–36.

Boyacıoğlu, Levent. "Tek Parti Döneminde İnkilap Temsilleri-II." *Tarih ve Toplum*, no. 103 (July 1992): 30–35.

Boyacıoğlu, Levent. "Tek Parti Döneminde İnkilap Temsilleri-III." *Tarih ve Toplum*, no. 104 (August 1992): 26–33.

Boyacıoğlu, Levent. "Tek Parti Döneminde İnkilap Temsilleri-IV." *Tarih ve Toplum*, no 105 (September 1992): 13-22.

Bozdağ, İsmet. *Atatürk'ün Fikir Sofrası*. Istanbul: Tekin Yayınevi, 1998.

Bozdoğan, Sibel. "Introduction." In Bozdoğan and Kasaba, *Rethinking the Project of Modernity and National Identity*, 3–14.

Bozdoğan, Sibel. *Modernism and Nation-Building: Turkish Architectural Culture in the Early Republic*. Seattle: University of Washington Press, 2001.

Bozdoğan, Sibel. "'Sıhhatli, Konforlu, Kullanışlı Evler': 1930'lar Mimarlığında Modernlik Söylemi." In *Osmanlı'dan Cumhuriyete*, edited by Hamdi Can Tuncer, 344–52. Istanbul: Tarih Vakfı Yurt Yayınları, 1998.

Bozdoğan, Sibel, and Reşat Kasaba. *Rethinking Modernity and National Identity in Turkey*. Seattle: University of Washington Press, 1997.

Braude, Benjamin, and Bernard Lewis. *Christians and Jews in the Ottoman Empire: The Functioning of a Plural Society*. New York: Holmes and Meier, 1982.

Brenner, Neil, Bob Jessop, Martin Jones, and Gordon Macleod. *State/Space: A Reader*. Oxford: Blackwell, 2003.

Breuilly, John. *Nationalism and the State*. Chicago: University of Chicago Press, 1985.

Brockett, Gavin D. "Collective Action and the Turkish Revolution: Towards a Framework for the Social History of the Atatürk Era, 1923–38." *Middle Eastern Studies* 34, no. 4 (1998): 44–66.

Brubaker, Rogers. *Citizenship and Nationhood in France and Germany*. Cambridge, MA: Harvard University Press, 1992.

Bulaç, Ahmet. *Din ve Modernizm*. Istanbul: Beyan Yayınları, 1992.

Büge, Salahaddin. "Cumhuriyet Devrinde Nafia İşleri." In *Cumhuriyetin 16: Yıldönümünde Hitabeler ve Konferanslar*, 46–53. Ankara: Ulus Basımevi, 1939.

Cağaptay, Soner. "Citizenship Policies in Interwar Turkey." *Nations and Nationalism* 9, no. 4 (2003): 601–19. doi:10.1111/1469-8219.00129.

Cağaptay, Soner. *Islam, Secularism and Nationalism in Modern Turkey*. London: Routledge, 2007.

Can, Bilmez Bülent. *Demiryolundan Petrole Chester Projesi (1908–1923)*. Istanbul: Tarih Vakfı Yurt Yayınları, 2000.

Cantek, Funda Şenol. *Sanki Viran Ankara*. Istanbul: İletişim Yayınları, 2006.

Cantek, Funda Şenol. *Yaban'lar ve Yerliler: Başkent Olma Sürecinde Ankara*. Istanbul: İletişim Yayınları, 2003.

Carter, Paul. *The Road to Botany Bay: An Exploration of Landscape History*. Chicago: University of Chicago Press, 1989.

Çavdar, Tevfik. "Halkevleri." In *Cumhuriyet Dönemi Türkiye Ansiklopedisi*, 878–84. Istanbul: İletişim Yayınları, 1981.

Caymaz, Birol. *Türkiye'de Vatandaşlık: Resmi İdeoloji ve Yansımaları*. Istanbul: Bilgi Üniversitesi Yayınları, 2007.

Cebesoy, Ali Fuat. *Milli Mücadele Hatıraları*. Istanbul: Vatican Neşriyatı, 1953.

Çeçen, Anıl. *Atatürk'ün Kültür Kurumu: Halkevleri*. 2nd rev. ed. Istanbul: Cumhuriyet Kitapları, 2000.

Çelik, G. Necmi. "Türkiye'de Tek Partili Dönemde Siyasal Bütünlesme ve Siyasal Davranışın Oluşumu Sürecinde Halkevlerinin İşlevi." PhD diss., Istanbul University, 1986.

Çelik, Resit. "Vakıflar Genel Müdürlüğündeki Kayıtlara Göre II: Meşrutiyet Döneminden Cumhuriyetin İlanına Kadar Tesis Edilen Eğitim ve Kültür Müesseseleri." T. C. Başbakanlık Cumhuriyet Devlet Arşivi, 1986.

Çelik, Zeynep. *Empire, Architecture, and the City: French–Ottoman Encounters, 1830–1914*. Seattle: University of Washington Press, 2008.

Çelik, Zeynep. *The Remaking of Istanbul: Portrait of an Ottoman City 1838–1908*. Seattle: University of Washington Press, 1986.

Cengizkan, Ali. *Ankara'nin İlk Planı/1924–1925 Lörcher Planı*. Ankara: Arkadaş Yayınevi, 2004.

Çerkezyan, Sarkis. *Dünya Hepimize Yeter*. Istanbul: Belge Yayınları, 2003.

Çetin, Fethiye. *Anneannem*. Istanbul: Metis Yayınları, 2004.

Çetin, Zafer. "Tales of Past, Present and Future." *Journal of Muslim Minority Affairs* 24, no. 2 (2004): 347–65.

Çetinoğlu, Sait. *Ekonomik ve Kültürel Jenosit: Varlık Vergisi 1942–1944*. 1st ed. Istanbul: Belge Yayınları, 2008.

Chakrabarty, Dipesh. "The Difference–Deferral of a Colonial Modernity: Public Debates on Domesticity in British Bengal." In Stoler and Cooper, *Tensions of Empire*, 373–405.

Chatterjee, Partha. *Nationalist Thought and the Colonial World: A Derivative Discourse*. Minneapolis: University of Minnesota Press, 1993.

Chatterjee, Partha. *The Nation and Its Fragments: Colonial and Postcolonial Histories*. Princeton, NJ: Princeton University Press, 1993.

C. H. F. Büyük Kongre (10–18 Mayis 1931) Zabıtları. Istanbul: Devlet Matbaası, 1931.

Childress, Faith. "Republican Lessons: Education and the Making of Modern Turkey." PhD diss., University of Utah, 2001.

Choay, Françoise. *Modern City Planning in the 19th Century*. New York: George Brazillier, 1969.

Cin, Halil. *Osmanlı Toprak Düzeni ve Bu Düzenin Bozulması*. Konya: Selçuk Üniversitesi Yayınları, 1992.

Çınar, Alev. *Modernity, Islam, and Secularism in Turkey: Bodies, Places, and Time*. Minneapolis: University of Minnesota Press, 2005.

Clark, Edward C. "The Turkish Varlık Vergisi Reconsidered." *Middle Eastern Studies* 8, no. 2 (May 1972): 205–16. doi:10.1080/00263207208700205.

Clark, Timothy J. *The Painting of Modern Life*. Princeton, NJ: Princeton University Press, 1989.

Conekin, Becky. *The Autobiography of a Nation: The 1951 Festival of Britain*. Manchester: Manchester University Press, 2003.

Copeaux, Etienne. *Tarih Ders Kitaplarinda (1931–1993): Türk Tarih Tezinden Türk İslam Sentezine*. Istanbul: Tarih Vakfı Yurt Yayınları, 1998.

Corrigan, Philip Richard, and Derek Sayer. *The Great Arch: English State Formation or Cultural Revolution*. Oxford: Blackwell, 1985.

Çorumda Cumhuriyetin On Beş Yılı. Istanbul: Resimli Ay Matbaası, 1938.

Cosgrove, Dennis E. *Social Formation and Symbolic Landscape*. Madison: University of Wisconsin Press, 1998.

Crane, Howard. "Ottoman Sultan's Mosques: Icons of Imperial Legitimacy." In *The Ottoman City and Its Parts: Urban Structure and Social Order*, edited by Irene Bierman, R. Abou El-Hajj, and Donald Preziosi, 173–243. New Rochelle: A. D. Caratzas, 1991.

Cronon, William. *Nature's Metropolis: Chicago and the Great West*. New York: Norton, 1991.

Cuda, Alfred. 'Professor Jansens Arbeiten Für Die Türkei'. *Deutsche Bauzeitung* 70:1, no. 4 (1936): 65–67.

Cuda, Alfred. "Stadtaufbau in Der Türkei." *Die Welt Des Islams* 21 (January 1, 1939), 1–84. doi:10.2307/1569072.

Cümhuriyetin 15 inci Yılı Anması Kastamonu Yıllığı. Istanbul: Tan Matbaası, 1938.

Cumhuriyetin 15. Yılında Aydın. Aydın: C. H. P. Basımevi, 1938.

Cumhuriyetin 15 inci Yılında Bolu. Bolu: Vilâyet Matbaası, 1938.

Cumhuriyetin 15. Yılında Denizli. Denizli: Cumhuriyet Matbaası, 1938.

Cumhuriyetin 15 inci Yılında Diyarbakır. Diyarbakır: Diyarbakır Matbaası, 1938.

Cumhuriyetin 25. Yılında Konya. Istanbul: Cumhuriyet Basımevi, 1938.

Cumhuriyetin 15 inci Yılında Malatya. Istanbul: Kenan Basımevi, 1938.

Cumhuriyetin 15. Yılında Manisa, 1938. Istanbul: Kemal Matbaası, 1938.

Cumhuriyetin 15. Yılında Yozgat. Yozgat: Vilâyet Matbaası, 1938.

Cumhuriyetin 16. Yıldönümünde Hitabeler ve Konferanslar. Ankara: Ulus Basımevi, 1939.

Cumhuriyetin 25. Yılında Eskisehir'e Bakış. Eskisehir: Bakış Müessesi ve Matbaası, 1948.

Curtis, William. *Modern Architecture since 1900.* Englewood Cliffs, NJ: Prentice Hall, 1987.

Danış, Didem, and Ebru Kayaalp. *Elmadağ: A Neighborhood in Flux.* Istanbul: IFEA, 2004.

Darkot, Besim, and Cemal Arif Alagöz. *Cumuriyet Çocuklarına Yeni Coğrafya Dersleri, Sınıf 4.* Istanbul: Türk Kitapçılığı Limitet Sosyetesi, 1936.

Davison, Graeme. "Cities and Ceremonies: Nationalism and Civic Ritual in Three New Lands." *New Zealand Journal of History* 24, no. 2 (1990): 97–117.

de Certeau, Michel. *The Practices of Everyday Life.* Berkeley: University of California Press, 1984.

Demirhan, Nezahat. "Türkiye Cumhuriyeti'nin Onuncu Yıl Kutlamaları." *Atatürk Araştırma Merkezi Dergisi,* August 20, 2007. http://www.atam.gov.tr/index.php?-Page=Print&DergiIcerikNo=682&Yer=DergiIcerik.

Derin, Haldun. *Çankaya Özel Kalemini Anımsarken (1933–1951).* Istanbul: Tarih Vakfı Yurt Yayınları, 1995.

Deringil, Selim. *The Well-Protected Domains: Ideology and the Legitimation of Power in the Ottoman Empire, 1876–1909.* New York: Palgrave Macmillan, 1998.

Dobrenko, Evgeny, and Eric Naiman. *The Landscape of Stalinism: The Art and Ideology of Soviet Space.* Seattle: University of Washington Press, 2003.

Dovey, Kim. *Framing Places: Mediating Power in Built Form.* London: Routledge, 1999.

Dragonas, Thalia, and Faruk Birtek. *Citizenship and the Nation-State in Greece and Turkey.* London: Routledge, 2005.

Duben, Alan, and Cem Behar. *Istanbul Households: Marriage, Family and Fertility 1880–1940.* Cambridge: Cambridge University Press, 1991.

Dumont, Paul. "Devrim Selanik'ten Başlar." In Veinstein, *Selânik 1850–1918,* 239–60.

Dumont, Paul. *Mustafa Kemal invente la Turquie moderne: 1919–1924.* Brussels: Editions Complexe, 1983.

Duncan, James S., and Nancy G. Duncan. *Landscapes of Privilege.* London: Routledge, 2004.

Dündar, Can. *Özel Arşivinden Belgeler ve Anılarla Vehbi Koç.* Istanbul: Doğan Kitap, 2006.

Duyguluer, Feridun. *Imar Mevzuatinin Cumhuriyet Dönemi Mimarlığına ve Şehir Planlamasına Etkileri.* Ankara: TBMM Kültür, Sanat ve Yayın Kurulu Yayınları, 1989.

Eccles, Jacquelynne S. "The Development of Children Ages 6 to 14." *Future of Children* 9, no. 1 (1999): 30–44.

El-Haj, Nadia Abu. *Facts on the Ground: Archaeological Practice and Territorial Self-Fashioning in Israeli Society.* Chicago: University of Chicago Press, 2008.

Ellison, Grace. *An English Woman in Angora.* London: Hutchinson, 1923.

Ellison, Grace. *Turkey To-Day.* London: Hutchinson, 1928.

Emiroğlu, Kudret, and Ahmet Yüksel. *Ankara Vilayeti Salname-i Resmisi 1325 (1907).* Ankara: Ankara Enstitüsü Vakfı Yayınları, 1995.

Emrence, C. "Politics of Discontent in the Midst of the Great Depression: The Free Republican Party of Turkey (1930)." *New Perspectives on Turkey* 23 (2000): 31–52.

Erdem, Cevat. *Ticaret Yıllığı Mecmuası*. Istanbul: Milli Ülkü Neşriyat Yurdu, 1946.

Erdim, Burak. "Lost in Translation: The Encounter between Bruno Taut and the Turkish Republic from 1936–38." MA Thesis, University of Virginia, 2004.

Ergin, Osman. *Türkiye'de Şehirciliğin Tarihi İnkişafı*. Istanbul: Cumhuriyet Gazete ve Matbaası, 1936.

Ergin, Osman. *Türk Şehirlerinde İmaret Sistemi*. Istanbul: Cumhuriyet Matbaası, 1939.

Erkin, Feridun Cemal. *Türk-Sovyet İlişkileri ve Boğazlar Meselesi*. Ankara: Başnur Matbaası, 1968.

Erman, Deniz Onur. "Cumhuriyet Sonrası Türk Seramik Sanatının Çağdaşlaşma Süreci." Accessed December 19, 2014. http://sanatvetasarim.gazi.edu.tr/web/makaleler/6_deniz.pdf.

Esendal, Memduh. *Ayaşlı ile Kiracıları*. 2nd ed. Ankara: Dost Yayınevi, 1957.

Esengin, Kenan. *Milli Mücadelede İç Ayaklanmalar*. Istanbul: Ağrı Yayınları, 1975.

Etlin, Richard. *Modernism in Italian Architecture 1890–1940*. Cambridge, MA: MIT Press, 1991.

Evin, Ahmet. "Communitarian Structures and Social Change." In *Modern Turkey: Continuity and Social Change*, edited by Ahmet Evin, 11–24. Opladen: Leske und Bundrich, 1984.

Evliyagil, Necdet. *Çankaya*. Ankara: Ajans-Türk Matbaası, 1986.

Evren, Burçak. *Yirmili Yılların Bozkır Kasabası Ankara*. Istanbul: Doğan Kitapçılık, 1998.

Evyapan, Gönül Aslanoğlu. *Kentleşme Olgusunun Hızlanması Nedeniyle Yapılar Yakın Çevresi Düzeyinde Açık Alan ve Mekanların Değişimi*. Ankara: Orta Doğu Teknik Üniversitesi Mimarlık Fakültesi, 1980.

Fabian, Johannes. *Time and the Other: How Anthropology Makes Its Object*. New York: Columbia University Press, 1983.

Falasca-Zamponi, Simonetta. *Fascist Spectacle: The Aesthetics of Power in Mussolini's Italy*. Berkeley: University of California Press, 1997.

Faroqhi, Suraiya. "New Approaches to State and Peasant in Ottoman History: An Introduction." *Journal of Peasant Studies* 18 (April–July 1991): 3–17.

Faubion, James. *Modern Greek Lessons: A Primer in Historical Constructivism*. Princeton Studies in Culture/Power/History. Princeton, NJ: Princeton University Press, 1993.

Findley, Carter Vaughn. *Turkey, Islam, Nationalism, and Modernity: A History, 1789–2007*. New Haven, CT: Yale University Press, 2010.

Fırkası, Cumhuriyet Halk. *CHF Halk Hatipleri Teşkilatı Talimatı*. Istanbul: Devlet Matbaası, 1931.

Fortna, Benjamin Carr. "Change in the School Maps of the Late Ottoman Empire." *Imago Mundi* 57 (2005): 23–34.

Foucault, Michel. *Discipline and Punish: The Birth of the Prison*. New York: Penguin, 1988.

Foucault, Michel. "Governmentality." In *The Anthropology of the State: A Reader*, edited by Aradhana Sharma and Akil Gupta, 131–43. London: Blackwell, 2006.

Foucault, Michel. "Of Other Spaces." *Diacritics* 16, no. 1 (1986): 22–27.

Foucault, Michel. "Space, Knowledge, and Power." In *The Foucault Reader*, edited by Paul Rabinow. Hammondsworth: Penguin Books, 1991.

Frijda, Nico H. "Commemorating." In Pennebaker, Paez, and Rimé, *Collective Memory of Political Events*, 103–27.

Galanti, Avram. *Ankara Tarihi*. Istanbul: Tan Matbaası, 1950.

Galanti, Avram. *Vatandaş Türkçe Konuş (Yahut Türkçe'nin Tamimi Meselesi)*. Istanbul: Hasan Tabiat Matbaası, 1928.

Garavaryan, Ohannes. "6–7 Eylül 1955: Ohannes Garavaryan Anlatıyor." Interview by Kemal Yalçın, April 3, 2004. http://www.kemalyalcin.com/index.php/menu-oge-si-soylesiler/170-6-7-eyluel-1955-ohannes-garavaryan-anlatyor.

Garner, Alice. *A Shifting Shore: Locals, Outsiders, and the Transformation of a French Fishing Town, 1823–2000*. Ithaca, NY: Cornell University Press, 2005.

Garnett, Lucy Mary Jane. *Mysticism and Magic in Turkey: An Account of the Religious Doctrines, Monastic Organisation, and Ecstatic Powers of the Dervish Orders*. London: Pitman, 1912.

Gaziantep '97: Kültür, Tarih, Arkeoloji. Gaziantep: Gaziantep İl Turizm Müdürlüğü, 1997.

Gellner, Ernest. *Nations and Nationalism*. Ithaca, NY: Cornell University Press, 1983.

Gershoni, Israel, Amy Singer, and Y. Hakan Erdem. *Middle East Historiographies: Narrating the Twentieth Century*. Seattle: University of Washington Press, 2006.

Ghirardo, Diane. *Building New Communities: New Deal America and Fascist Italy*. Princeton, NJ: Princeton University Press, 1989.

Giddens, Anthony. *The Consequences of Modernity*. Stanford, CA: Stanford University Press, 1990.

Giddens, Anthony. *The Nation-State and Violence*. Berkeley: University of California Press, 1987.

Giresun Ticaret ve Sanayi Odası Cumhuriyetin 10. Yılında (1923–1933). Giresun: Işık Matbaası, 1933.

Göçek, Fatma Müge. "Ethnic Segmentation, Western Education, and Political Outcomes: Nineteenth-Century Ottoman Society." *Poetics Today* 14, no. 3 (1993): 507–38.

Göçek, Fatma Müge. *Rise of the Bourgeoisie, Demise of Empire: Ottoman Westernization and Social Change*. New York: Oxford University Press, 1996.

Goffman, Daniel. "Ottoman Millets in the Early Seventeenth Century." *New Perspectives on Turkey*, no. 11 (1994): 135–58.

Goffman, Erving. *The Presentation of Self in Everyday Life*. Gloucester, MA: Peter Smith, 1999.

Gökaçtı, M. Ali. *Nüfus Mübadelesi: Kayıp bir Kuşağın Hikâyesi*. Istanbul: İletişim, 2003.

Gökay, Bülent. *British Documents on Foreign Affairs: Reports and Papers from the Foreign Office Confidential Print, Series B: Turkey, Iran, and the Middle East 1918–1939. Vol. 29: Turkey, August 1922–July 1923*. Frederick, MD: University Publications of America, 1997.

Gökay, Bülent. *British Documents on Foreign Affairs: Reports and Papers from the Foreign Office Confidential Print, Series B: Turkey, Iran, and the Middle East 1918–1939. Vol. 30: Turkey, August 1923–February 1927*. Frederick, MD: University Publications of America, 1997.

Gökay, Bülent. *British Documents on Foreign Affairs: Reports and Papers from the Foreign Office Confidential Print, Series B: Turkey, Iran, and the Middle East 1918–1939. Volume 31: Turkey, March 1927–December 1929*. Frederick, MD: University Publications of America, 1997.

Gökay, Bülent. *British Documents on Foreign Affairs: Reports and Papers from the*

Foreign Office Confidential Print, Series B: Turkey, Iran, and the Middle East 1918–1939. Vol. 32: Turkey, January 1930–December 1932. Frederick, MD: University Publications of America, 1997.

Gökay, Bülent. *British Documents on Foreign Affairs: Reports and Papers from the Foreign Office Confidential Print, Series B: Turkey, Iran, and the Middle East 1918–1939. Vol. 33: Turkey, December 1932–November 1935.* Frederick, MD: University Publications of America, 1997.

Göle, Nilüfer. *The Forbidden Modern: Civilization and Veiling.* Critical Perspectives on Women and Gender. Ann Arbor: University of Michigan Press, 1996.

Goloğlu, Mahmut. *Atatürk ve Anadolu Kulübü.* Ankara: Ajans-Türk Matbaası, 1981.

Goloğlu, Mahmut. *Devrimler ve Tepkileri (1924–1930).* Türkiye Cumhuriyeti Tarihi. Ankara: Turhan Kitabevi, 1972.

Goloğlu, Mahmut. *Tek Partili Cumhuriyet (1931–1938).* Türkiye Cumhuriyeti Tarihi. Ankara: Turhan Kitabevi, 1974.

Gölpınarlı, Abdülbâki. *Mevlânâ'dan sonra Mevlevîlik.* Istanbul: İnkılâp Kitabevi, 1953.

Gölpınarlı, Abdülbaki. *Yurt Bilgisi.* Istanbul: Türk Neşriyat Yurdu, 1927.

Gordon, Leland James. *American Relations with Turkey 1830–1930: An Economic Interpretation.* Philadelphia: University of Pennsylvania Press, 1932.

Gournay, Isabelle, and Jane C. Loeffler. "Washington and Ottawa: A Tale of Two Embassies." *Journal of the Society of Architectural Historians* 61, no. 4 (2002): 480–507.

Granda, Cemal. *Atatürk'ün Uşağı Idim.* Istanbul: Hürriyet Yayınları, 1973.

Grazia, Victoria de. *How Fascism Ruled Women.* Berkeley: University of California Press, 1992.

Greenfeld, Liah. *Nationalism: Five Roads to Modernity.* Cambridge, MA: Harvard University Press, 1992.

Grew, Joseph C. *The Turbulent Era: A Diplomatic Record of Forty Years 1904–1945.* Vol. 2. Boston: Houghton Mifflin, 1952.

Gross, David. "Critical Synthesis on Urban Knowledge: Remembering and Forgetting in the Modern City." *Social Epistemology* 4, no. 1 (1990): 3–22.

Güçhan, Neriman Şahin. "Tracing the Memoir of Dr Şerafeddin Magmumi for the Urban Memory of Ayvalık." *METU Journal of the Faculty of Architecture* 25, no. 1 (2008): 53–80.

Gül, Murat. *The Emergence of Modern Istanbul: Transformation and Modernisation of a City.* London: Tauris, 2009.

Gül, Murat, John Dee, and Cahide Nur Cünük. "Istanbul's Taksim Square and Gezi Park: The Place of Protest and the Ideology of Place." *Journal of Architecture and Urbanism* 38, no. 1 (2014): 63–72.

Gülekli, Nurettin Can. *Ankara Rehberi: The Guide of Ankara.* Ankara Spor Kulübü Yayınları. Istanbul: Pulhan Matbaası, 1949.

Gülersoy, Çelik. *Taksim: The Story of a Square.* İstanbul: Kitaplığı, 1991.

Güneş, Günver. "Serbest Cumhuriyet Fırkası Döneminde Türk Ocakları ve Siyaset." *Toplumsal Tarih* (May 1999): 11–18.

Güneş, İhsan. *Birinci Meclisin Düşünce Yapısı.* Ankara: İş Bankası Kültür Yayınları, 1985.

Gürallar Yeşilkaya, Neşe. *Halkevleri: İdeoloji ve Mimarlık.* Istanbul: İletişim, 1999.

Güvelioğlu, İshak Güven. "Rize Meşayihi." *Tasavvuf: İlmî ve Akademik Araştırma Dergisi,* no. 17 (2006): 191–216.

Güven, Dilek. *Cumhuriyet Dönemi Azınlık Politikaları Bağlamında 6–7 Eylül Olaylari*. Istanbul: Tarih Vakfı Yurt Yayınları, 2005.

Güven, Zühtü. *Anzavur İsyanı: İstiklal Savaşı Hatıralarından Acı Bir Safha*. Ankara: Türkiye İş Bankası Yayınları, 1965.

Haas, Ernst. "Nationalism: An Instrumental Social Construction." *Millennium: Journal of International Studies* 22 (winter 1993): 505–45.

Habermas, Jürgen. "Legitimation Problems in the Modern State." In *Communication and the Evolution of Society*, edited by Jürgen Habermas, 178–205. Boston: Beacon Press, 1979.

Haker, Erol. *Bir Zamanlar Kırklareli'de Yahudiler Yaşardı*. Istanbul: İletişim Yayınları, 2002.

Hakko, Vitali. *Hayatım, Vakko*. 2nd ed. Istanbul: s.n., 1997.

Halbwachs, Maurice. *The Collective Memory*. New York: Harper Colophon Books, 1980.

Halkevleri ve Halkodaları. Istanbul: Alaeddin Kıral Matbaası, 1942.

Hall, Peter. *Cities of Tomorrow*. Oxford: Basil Blackwell Ltd., 1988.

Hallı, Resat. *Türkiye Cumhuriyetinde Ayaklanmalar (1924–1938)*. Ankara: Genel Kurmay Harp Tarihi Başkanlığı Yayınları, 1972.

Hanioğlu, M. Şükrü. *A Brief History of the Late Ottoman Empire*. Princeton, NJ: Princeton University Press, 2008.

Hanioğlu, M. Şükrü. "The Second Constitutional Period (1908–18)." In Kasaba, *The Cambridge History of Turkey: Volume 4*, 62–111. Cambridge: Cambridge University Press, 2008.

Hanioğlu, M. Şükrü. *The Young Turks in Opposition*. Oxford: Oxford University Press, 1995.

Harley, John Brian. "The Map and the Development of the History of Cartography." In *The History of Cartography, Volume 1*, edited by David Woodward and John Brian Harley, 1–42. Accessed 22 June 2012. http://www.press.uchicago.edu/ucp/books/book/chicago/H/bo3620863.html.

Hartalı Ankara Rehberi. Ankara: Ankara Şoför Okulu Yayınları, 1949.

Harvey, David. *The Condition of Postmodernity: An Enquiry into the Origins of Cultural Change*. Cambridge, MA: Blackwell, 1989.

Harvey, David. *Justice, Nature and the Geography of Difference*. Cambridge, MA: Blackwell, 1996.

Harvey, David. *The Urban Experience*. Baltimore: Johns Hopkins University Press, 1989.

Hayden, Dolores. *The Power of Place: Urban Landscapes as Public History*. Cambridge, MA: MIT Press, 1995.

Hayes, Carlton J. H. *Nationalism: A Religion*. New York: Macmillan, 1960.

Heper, Metin. *The State Tradition in Turkey*. Atlantic Highlands, NJ: Eothen Press, 1985.

Herf, Jeffrey. *Divided Memory: The Nazi Past in the Two Germanys*. Cambridge, MA: Harvard University Press, 1997.

Herf, Jeffrey. *Reactionary Modernism: Technology, Culture, and Politics in Weimar and the Third Reich*. Cambridge: Cambridge University Press, 1984.

Hetherington, Kevin. *The Badlands of Modernity: Heterotopia and Social Ordering*. London: Routledge, 1997.

Hirsch, Herbert. *Genocide and the Politics of Memory: Studying Death to Preserve Life*. Chapel Hill: University of North Carolina Press, 1995.

Hirschon, Renee. *Crossing the Aegean: An Appraisal of the 1923 Compulsory Popula-tion Exchange between Greece and Turkey*. Oxford: Berghahn Books, 2003.

Hirschon, Renee. *Heirs of the Greek Catastrophe: The Social Life of Asia Minor Refu-gees in Piraeus*. Oxford: Clarendon Press, 1989.

Hobsbawm, E. J. *Nations and Nationalism since 1780: Programme, Myth, Reality*. 2nd ed. Cambridge: Cambridge University Press, 2012.

Hobsbawm, Eric, and Terence Ranger. *The Invention of Tradition*. Past and Present Publications. Cambridge: Cambridge University Press, 1984.

Holston, James. *The Modernist City: An Anthropological Critique of Brasilia*. Chicago: University of Chicago Press, 1989.

Hooper-Greenhill, Eilean. *Museums and the Shaping of Knowledge*. Edited by Andrew Wheatcroft. The Heritage Care and Preservation Management. London: Rout-ledge, 1992.

Horn, David G. *Social Bodies: Science, Reproduction, and Italian Modernity*. Prince-ton, NJ: Princeton University Press, 1994.

Hunt, Lynn. *Politics, Culture and Class in the French Revolution*. Berkeley: University of California Press, 1984.

Huntington, Samuel P. *Political Order in Changing Societies*. New Haven, CT: Yale University Press, 1968.

"I. Türk Tarih Kongresi." In *Türk Tarih Kongresi*. Ankara: T.C. Maarif Vekaleti, 1932.

İçduygu, Ahmet, and B. Ali Soner. "Turkish Minority Rights Regime: Between Difference and Equality." *Middle Eastern Studies* 42, no. 3 (2006): 447–68.

İçduygu, Ahmet, and Özlem Kaygusuz. "The Politics of Citizenship by Drawing Borders: Foreign Policy and the Construction of National Citizenship Identity in Turkey." *Middle Eastern Studies* 40, no. 6 (2004): 26–50.

İçduygu, Ahmet, Şule Toktaş, and B. Ali Soner. "The Politics of Population in a Nation-Building Process: Emigration of Non-Muslims from Turkey." *Ethnic and Racial Studies* 31, no. 2 (2007): 358–89.

İğdemir, Uluğ. *Biga Ayaklanmasi ve Anzavur Olaylari: Günlük Anılar*. Ankara: Türk Tarih Kurumu Basımevi, 1989.

İğdemir, Uluğ. "Halkevleri ve Halkodaları." *Aylık Ansiklopedi* (March 1945).

Iheduru, Obioma M. *Contending Issues in African Development: Advances, Challenges, and the Future*. Westport, CT: Greenwood, 2001.

İlk Mektep Planları Albümü. Ankara: Maarif Vekaleti İlk Tedrisat Dairesi, 1933.

İmece, Mustafa Selim. *Atatürk'ün Sapka Devriminde Kastamonu ve İnebolu Seyahat-leri*. Ankara: Türkiye İş Bankası Kültür Yayınları, 1975.

İnan, M. Rauf. "Atatürk'ün Halkçılık Ülküsü: Halkevi Gerçeği ve Tragedyası." In Ka-plan, *Atatürk ve Halkevleri*, 95–115.

İnan, Süleyman. "Varlık Vergisi Ile İlgili Değerlendirmelere Türk Ekonomisi Açısın-dan Kısa Bir Bakış." *Türk Yurdu* 22, no. 182 (2001): 30–38.

İpşiroğlu, Mazhar Şevket. *Ahtamar Kilisesi: Işıkla Canlanan Duvarlar*. Istanbul: Yapı ve Kredi Yayınları, 2003.

Irving, Robert Grant. *Indian Summer: Lutyens, Baker, and Imperial Delhi*. New Haven, CT: Yale University Press, 1981.

İsmail, Osman Mükerrem Bin. *Teceddüd Mekteb Atlası: Coğrafyaya Mütealik Hülasa ve Hatıra*. Istanbul: İkbal Kütüphanesi, 1925.

İzet, Hakkı. "Coğrafya Tedrisatında Resimden İstifade." *İlköğretim Haftası* (1939): 262–68.

Jacoby, Henry. *The Bureaucratization of the World*. Berkeley: University of California Press, 1973.

Jansen, Hermann. *Ankara İli İmar Planı*. Istanbul: Alaaddin Kıral Matbaası, 1937.

Jaussely, M., and Herman Jansen. *Ankara Sehrinin Profesör M. Jaussely, Jansen ve Brix Tarafından Yapılan Plan ve Projelerine Ait Izahnameler*. Ankara: T. C. Ankara Sehremaneti, 1929.

Jongerden, Joost. *The Settlement Issue in Turkey and the Kurds: An Analysis of Spatical Policies, Modernity and War*. Leiden: Brill, 2007.

Joseph, M. *Nomadic Identities: The Performance of Citizenship*. Minneapolis: University of Minnesota Press, 1999.

Kabasakal, Mehmet. *Türkiye'de Siyasal Parti Örgütlenmesi (1908–1960)*. Istanbul: Tekin Yayınevi, 1991.

Kalustian, Shnork. "Statement of His Holiness the Patriarch of the Armenians of Turkey." *Armenian Review* 31, no. 1 (1978): 88–90.

Kami, Ali. *Yurt Bilgisi Ilk Mektep 5. Sınıf*. Istanbul: Hilmi Kütüphanesi, 1930.

Kandiyoti, Deniz. *Cariyeler, Bacılar, Yurttaslar: Kimlikler ve Toplumsal Dönüsümler*. Istanbul: Metis Kadın Yayınları, 1996.

Kandiyoti, Deniz. *Gendering the Middle East: Emerging Perspectives*. Syracuse, NY: Syracuse University Press, 1996.

Kandiyoti, Deniz. "Gendering the Modern: On Missing Dimensions in the Study of Turkish Modernity." In Bozdoğan and Kasaba. *Rethinking Modernity and National Identity*, 113–32.

Kandiyoti, Deniz, and Ayşe Saktanber. *Fragments of Culture: The Everyday of Modern in Turkey*. London: Tauris, 2005.

Kansu, Aykut. "Kemalist 'Yeni Düzen' Projesine Giris (1920–1923)." In Koçak, *Birinci Meclis*, 135–61.

Kansu, Aykut. *1908 Devrimi*. Istanbul: İletişim Yayınları, 1995.

Kansu, Aykut. *The Revolution of 1908 in Turkey*. Leiden: Brill, 1997.

Kansu, Mazhar Müfit. *Erzurum'dan Ölümüne Kadar Atatürk'le Beraber*. Ankara: Türk Tarih Kurumu Yayınları, 1968.

Kaplan, Kadri. *Atatürk ve Halkevleri: Atatürkçü Düsünce Üzerine Denemeler*. Ankara: Türk Tarih Kurumu Basımevi, 1974.

Kaplan, Kadri. "Halkevleri." In Kaplan, *Atatürk ve Halkevleri*, 131–41.

Karabekir, Kâzım, and Faruk Özerengin. *Ankara'da Savaş Rüzgarları: II. Cihan Harbi: CHP Grup Tartışmaları*. Vol. 18. Yakın Tarih Serisi 18. Cağaloğlu. Istanbul: Emre Yayınları, 1994.

Karaca, Zafer, ed. *6–7 Eylül Olayları: Fotoğraflar Belgeler, Fahri Çoker Arşivi*. Istanbul: Tarih Vakfı Yurt Yayınları, 2005.

Karagueuzian, Hrayr S. *Genocide and Life Insurance: The Armenian Case*. La Verne: University of La Verne Press, 2006.

Karajian, Sarkis J. "An Inquiry into the Statistics of the Genocide of the Turkish Genocide of the Armenians 1915–1918." *Armenian Review* 25 (winter 1972): 3–44.

Karakus, Emin. *40 Yıllık Bir Gazeteci Gözü ile İşte Ankara*. Istanbul: Hür Yayın ve Ticaret, 1977.

Karaosmanoğlu, Yakup Kadri. *Ankara*. Istanbul: İletişim Yayınları, 1991.

Karaosmanoğlu, Yakup Kadri. *Panorama*. Istanbul: Remzi Kitabevi, 1953.

Karaosmanoğlu, Yakup Kadri. *Yaban*. Istanbul: Remzi Kitabevi, 1932.

Karay, Refik Halit. *Deli*. Istanbul: Semih Lütfi Kitabevi, 1939.

Karpat, Kemal H. "The Impact of the People's Houses on the Development of Communication in Turkey: 1931–1951." *Die Welt des Islams* 15, nos. 1–4 (1974), 69–84.

Karpat, Kemal. *An Inquiry into the Social Foundations of Nationalism in the Ottoman State: From Social Estates to Classes, from Millets to Nations*. Princeton, NJ: Center for International Studies: Woodrow Wilson School of Public and International Affairs, Princeton University, 1973.

Karpat, Kemal. *Osmanlı Nüfusu 1830–1914 (Demografik ve Sosyal Özellikleri)*. Istanbul: Tarih Vakfı Yurt Yayınları, 2003.

Karpuz, Hasim. *Rize*. Tanıtma Eserleri Dizisi. Ankara: Kültür Bakanlığı Yayınları, 1992.

Kasaba, Reşat. *The Cambridge History of Turkey: Volume 4, Turkey in the Modern World*. 1st ed. Cambridge: Cambridge University Press, 2008.

Kasaba, Reşat. "Izmir 1922: A Port City Unravels." In *Modernity and Culture: From the Mediterranean to the Indian Ocean*, edited by Leila Fawaz, C. A. Bayly, and Robert Ilbert, 204–30. New York: Columbia University Press, 2002.

Kasaba, Reşat. "Kemalist Certainties and Modern Ambiguities." In Bozdoğan and Kasaba, *Rethinking Modernity and National Identity*, 15–36.

Kasaba, Reşat. *A Moveable Empire: Ottoman Nomads, Migrants, and Refugees*. Seattle: University of Washington Press, 2009.

Kasaba, Reşat. *The Ottoman Empire and the World Economy: The Nineteenth Century*. Albany: State University of New York Press, 1988.

Kasaba, Reşat, Çağlar Keyder, and Faruk Tabak. "Eastern Mediterranean Port Cities and Their Bourgeoisies: Merchants, Political Projects, and Nation-States." *Fernand Braudel Center Review* 10 (1986), 121–35.

Kasparian, Alice Odian. *The History of the Armenians of Angora and Stanos (From Prechristian and Galatian Periods up to 1918)*. Beirut: Doniguian Press, 1968.

Kaya, Kemal. *İlkokulda Coğrafya Öğretimi*. T. C. Maarif Vekilliği İlkokul Öğretmeni Kılavuzları. Istanbul: Maarif Matbaası, 1942.

Kaya, Kemal. *Yurt Tetkiki ve Cografya: İlk ve Ortaokul Öğretmenleri için Tedris Usülü Kitabi*. Istanbul: Muallim Ahmet Halim Kitaphanesi, 1933.

Kayalı, Hasan. *Arabs and Young Turks: Ottomanism, Arabism, and Islamism in the Ottoman Empire, 1908–1918*. Berkeley: University of California Press, 1997.

Kayaoğlu, I. Gündağ, and Mustafa Duman. *Trabzon 88–89 Kültür Sanat Yıllığı*. Istanbul: Trabzonlular Kültür ve Yardımlaşma Derneği, 1989.

Kayra, Cahit. *Savaş Türkiye Varlık Vergisi*. 1st ed. Istanbul: Tarihçi Kitabevi, 2011.

Kebabcıyan, Raffi. *Konuş Halil Bey Konuş*. Istanbul: Aras Yayıncılık, 2000.

Keleş, Ruşen. *Eski Ankara'da Bir Sehir Tipolojisi*. Ankara: Ankara Üniversitesi Siyasal Bilgiler Fakültesi Yayınları, 1971.

Kemal, Mehmed. *Türkiye'nin Kalbi Ankara*. Istanbul: Çağdas Yayınları, 1983.

Kemali, Ali. *Erzincan: Tarihi, Coğrafi, İçtimai, Etnoğrafi, İdari, İhsai Tetkikat Tecrübesi*. Istanbul: Resimli Ay Matbaası, 1932.

Kerimoğlu, Hasan Taner. "1913–1914 Rumlara Karşı Boykot Ve Hüseyin Kazım Bey'in Bir Risalesi." *Çağdaş Türkiye Tarihi Araştırmaları Dergisi*, no. 13 (2006): 91–107.

Keyder, Çağlar. "A History and Geography of Turkish Nationalism." Dragonas and Birtek, *Citizenship and the Nation-State in Greece and Turkey*, 3–17.

Keyder, Çağlar. *Memaliki Osmaniye'den Avrupa Birligi'ne*. Istanbul: İletişim Yayınları, 2003.

Keyder, Çağlar. "Nüfus Mübadelesinin Türkiye Açısından Sonuçları." In *Memalik-i*

Osmaniye'den Avrupa Birliği'ne Türkiye, edited by Çağlar Keyder, 97–119. Istanbul: İletişim Yayınları, 2003.

Keyder, Çağlar. "The Ottoman Empire." In Barkey and von Hagen, *After Empire*, 30–44.

Keyder, Çağlar. "Port Cities in the Ottoman Empire: Some Theoretical and Historical Perspectives." *Fernand Braudel Center Review* 16, no. 4 (Special Issue: Port Cities of the Eastern Mediterranean) (1993): 519–58.

Keyder, Çağlar. *State and Class in Turkey: A Study in Capitalist Development*. London: Verso, 1987.

Keyder, Çağlar. "Whither the Project of Modernity? Turkey in the 1990s." In Bozdoğan and Kasaba, *Rethinking Modernity and National Identity*, 37–51.

Keyder, Çağlar, and Faruk Tabak. *Landholding and Commercial Agriculture in the Middle East*. Albany: State University of New York Press, 1991.

Kezer, Zeynep. "Contesting Urban Space in Early Republican Ankara." *Journal of Architectural Education* 52 (September, 1998): 11–19.

Kezer, Zeynep. "An Imaginable Community: The Material Culture of Nation-Building in Early Republican Turkey." *Environment and Planning D: Society and Space* 27, no. 3 (2009): 508–30. doi:10.1068/d10907.

Kezer, Zeynep. "The Making of a National Capital: Ideology and Socio-Spatial Practices in Early Republican Ankara." PhD diss., University of California at Berkeley, 1999.

Kezer, Zeynep. "Molding the Republican Generation: The Landscapes of Learning in Early Republican Turkey." In *Designing Modern Childhoods*, edited by Marta Gutman and Ning de Coninck-Smith, 128–51. Piscataway, NJ: Rutgers University Press, 2008.

Kieser, Hans-Lukas. *Iskalanmış Barış: Doğu Vilayetlerinde Misyonerlik, Etnik Kimlik ve Devlet 1839–1938*. Translated by Atilla Dirim. Istanbul: İletişim, 2005.

Kısakürek, Necip Fazil. *Son Devrin Din Mazlumlari*. Istanbul: Toker Yayınları, 1969.

Kırlı, Biray Kolluoğlu. "Forgetting the Smyrna Fire." *History Workshop Journal* 60, no. 1 (2005): 25–44.

Kırlı, Biray Kolluoğlu. "From Ottoman Empire to Turkish Nation-State: Reconfiguring Spaces and Geobodies." PhD diss., State University of New York–Binghamton, 2002.

Kırlı, Biray Kolluoğlu. "The Play of Memory, Counter Memory: Building Izmir on Smyrna's Ashes." *New Perspectives on Turkey* 26 (spring 2002): 1–28.

Kız Enstitüleri ve Sağnat Okulları. Ankara: Devlet Matbaası, 1938.

Koç, Vehbi. *Hayat Hikayem*. Istanbul: Apa Ofset Basımevi, 1973.

Kocabaşoğlu, Uygur. "Bir Devir, Bir Şehir, Bir Adam: 1929–1946 Ankara'sı ve Nevzat Tandoğan." In Tekeli, *Türk Belediyeciliğinde 60 Yıl*, 193–213.

Kocabaşoğlu, Uygur. "Birinci Türkiye Büyük Millet Meclisinden 'Sol' Portreler!" In *Birinci Meclis*, edited by Cemil Koçak, 165–87. Istanbul: Sabancı Üniversitesi, 1998.

Koçak, Cemil. "Ayın Karanlık Yüzü: Tek-Parti Döneminde Gayri Müslim Azınlıklar Hakkında Açılan Türklüğü Tahkir Davaları." *Tarih ve Toplum Yeni Yaklaşımlar*, no. 1 (2005): 147–208.

Koçak, Cemil. *Belgelerle Heyet-i Mahsusalar*. Istanbul: İletişim Yayınları, 2005.

Koçak, Cemil. *Geçmişiniz İtinayla Temizlenir*. İstanbul: İletişim Yayınları, 2009.

Koçak, Cemil. *Türkiye'de Milli Şef Dönemi (1938–1945)*. 2 vols. Istanbul: İletişim Yayınları, 1996.

Koçak, Cemil. *Umumi Müfettişlikler (1927–1952)*. Istanbul: İletişim Yayınları, 2003.

Kocaoğlu, Bünyamin. "Atatürk Dönemi Laiklik Uygulamalarına Yönelik Bazı Toplumsal Tepkiler." *Turkish Studies* 2, no. 4 (fall 2007): 1297–307.

Köçer, Mehmet. "Bolşevik İhtilali Sonrasında Afganistan Üzerinde İngiliz-Rus Mücadelesi." *İlahiyat Fakültesi Dergisi*, August 19, 2007. http://www.firat.edu.tr/ilahiyat/DergiYazilari/09-1_2004/05MehmetKocer.pdf.

Kohl, Philip L., and Clare P. Fawcett. *Nationalism, Politics, and the Practice of Archaeology.* Cambridge: Cambridge University Press, 1995.

Köklü, Nusret. *Dünkü Manisa.* Ankara: Ayyıldız Matbaası A.Ş., 1970.

Konyalı, Ibrahim Hakkı. *Ankara Camileri.* Ankara: Vakıflar Genel Müdürlüğü Yayınları, 1978.

Kop, Kadri Kemal. *Atatürk Diyarbakır'da ve 'O'nun Hatıraları.* Istanbul: Cumhuriyet Matbaası, 1938.

Körükçü, Muhtar. *Köyden Haber.* İstanbul: Varlık Yayınları, 1950.

Kotkin, Stephen. "Coercion and Identity: Workers' Lives in Stalin's Showcase City." In *Making Workers Soviet: Power, Class and Identity*, edited by Ronald Grigor Suny and Lewis Siegelbaum. Ithaca, NY: Cornell University Press, 1995.

Kreiser, Klaus. "Dervish Living." In Lifchez, *The Dervish Lodge*, 49–56.

Kuban, Doğan. *Çağlar Boyunca Türkiye Sanatının Anahatları.* Istanbul: Yapı ve Kredi Yayınları, 2002.

Kunter, Halim Baki. "Türk Vakıfları ve Vakfiyeleri." *Vakıflar Dergisi*, 1934.

Kürkçüoğlu, Ömer. *Türk İngiliz Iliskileri (1919–1926).* Ankara: Ankara Üniversitesi Siyasal Bilgiler Fakültesi Yayınları, 1978.

Kürkçüoğlu, Ömer. "Turco-British Relations since the 1920s." In *Four Centuries of Turco-British Relations: Studies in Diplomatic, Economic and Cultural Affairs*, edited by Ali İhsan Bağış and William Hale, 80–102. North Humberside: Eothen Press, 1984.

Kushikian, B. "One Month in Turkey." *Armenian Review* 6, no. 2 (1953): 115–25.

Kutay, Cemal. *Mesken Meselesi Nasıl Halledilir?* Ankara: Büyük Davalar Serisi, 1939.

Ladd, Brian. *Ghosts of Berlin: Confronting German History in the Urban Landscape.* Chicago: University of Chicago Press, 1997.

Lambert, Jacques H. "Ankara Kamaliste." *La Construction Moderne* 51 (August 1936): 907–16.

Landau, Jacob. *Atatürk and the Modernization of Turkey.* Boulder, CO: Westview Press, 1984.

Lane, Barbara Miller. *Architecture and Politics in Germany, 1918–1945.* Cambridge, MA: Harvard University Press, 1966.

Lapidot, Anat. "Islamic Activism in Turkey since the 1980 Military Takeover." *Terrorism and Political Violence* 8, no. 2 (1996): 62–74. doi:10.1080/09546559608427346.

Laprade, Alfred. "Embassade de France a Ankara." *L'Architecture d'Aujourd'hui*, 1931.

Laqueur, Hans Peter. "Dervish Gravestones." In Lifchez, *The Dervish Lodge*, 284–95.

Lasansky, D. Medina. *The Renaissance Perfected: Architecture, Spectacle, and Tourism in Fascist Italy.* University Park: Pennsylvania State University Press, 2004.

Latour, Bruno. *Reassembling the Social: An Introduction to Actor-Network-Theory.* New ed. Oxford: Oxford University Press, 2007.

Lausanne Peace Treaty. Accessed December 16, 2014. http://www.mfa.gov.tr/lausanne-peace-treaty.en.mfa.

Lausanne Peace Treaty VI. Convention Concerning the Exchange of Greek and Turkish Populations Signed at Lausanne, January 30, 1923. Accessed December 16, 2014.

http://www.mfa.gov.tr/lausanne-peace-treaty-vi_-convention-concerning-the-exchange-of-greek-and-turkish-populations-signed-at-lausanne_.en.mfa.

Lee, Rose. "New Turkey Progresses at High Speed under the Guidance of Mustapha Kemal the Nation Is Reorganizing Its Life along Modern Lines." *New York Times Magazine*, May 30, 1926.

Lefebvre, Henri. *The Production of Space*. Oxford: Blackwell, 1991.

Lefebvre, Henri. "Space and the State." In Brenner, Jessop, Jones, and Macleod, *State/Space*, 84–100.

Lekka, A. "Legislative Provisions of the Ottoman/Turkish Governments Regarding Minorities and Their Properties." *Mediterranean Quarterly* 18, no. 1 (2007): 135–54.

Lerner, David. *The Passing of the Traditional Society*. New York: Free Press, 1958.

Levi, Avner. *Türkiye Cumhuriyeti'nde Yahudiler*. Istanbul: İletişim Yayınları, 1996.

Lewis, Bernard. *The Emergence of Modern Turkey*. Oxford: Oxford University Press, 1962.

Lifchez, Raymond. *The Dervish Lodge*. Berkeley: University of California Press, 1992.

"L'Institut de Jeunes Filles d'Ismet İnönü." *La Turquie Kamaliste*, no. 6 (April 1935).

"A List of Those Responsible for the Massacres and Deportations of the Armenians (Part I)." *Armenian Review* 35 (autumn 1982): 290–312.

"A List of Those Responsible for the Massacres and Deportations of the Armenians (Part II)." *Armenian Review* 35 (winter 1982): 438–49.

Loeffler, Jane C. "The Architecture of Diplomacy: Heyday of the United States Embassy Building Program, 1954–1960." *Journal of the Society of Architectural Historians* 49, no. 3 (1990): 251–78.

Loizos, Peter. "Ottoman Half-Lives: Long Term Perspectives on Particular Forced-Migrations." *Journal of Refugee Studies* 12, no. 3 (1999): 237–63.

Lörcher, Carl C. "Das Neue Regierungsviertel Der Stadt Angora." *Städtebau*, 1925.

Lowenthal, David. *The Past Is a Foreign Country*. Cambridge: Cambridge University Press, 1985.

Maarif Sergisi Rehberi. Ankara: Maarif Vekaleti, 1933.

Mahçupyan, Etyen. *İçimizdeki Öteki*. Istanbul: İletişim Yayınları, 2005.

Mamboury, Ernest. *La Guide Touristique de Ankara*. Ankara : Ministère Turc de l'Intérieur 1934.

Mann, Michael. "The Autonomous Power of the State: Its Origins, Mechanisms and Results." In Brenner, Jessop, Jones, and Macleod, *State/Space*, 53–64.

Marashi, Afshin. *Nationalizing Iran: Culture, Power, and the State, 1870–1940*. Seattle: University of Washington Press, 2008.

Marchand, Suzanne L. *Down from Olympus: Archaeology and Philhellenism in Germany, 1750–1970*. Princeton, NJ: Princeton University Press, 2003.

Mardin, Serif. "The Ottoman Empire." In Barkey and von Hagen, *After Empire*, 115–28.

Mardin, Serif. *Religion and Social Change in Modern Turkey*. Albany: State University of New York Press, 1989.

Margosyan, Mıgırdiç. *Biletimiz İstanbul'a Kesildi*. Istanbul: Aras Yayıncılık, 1998.

Margosyan, Mıgırdiç. *Gâvur Mahallesi*. Istanbul: Aras Yayıncılık, 1994.

Margosyan, Mıgırdiç. *Söyle Margos Nerelisen*. Istanbul: Aras Yayıncılık, 1995.

Margosyan, Mıgırdiç. *Tespih Taneleri*. Istanbul: Aras Yayıncılık, 2006.

Marzari, Frank. "Western-Soviet Rivalry in Turkey, 1939-I." *Middle Eastern Studies* 7, no. 1 (1971): 63–79.

Marzari, Frank. "Western Soviet Rivalry in Turkey, 1939-II." *Middle Eastern Studies* 7, no. 2 (1971): 201–20.

Matossian, Mary Kilbourne, and Susie Hoogasian Villa. *Anlatılar ve Fotoğraflarla 1914 Öncesi Ermeni Köy Hayatı.* Istanbul: Aras Yayıncılık, 2006.

Mazower, Mark. *Salonica, City of Ghosts: Christians, Muslims and Jews, 1430–1950.* 1st American ed. New York: Knopf, 2005.

McCarthy, Justin. "Foundations of the Turkish Republic: Social and Economic Change." *Middle Eastern Studies* 19, no. 2 (1983): 139–51.

McCarthy, Justin. *Muslims and Minorities: The Population of Ottoman Anatolia at the End of the Empire.* New York: New York University Press, 1983.

McCartney, R. H. "Ankara, the Capital of Modern Turkey." *Builder* 152 (June 4, 1937): 1171–74.

McClintock, Anne. *Imperial Leather: Race Gender and Sexuality in the Colonial Context.* New York: Routledge, 1995.

McCormick, Anne O'Hare. "The High Adventure of Angora: Going It Alone on the Original Turkish Plan of Being Western without Western Advice." *New York Times Magazine,* May 25, 1924.

McCormick, Anne O'Hare. "The Self-Determined Turk: From His Mud Village of Angora He Has Declared His Independence of East and West." *New York Times Magazine,* May 4, 1925.

McNeely, Connie L. *Constructing the Nation-State: International Organization and Prescriptive Action.* Westport, CT: Greenwood Press, 1995.

Migdal, Joel. *State in Society: Studying How States and Societies Transform and Constitute One Another.* Cambridge: Cambridge University Press, 2001.

Migdal, Joel. *Strong Societies and Weak States: State-Society Relations and State Capabilities in the Third World.* Princeton, NJ: Princeton University Press, 1988.

Millas, Herkül. *Göç: Rumlar'ın Anadolu'dan Mecburi Ayrılışı.* Istanbul: İletişim Yayınları, 2001.

Miller, Daniel. *Materiality.* Durham, NC: Duke University Press, 2005.

Minassian, Anahide Ter. *Ermeni Kültürü ve Modernleşme: Şehir, Oyun, Mizah, Aile Dil.* Istanbul: Aras Yayınları, 2006.

Mitchell, Timothy. *Colonizing Egypt.* Berkeley: University of California Press, 1991.

Mitchell, Timothy. *Questions of Modernity.* Minneapolis: University of Minnesota Press, 2000.

Mitchell, W. J. T. *Landscape and Power.* Chicago: University of Chicago Press, 1994.

Mıntzuri, Hagop. *İstanbul Anıları (1897–1940).* Istanbul: Tarih Vakfı Yurt Yayınları, 1993.

Moltke, Helmuth Graf von. *Briefe uber Zustande und Begebenheiten in Der Turkei aus den jahren 1835 bis 1839.* Berlin: E. S. Mittler, 1893.

Monmonier, Mark S. *How to Lie with Maps.* Chicago: University of Chicago Press, 1996.

Moore, Barrington. *Social Origins of Dictatorship and Democracy: Lord and Peasant in the Making of the Modern World.* Boston: Beacon Press, 1966.

Morton, Patricia A. *Hybrid Modernities: Architecture and Representation at the 1931 Colonial Exposition, Paris.* Illustrated ed. Cambridge, MA: MIT Press, 2000.

Mosse, George. *The Nationalization of the Masses.* Ithaca, NY: Cornell University Press, 1991.

Müderrisoğlu, Alptekin. *Kurtuluş Savaşında Ankara.* Ankara: Ankara Büyükşehir Belediyesi Yayınları, 1993.

Muğulkoç, Ziya G. "Halkevlerinin Gelişme Dönemi: Sosyal Bir İnceleme." In Kaplan, *Atatürk ve Halkevleri*, 142–58.

Mukerji, Chandra. "The Political Mobilization of Nature in Seventeenth-Century French Formal Gardens." *Theory and Society* 23, no. 5 (1994): 651–77.

Mukerji, Chandra. *Territorial Ambitions and the Gardens of Versailles*. Cambridge: Cambridge University Press, 1997.

Mustafa Aydin, Nail Alkan. *An Extensive Bibliography of Studies in English, German and French on Turkish Foreign Policy (1923–1997)*. SAM Papers. Ankara: Center for Strategic Research, 1997.

Nadolny, Rudolf. *Mein Beitrag: Erinnerungen eines Botschafters des Deutschen Reiches*. Cologne: DME-Verlag, 1985.

Nafia Sergisi. Ankara: Devlet Basımevi, 1942.

Nalbantoğlu, Gülsüm Baydar. "An Architectural and Historical Survey on the Development of the 'Apartment Building' in Ankara (1923–1950)." MA thesis, Middle East Technical University, 1981.

Navaro, Yael. "'Using the Mind' at Home: The Rationalization of Housewifery in Early Republican Turkey (1928–1940)." Thesis, Brandeis University, 1991.

Navaro-Yashin, Yael. *Faces of the State: Secularism and Public Life in Turkey*. Princeton, NJ: Princeton University Press, 2002.

Nedim, Ahmed. *Ankara Istiklal Mahkemesi Zabıtları 1926*. Edited by Belgelerle Kurtuluş Savaşı. Istanbul: İşaret Yayınları, 1993.

Nereid, Camilla T. "Kemalism on the Catwalk: The Turkish Hat Law of 1925." *Journal of Social History* 44, no. 3 (2011): 707–28. doi:10.1353/jsh.2011.0003.

Neyzi, Leyla. *İstanbul'da Hatırlamak ve Unutmak*. Istanbul: Tarih Vakfı Yayınları, 1999.

Nicolai, Bernd. *Moderne und Exil: Deutschsprachige Architekten in der Türkei, 1925–1955*. Berlin: Verlag fur Bauwesen, 1998.

Norton, John. "Faith and Fashion in Turkey." In *Languages of Dress in the Middle East*, edited by Nancy Lindisfarne-Tapper, 149–77. Surrey: Curzon Press (in Association with the Center for Near and Middle Eastern Studies SOAS), 1997.

Odabaşıoğlu, Cumhur. *Trabzon 1869–1933 Yılları Yaşantısı*. Ankara: İlk-San Matbaası, 1985.

Oğuz, Dicle, and Renan Erdogan. *Ankara Kentinde Ender Bulunan Ağaç Türleri Üzerine Bir Araştırma*. Ankara: Ankara Üniversitesi Araştırma Fon Müdürlüğü, 2002.

Ökte, Faik. *Varlık Vergisi Faciası*. Istanbul: Nebioğlu Yayınevi, 1951.

Öktem, Kerem. *Angry Nation: Turkey since 1989*. London: Zed Books, 2011.

Öktem, Kerem. *Creating the Turk's Homeland: Modernization, Nationalism and Geography in Southeast Turkey in the Late 19th and 20th Centuries*. 2006. http://www.ksg.harvard.edu/kokkalis/GSW5/oktem.pdf.

Öktem, Kerem. "Incorporating the Time and Space of the Ethnic 'Other': Nationalism and Space in Southeast Turkey in the Nineteenth and Twentieth Centuries." *Nations and Nationalism* 10, no. 4 (2004): 559–78. doi:10.1111/j.1354-5078.2004.00182.x.

Öktem, Kerem. "The Nation's Imprint: Demographic Engineering and the Change of Toponyms in Republican Turkey." *European Journal of Turkish Studies*, Thematic Issue 7 (Demographic Engineering, part 1) (February 23, 2009). http://www.ejts.org/document2243.html.

Okuma 4. Sınıf. Istanbul: Türkiye Cumuriyeti [*sic*] Kültür Bakanlığı, 1936.

Okuma Kitabi 2: Ikinci Sınıf. Istanbul: Türkiye Cumuriyeti [*sic*] Kültür Bakanlığı, 1937.

Okuma Kitabı Dördüncü Sınıf. Istanbul: Türkiye Cumhuriyeti Kültür Bakanlığı, 1935.

Okutan, M. Çağatay. *Tek Parti Döneminde Azınlık Politikaları*. 1st ed. Istanbul: Bilgi Üniversitesi Yayınları, 2004.

Olgun, Tahir. *Matbuat Alemindeki Hayatım ve Istiklal Mahkemeleri*. Istanbul: Nehir Yayınları, 1990.

Olson, Robert. "The Kurdish Rebellions of Sheikh Said (1925), Mt. Ararat (1930), and Dersim (1937–8): Their Impact on the Development of the Turkish Air Force and on Kurdish and Turkish Nationalism." *Welt des Islams* 40, no. 1 (2000): 67–94.

Önder, Mehmet. *Atatürk'ün Yurt Gezileri*. Ankara: Türkiye, 1998.

Oran, Baskın. *Atatürk Milliyetçiliği : Resmi İdeoloji Dışı Bir İnceleme*. Ankara: Dost Kitabevi, 1988.

Oran, Baskın. *Azgelişmiş Ülke Milliyetçiliği : Kara Afrika Modeli*. Ankara: Ankara Üniversitesi Siyasal Bilgiler Fakültesi Yayınları, 1977.

Oran, Baskın. *Türkiye'de Azınlıklar: Kavramlar, Teori, Lozan, İç Mevzuat, İçtihat, Uygulama*. Istanbul: İletişim Yayınları, 2004.

Orhonlu, Cengiz. *Osmanlı İmparatorluğu'nda Aşiretlerin İskanı*. Istanbul: Eren Yayıncılık ve Kitapçılık, 1987.

Orhun, Hayri, and Celal Kasaroğlu. *Meşhur Valiler*. Ankara: İçisleri Bakanlığı Merkez Valileri Bürosu Yayınları, 1969.

Orkon, Cenap Refik. *Manisa Coğrafyası*. Istanbul: Resimli Ay Matbaası, 1937.

Örs, İlay Romain. "Genie in the Bottle: Gezi Park, Taksim Square, and the Realignment of Democracy and Space in Turkey." *Philosophy and Social Criticism* 40, nos. 4–5 (May 2014): 489–98. doi:10.1177/0191453714525390.

Osborne, Brian S. "Constructing Landscapes of Power: The George Etienne Cartier Monument, Montreal." *Journal of Historical Geography* 24 (1998): 431–58.

Özacun, Orhan. "Halkevlerinin Dramı." *Kebikeç* 2, no. 3 (1996): 87–95.

Özbay, Ferhunde. "Gendered Space: A New Look at Turkish Modernisation." *Gender and History* 11, no. 3 (1999): 555–68.

Özbudun, Ergun. *Social Change and Political Participation in Turkey*. Princeton, NJ: Princeton University Press, 1976.

Özcan, Selim. "XX Yüzyıl Başlarında, Canik (Samsun) Sancağında İsimleri Değiştirilmek İstenen Kaza, Köy, Mahaleler ve Yeni İsimleri." In *Geçmişten Geleceğe Samsun*, edited by Cevdet Yılmaz, 671–85. Samsun: Samsun Büyükşehir Belediyesi Kültür ve Eğitim Hizmetleri Daire Başkanlığı, 2006.

Özemre, Ahmed Yüksel. *Hasretini Çektiğim Üsküdar*. 1st ed. Istanbul: Kubbealtı Neşriyâtı, 2007.

Ozouf, Mona. *Festivals and the French Revolution*. Cambridge, MA: Harvard University Press, 1988.

Öztürk, Nazif. *Menşei ve Tarihi Açısından Vakıflar*. Ankara: Vakıflar Genel Müdürlüğü Yayınları, 1983.

Öztürk, Nazif. *Türk Yenileşme Çerçevesinde Vakıf Müessesi*. Ankara: Diyanet Vakfı Yayınları, 1995.

Öztürk, Nazif. *Vakıfların İdaresi ve Teskilat Yapısı Üzerine Düşünceler*. Ankara: Vakıflar Genel Müdürlüğü Yayınları, 1983.

Öztürk, Serdar. "The Struggle over Turkish Village Coffeehouses (1923–45)." *Middle Eastern Studies* 44, no. 3 (May 2008): 435–54.

Öztürk, Yaşar Nuri. *Tasavvufun Ruhu ve Tarikatler*. Istanbul: Sidre Yayıncılık, 1988.

Öztürkmen, Arzu. "Politics of National Dance in Turkey." *Yearbook for Traditional Music* 33 (2001): 139–43.

Öztürkmen, Arzu. "Remembering through Material Culture: Local Knowledge of Past Communities in a Turkish Black Sea Town." *Middle Eastern Studies* 39, no. 2 (2003): 179–93.

Öztürkmen, Arzu. *Türkiye'de Folklor ve Milliyetçilik*. Istanbul: İletişim Yayınları, 1998.

Özyürek, Esra. *Nostalgia for the Modern: State Secularism and Everyday Politics in Turkey*. Durham, NC: Duke University Press, 2006.

Parla, Taha. *Türkiyede Siyasal Kültürün Resmi Kaynakları*. Istanbul: İletişim Yayınları, 1992.

Parla, Taha, and Andrew Davison. *Corporatarist Ideology in Kemalist Turkey: Progress or Order*. Syracuse, NY: Syracuse University Press, 2004.

Partisi, Cumhuriyet Halk. *On Beşinci Yıl Kitabı*. Ankara: Cumhuriyet Matbaası, 1938.

Partisi, Cumhuriyet Halk, and Eskişehir. *Cumhuriyetin 15 inci Yılında Eskişehir*. Istanbul: Kültür Matbaası, 1938.

Pearce, Susan. *Museums, Objects and Collections*. Washington, DC: Smithsonian Institution Press, 1992.

Pennebaker, James W., Dario Paez, and Bernard Rimé. *Collective Memory of Political Events: Social Psychological Perspectives*. Mahwah, NJ: Lawrence Erlbaum, 1997.

Phrankoudakē, Anna, and Çağlar Keyder. *Ways to Modernity in Greece and Turkey Encounters with Europe, 1850–1950*. London: Tauris, 2007.

Pinon, Pierre, and Korkut Erdur. *Albert Gabriel (1883–1972): Mimar, Arkeolog, Ressam, Gezgin*. Istanbul: Yapı ve Kredi Yayınları, 2006.

Poggi, Gianfranco. *The Development of the Modern State: A Sociological Introduction*. Stanford, CA: Stanford University Press, 1978.

Poulantzas, Nicos. "The Nation." In Brenner, Jessop, Jones, and Macleod, *State/Space*, 65–83.

Pratt, Mary Louise. *Imperial Eyes: Travel Writing and Transculturation*. New York: Routledge, 1992.

Program Accepted by the Fourth Grand Congress of the Party. Ankara: Republican People's Party, 1935.

Pur, Hüseyin Perviz. *Varlık Vergisi ve Azınlıklar*. Istanbul: Eren Yayıncılık, 2007.

Rabinow, Paul. *French Modern: Norms and Forms of the Social Environment*. Cambridge, MA: MIT Press, 1989.

Rae, Heather. *State Identities and the Homogenisation of Peoples*. Cambridge: Cambridge University Press, 2002.

Rae, Heather. "Theories of State Formation." In *International Relations Theory for the Twenty-First Century*, edited by Martin Griffiths, 123–34. Abingdon, Oxon, 2007.

"Remnants of the Turkish Genocide." *Armenian Review* 50 (winter 1949): 49–53.

Rizk, Yunan Labib. 'The Ambassador's Tarboush'. *Al Ahram Weekly Online*, 7 August 2003. http://weekly.ahram.org.eg/2003/650/chrncls.htm.

Ronaldshay, Earl of. *The Life of Lord Curzon, Being the Authorized Biography of George Nathaniel Marquess Curzon of Keddleston, K.G.* London: Ernest Benn, 1928.

Rustow, Dankwart A. *Political Modernization in Japan and Turkey*. Princeton, NJ: Princeton University Press, 1964.

Saatçi, Mustafa. "Nation-States and Ethnic Boundaries: Modern Turkish Identity and Turkish-Kurdish Conflict." *Nations and Nationalism* 8, no. s4 (2002): 549–64. doi:10.1111/1469-8219.00065.

Sabahattin, Selek. *Anadolu İhtilali*. Istanbul: Cem Yayınevi, 1976.

Sahil, Sare. "Cumhuriyet Sonrasi Türk Toplumsal Yapi Degisimlerinin Ankara Atatürk Bulvarı Mekansal Yapısında Örneklenmesi." PhD diss., Gazi Üniversitesi, 1986.

Said, Edward. *Orientalism*. New York: Vintage Books, 1978.

Sakallı, Bayram. *Milli Mücadelenin Sosyal Tarihi*. Istanbul: İz Yayıncılık, 1997.

Sakallı, Bayram. "Tekke, Zaviye ve Türbelerin Türk Toplumundaki Rolleri, Kapatılmaları ve Tepkiler." *Türkiye Günlüğü* (July–August 1994): 202–21.

Salman, Mustafa. *Balıkesir Tarihi, Coğrafyası*. Balıkesir: Türk Dili Matbaası, 1955.

Salmoni, Barak. "The 'Teachers' Army' and Its Miniature Republican Society: Educators' Traits and School Dynamics in Turkish Pedagogical Prescriptions, 1923–1950." *Comparative Studies of South Asia, Africa, and the Middle East* 21, nos. 1 and 2 (2001): 61–72.

Salmoni, Barak. "Women in the Nationalist-Educational Prism: Turkish and Egyptian Pedagogues and Their Endered Agenda, 1920–1952." *History of Education Quarterly* 18 (October 2006): 483–516.

Saltık, Hasan. *Trabzon*. Tanıtma Eserleri Dizisi. Istanbul: T. C. Turizm Bakanlığı Yayımlar Dairesi Baskanlığı, 1996.

Sarafyan, Ara. *United States Official Documents on the Armenian Genocide*. Archival Collections on the Armenian Genocide, Volume 1: Lower Euphrates. Watertown, MA: Armenian Review, 1994.

Sarafyan, Ara. *United States Official Documents on the Armenian Genocide*. Archival Collections on the Armenian Genocide, Volume 2: The Peripheries. Watertown, MA: Armenian Review, 1994.

Sarafyan, Ara. *United States Official Documents on the Armenian Genocide*. Archival Collections on the Armenian Genocide, Volume 3: The Central Lands. Watertown, MA: Armenian Review, 1994.

Sarıkaya, Yasar. *Medreseler ve Modernleşme*. Istanbul: İz Yayıncılık, 1997.

Sarınay, Yusuf. *Türk Milliyetciliğinin Tarihi Gelişimi ve Türk Ocakları*. Istanbul: Ötüken Neşriyat, 1994.

Schivelbusch, Wolfgang. *The Railway Journey: The Industrialization of Time and Space in the 19th Century*. Berkeley: University of California Press, 1987.

Scott, James C. *Seeing like a State: How Certain Schemes to Improve the Human Condition Have Failed*. New Haven, CT: Yale University Press, 1998.

Şehremaneti, Ankara. *Ankara Sehrinin Jausseley, Jansen, ve Brix Plan ve Projelerine Ait İzahnameler*. Ankara: Hakimiyet-i Milliye Matbaası, 1929.

Sekizli, Ubeydullah. "Çorum'da Bir Mûsikîşinas Hâfız Recep Camcı." *İstanbul Üniversitesi İlahiyat Fakültesi Dergisi*, no. 22 (2012): 267–84.

Şenyapılı, Önder. "Ankara '70." *Mimarlik* (March 1970), 26–44.

Şenyapılı, Tansı. *Ankara Kentinde Gecekondu Gelişimi*. Ankara: Kent-Koop Yayınları, 1985.

Şerif, Ahmet. *Anadolu'da Tanin*. Edited by Ç. Börekçi. Istanbul: Broy Yayınevi, 1977.

Sertel, Cemal Hidayet. "Türk Demiryolculuğu." In *Cumhuriyetin 16. Yıldönümünde Hitabeler ve Konferanslar*. Ankara: Ulus Kitabevi, 1939.

Sertel, Zekeriya. "Harb Zengini Kimdir ve Onu Nasıl Bulacağız?" *Tan*, May 30, 1942.

Seyhan Cumhuriyetin 15 Yılı İçinde. Istanbul: Tan Matbaası, 1938.

Sharma, Aradhana, and Akhil Gupta. *The Anthropology of the State: A Reader*. Malden, MA: Blackwell, 2009.

Shaw, Stanford. *History of the Ottoman Empire and Modern Turkey*. Cambridge: Cambridge University Press, 1976.

Sherrill, Charles Hitchcock. *Gazi Mustafa Kemal Nezdinde Bir Yıl Elçilik*. Istanbul: Muallim Ahmet Halit Kitaphanesi, 1935.

Sherrill, Charles Hitchcock. *A Year's Embassy to Mustafa Kemal*. New York: Scribner's, 1934.

Shotwell, James, and Francis Deák. *Turkey at the Straits: A Short History*. New York: Macmillan, 1940.

Şimşek, Sefa. *Bir Ideolojik Seferberlik Deneyimi: Halkevleri, 1932–1951*. Istanbul: Boğaziçi Üniversitesi Yayınevi, 2002.

Şimşir, Bilal. *Ankara . . . Ankara: Bir Başkentin Doğuşu*. Ankara: Bilgi Yayınevi, 1988.

Şimşir, Bilal. "Fes Olayı, Türkiye-Mısır İlişkilerinden Bir Sayfa (1932–1933)." *Belleten* 48, nos. 189–90 (1984): 1–54.

Skocpol, Theda. *States and Social Revolutions: A Comparative Analysis of France, Russia, and China*. Cambridge: Cambridge University Press, 1979.

Smith, Anthony. *National Identity*. Reno: University of Nevada Press, 1991.

Smith, Thomas W. "Civic Nationalism and Ethnocultural Justice in Turkey." *Human Rights Quarterly* 27, no. 2 (2005): 436–70.

Soja, Edward. *Postmodern Geographies: The Reassertion of Space in Critical Social Theory*. London: Verso, 1989.

Somel, Selçuk Akşin. "Osmanlı Ermenilerinde Kültür Modernleşmesi, Cemaat Okulları ve Abdülhamid Rejimi." *Tarih ve Toplum: Yeni Yaklaşımlar*, no. 5 (2007): 71–92.

"Statement on Conditions (1974) by the Chancellory of the Armenian Patriarchy in Turkey." *Armenian Review* 30, no. 3 (1977): 302–5.

Stokes, Martin. *The Arabesk Debate: Music and Musicians in Modern Turkey*. Oxford: Clarendon Press, 1992.

Stoler, Ann Laura, and Frederick Cooper. "Between Metropole and Colony: Rethinking a Research Agenda." In Stoler and Cooper, *Tensions of Empire*, 1–56.

Stoler, Ann Laura, and Frederick Cooper, eds. *Tensions of Empire: Colonial Cultures in a Bourgeois World*. Berkeley: University of California Press, 1997.

Suny, Ronald Grigor, Fatma Müge Göçek, and Norman M Naimark. *A Question of Genocide: Armenians and Turks at the End of the Ottoman Empire*. New York: Oxford University Press, 2013.

Tabak, Faruk. "Agrarian Fluctuations and the Modes of Labor Control in the Western Arc of the Fertile Crescent Cc. 1700–1850." In Keyder and Tabak, *Landholding and Commercial Agriculture in the Middle East*, 135–54.

Tan, Mine Göğüş, Özlem Şahin, Mustafa Sever, and Aksu Bora. *Cumhuriyet'ye Çocuktular*. Istanbul: Boğaziçi Üniversitesi Yayınevi, 2007.

Tankut, Gönül. *Bir Başkentin İmari Ankara (1929–1939)*. Ankara: Orta Doğu Teknik Üniversitesi Yayınları, 1990.

Tankut, Gönül. "Cumhuriyet Döneminin İlk Toplu İmar Deneyimi: Ankara." *Amme İdaresi Dergisi* 14 (December 1981): 113–19.

Tankut, Gönül. *Jansen Planı Uygulama Sorunları*. Edited by Ümit Nevzat Uğurel. Tarih İçinde Ankara. Ankara: Orta Doğu Teknik Üniversitesi Yayınları, 1981.

Tanman, Baha. "Settings for the Veneration of the Saints." In Lifchez, *The Dervish Lodge*, 130–71.

Tanör, Bülent. *Türkiye'de Kongre Iktidarlari*. Istanbul: Yapi Kredi Kültür Sanat Yayıncılık Ticaret ve Sanayi A.Ş., 1998.

Tanrıöver, Hamdullah Suphi. "Türk Ocağı'nin Tarihçesi ve İftiralara Karşı Cevaplarımız." *Türk Yurdu* 5, no. 36 (1930): 2–23.

Tanrıöver, Hamdullah Suphi. "Türk Ocakları Merkez Binasının Açılmasında Hamdullah Suphi Beyin Söylediği Nutuk." *Türk Yurdu* 29, no. 223 (May 1930): 4–24.

Tanrıverdi, Fuat. *Erzurum Şehri Gelişmesinde Peyzaj Mimarisi Bakımından Gözönüne Alınması Lazım Gelen Temel Problemler.* Erzurum: Atatürk Üniversitesi Yayınları, 1973.

Tanyu, Hikmet. *Ankara ve Çevresinde Adak Yerleri.* Ankara: Ankara Üniversitesi İlahiyat Fakültesi Yayınları, 1967.

Türk Tarihini Tetkik Cemiyeti. *Tarih IV.* Istanbul: Maarif Vekaleti (Devlet Matbaası), 1934.

Taylor, Peter J. "The State as Container: Territoriality in the Modern World System." In Brenner, Jessop, Jones, and Macleod, *State/Space,* 101–14.

Taylor, Robert. *The Word in Stone: The Role of Architecture in the National Socialist Ideology.* Berkeley: University of California Press, 1974.

T. C. Kültür Bakanlığı. *Cimnastik Şenlikleri Talimatnamesi.* Istanbul: Devlet Basımevi, 1938.

T. C. Kültür Bakanlığı. *Okullarda Kullanılacak Milli Bayrak ve Okul Filaması Hakkında Talimatname.* Istanbul: Devlet Basımevi, 1938.

Tekeli, İlhan. "Cumhuriyetin Altmış Yıllık Belediyecilik Deneyiminin Değerlendirilmesi Üzerine." In Tekeli, *Türk Belediyeciliğinde 60,* 328–46.

Tekeli, İlhan. "1923–1950 Döneminde Muğla'da Olan Gelişmeler." In Tekeli, *Tarih İçinde Muğla,* 114–87.

Tekeli, İlhan. *Tarih İçinde Muğla.* Ankara: Orta Doğu Teknik Üniversitesi Yayınları, 1993.

Tekeli, İlhan. *Türkiye'de Kentleşme Yazıları.* Ekonomik ve Sosyal Arastirmalar. Ankara: Turhan Yayınevi, 1982.

Tekeli, İlhan. "Türkiye'de Kent Planlamasinin Tarihsel Kökleri." In *Türkiye'de İmar Planlaması Konferansı,* edited by Tamer Gök, 8–112. Ankara: Orta Teknik Üniversitesi Şehir ve Planlama Bölümü, 1980.

Tekeli, İlhan, ed. *Türk Belediyeciliğinde 60 Yıl Uluslararası Sempozyumu.* Ankara: Metropol İmar A.S. Ankara Büyükşehir Belediyesi, 1990.

Tekeli, İlhan, and Selim İlkin. *Bahçeli Evlerin Öyküsü: Bir Batı Kurumunun Yeniden Yorumlanması.* Ankara: Kent Koop Yayınları, 1984.

Tekeli, İlhan, and Selim İlkin. *Cumhuriyetin Harcı.* Istanbul: Bilgi Üniversitesi Yayınları, 2003.

Tekeli, İlhan, and İlber Ortaylı. *Türkiye'de Belediyeciliğin Evrimi.* Ankara: Ayyıldız Matbaası, 1978.

Tekiner, Ü. Aylin. *Atatürk Heykelleri: Kültür, Estetik, Siyaset.* Istanbul: İletişim Yayınları, 2010.

Tezcan, Mahmut. *Türk Ailesi Antropolojisi.* 1st ed. Kızılay, Ankara: İmge Kitabevi, 2000.

Timur, Taner. *Osmanlı Çalışmaları: İlkel Feodalizmden Yarı Sömürge Ekonomisine.* Ankara: V Yayınları, 1989.

Timur, Taner. *Türk Devrimi ve Sonrası.* Ankara: İmge Yayınevi, 1994.

Tiregöl, Jessica Selma. "The Role of Primary Education in Nation-State Building: The Case of the Early Turkish Republic (1923–1938)." PhD diss., Princeton University, 1998.

Toprak, Zafer. *Bir Yurttaş Yaratmak: Muasır Bir Medeniyet İçin Seferberlik Bilgileri.* Istanbul: Yapı Kredi Kültür ve Sanat Yayıncılık, 1998.

Trask, Roger R. *The United States Response to Turkish Nationalism and Reform.* Minneapolis: University of Minnesota Press, 1971.

Trimberger, Ellen Kay. *Revolution from Above: Military Bureaucrats and Development in Japan, Turkey, Egypt, and Peru*. New Brunswick, NJ: Transaction Books, 1978.

Trimberger, Ellen Kay. "A Theory of Elite Revolutions." *Studies in Comparative International Development* 7, no. 3 (September 1972): 191–207. doi:10.1007/BF03041090.

Tucker, Robert C. "The Emergence of Stalin's Foreign Policy." *Slavic Review* 36, no. 4 (1977): 563–89.

Tunaya, Tarık Zafer. *Türkiye'de Siyasal Partiler, Cilt III: İttihat ve Terakki: Bir Çağın, Bir Kuşağın, Bir Partinin Tarihi*. Istanbul: Hürriyet Vakfı Yayınları, 1989.

Tunçay, Mete. *Türkiye'de Tek Parti Yönetiminin Kurulması (1923–1931)*. 3rd rev. ed. Istanbul: Tarih Vakfı Yurt Yayınları, 1999.

Tunçel, Harun. "Türkiye'de İsmi Değiştirilen Köyler." *Fırat Üniversitesi Sosyal Bilimler Dergisi/Fırat University Journal of Social Science* 10, no. 2 (2000): 23–34.

Turan, Ömer. "Kırklareli (Kırk Kilise)." *Encyclopedia of Jews in the Islamic World*. Brill Online, 2014. http://referenceworks.brillonline.com/entries/encyclopedia-of-jews-in-the-islamic-world/k-rklareli-k-rk-kilise-SIM_0013010/.

Türkiye Cumhuriyeti Maarif Vekaleti İlk Mektepler Talimatnamesi. Istanbul: Devlet Matbaası, 1929.

Türkiye Cumhuriyeti Maarif Vekaleti İsmet Paşa Kız Enstitüsü. Ankara: Hakimiyet-i Milliye Matbaası, n.d.

Türkiye Cumuriyeti [*sic*] Kültür Bakanlığı, ed. *İlkokul Programı*. Istanbul: Devlet Basımevi, 1936.

Türkoğlu, Ömer. "Halkevlerinin Kuruluş Amaçları, Örgütsel Yapısı ve Bazı Uygulamaları." *Kebikeç* 2, no. 3 (1996): 97–106.

Türköz, Meltem. "Surname Narratives and the State–Society Boundary: Memories of Turkey's Family Name Law of 1934." *Middle Eastern Studies* 43, no. 6 (2007): 893–908.

Tversky, Barbara. "Cognitive Maps, Cognitive Collages, and Spatial Mental Models." In *Spatial Information Theory: A Theoretical Basis for GIS*, edited by Andrew U. Frank and Irene Campari, 14–24. Lecture Notes in Computer Science 716. Berlin: Springer, 1993. http://link.springer.com/chapter/10.1007/3-540-57207-4_2.

Tversky, Barbara. "Remembering Spaces." In *Handbook of Memory*, edited by E. Tulving and F. I. M. Craik, 363–78. New York: Oxford University Press, 2000.

Ülker, Erol. "Assimilation, Security and Geographical Nationalization in Interwar Turkey: The Settlement Law of 1934." In *European Journal of Turkish Studies*, Demographic Engineering Part 1, edited by Nikos Sigalas and Alexandre Toumarkine, no. 7 (December 11, 2008). http://ejts.revues.org/index2123.html.

Uludağ, Zeynep. "Cumhuriyet Döneminde Rekreasyon ve Gençlik Parkı Örneği." In *75 Yılda Değişen Kent ve Mimarlık*, edited by Yıldız Sey, 65–74. Istanbul: Tarih Vakfı Yayınları, 1998.

Uluğ, Naşit Hakkı. *Tunceli Medeniyete Açılıyor*. Istanbul: Cumhuriyet Matbaası, 1939.

Umar, Bilge. *Türkiye'deki Tarihsel Adlar*. Istanbul: İnkilap Kitabevi, 1993.

Üngör, Uğur Ü. "Geographies of Nationalism and Violence: Towards a New Understanding of Young Turk Social Engineering." *European Journal of Turkish Studies*, Thematic Issue no. 7, Demographic Engineering, Part 1 (March 10, 2008). http://www.ejts.org/document2583.html.

Üngör, Uğur Ü. *The Making of Modern Turkey: Nation and State in Eastern Anatolia, 1913–1950*. Oxford: Oxford University Press, 2011.

Üngör, Uğur Ü. "Organizing Oblivion in the Aftermath of Mass Violence." *Armenian Weekly*, March 12, 2008. http://www.hairenik.com/armenianweekly/gin_041608_06.htm.

Üngör, Uğur Ü. "A Reign of Terror: CUP Rule in Diyarbekir Province 1913–1923." MA thesis, University of Amsterdam, 2005.

Üngör, Uğur Ü. "Seeing like a Nation-State: Young Turk Social Engineering in Eastern Turkey." *Journal of Genocide Research* 10, no. 1 (2008): 15–39.

Upton, Dell. "Another City." In *Everyday Life in the Early Republic*, edited by Catherine E. Hutchins, 61–117. Winterthur: Winterthur Museum, 1994.

Upton, Dell. "The Self in Space: The City as Material Culture." In *The Art and the Mystery of Material Culture*, edited by Anne Elizabeth Yentsch and Marie Beaudry, 51–63. Boca Raton, FL: CRC Press, 1992.

Üremiş, Ali. "Türkiye Selçuklularında Bazı Sünni Tasavvuf Hareketleri." *Selçuk Üniversitesi Türkiyat Araştırmaları Dergisi*, no. 28. Accessed 9 December 2013. http://www.turkiyat.selcuk.edu.tr/pdfdergi/s28/uremis.pdf.

Üstel, Füsun. *İmparatorluktan Ulus-Devlete Türk Milliyetçiliği: Türk Ocakları (1912–1931)*. Istanbul: İletişim Yayınları, 1997.

Uz, Behçet, and L. Ece Sakar. *Atatürk'ün İzmir'i: Bir Kentin Yeniden Doğuşu*. Istanbul: Türkiye İş Bankası, 2007.

Vale, Lawrence. *Architecture, Power and National Identity*. New Haven, CT: Yale University Press, 1992.

van Bruinessen, Martin. *Agha, Shaikh, and State: The Social and Political Structures of Kurdistan*. London: Zed Books, 1992.

van Bruinessen, Martin. "'Aslını İnkar Eden Haramzadedir': The Debate on the Ethnic Identity of the Kurdish Alevis." *Syncretistic Religious Communities in the Near East*, 1–23. Leiden: Brill, 1997.

Vasilian, Hampartzoum. "Two Months in the Interior of Turkey." *Armenian Review* 5, no. 1 (1952): 113–19.

Veinstein, Gilles, ed. *Selânik 1850–1918: "Yahudilerin Kenti" ve Balkanlar'ın Uyanışı*. 2 vols. Istanbul: İletişim, 1999.

Velidedeoğlu, Hıfzı Veldet. *İlk Meclis ve Milli Mücadele'de Anadolu*. Istanbul: Çağdaş Yayınları, 1990.

Vick, Brian. "The Origins of the German Volk: Cultural Purity and National Identity in Nineteenth-Century Germany." *German Studies Review* 26, no. 2 (May 2003): 241–56. doi:10.2307/1433324.

Vilayetler Albümü. Ankara: Dahiliye Vekaleti, 1929.

Walkowitz, Daniel J., and Lisa Maya Knauer. *Memory and the Impact of Political Transformation in Public Space*. Durham, NC: Duke University Press, 2004.

Walzer, Michael. *The Revolution of the Saints: A Study in the Origins of Radical Politics*. New York: Atheneum Press, 1970.

Weber, Eugen. *My France: Politics, Culture, Myth*. Cambridge, MA: Belknap Press of Harvard University Press, 1991.

Weber, Eugen. *Peasants into Frenchmen: The Modernization of Rural France 1870–1914*. Stanford, CA: Stanford University Press, 1977.

Weber, M., and S. N. Eisenstadt. *On Charisma and Institution Building*. Chicago: University of Chicago Press, 1968.

White, Jenny B. *Muslim Nationalism and the New Turks*. With a new afterword. Princeton, NJ: Princeton University Press, 2014.

White, Jenny B. "State Feminism, Modernization and the Turkish Republican Woman." *NWSA Journal* 15, no. 3 (2003): 145–59.

Will, Brandon Taylor, and Wilfried Van der Will. *The Nazification of Art: Art, Design, Music, Architecture, and Film in the Third Reich*. Winchester, ON: Winchester Press, 1990.

Wright, Gwendolyn. *The Politics of French Colonial Urbanism*. Chicago: University of Chicago Press, 1991.

Yalçın, Kemal. *You Rejoice My Heart*. Translated by Paul Bessemer. Watertown, MA: Garod Books, 2007 (1952).

Yavuz, Erdal, and Ümit Nevzat Uğurel. *Tarih Içinde Ankara*. Ankara: Orta Doğu Teknik Üniversitesi Yayınları, 1981.

Yavuz, Fehmi. *Ankara' nın İmarı ve Sehirciliğimiz*. Ankara: Ankara Üniversitesi Siyasal Bilgiler Fakültesi Yayınları, 1952.

Yavuz, Yıldırım. *Mimar Kemalettin ve Birinci Ulusal Mimarlık Dönemi*. Ankara: Orta Doğu Teknik Üniversitesi Yayınları, 1981.

Yeğen, Mesut. *Devlet Söyleminde Kürt Sorunu*. 1st ed. Cağaloğlu, Istanbul: İletişim Yayınları, 1999.

Yeğenoğlu, Meyda. *Colonial Fantasies: Towards a Feminist Critique of Orientalism*. Cambridge: Cambridge University Press, 1998.

Yerasimos, Stefanos. *Az Gelismislik Sürecinde Türkiye*. 3 vols. Bilim Araştırma Dizisi. Istanbul: Gözlem Yayınları, 1974–1976.

Yerasimos, Stefanos. *Milliyetler ve Sınırlar: Balkanlar, Kafkasya ve Ortadogu*. Istanbul: İletişim Yayınları, 1994.

Yerasimos, Stefanos. "The Monoparty Period." In *Turkey in Transition: New Perspectives*, edited by Ahmet Ertuğrul Tonak and Irvin C. Schick, 66–100. New York: Oxford University Press, 1987.

Yerasimos, Stefanos. "Tanzimatin Kent Reformları Üzerine." In *Modernlesme Sürecinde Osmanli Kentleri*. Istanbul: Tarih Vakfı Yurt Yayınları, 1996.

Yerasimos, Stefanos. *Türk Sovyet Ilişkileri*. Istanbul: Gözlem Yayınları, 1979.

Yeşil, Sevim. "Unfolding Republican Patriarchy: The Case of Young Kurdish Women at the Girls' Vocational Boarding School in Elazığ." MA thesis, Middle East Technical University, 2003.

Yiğit, Nuyan. *Atatürk'le 30 Yıl : İbrahim Süreyya Yiğit'in Öyküsü*. 2nd ed. Istanbul: Remzi Kitabevi, 2004.

Yıldız, Ahmet. *Ne Mutlu Türküm Diyebilene: Türk Ulusal Kimliginin Etno-Seküler Sınırları*. Istanbul: İletişim Yayınları, 2001.

Yılmaz, Şuhnaz. "Challenging Stereotypes: Turkish-American Relations in the Inter-War Era." *Middle Eastern Studies* 42, no. 2 (2006): 223–37.

Young, James E. *The Texture of Memory: Holocaust Memorials and Meaning*. New Haven, CT: Yale University Press, 1993.

Yüksel, Ahmet. *Ankara Şehri Salnamesi 1325/1907*. Ankara: Ankara Araştırmaları Vakfı, 1995.

Yüksel, Ahmet. "Merzifon Halkevi ve Taşan Dergisi." *Kebikeç* 2, no. 3 (1996): 169–88.

Yüksel, Metin. "The Encounter of Kurdish Women with Nationalism in Turkey." *Middle Eastern Studies* 42, no. 5 (2006): 777–802.

Yumul, Arus. "'A Prostitute Lodging in the Bosom of Turkishness': Istanbul's Pera and Its Representation." *Journal of Intercultural Studies* 30, no. 1 (2009): 57–72. doi:10.1080/07256860802579444.

Yutkevich, Sergei. *Türkiye'nin Kalbi Ankara (Ankara–Serdtse Turtsii)*. Film, Başbakanlık Basın Yayın Genel Müdürlüğü Film Merkezi, 1933.

Zacharia, Katerina, ed. *Hellenisms: Culture, Identity, and Ethnicity from Antiquity to Modernity*. Aldershot, Hampshire: Ashgate, 2008.

Zandi-Sayek, Sibel. *Ottoman Izmir: The Rise of a Cosmopolitan Port, 1840–1880*. Minneapolis: University of Minnesota Press, 2012.

Zilfi, Madeline C. *The Politics of Piety: The Ottoman Ulema in the Post-Classical Age (1600–1800)*. Minneapolis: Bibliotheca Islamica, 1988.

Ziya, Halid. "Belediyeler Nasıl Bir Haritaya Muhtaçtir?" *Belediyeler Dergisi*, 1934.

"Zum 70. Geburstag von Hermann Jansen." *Deutsche Bauzeitung* 73, no. 21 (1939): 165–72.

Zürcher, Erik J. *Savaş, Devrim ve Uluslaşma: Türkiye Tarihinde Geçiş Dönemi (1908–1938)*. Istanbul: Bilgi Üniversitesi Yayınları, 2005.

Zürcher, Erik J. *Turkey: A Modern History*. Rev. ed. London: Tauris, 2004.

Zürcher, Erik J. *The Young Turk Legacy and Nation Building: From the Ottoman Empire to Atatürk's Turkey*. London: Tauris, 2010.

Newspapers and Periodicals

Akşam
Arkitekt (aka *Mimar*)
Ayın Tarihi
Belediyeler Dergisi
Cumhuriyet
Hakimiyet-i Milliye (later *Ulus*)
İlköğretim Haftası
*La Turquie Kamaliste (*aka *La Turquie Kemaliste*)
London Times
New York Times
Resmi Gazete
Tan
Tevhid-i Efkâr
Time
Ülkü
Yedigün
Yeni Adam
Yeni Mecmua

INDEX

Note: Page references in *italic* refer to figures.